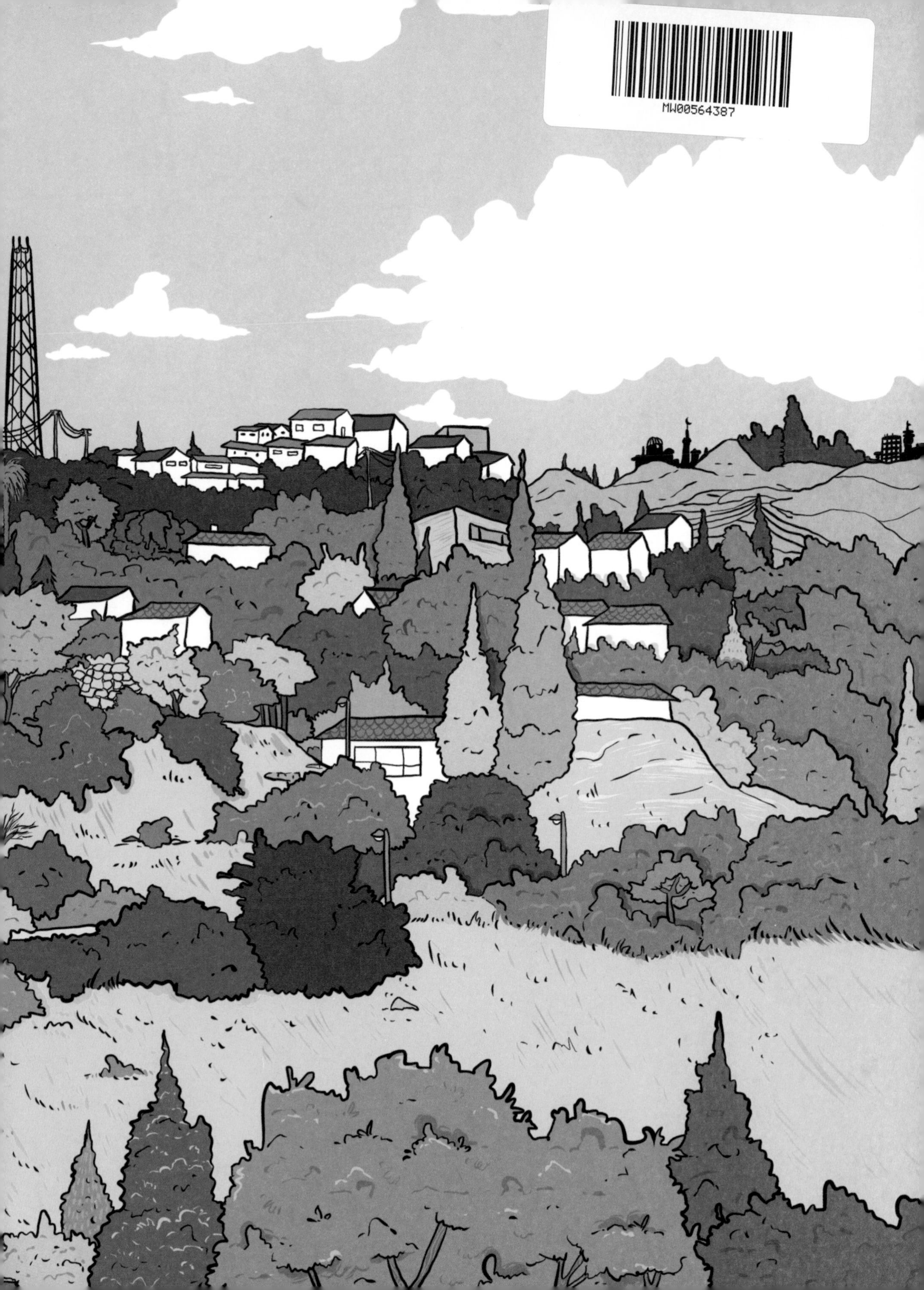

GOOD GIRLS GO TO HELL

Tohar Sherman-Friedman

Translated by Margaret Morrison

graphic mundi

I began creating this graphic novel in the midst of a global pandemic, as borders closed, fear gained momentum, and we were plunged deep into lockdown and social distancing.

The heavy atmosphere urged me toward my life story, and the weight of time and silence generated by Covid opened a small window onto my inner world, which took shape on paper.

This project would not have been possible without the incredible support I have received, and I would like to thank and pay tribute to those people without whom this graphic novel would not have been possible.
A huge thank-you…

To Daniel, my exceptional husband, who supports me with his infinite and unconditional love and superb calm, which is trusting, consistent, and supportive, and which gave me the strength to create this book.

To my parents, who, after all the upheavals I've experienced, are a strong and stable rock in my life, after all the storms I have made them go through… It is a great privilege to be your daughter.

To my sister, my wonderful Tiferett, who was generous enough to allow me to share part of her life story. Without you I would not be where I am today.

To all my brothers and sisters (each of whom is a beautiful world in themselves), Tehila, Tovi, Ouri, Talia, and David.

To my friend and artist Guy Schreiber; it was at his home that many pages of this book took shape.

To my closest friends who have supported me, with patience, throughout this journey along the paths of memory and nostalgia, Eden Tzur, Tehiya Ben Porat, Naomi Listenberg, Moriah Oron, and Matan Avigal.

To Nicolas Grivel and Leslie Perreaut, thank you for helping me to believe in myself before even I did. And of course to Delcourt Publishing and its wonderful team.

To Asaf Hanuka, my mentor, who trusted me and guided me through the creation of my final project in Shenkar and up to the moment of publishing the album. And to Hila Shaltieli, who pushed me to explore the boundaries of my work.

To Dorith Daliot, the one and only, who courageously translated this book from Hebrew to French. Thank you for carrying my words to a distant land in this pandemic.

It is a privilege to say thank you, and it is an even greater privilege to receive all this support and love from all of you. Toda!

TOHAR SHERMAN-FRIEDMAN

To my wonderful parents,
whom I love.

It is an honor
to be your daughter.

PROLOGUE

"THE SHOUTS OF JOY HAVE BEEN STILLED*"

Isaiah 16:9

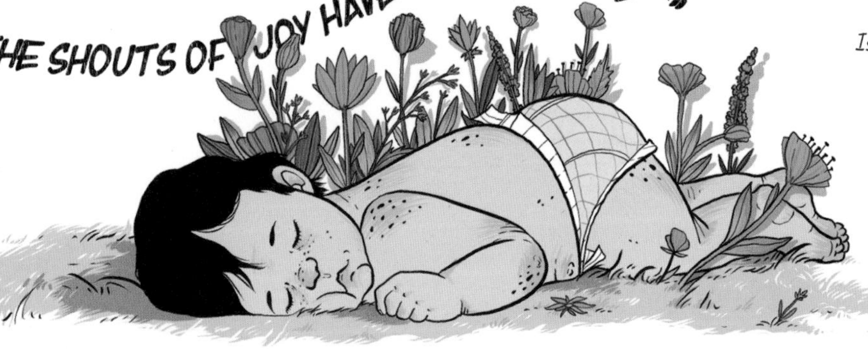

It's sad to die, and, perhaps, to be born, in midsummer.
As my mother was about to bring me into the world, her own mother was suffering in the advanced stages of cancer.

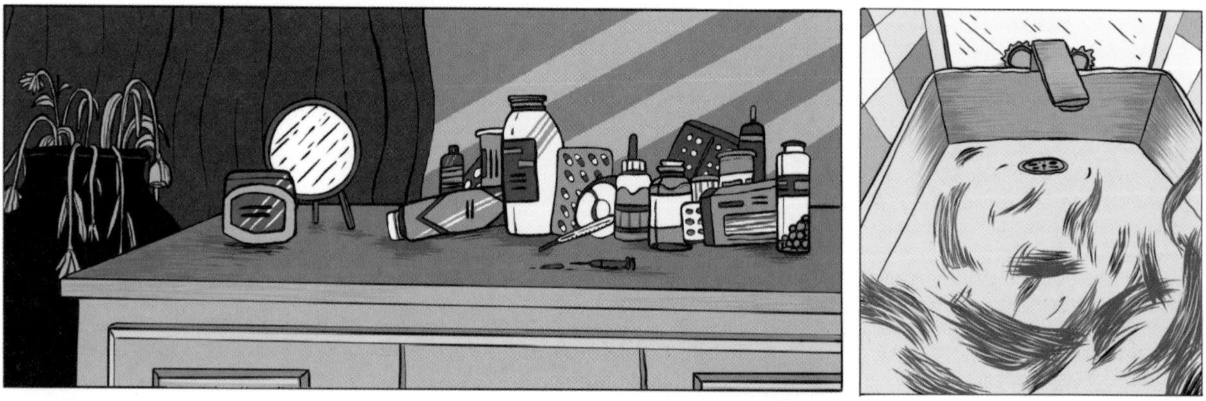

When I think about what my mom must have been feeling when she was carrying me inside her, I get an impression of finality. A routine cruelly cut off by the nature of things. I was born, my grandmother died.

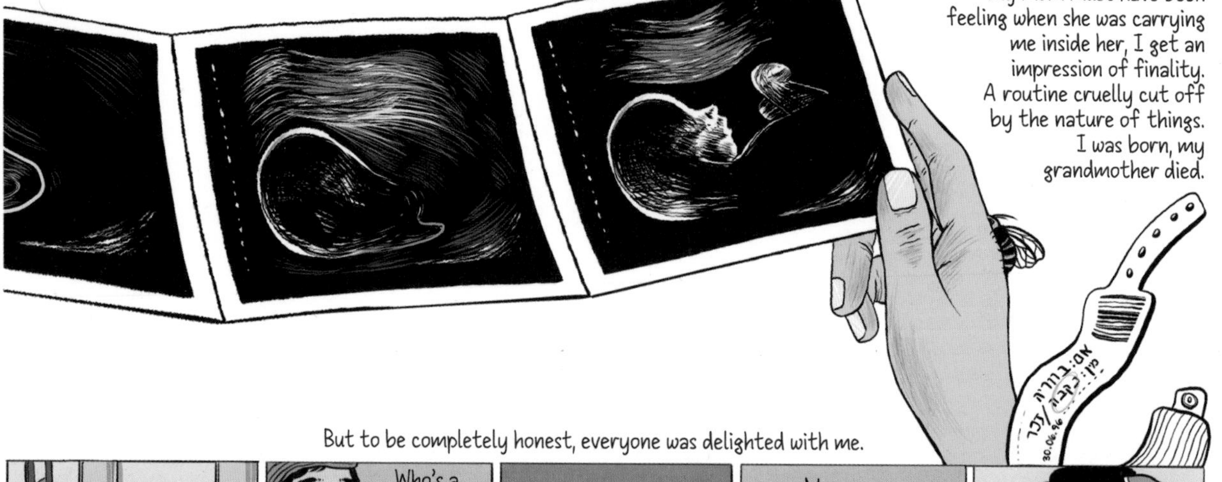

But to be completely honest, everyone was delighted with me.

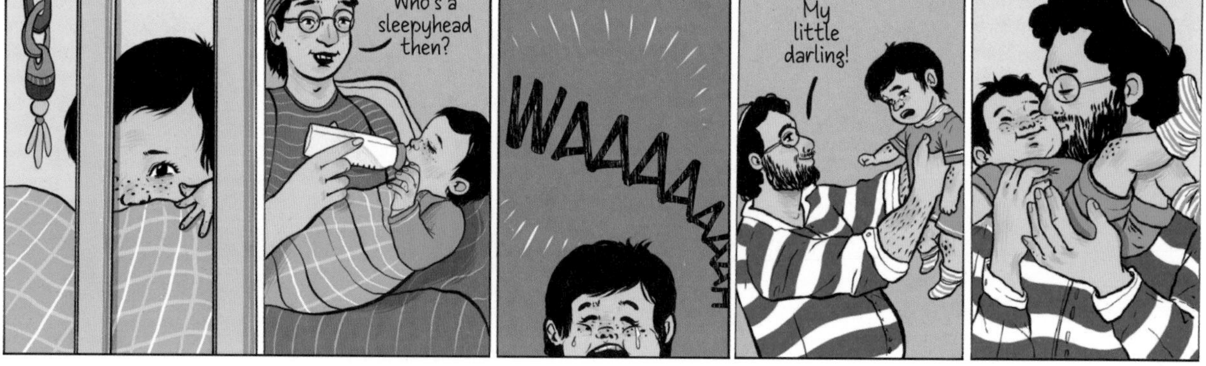
Who's a sleepyhead then?
WAAAAAAAH
My little darling!

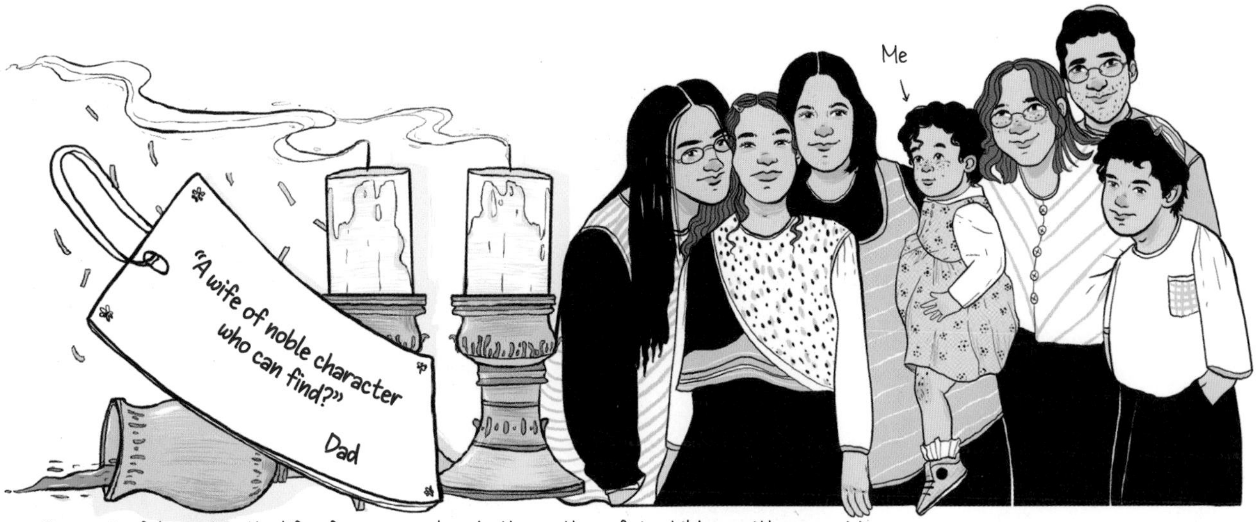
Me
“A wife of noble character who can find?”
Dad

I was a joyful event in the life of a woman, already the mother of six children, with a promising career, and a supportive and understanding husband.

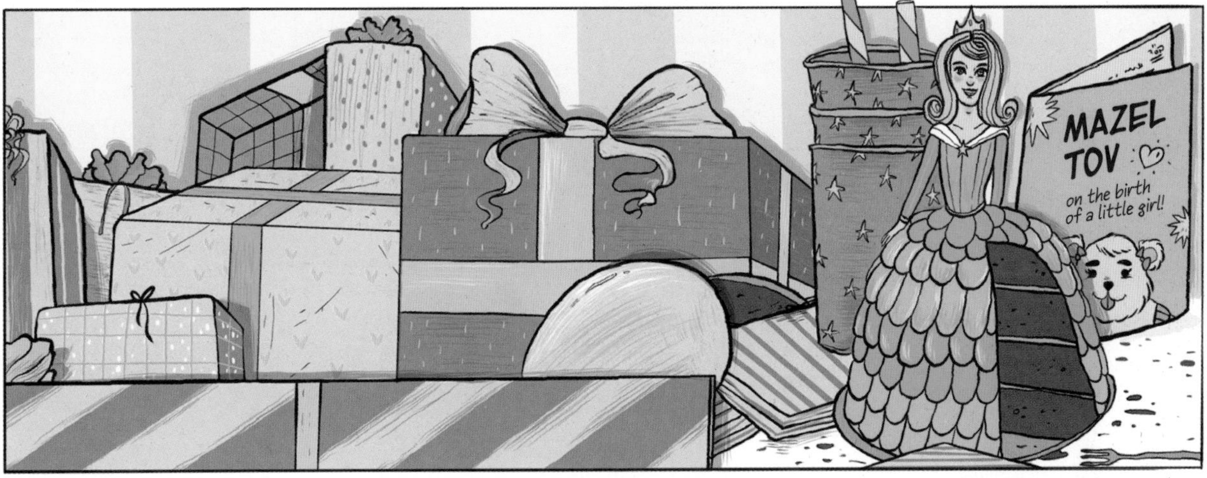
MAZEL TOV
on the birth of a little girl!

And perhaps a little bit of my mother's sadness and uncertainty ended up in me.
My mom's mom died just a year later, in the month of Tammuz*, my birth month.

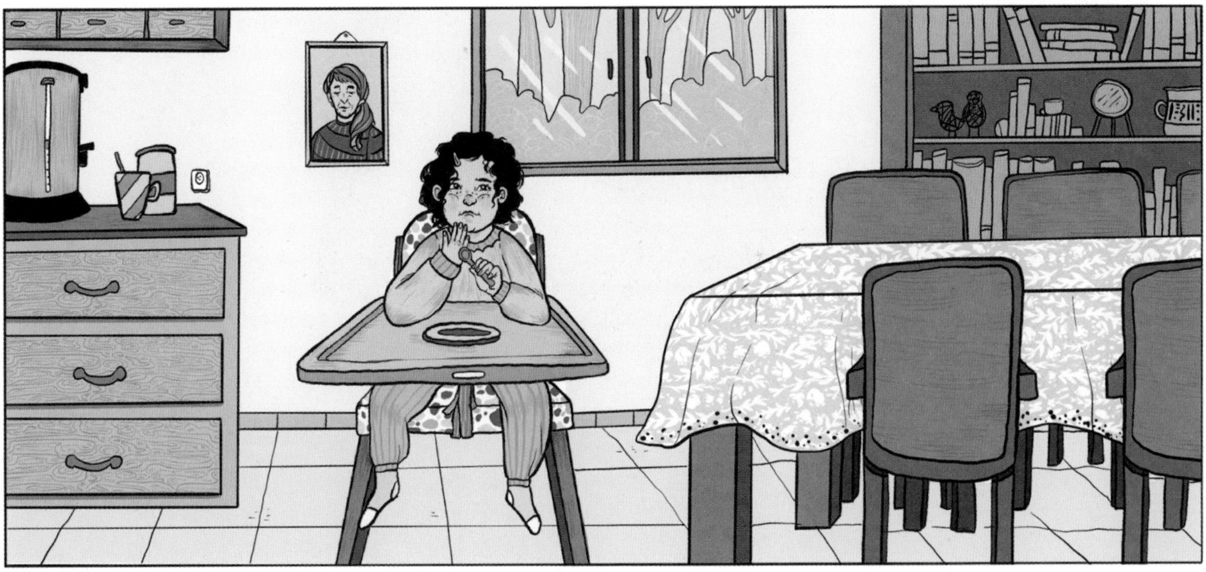

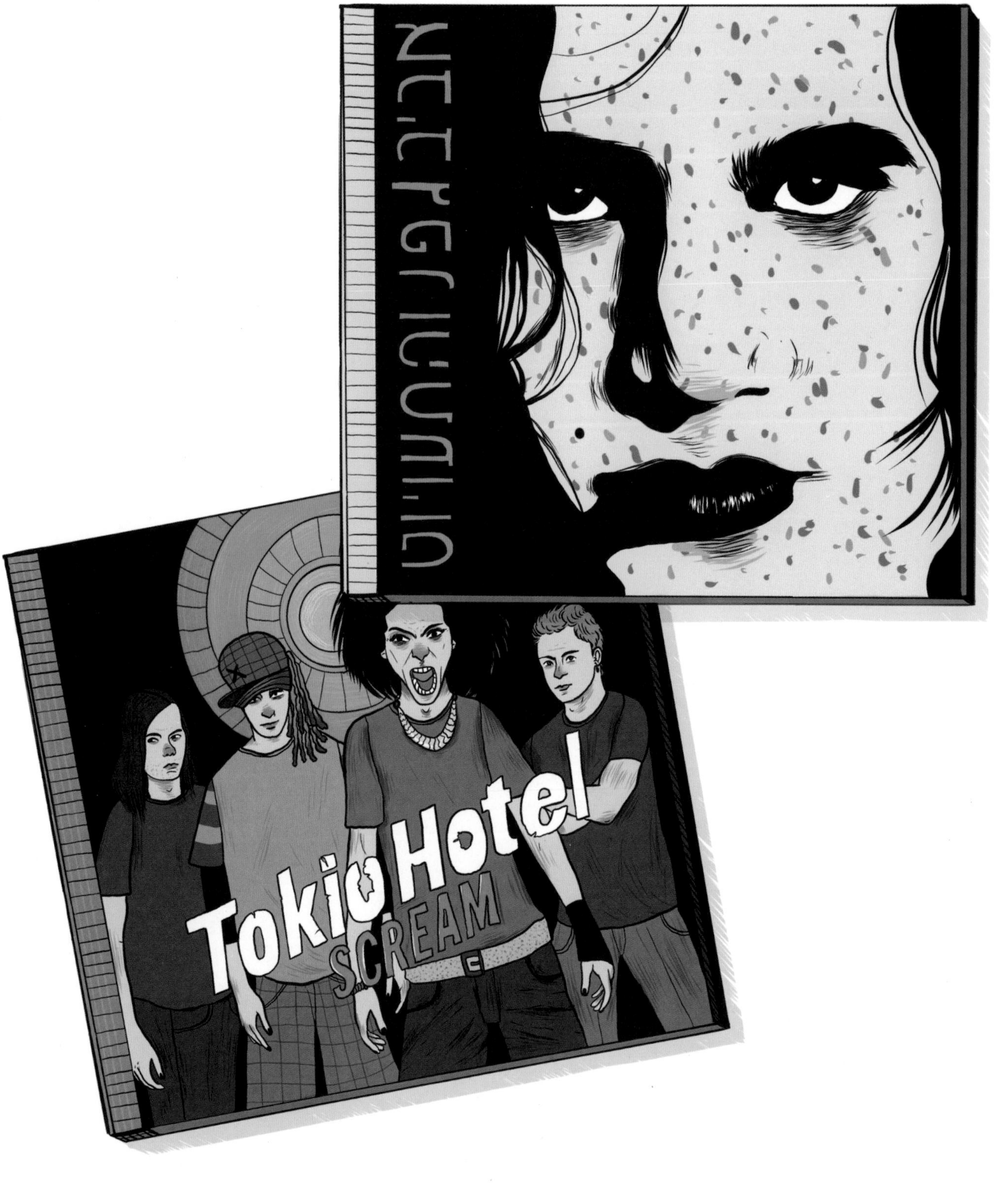
Tokio Hotel
SCREAM

PART ONE

A Billion Wanderers

NOT ALONE

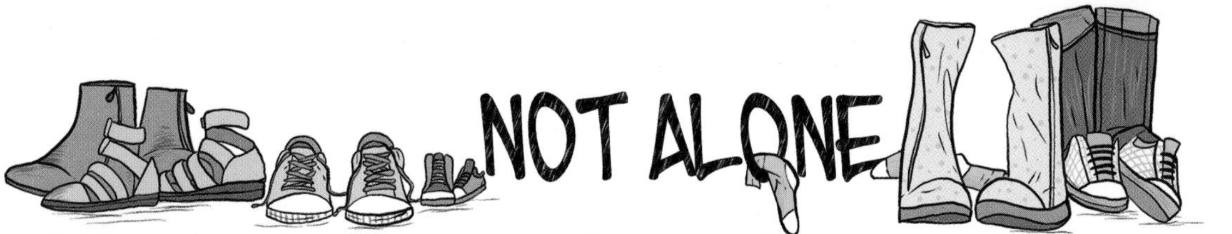

They say that the experiences we have at a very young age shape the person we are today.
Rather than experiences, I'd say events, or crucial moments. When I was 3, something happened.

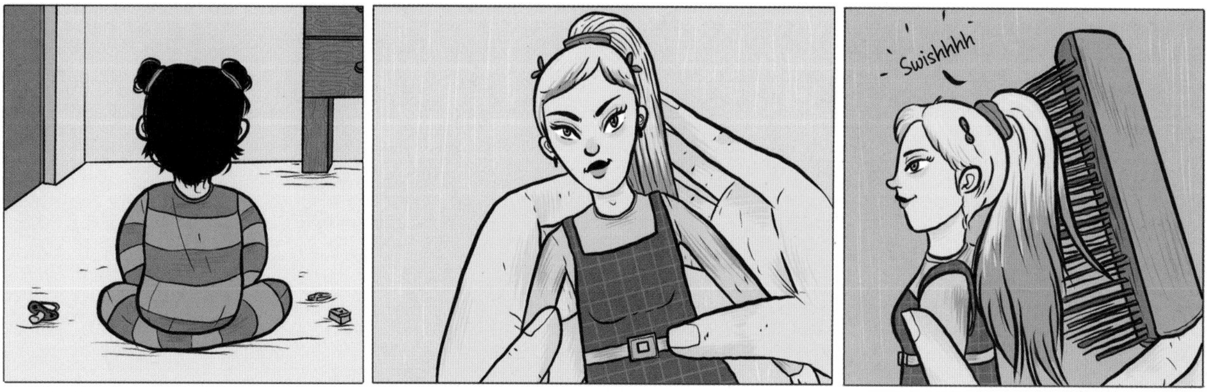

Swishhhh

You don't really remember from when you were 3, but I know that all my brothers and sisters, apart from my oldest sister, still lived at home.

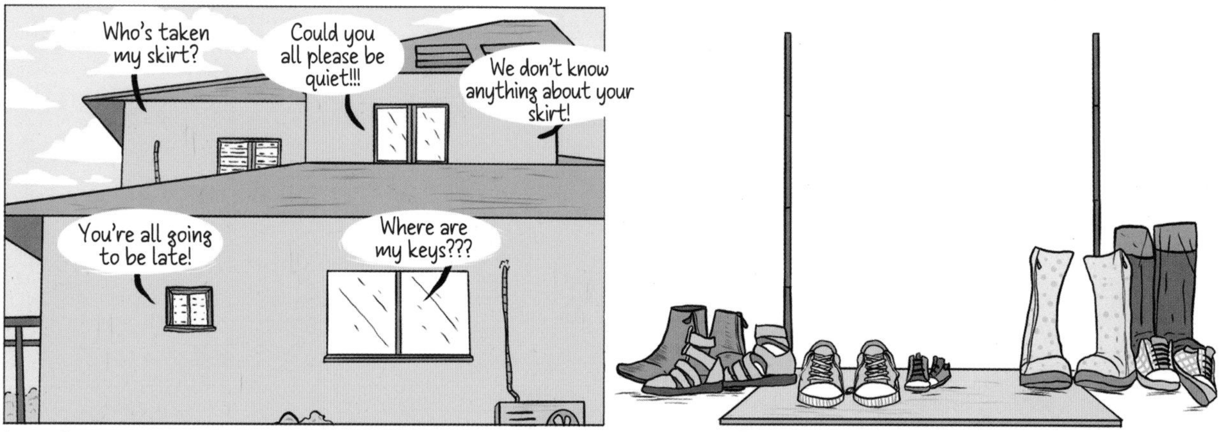

Who's taken my skirt?
Could you all please be quiet!!!
We don't know anything about your skirt!
You're all going to be late!
Where are my keys???

From first thing in the morning, a family with seven kids is chaos! The pile of dishes in the sink must have driven my mother crazy, along with the breadcrumbs on the kitchen counter. In a flurry of hasty goodbyes and schoolbags, everyone left, apart from me, the littlest and the last, 3 years old. In a corner of my room I played with my Barbie with the ends of her hair colored pink with felt pen.

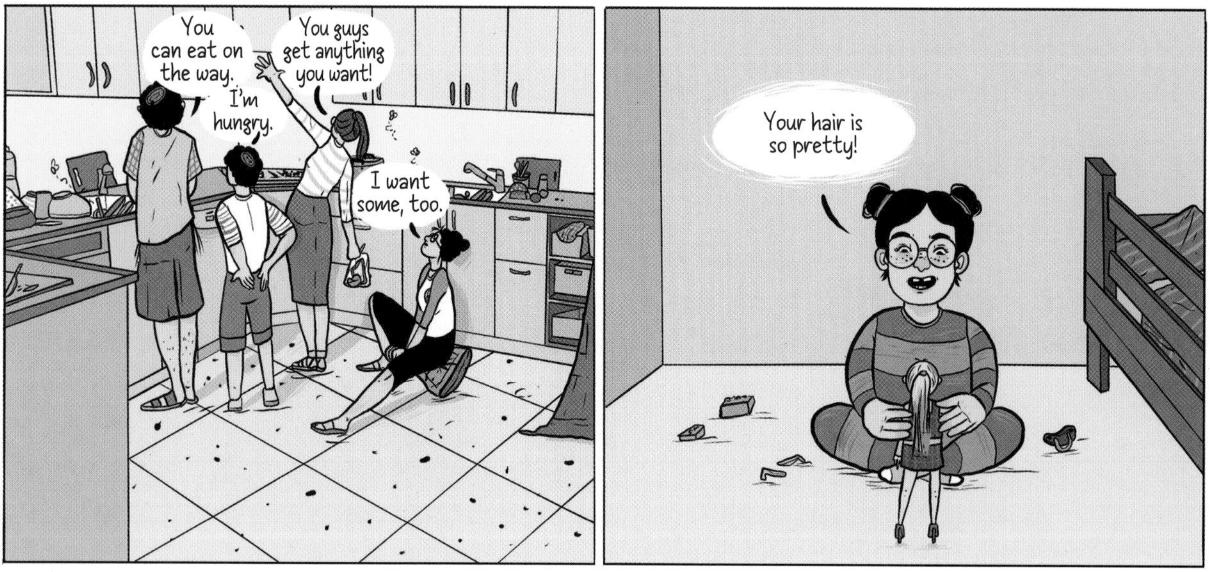

You can eat on the way.
I'm hungry.
You guys get anything you want!
I want some, too.
Your hair is so pretty!

That little girl must have liked the sudden peace in the house, because she was born into uproar. But if she'd known that throughout most of her childhood the house would be empty, she would have appreciated those noisy times.

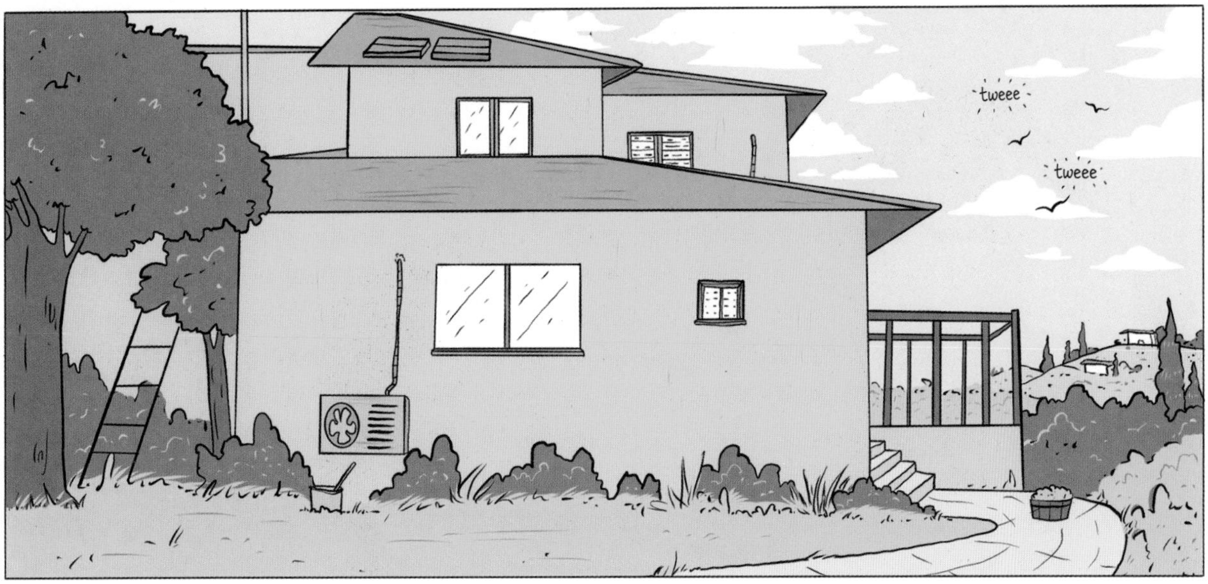
tweee
tweee

I wonder if she got scared when she realized that she was all alone, that she'd been forgotten. That I'd been forgotten.

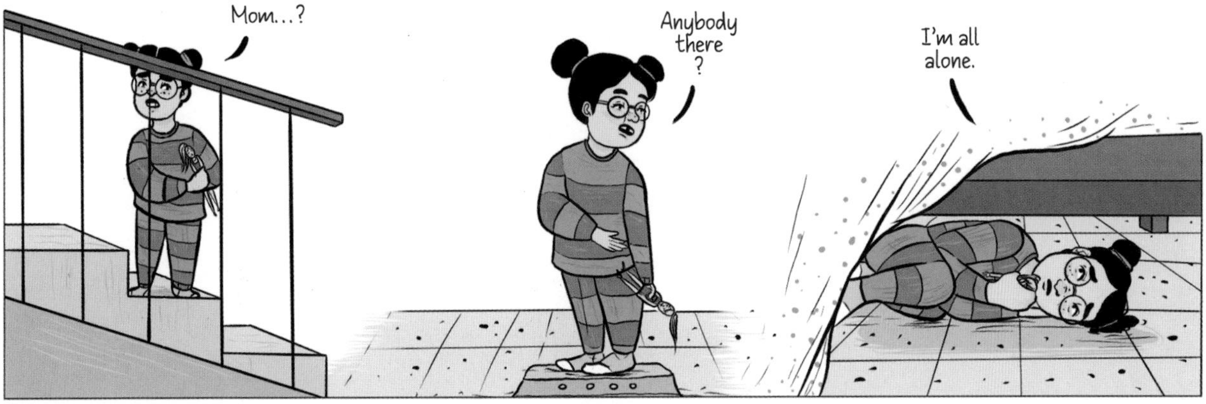
Mom...?
Anybody there ?
I'm all alone.

I wonder if she cried, if she screamed, if she knew that everyone had gone, or if she liked it.

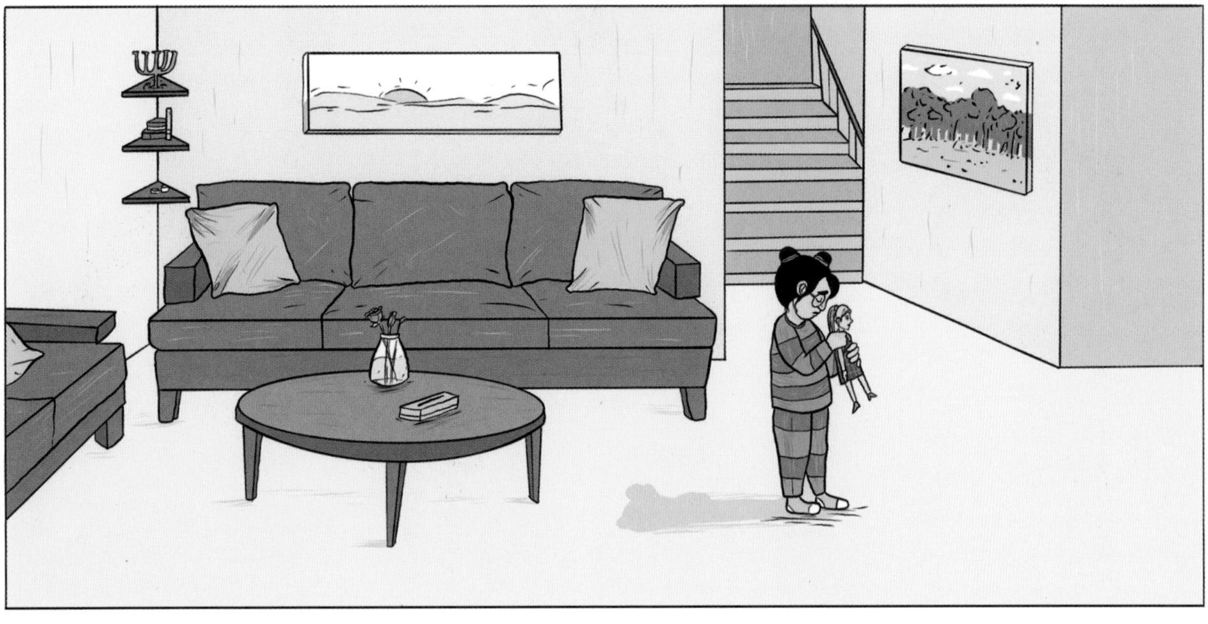

The year I was 9, we had renovation work done on the house. One evening, I was alone, and night was just falling. Suddenly I heard a series of little beeps coming from the living room. I tried to home in on where it was coming from.

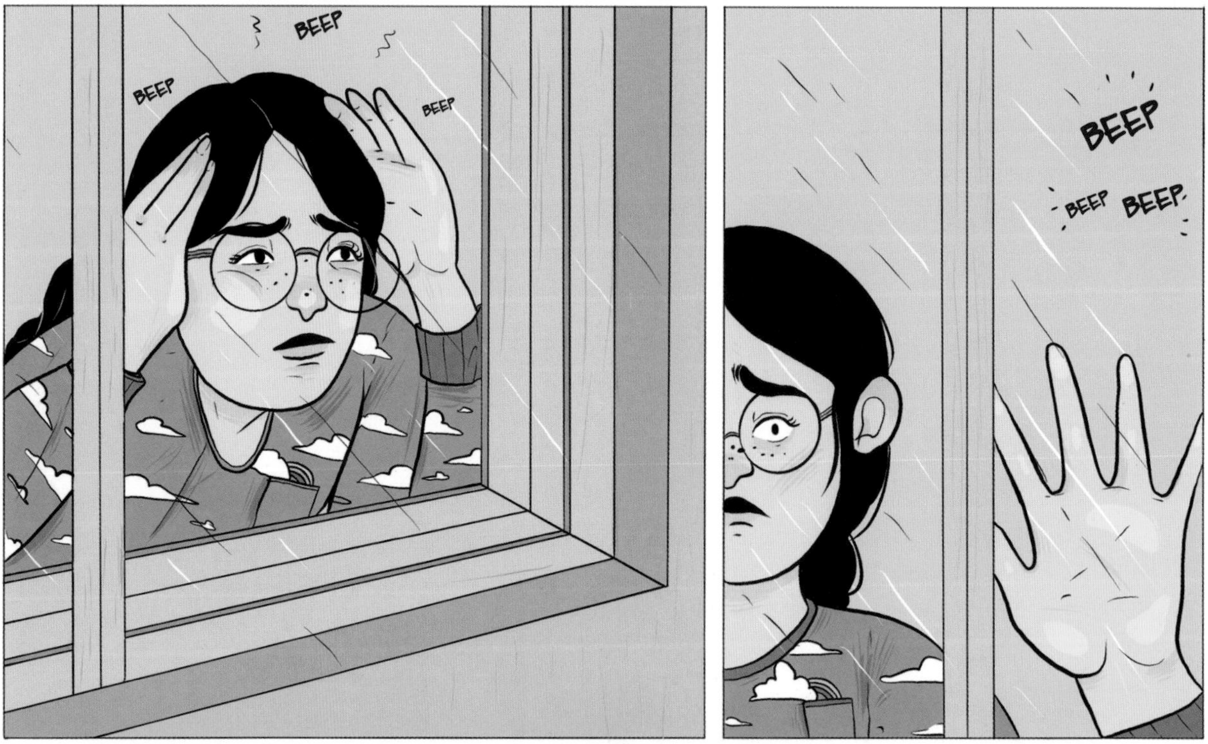

BEEP
BEEP
BEEP
BEEP
BEEP
BEEP

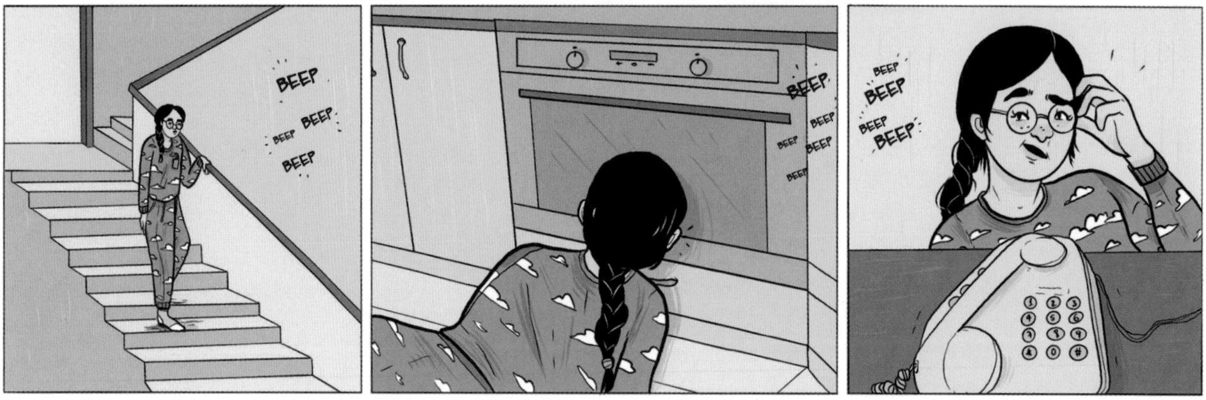

BEEP
BEEP
BEEP
BEEP
BEEP
BEEP
BEEP
BEEP
BEEP
BEEP
BEEP
BEEP
BEEP
BEEP

My gaze fell on the alarm screen, which was flashing green/yellow with the "Intrusion" alert. I knew that meant "Terror attack threat." I started sweating, afraid, as I tried to remember the procedure to follow when that happened.

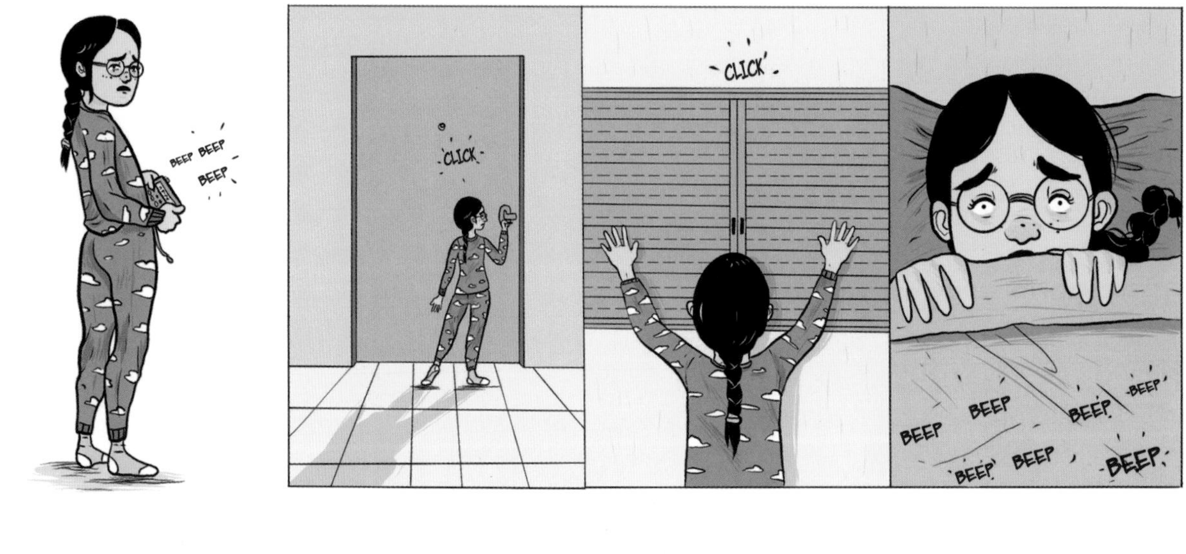

BEEP BEEP
BEEP
CLICK
CLICK
BEEP
BEEP
BEEP
BEEP
BEEP
BEEP
BEEP
BEEP

I curled up in a corner, terrified. I imagined all the methods a terrorist might use to attack me.

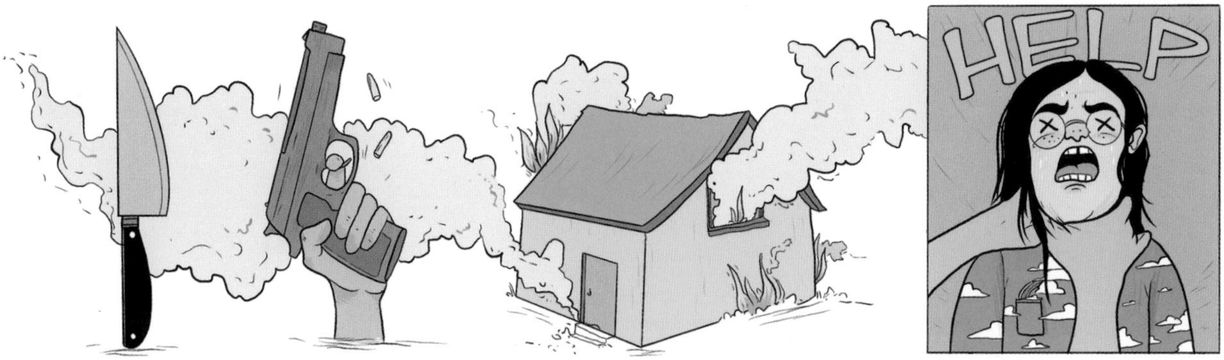
HELP

In my parents' bedroom, listening to the wind whistling outside, I thought about little 3-year-old Tohar.
And that's when I understood: she didn't want to be alone, and she was so happy to see her mother rushing to kiss her.

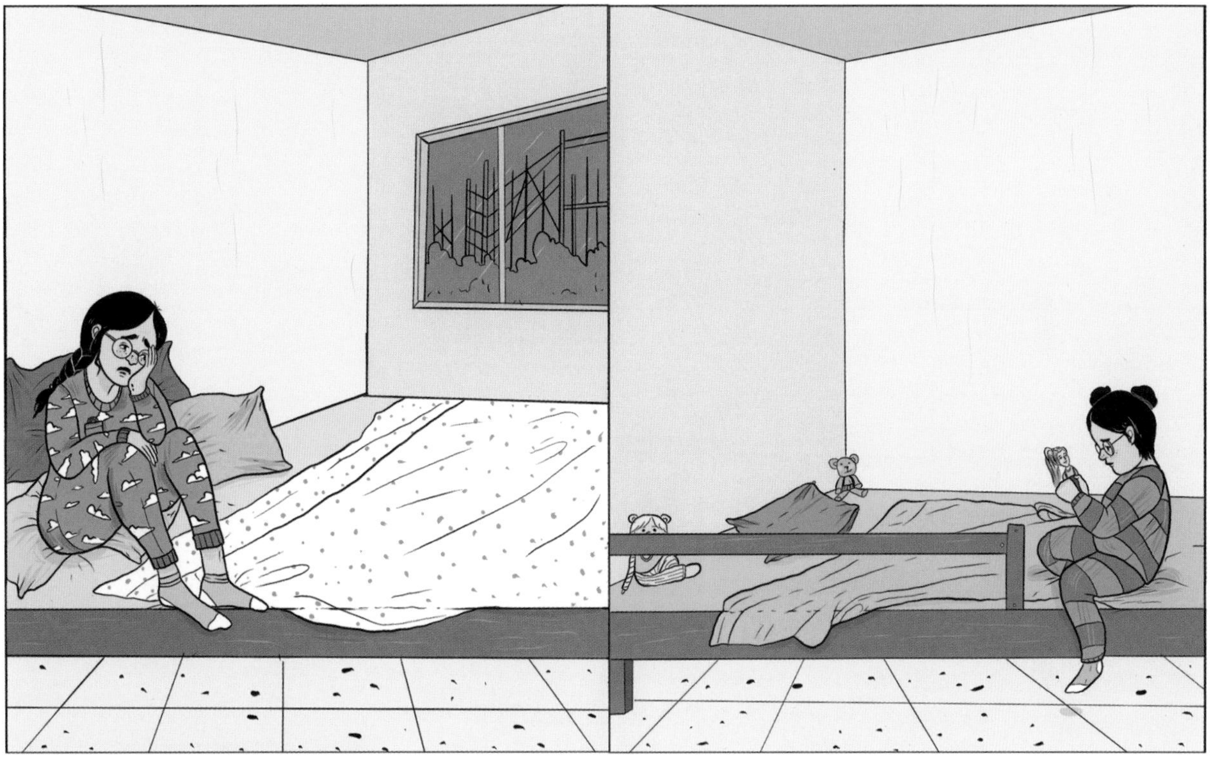

So I prayed with all my heart for someone to come and save me, and hug me tight ... And then the phone rang.

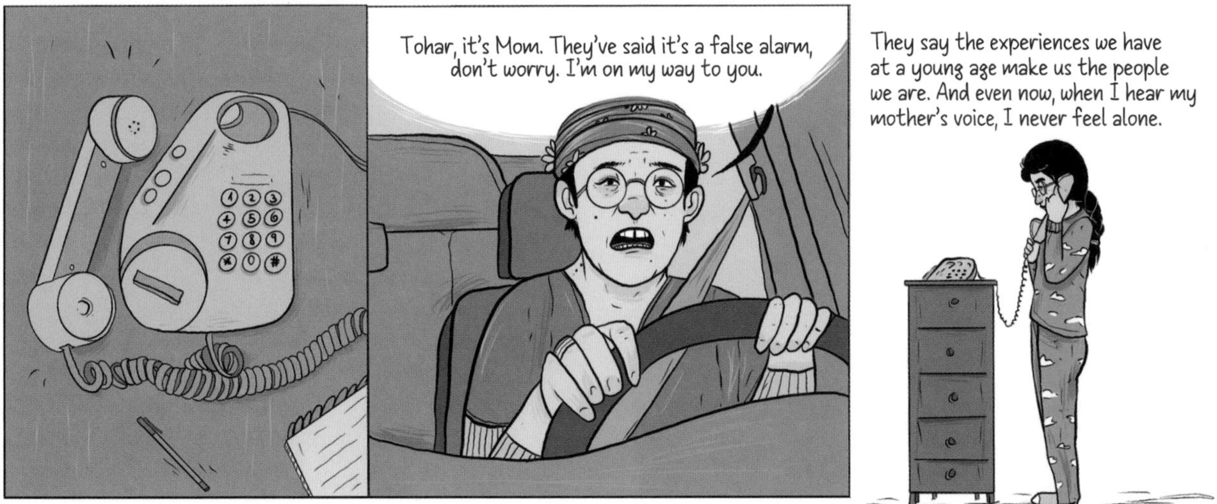
Tohar, it's Mom. They've said it's a false alarm, don't worry. I'm on my way to you.
They say the experiences we have at a young age make us the people we are. And even now, when I hear my mother's voice, I never feel alone.

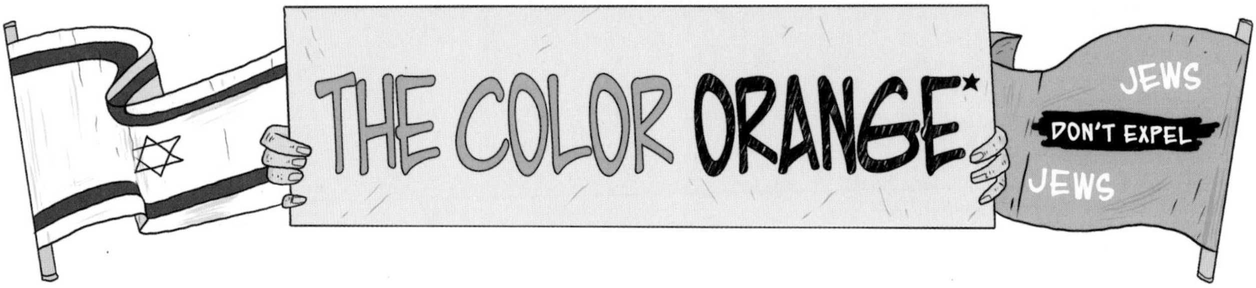
THE COLOR ORANGE*
JEWS
DON'T EXPEL
JEWS

2004, end of the summer. Under orders from Sharon, the Gaza settlements were evacuated. Orange ribbons fluttered everywhere as a sign of protest, while supporters of the Shalom Achshav movement's "Land for Peace" proposal wore blue ribbons.

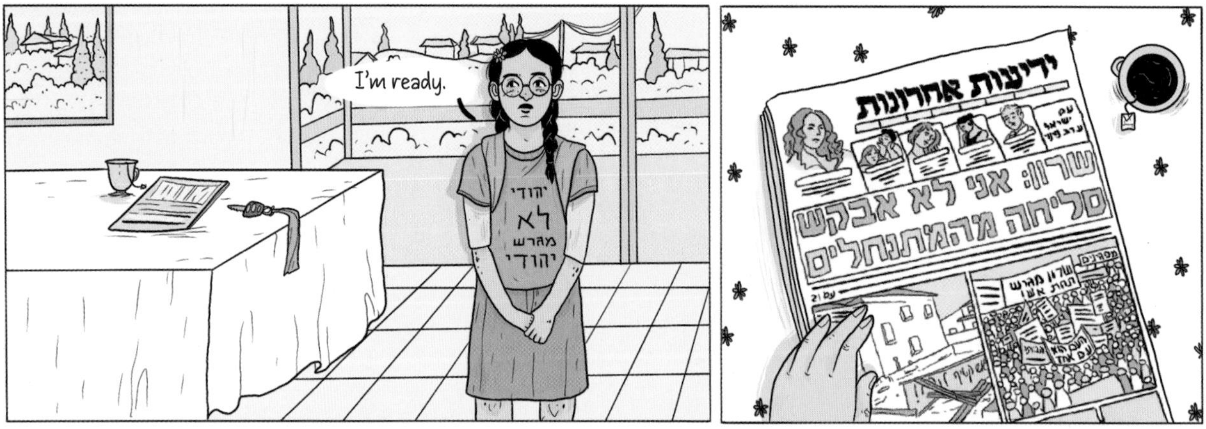
I'm ready.
יהודי לא מגרש יהודי
ידיעות אחרונות
שרון: אני לא אבקש סליחה מהמתנחלים

We set off. A blinding sun beat through the car windows. I tried to doze while my parents were having a heated discussion about the national situation. There was talk of a split, a civil war.

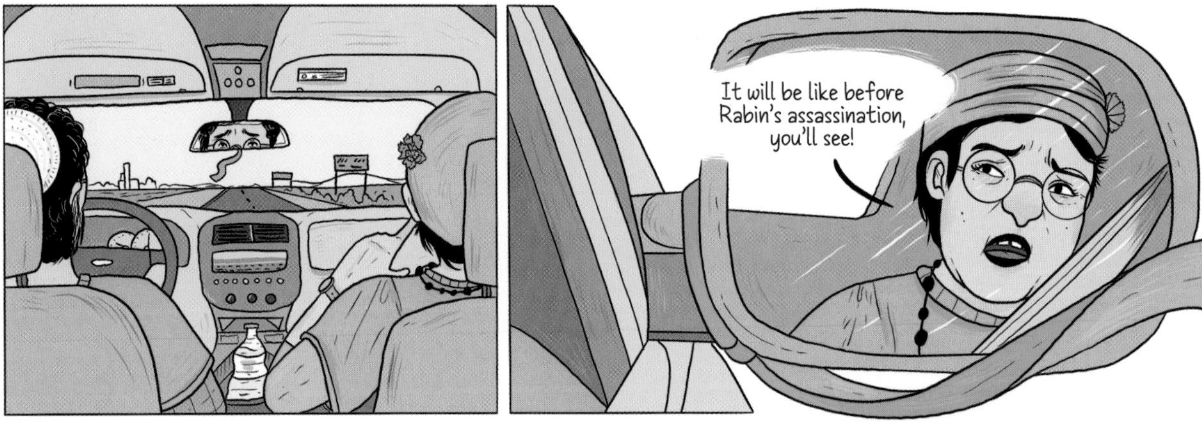
It will be like before Rabin's assassination, you'll see!

I wasn't really listening to them. My eyes were glued to the orange ribbon tied to the side-view mirror, which was floating in the summer breeze.

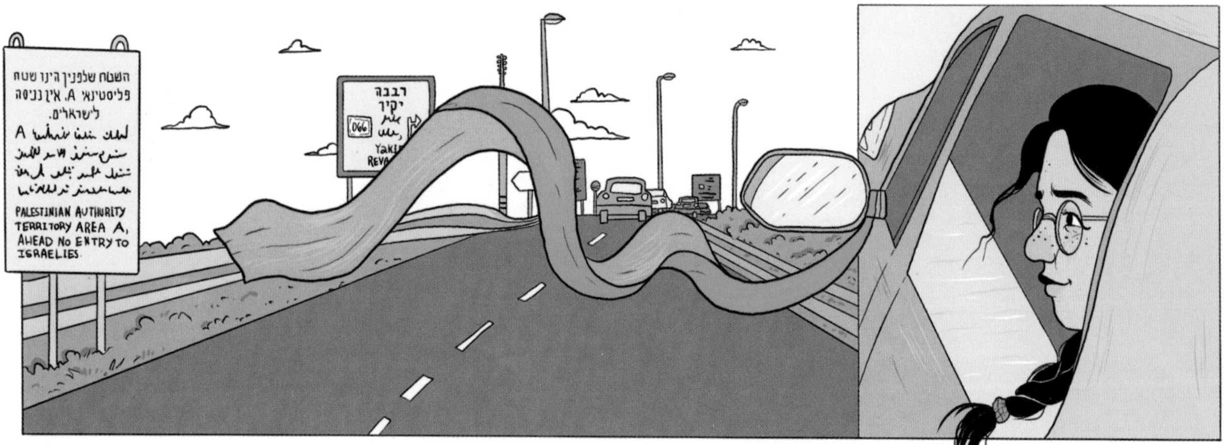
השטח שלפניך הינו שטח פליסטינאי A. אין כניסה לישראלים.
PALESTINIAN AUTHURITY TERRITORY AREA A, AHEAD NO ENTRY TO ISRAELIES.
רבבה
יקיר
066

That morning, I'd asked Dad where we were going. He talked about a protest. I didn't really understand, but I was happy to be going out. I could already recognize the road out of the settlement, as I had some landmarks and waypoints.

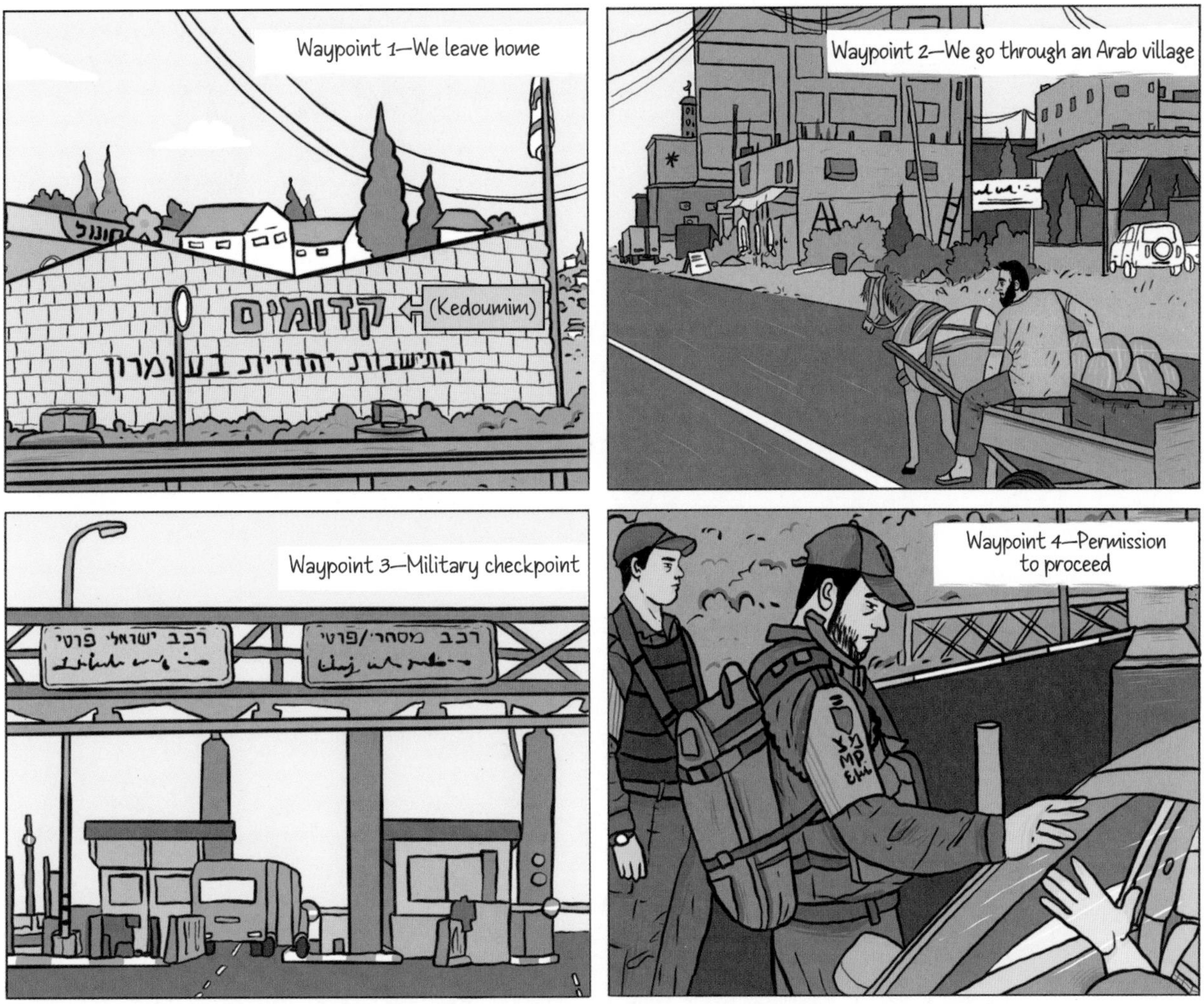
Waypoint 1—We leave home
קדומים
(Kedoumim)
התישבות יהודית בשומרון
Waypoint 2—We go through an Arab village
Waypoint 3—Military checkpoint
רכב ישראלי פרטי
רכב מסחרי/פרטי
Waypoint 4—Permission to proceed
MP

At the checkpoint, Dad opens the windows, greets the soldiers, and wishes them a good day or something like that before going on. I try to understand if there's a special code, because we go on, but some cars don't make it through. I get bored and count the vehicles with an orange ribbon. Suddenly I see one where it's blue.

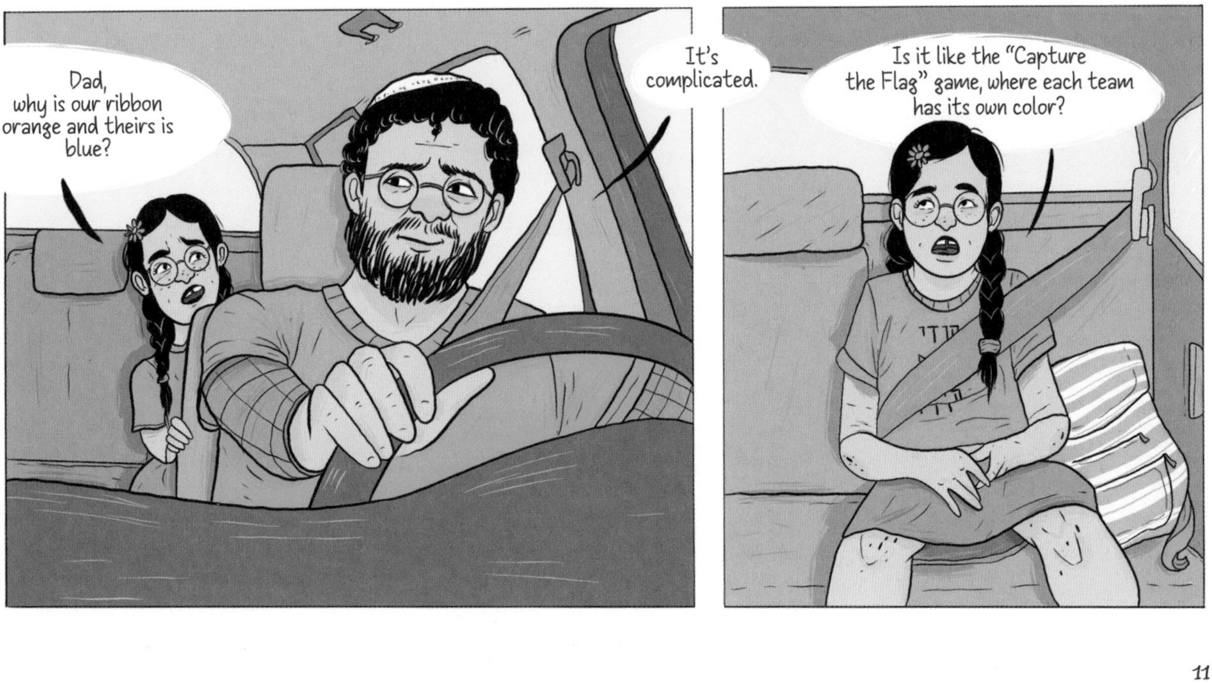
Dad, why is our ribbon orange and theirs is blue?
It's complicated.
Is it like the "Capture the Flag" game, where each team has its own color?

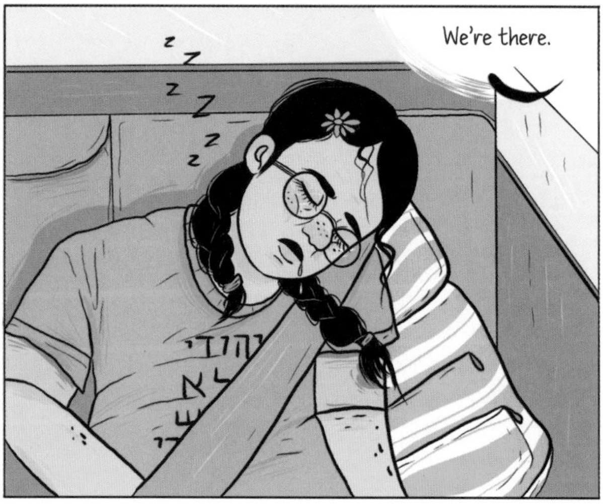
We're there.

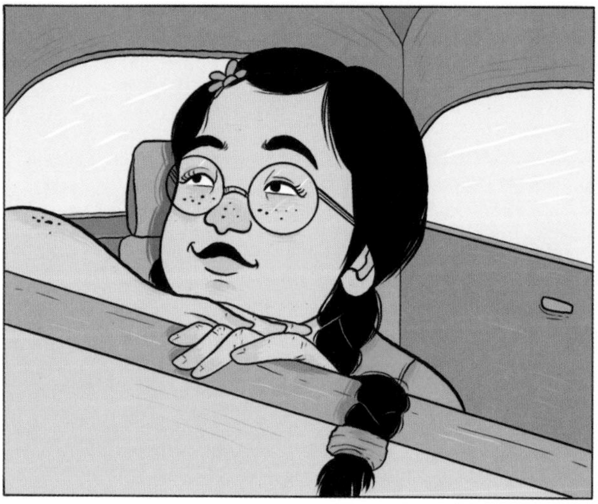

I was hungry. Settling down to eat an apple, I looked on the ground.

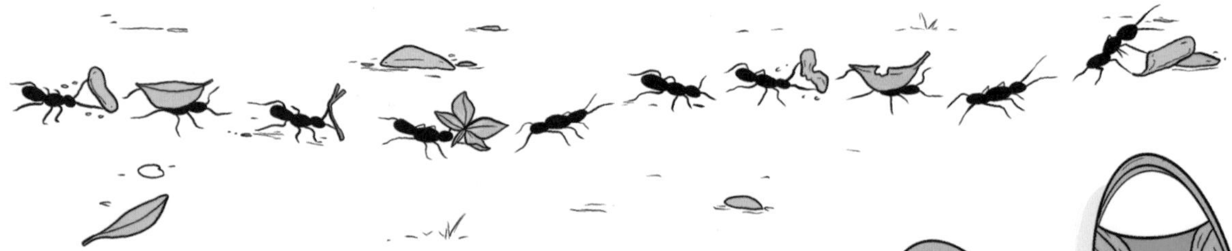

An ant colony was carrying bits of leaf, twigs, and crumbs of something that was almost gone. My mother's voice called me out of my thoughts. "Come on, Tohar, we're going to join everyone!"

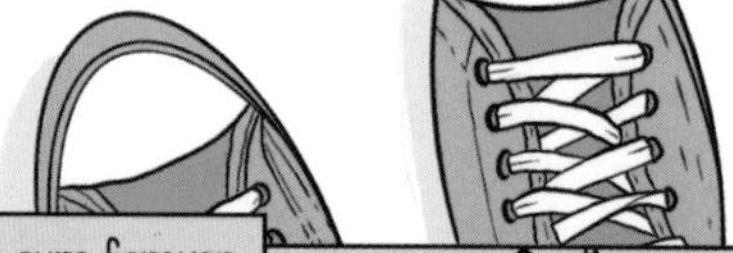

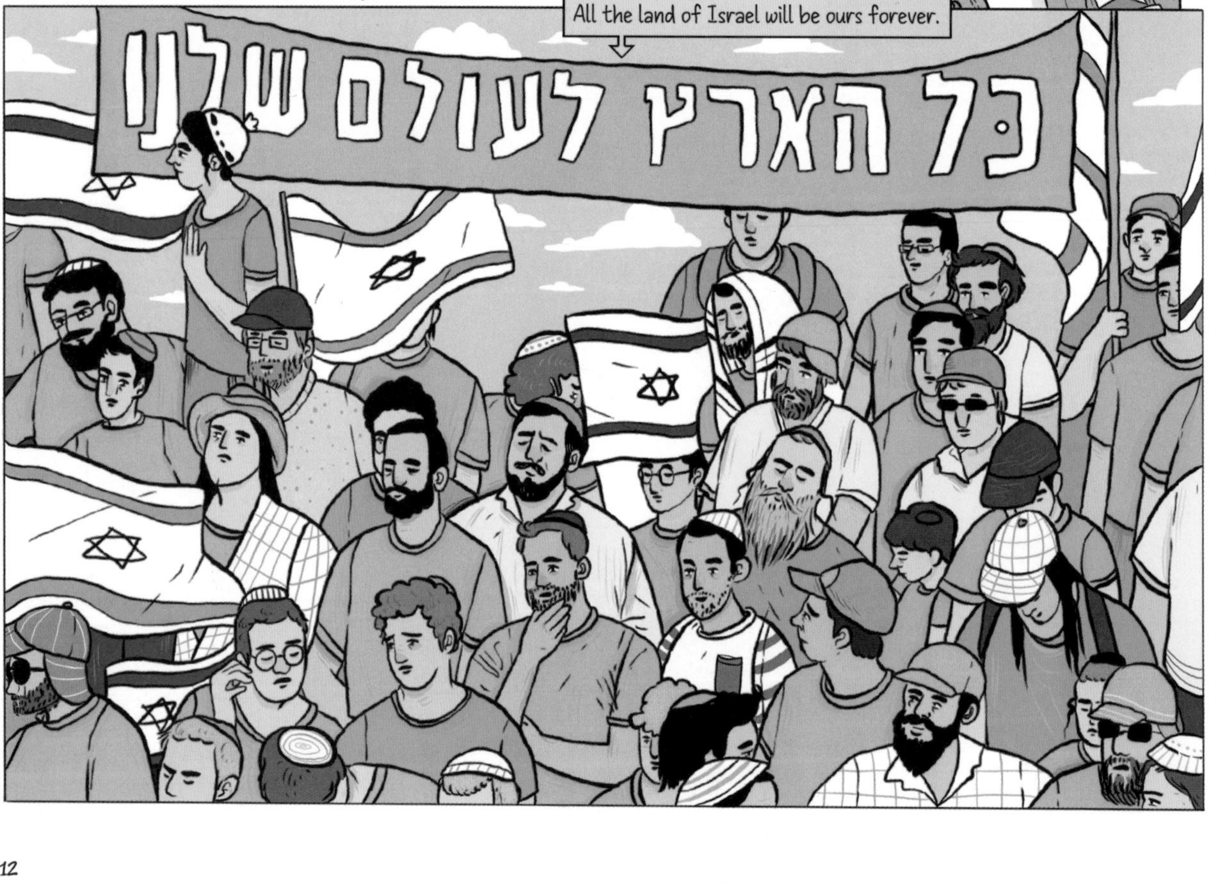
All the land of Israel will be ours forever.
כל הארץ לעולם שלנו

Dozens of people in T-shirts were holding hands. There were no familiar faces until I saw my sister Tovi and her family. We were so happy! We'd joined the orange chain!

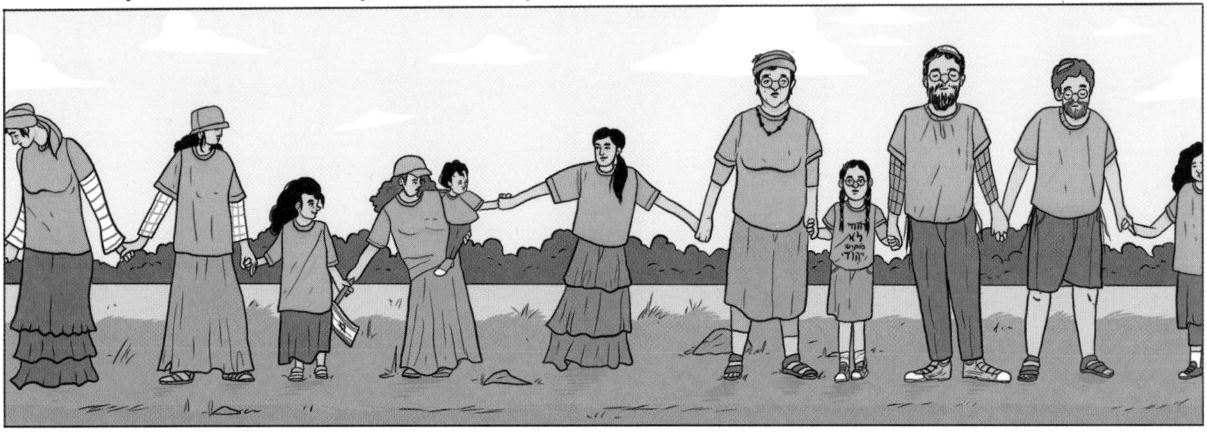

The sun was beating down. I remember my mother's hand, damp with sweat. I wanted to let go, but I didn't know if that was allowed. I looked around and everyone was holding hands. The Israeli flag was flying everywhere.

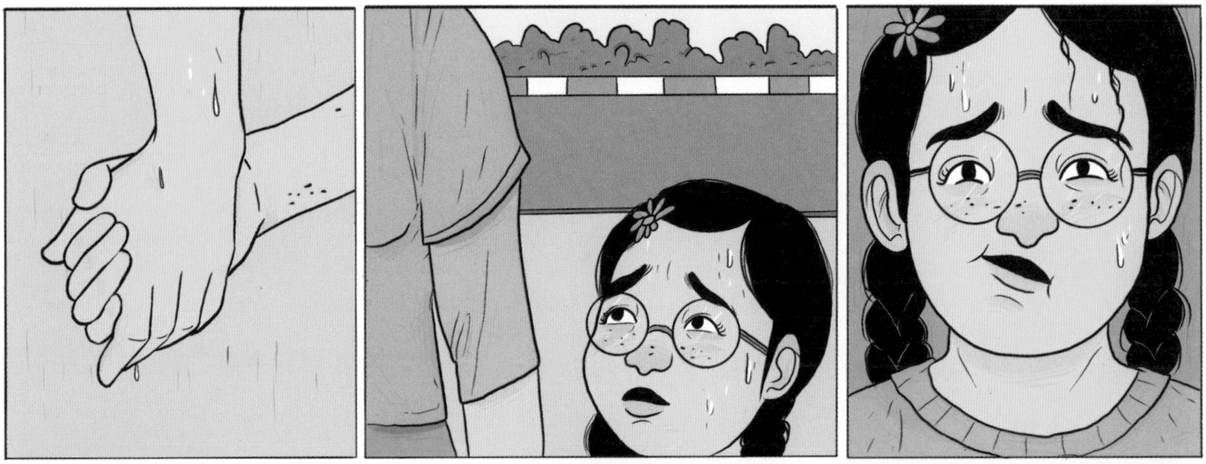

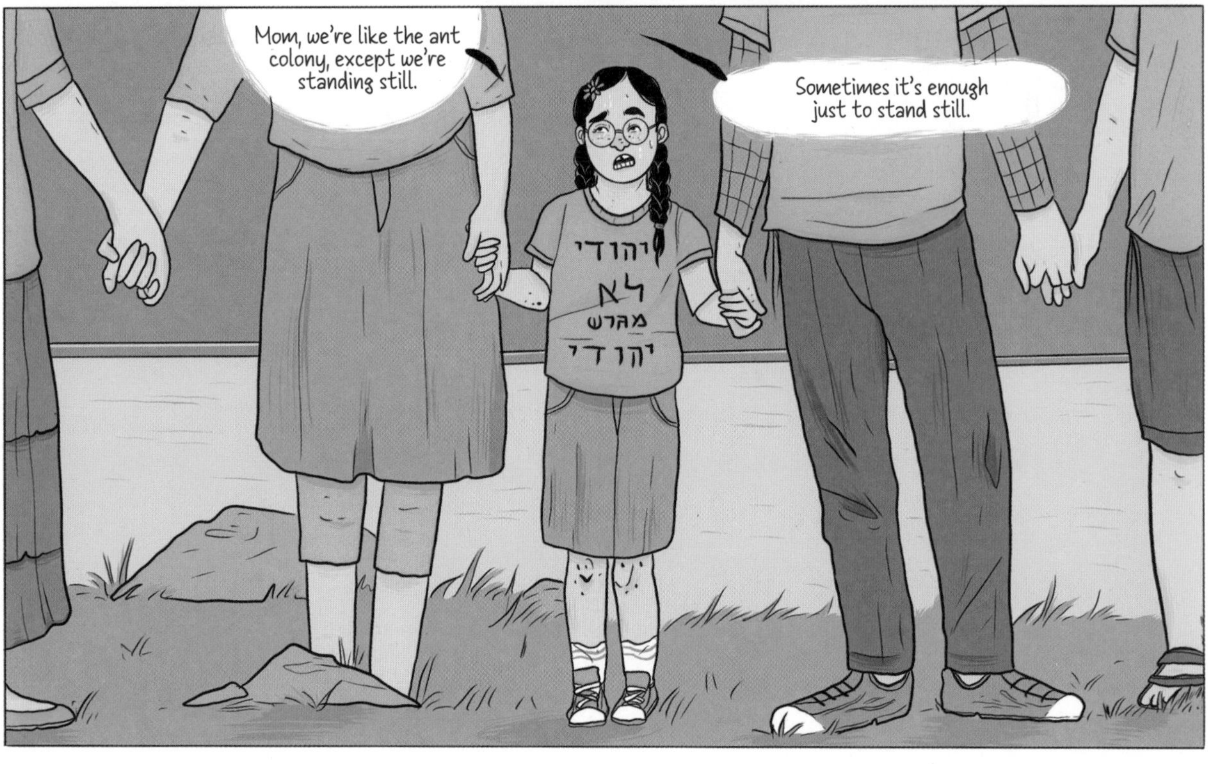
Mom, we're like the ant colony, except we're standing still.
Sometimes it's enough just to stand still.
יהודי
לא
מגרש
יהודי

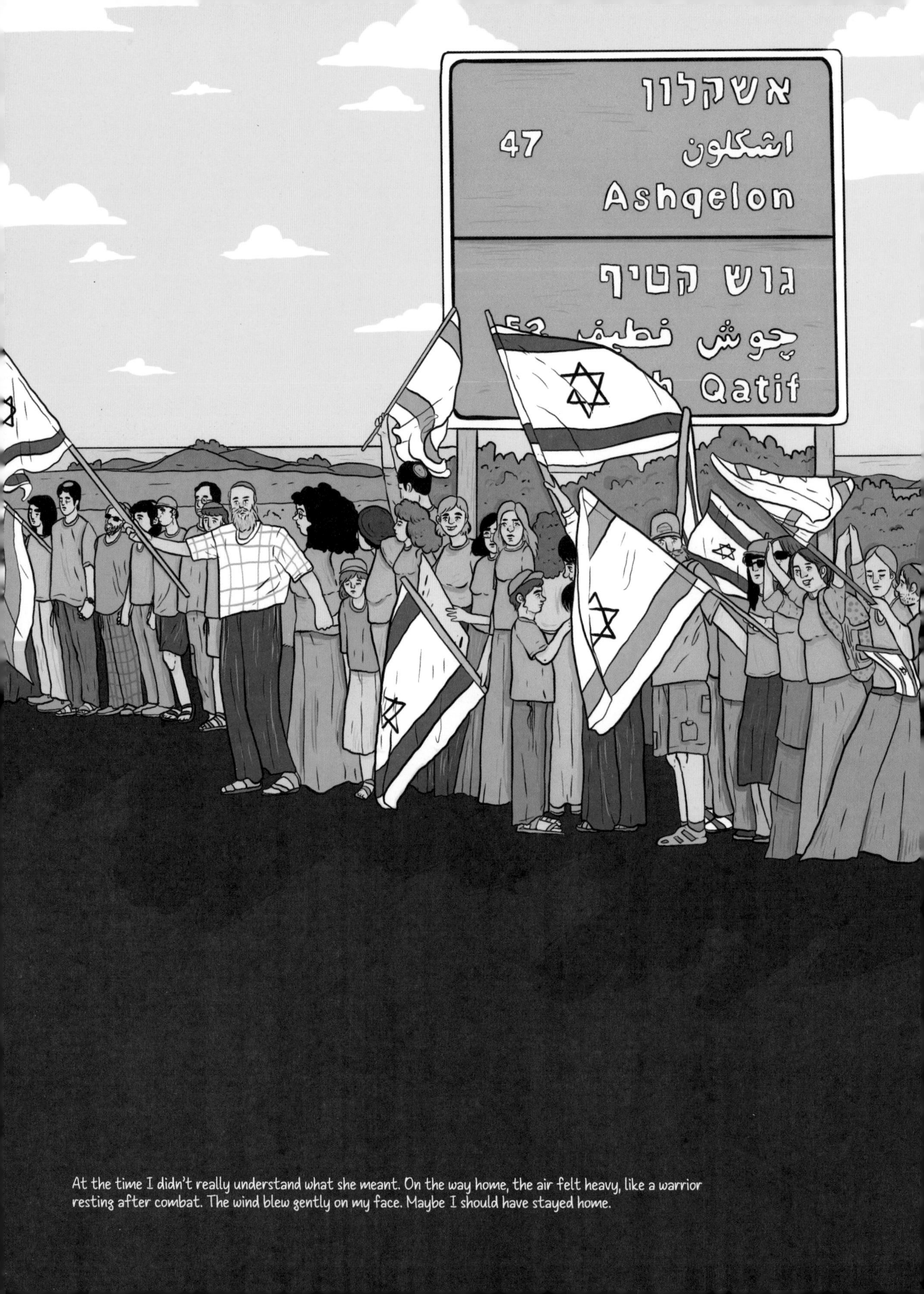

אשקלון
47
اشكلون
Ashqelon
גוש קטיף
Qatif
At the time I didn't really understand what she meant. On the way home, the air felt heavy, like a warrior resting after combat. The wind blew gently on my face. Maybe I should have stayed home.

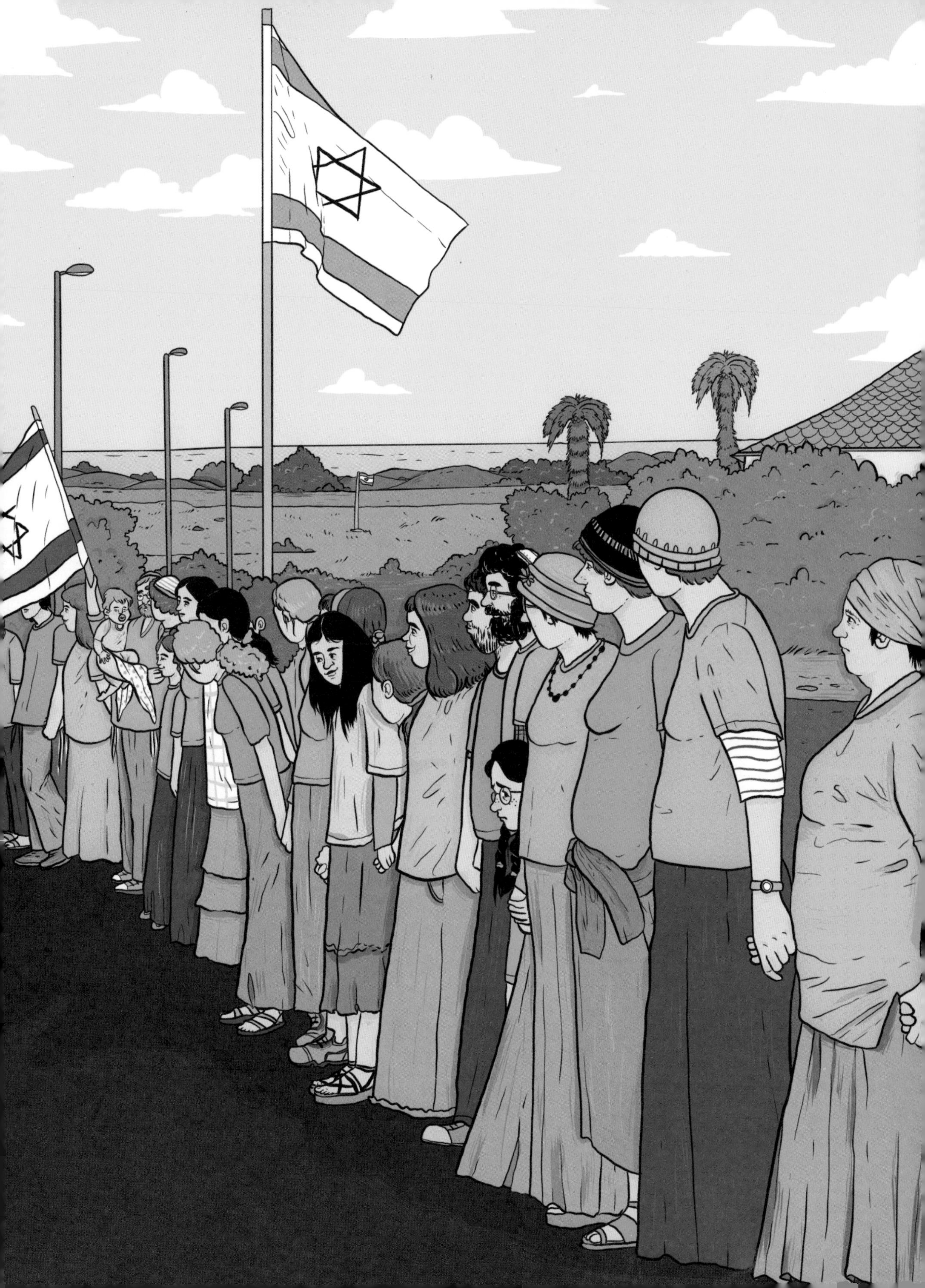

YOUR GENERATION IS SPOILED ROTTEN

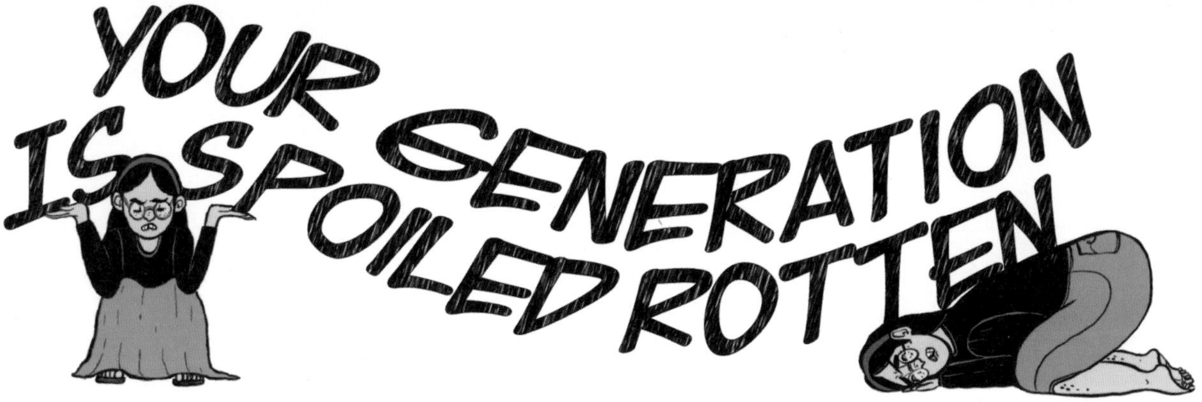

My generation grew up with the promise of a life with a little house and yard with a fence around it. All you had to do for it was live.

You just had to live up to their expectations, work hard, like our forefathers did, and prove that you were worthy, that you were good ... At least as good as them.

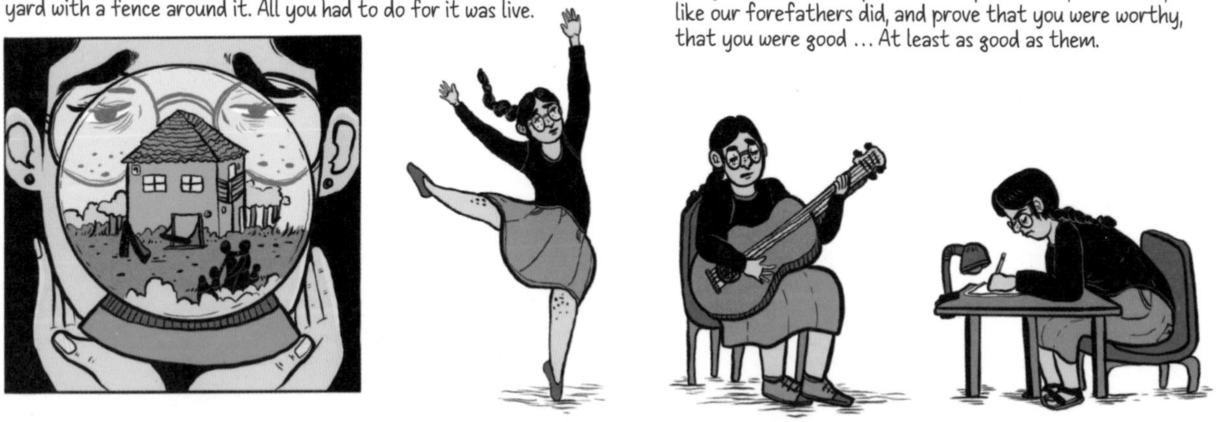

It seemed to me that I was a good girl. I always wanted to be the best. Mediocrity is unbearable—you can always do better. You have to move quickly, not waste time, and not invest too much emotion. "Now what's all this whining?"

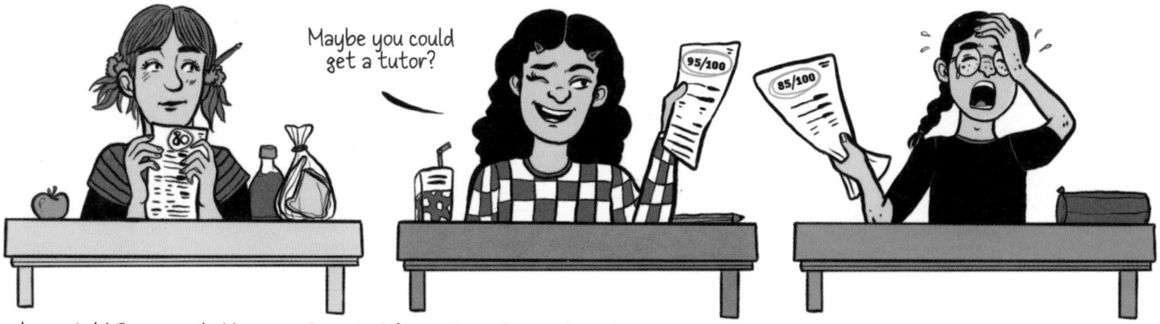
Maybe you could get a tutor?
95/100
85/100

I was always told I was spoiled because I wanted for nothing. But in fact, I grew up in a time when I had to fend for myself: going to school, being top of the class, going home, getting my own dinner, finding things to keep me busy, and especially not bothering the grown-ups in their marathon slog through life.

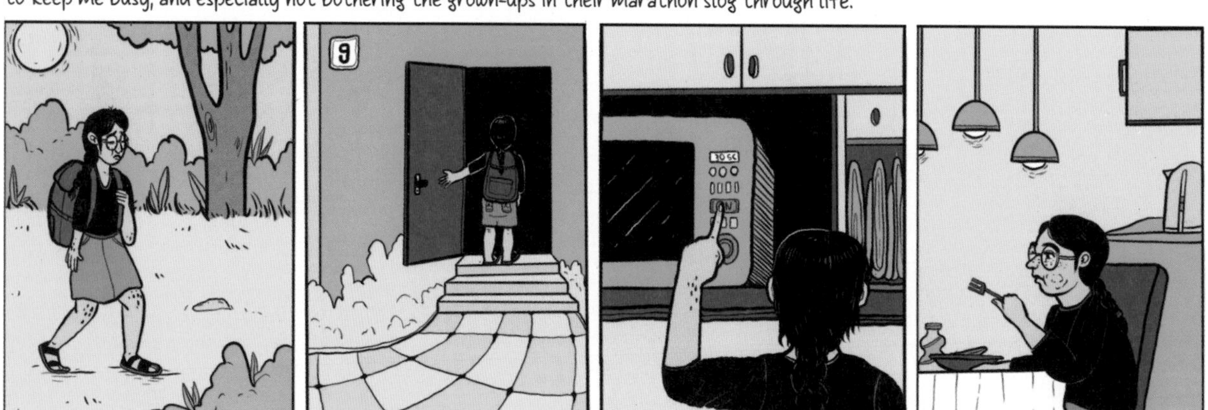
9

Throughout my childhood, I was obsessed by these aims, by this mad dash for success. I was a rather solitary girl. Not sad—more like stressed, in this race toward adolescence, toward glory, toward unattainable perfection.

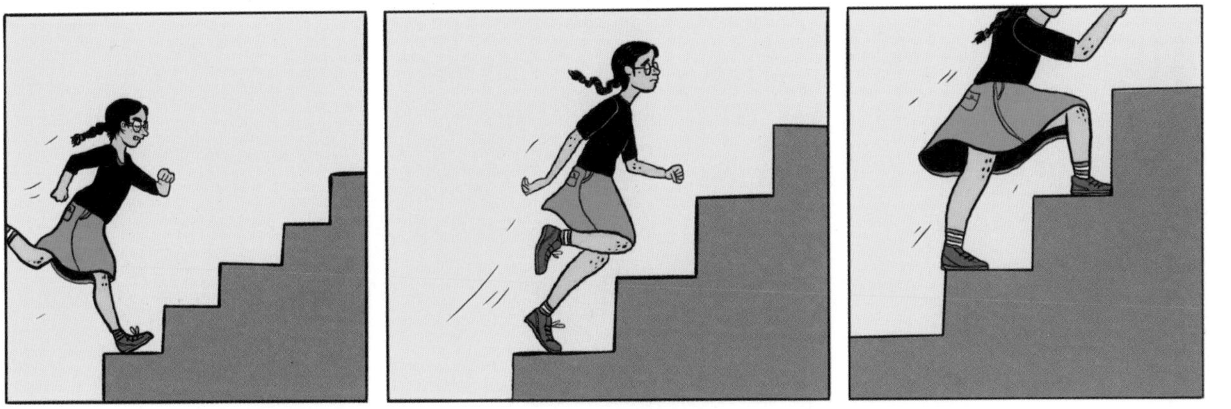

In hindsight, there were successes—music courses, exams, good grades, surprising maturity for my age, and the responsibility I'd taken on.

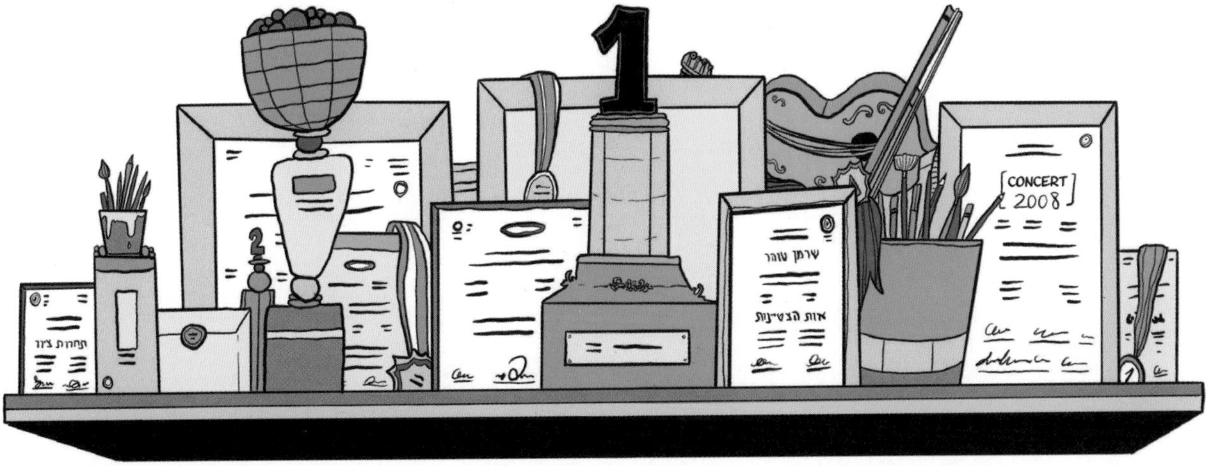
1
2
CONCERT 2008
שרמן טוהר
אות הצטיינות
תחרות ציור

But there was also the empty house, the fast food, the obsessive journal entries (as if someone understood me or was listening to me), the anti-terrorist attack alarm in the living room, the disappointment of my parents, anger, the reproaches from teachers.

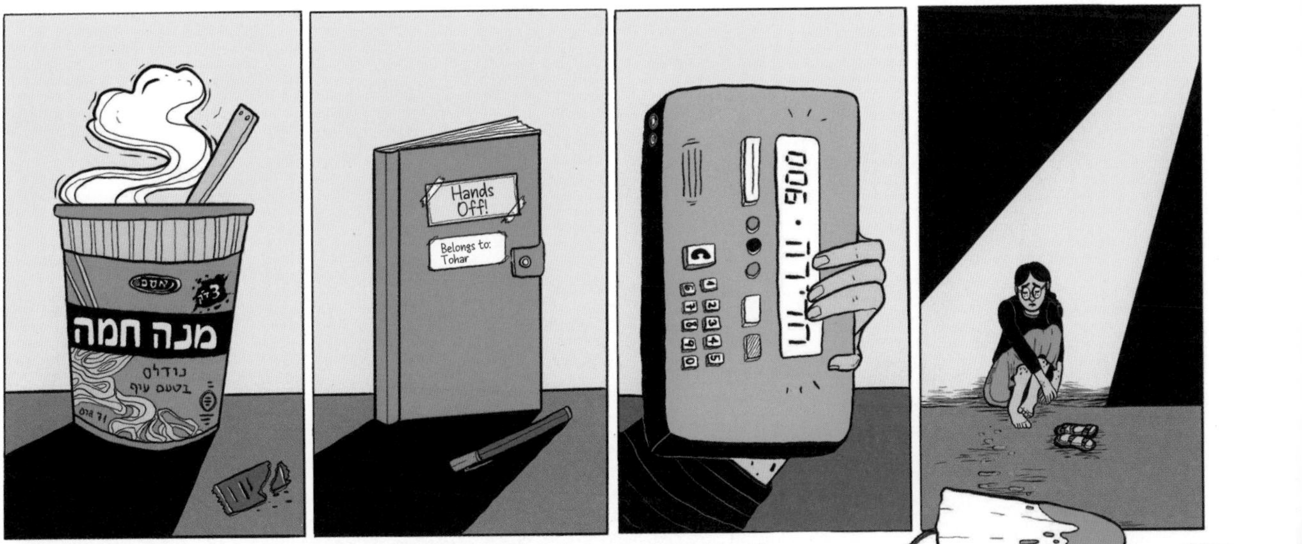
מנה חמה
Hands Off!
Belongs to: Tohar

There was also that young girl who got her period and didn't tell anyone about it until someone noticed, that girl who cried inside her own silence, in her bubble.

HE'S NOT LIKE EVERYONE ELSE
P.S.: neither am I

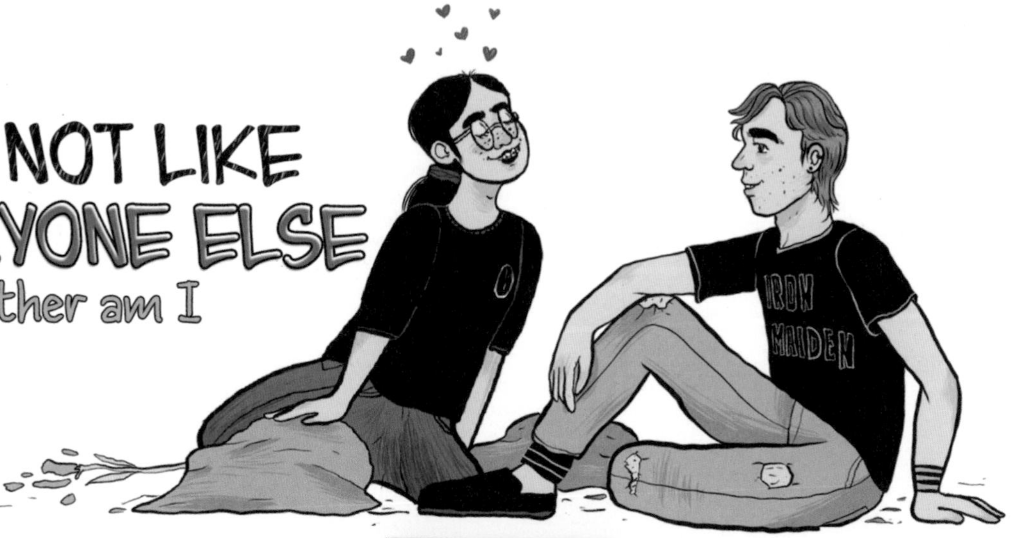
IRON MAIDEN

Spring 2008

You could see that he was different.

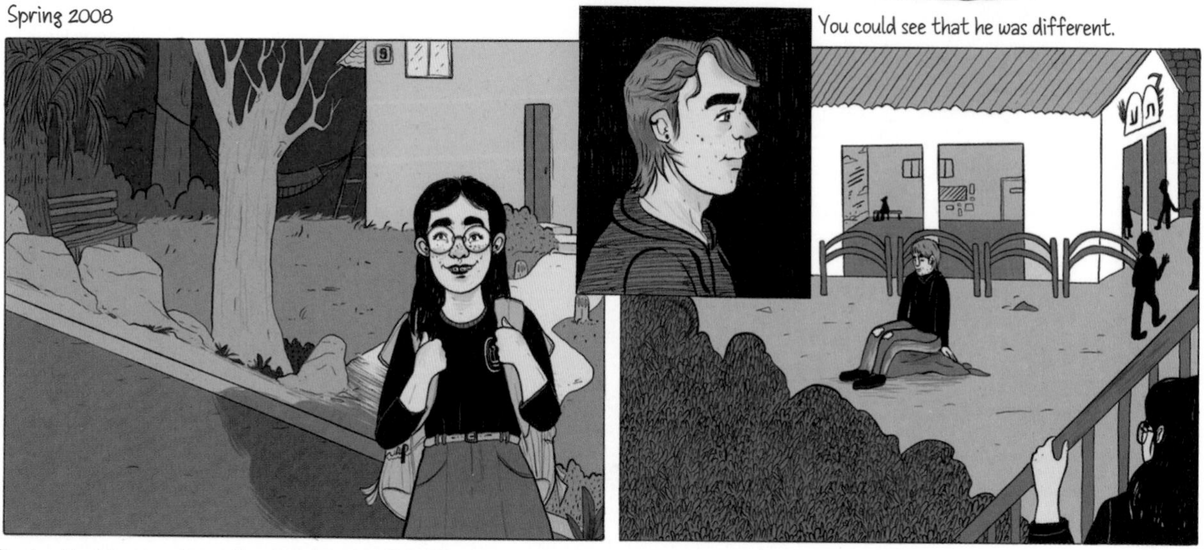

During the Movement meeting, I listened with half an ear to the leaders talking about fraternity, love for your fellow man, the feeling of being close to God. But I was looking at his T-shirt with a rock group logo on it. It felt like he came from somewhere else.

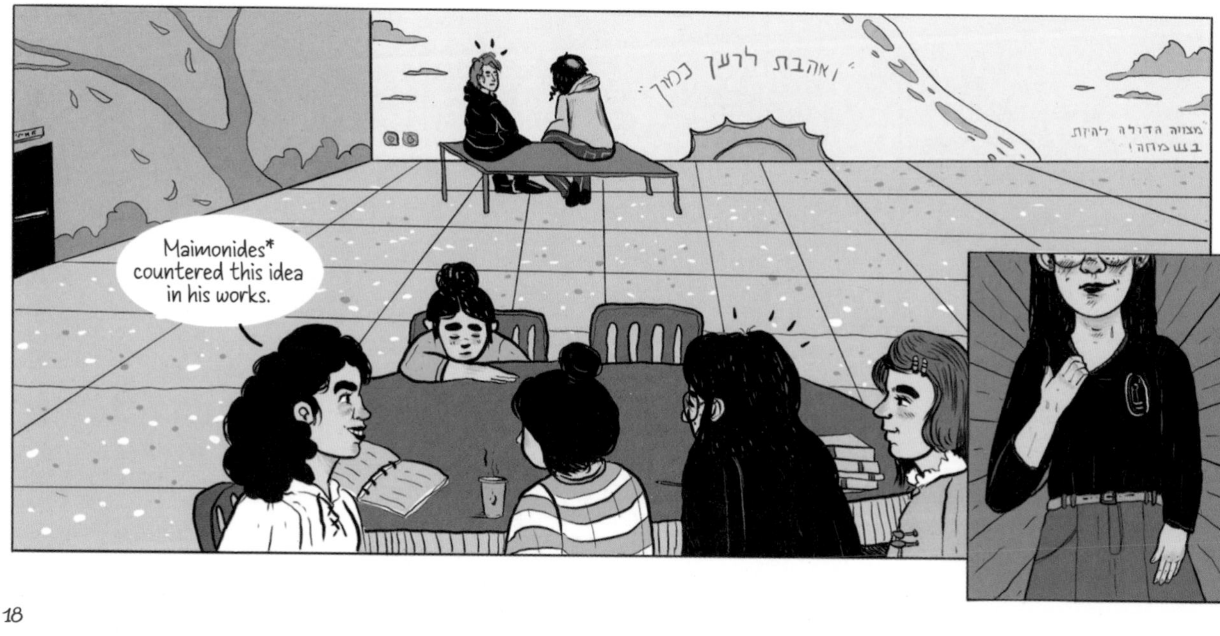
"ואהבת לרעך כמוך"
מצוה גדולה להיות בשמחה!
Maimonides* countered this idea in his works.

He was cute and gave off a certain air of mystery.
As for me, I was suffering from all the complexes you'd expect from an Orthodox girl living in a settlement.

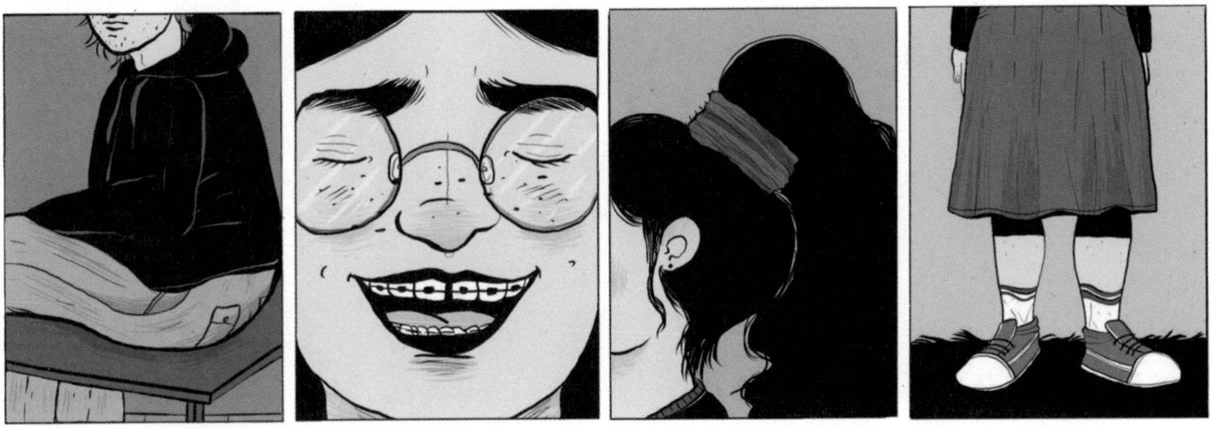

Music brought us together. Later on, I learned to understand his taste, which I took on as my own, Iron Maiden and Metallica—the soundtrack to our relationship. A real cliché—he played electric guitar, and I only had eyes for him!

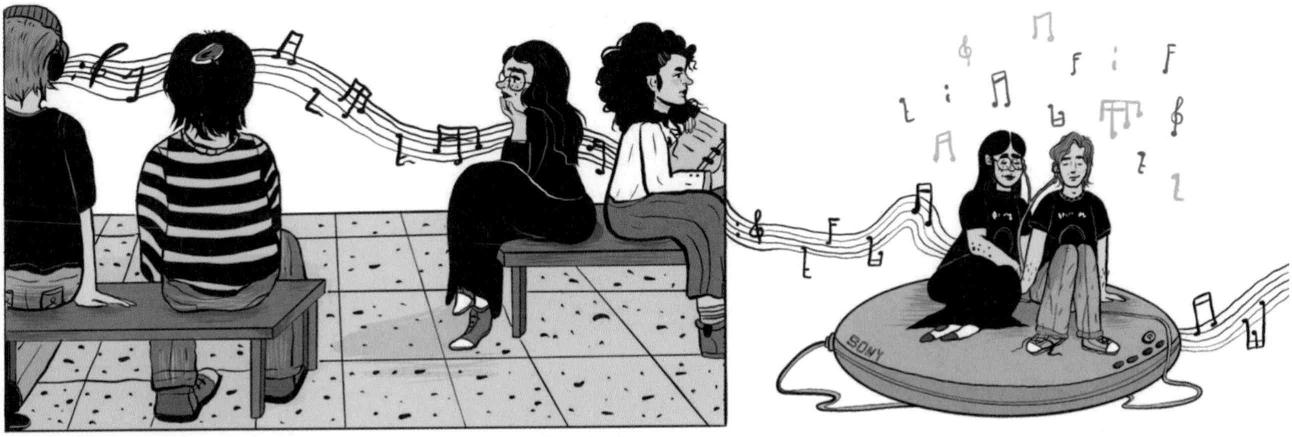
SONY

We started going out. He came to my house, and we played music till late into the night.
We talked, we laughed. As soon as my parents came home, he left via the window. In those moments, I forgot about my friends, school, the Almighty, and Tradition. I only thought about him.

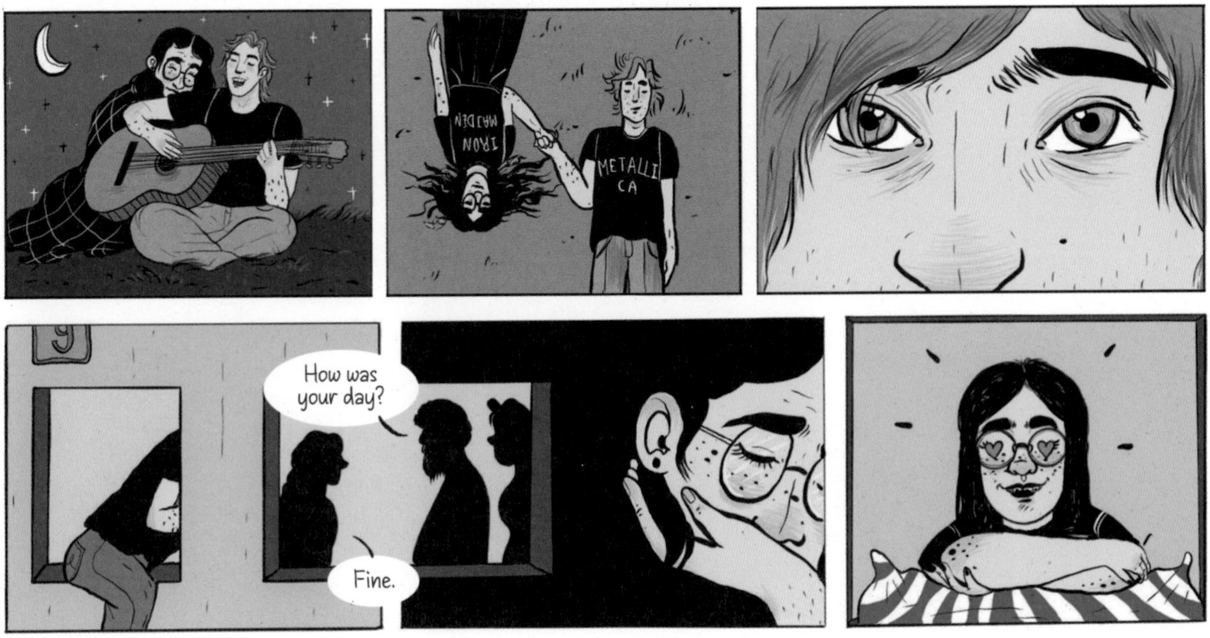
IRON MAIDEN
METALLI CA
How was your day?
Fine.

One evening, we met in an old abandoned building, on the outskirts of the Palestinian village of Kafr Qaddum …
He told me that I shouldn't fall in love with him, but I couldn't resist …

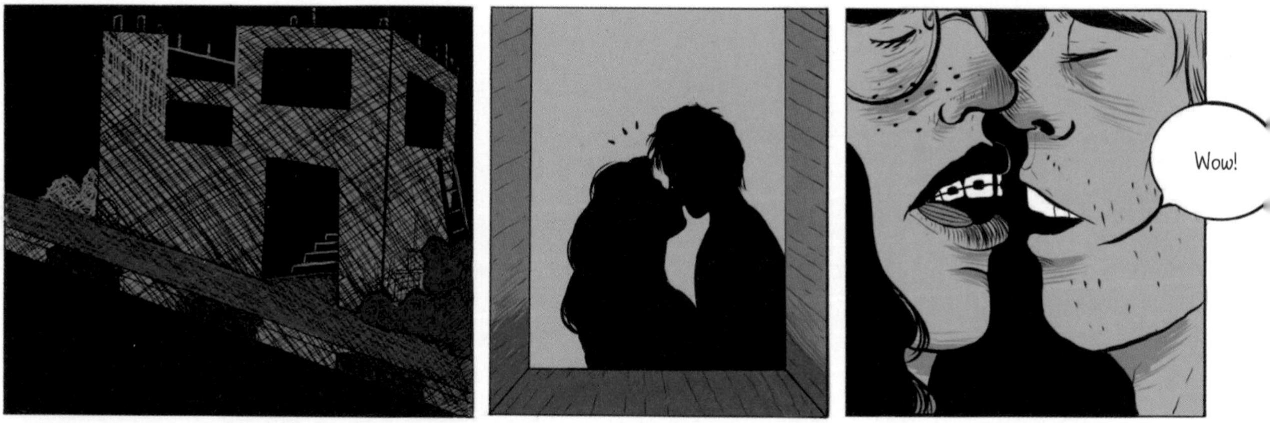
Wow!

I kissed him! I felt so strong, different from the others …

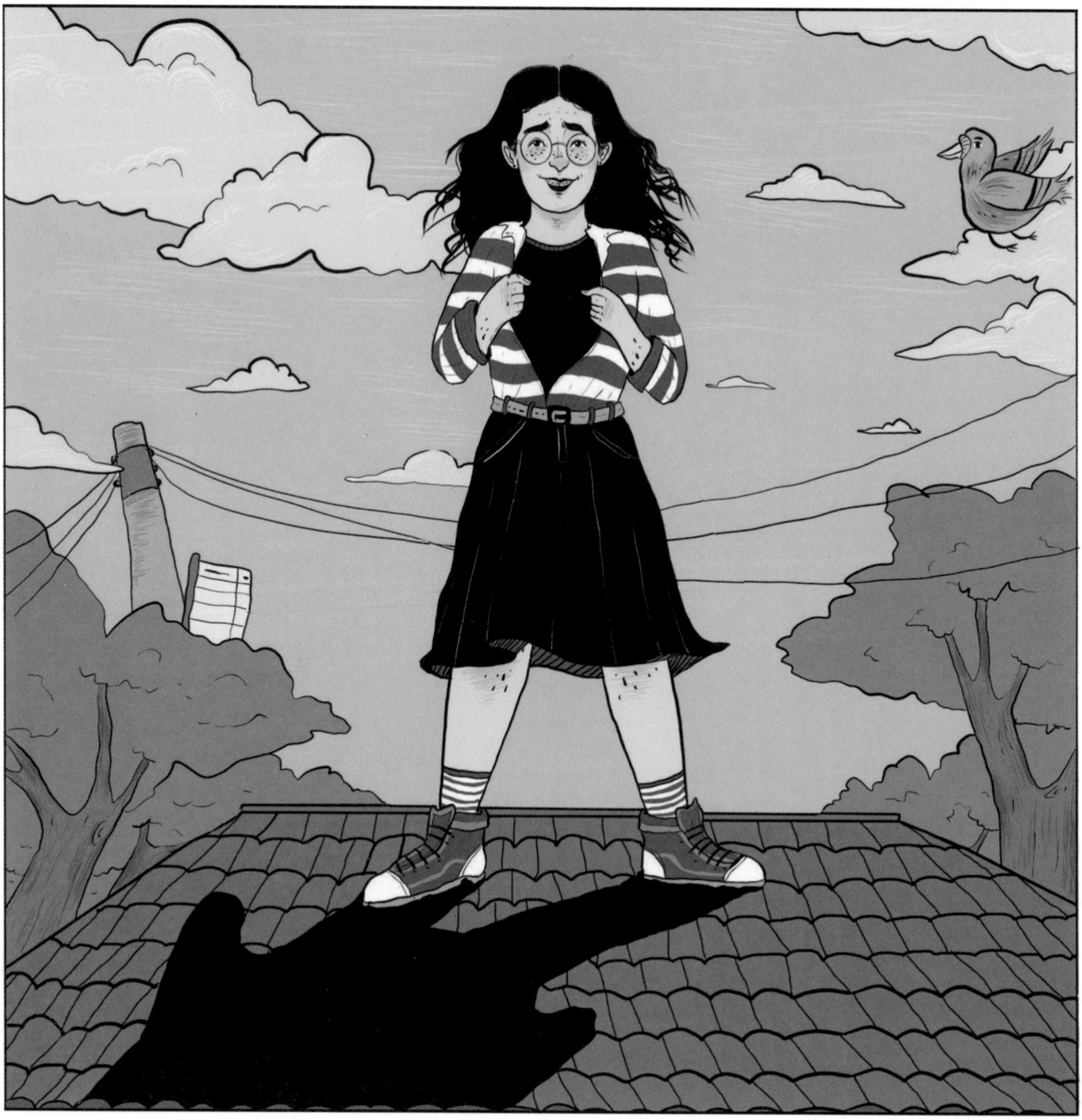

He was firm in his opinions. Bit by bit, I learned to defend mine. He breathed new life into my combative nature, and that's when I began to weigh the pros and cons of my life.

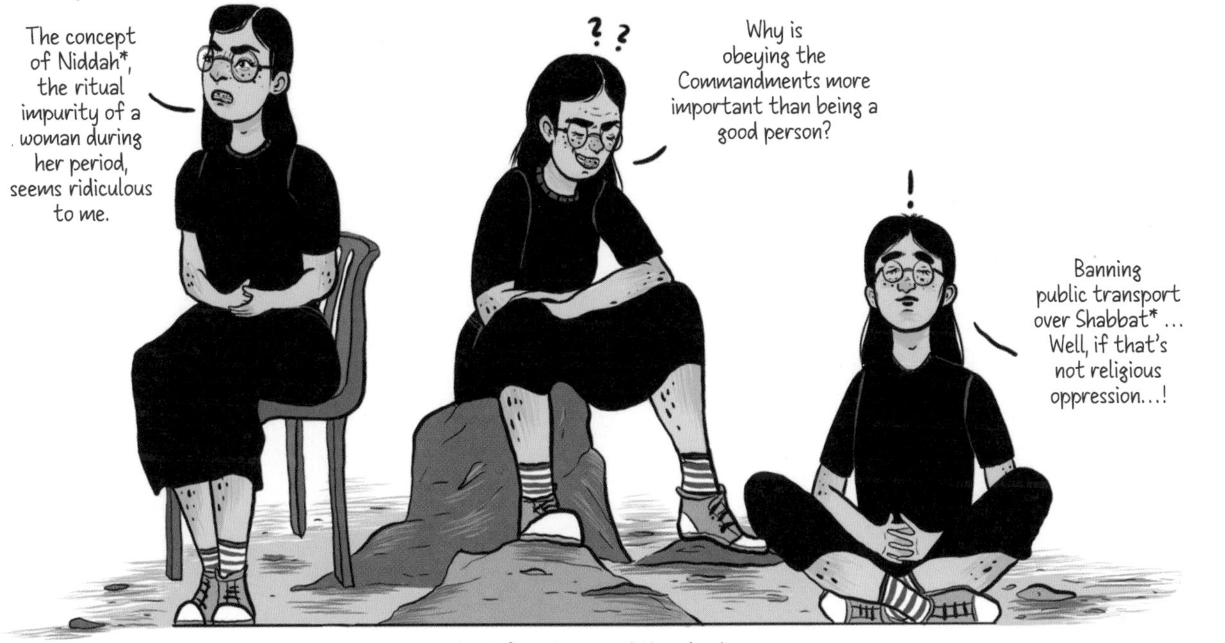
The concept of Niddah*, the ritual impurity of a woman during her period, seems ridiculous to me.
? ?
Why is obeying the Commandments more important than being a good person?
!
Banning public transport over Shabbat* … Well, if that's not religious oppression…!

The rumors spread very quickly. During recess my best friends turned their backs on me, exchanging meaningful looks with each other.

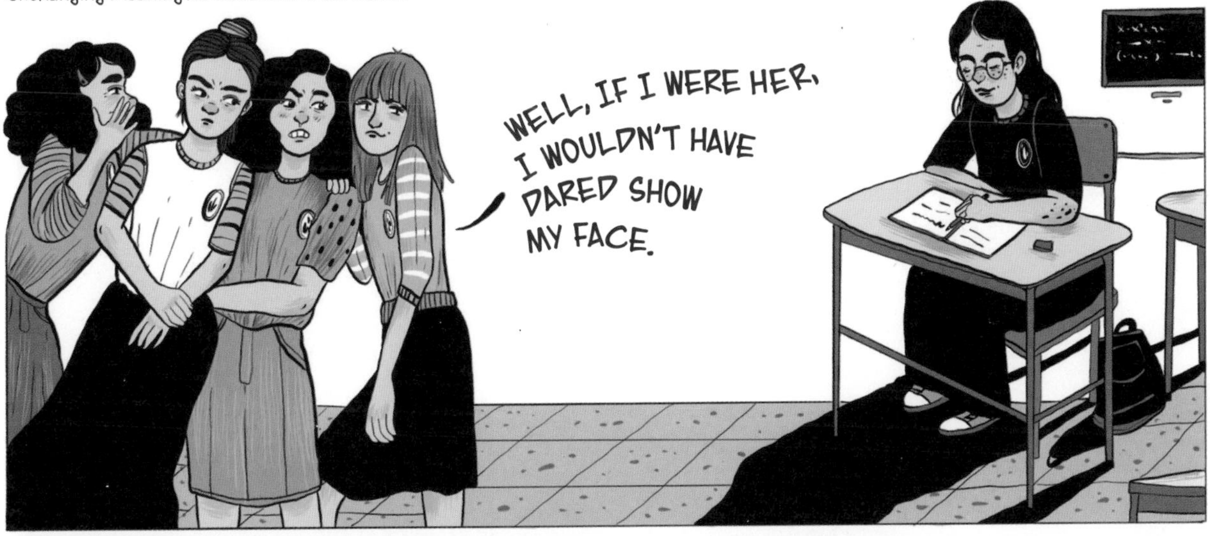
WELL, IF I WERE HER, I WOULDN'T HAVE DARED SHOW MY FACE.

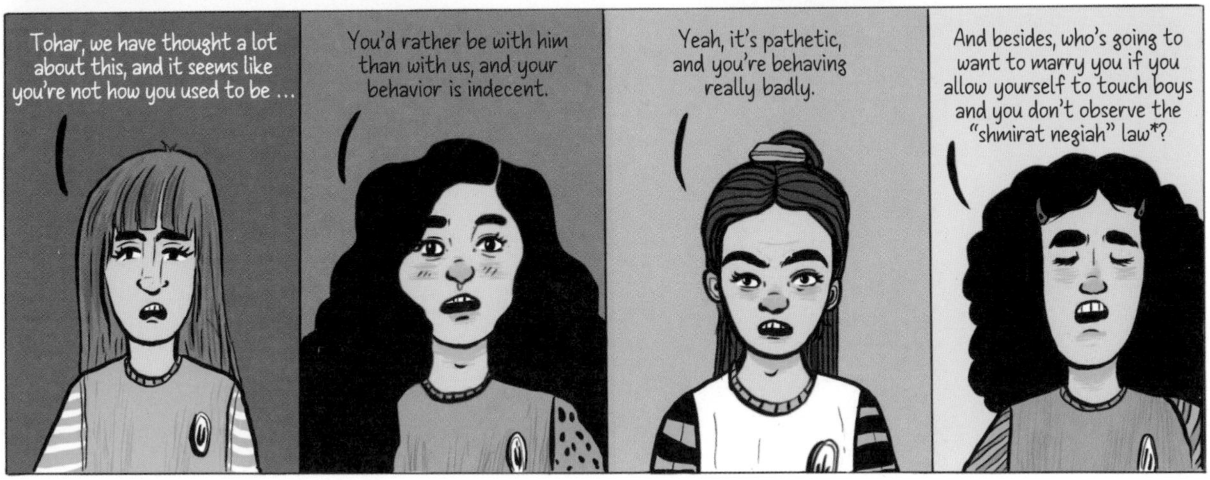
Tohar, we have thought a lot about this, and it seems like you're not how you used to be …
You'd rather be with him than with us, and your behavior is indecent.
Yeah, it's pathetic, and you're behaving really badly.
And besides, who's going to want to marry you if you allow yourself to touch boys and you don't observe the "shmirat negiah" law*?

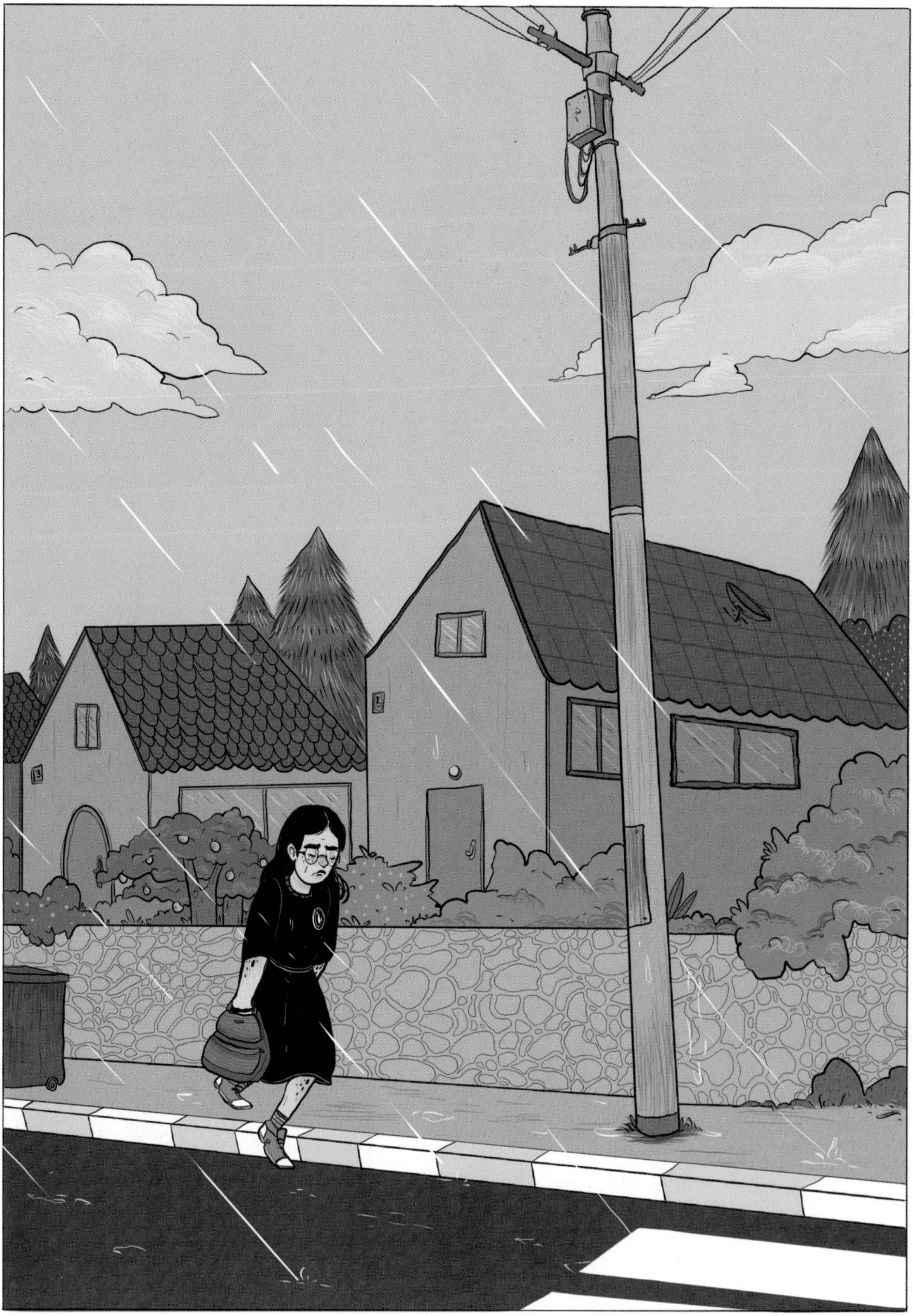

Being alone is hard. You see yourself in a different way, you discover such new feelings.
You feel weaker, you lose confidence in yourself and in the people who have turned their backs on you.

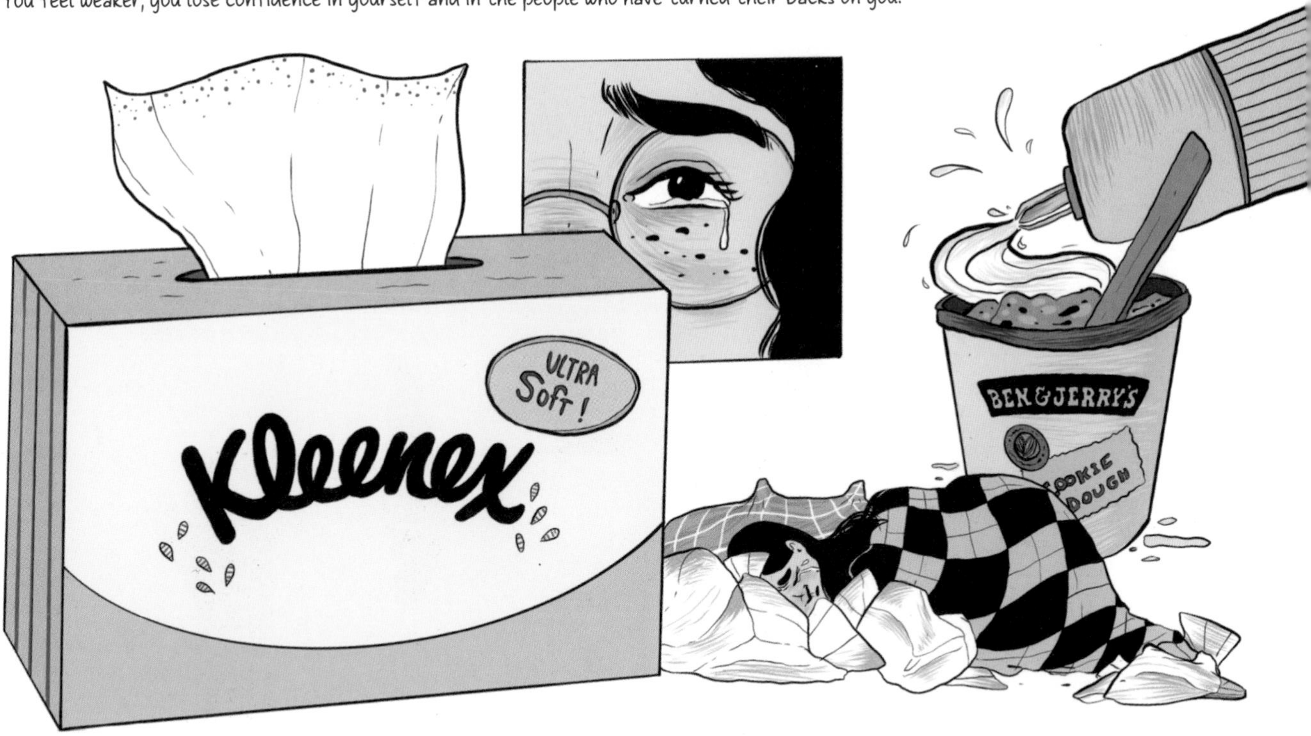
ULTRA Soft!
Kleenex
BEN&JERRY'S
COOKIE DOUGH

When I understood that it was me who was in the wrong, I freaked out. It was my fault, and it was up to me to pick up the pieces.

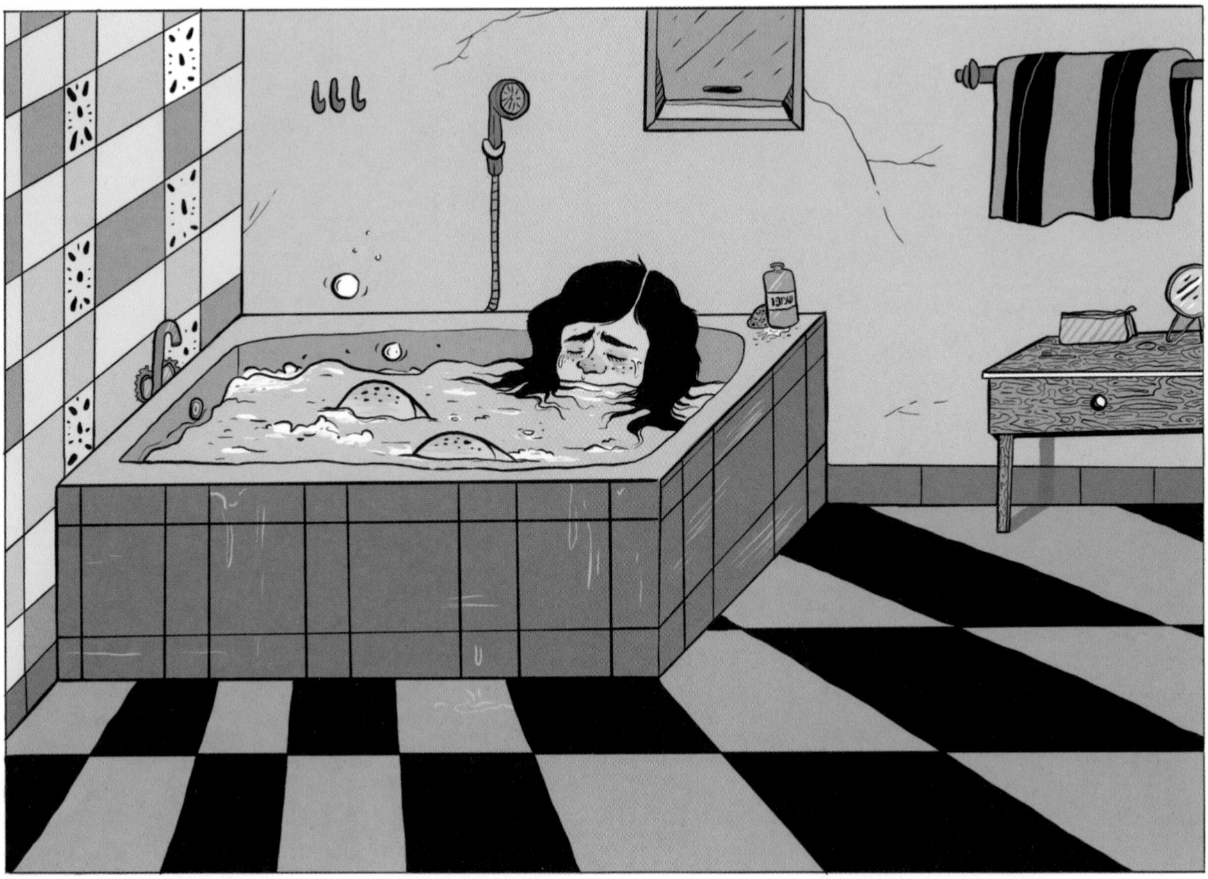

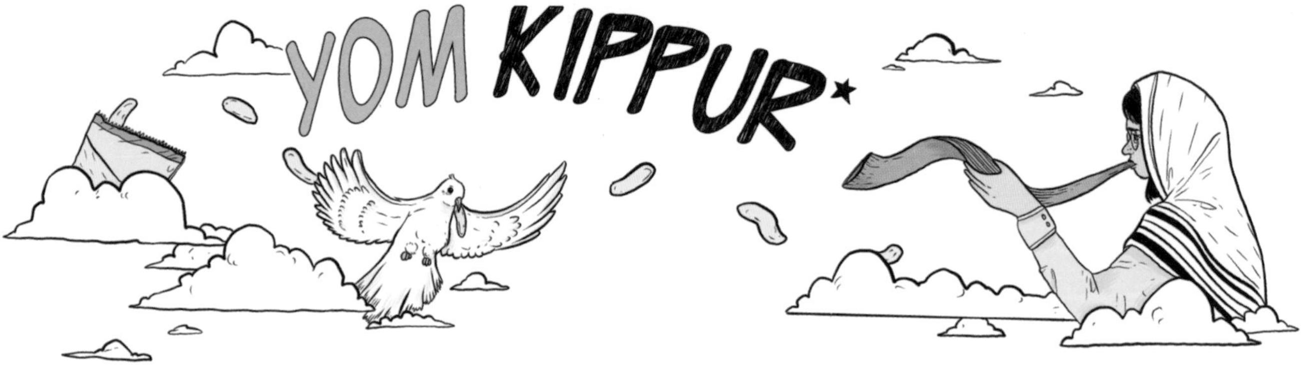
YOM KIPPUR

I hate fasting. On Yom Kippur, we fast and pray for forgiveness, and I think it rings pretty hollow! As if on that one day, by wearing white and praying for forgiveness and absolution, we could wipe out all our bad actions and hurtful words. I would be deep in these thoughts while the Movement leaders were talking and my stomach was protesting against the fast.

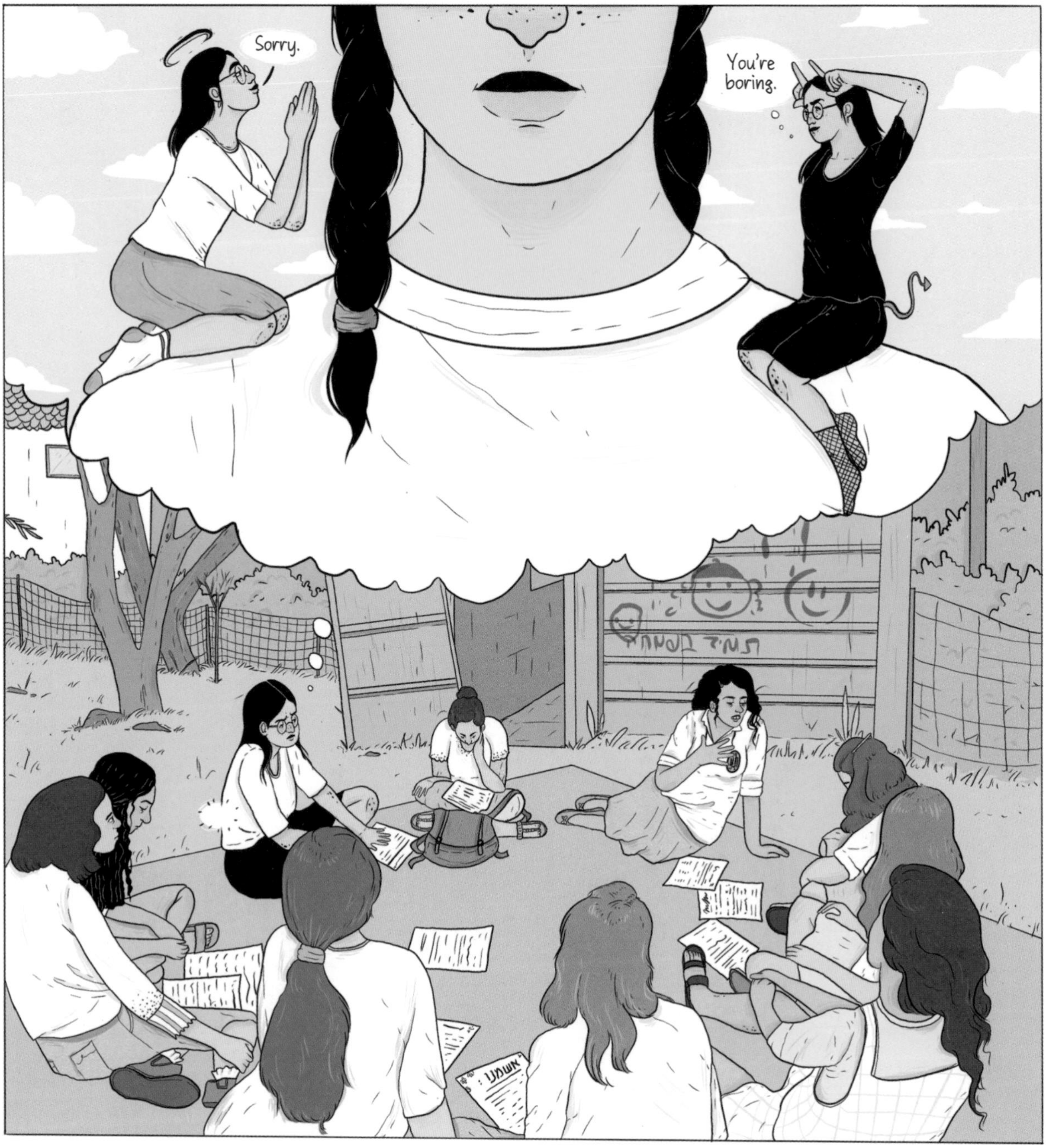
Sorry.
You're boring.

When the girls had gone, I stayed back with Atara, the youth leader. I felt like she wanted to go as well. During the meeting, I was determined to contradict her, to interrupt her when she talked about morals or faith, and to question everything.

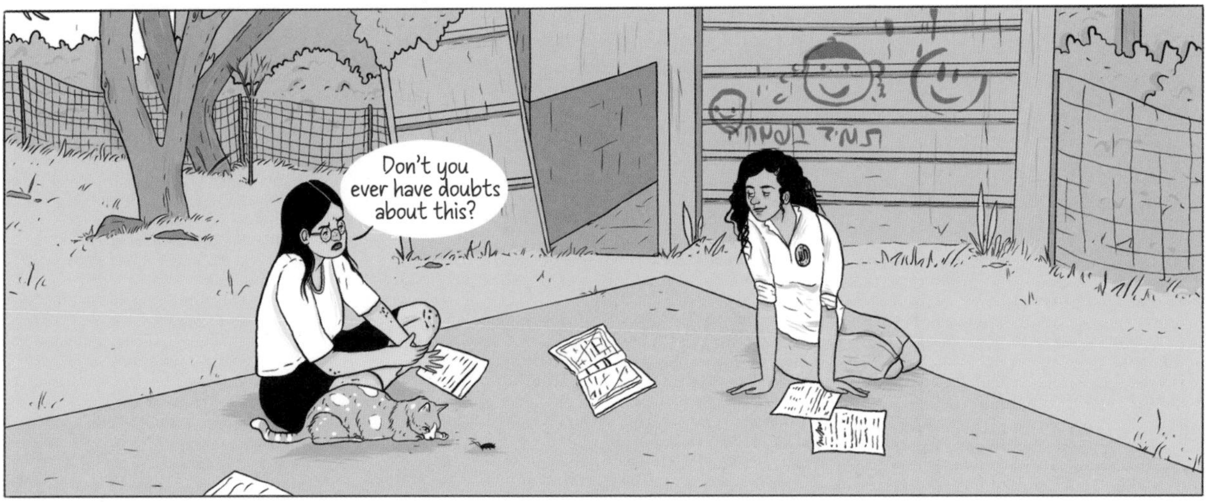
Don't you ever have doubts about this?

She gave me a compassionate look as she put away her notes in an old plastic folder.

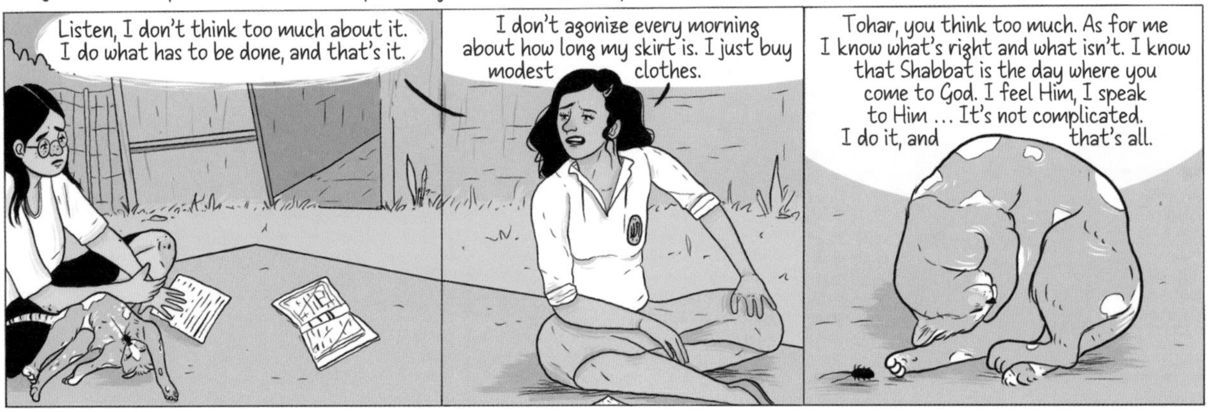
Listen, I don't think too much about it. I do what has to be done, and that's it.
I don't agonize every morning about how long my skirt is. I just buy modest clothes.
Tohar, you think too much. As for me I know what's right and what isn't. I know that Shabbat is the day where you come to God. I feel Him, I speak to Him … It's not complicated. I do it, and that's all.

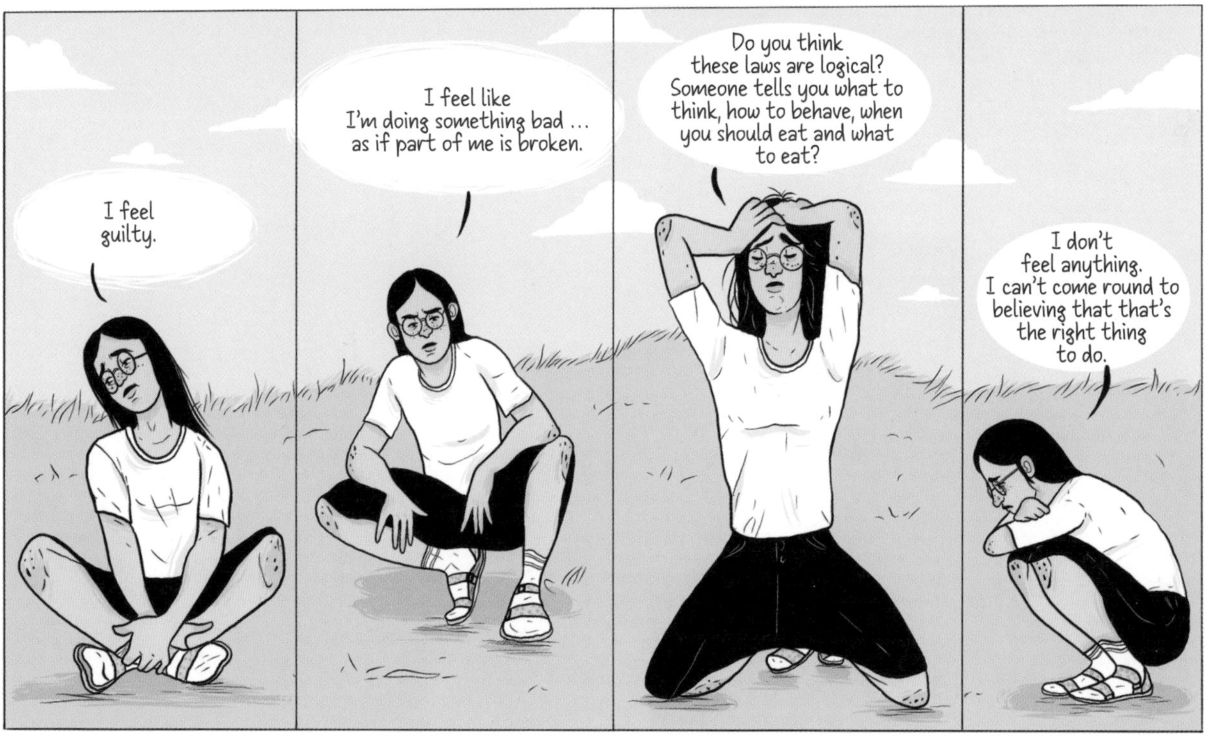
I feel guilty.
I feel like I'm doing something bad … as if part of me is broken.
Do you think these laws are logical? Someone tells you what to think, how to behave, when you should eat and what to eat?
I don't feel anything. I can't come round to believing that that's the right thing to do.

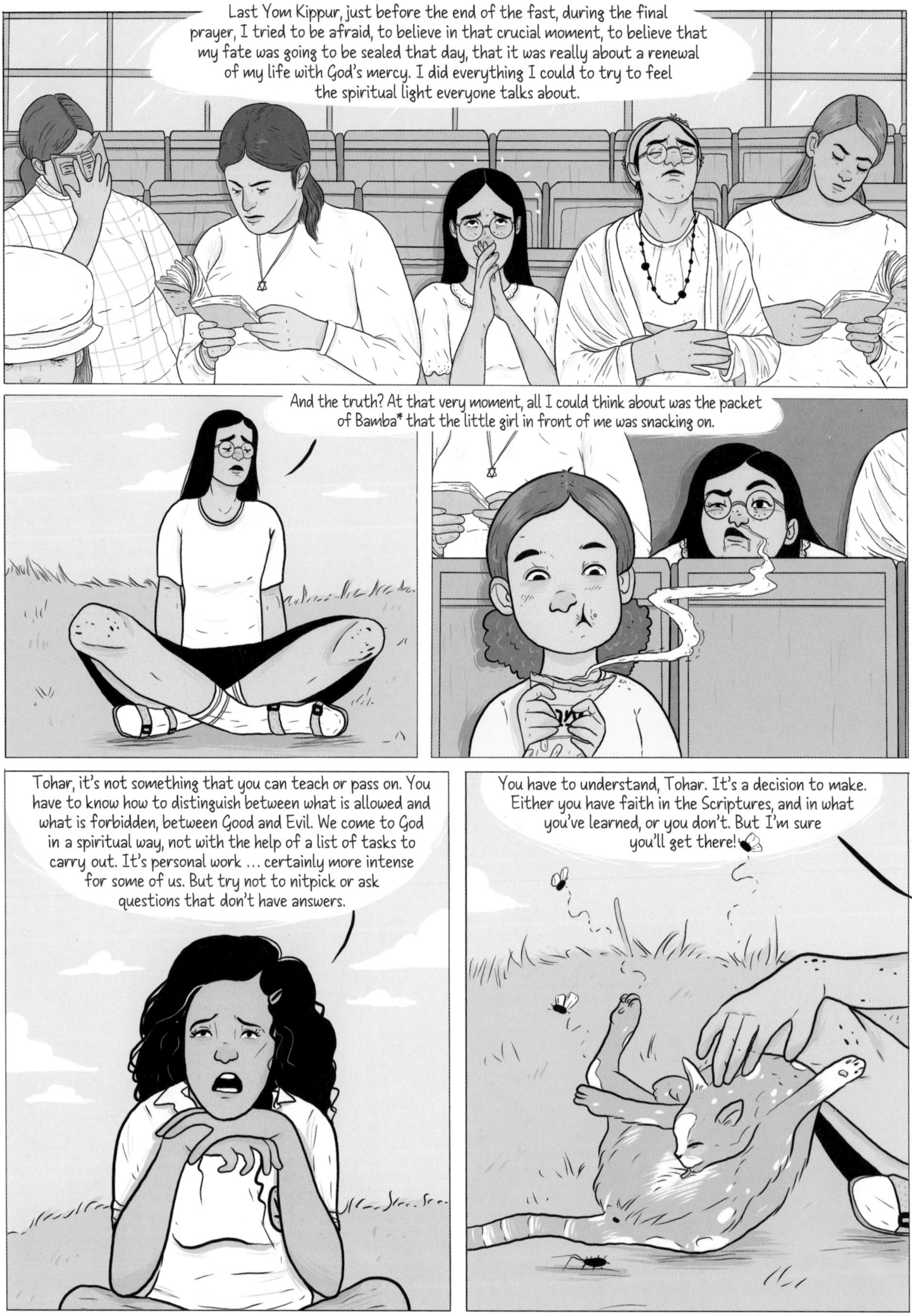
Last Yom Kippur, just before the end of the fast, during the final prayer, I tried to be afraid, to believe in that crucial moment, to believe that my fate was going to be sealed that day, that it was really about a renewal of my life with God's mercy. I did everything I could to try to feel the spiritual light everyone talks about.
And the truth? At that very moment, all I could think about was the packet of Bamba* that the little girl in front of me was snacking on.
Tohar, it's not something that you can teach or pass on. You have to know how to distinguish between what is allowed and what is forbidden, between Good and Evil. We come to God in a spiritual way, not with the help of a list of tasks to carry out. It's personal work ... certainly more intense for some of us. But try not to nitpick or ask questions that don't have answers.
You have to understand, Tohar. It's a decision to make. Either you have faith in the Scriptures, and in what you've learned, or you don't. But I'm sure you'll get there!

That's not enough. Nothing's enough. I ran home ...

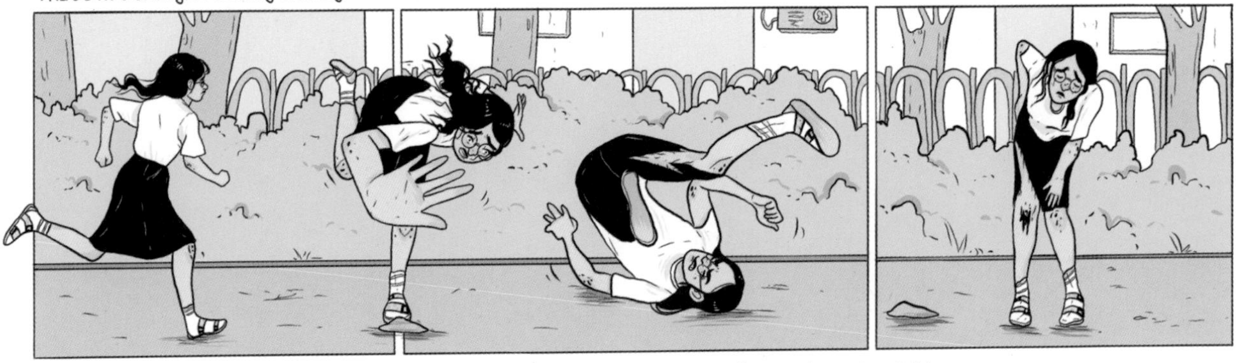

Ugh, what a pain! My skirt! But in the end it's easier walking like that, my knees free and my step lighter.
To tell you the truth, I hid from Atara that I hadn't been able to resist the Bamba that day. And nothing had happened.
Nothing tragic, nothing new under the sun. Everything is vanity.

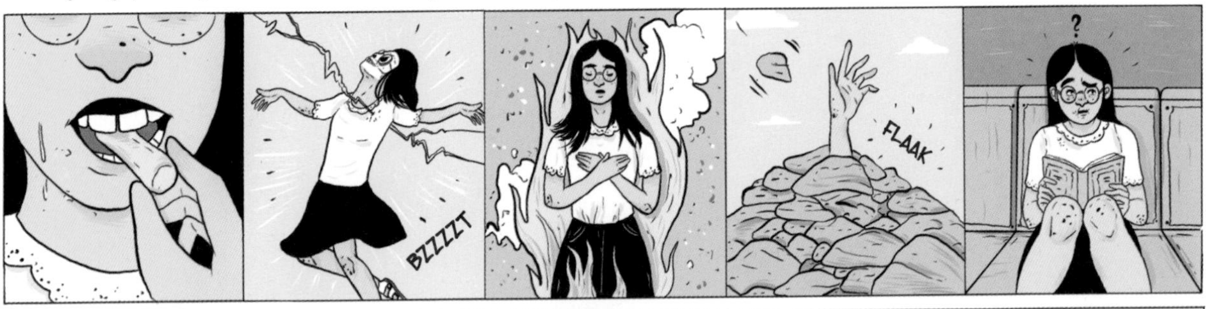
BZZZZT
FLAAK

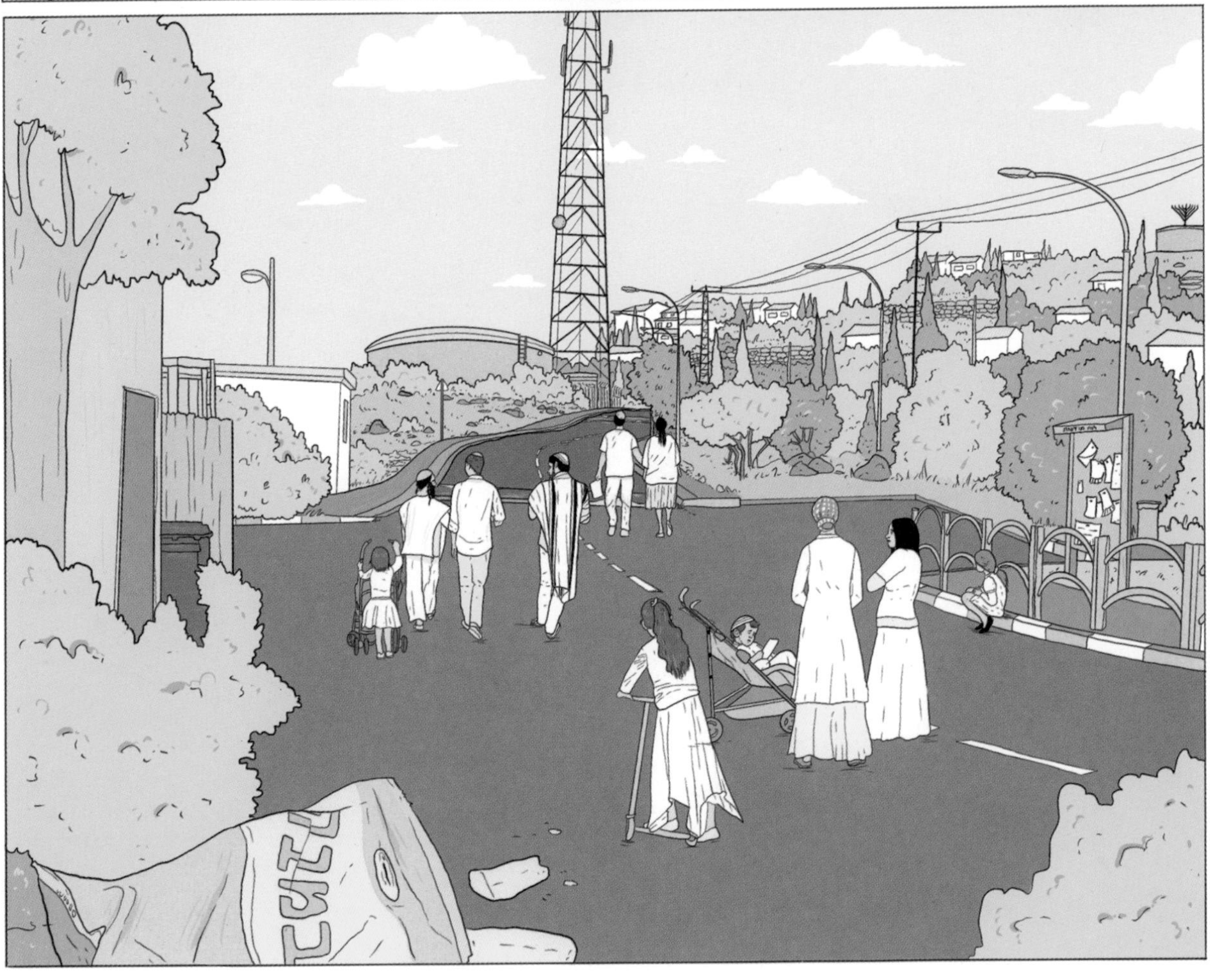

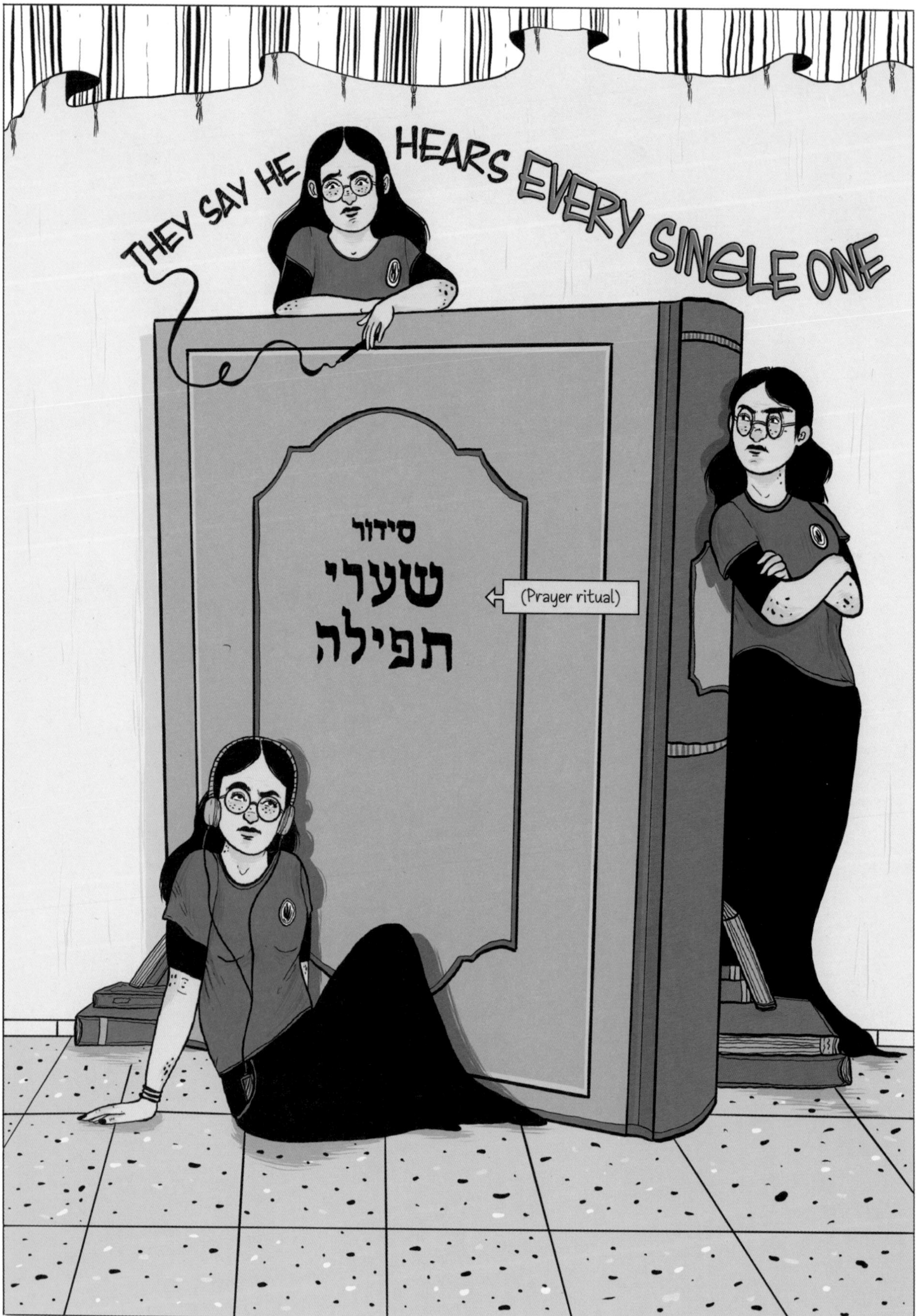
THEY SAY HE HEARS EVERY SINGLE ONE
סידור
שערי
תפילה
(Prayer ritual)

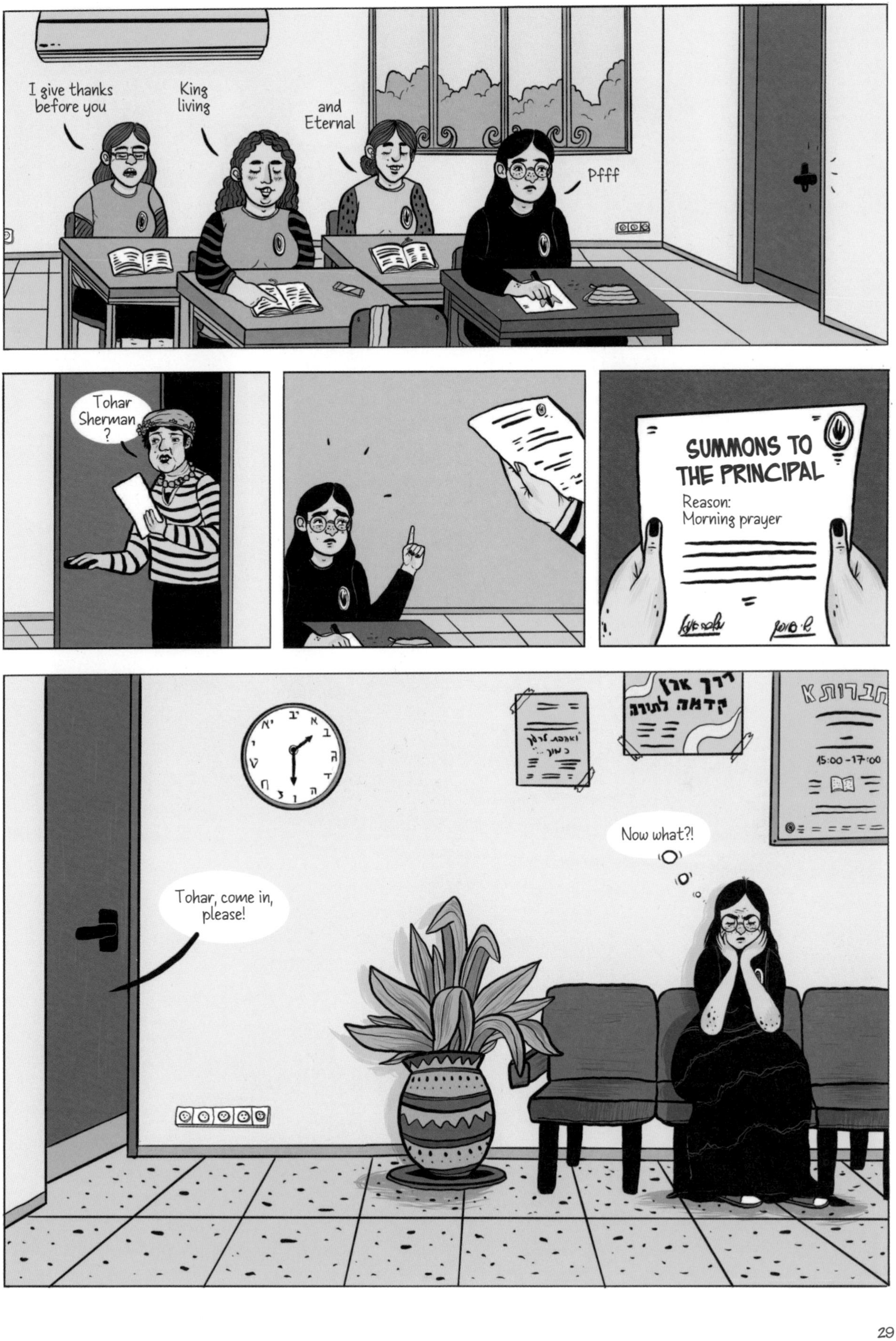
I give thanks before you
King living
and Eternal
Pfff
Tohar Sherman?
SUMMONS TO THE PRINCIPAL
Reason:
Morning prayer
דרך ארץ קדמה לתורה
חברות א
15:00 -17:00
Now what?!
Tohar, come in, please!

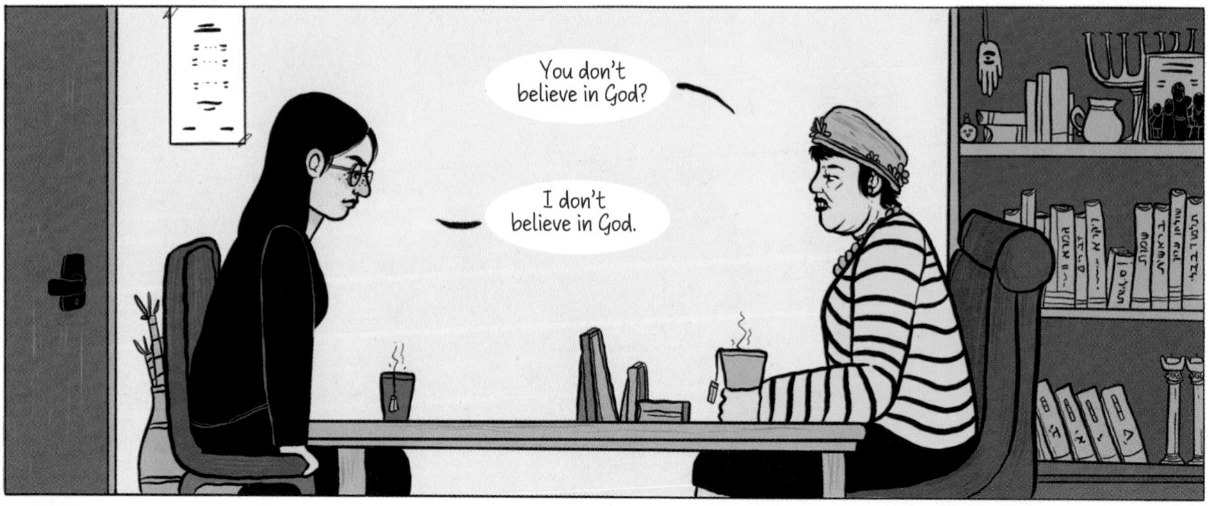
You don't believe in God?
I don't believe in God.

The fabric of my flounced skirt, the one that reached to the tips of my toes, gave me a shiver. It's like they found the exact fabric to match the feeling I got when I went through the doors of the Oulpena, the Orthodox high school for girls.

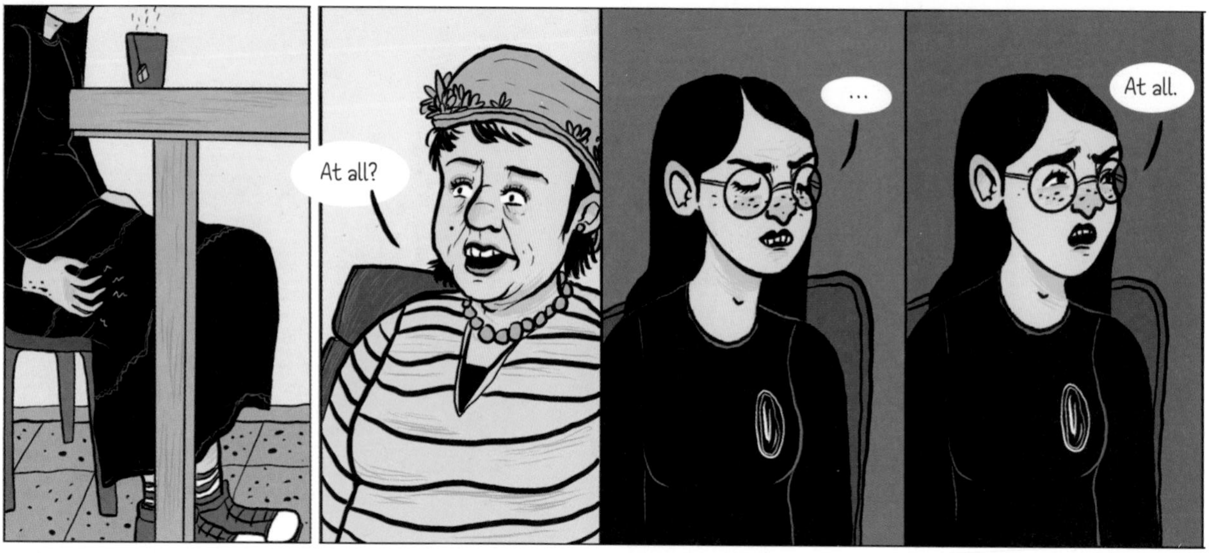
At all?
...
At all.

"Perhaps we should organize some joint prayer sessions to help you share the emotions that surround us."
I thought that if I rolled my eyes one more time, they'd be stuck in perpetual motion …

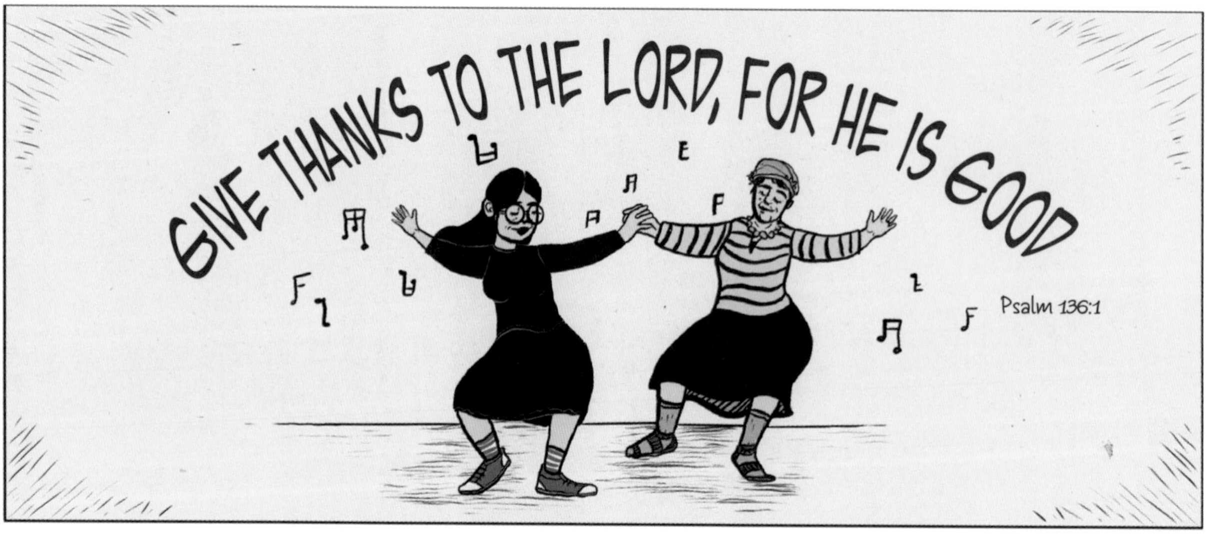
GIVE THANKS TO THE LORD, FOR HE IS GOOD
Psalm 136:1

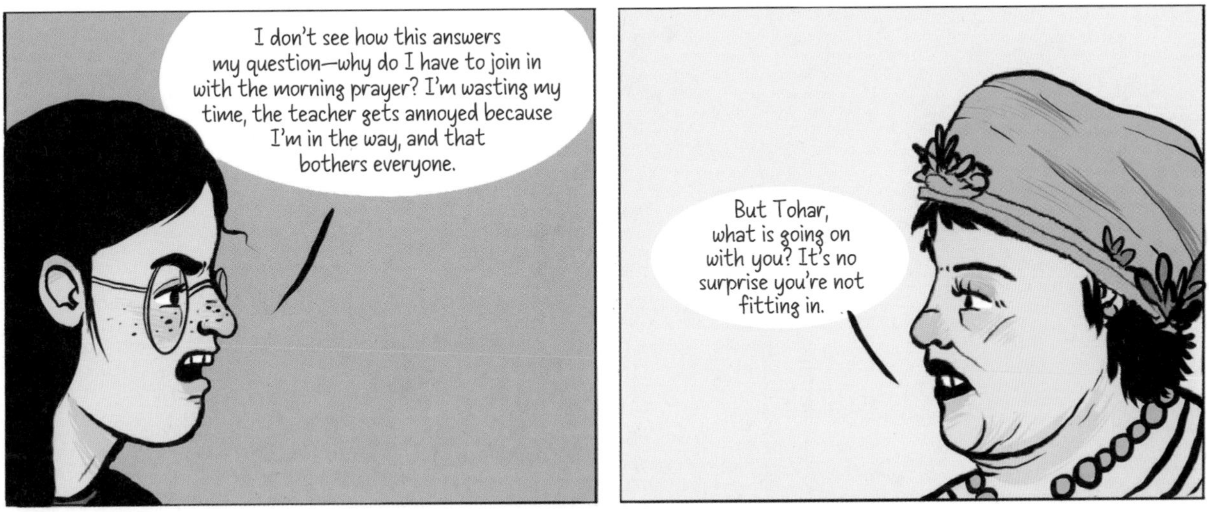
I don't see how this answers my question—why do I have to join in with the morning prayer? I'm wasting my time, the teacher gets annoyed because I'm in the way, and that bothers everyone.
But Tohar, what is going on with you? It's no surprise you're not fitting in.

I grabbed my things and left.

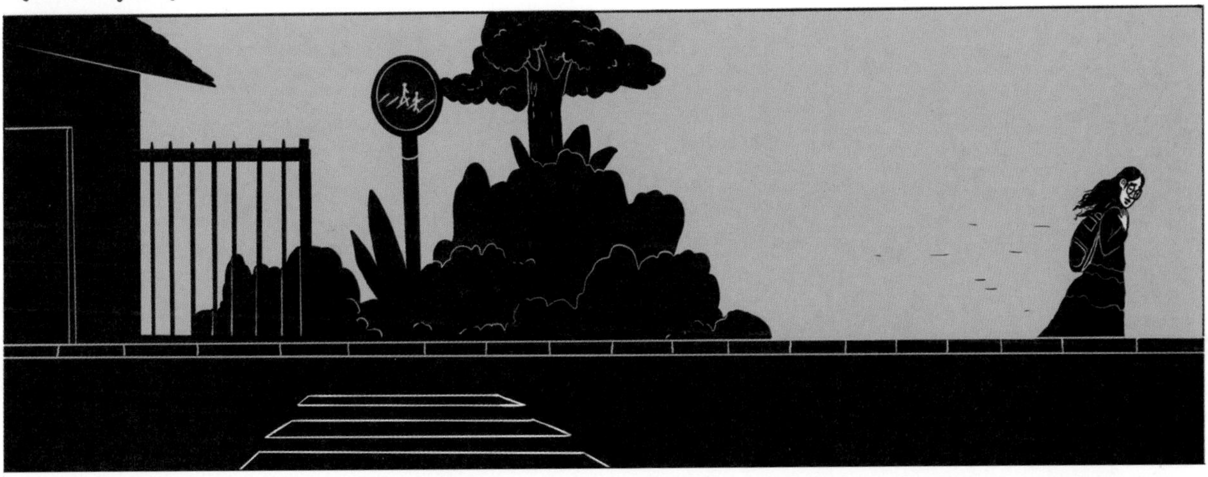

13 is a thankless age at the best of times. Getting ready in the morning had become an interminable chore, as I was obliged to bundle myself up in like a thousand layers of clothing and then see a shape in the mirror that I just didn't recognize. Even without God having to be the first person I spoke to in the morning, life was complicated enough already. That was the last day I prayed.

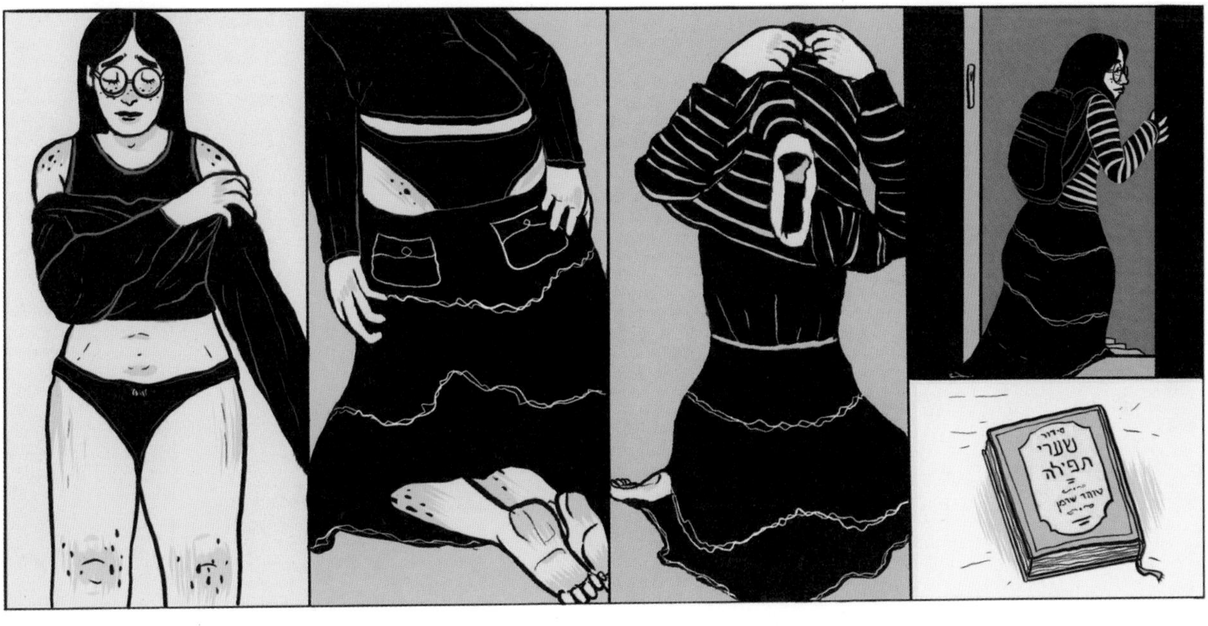
שערי
תפילה

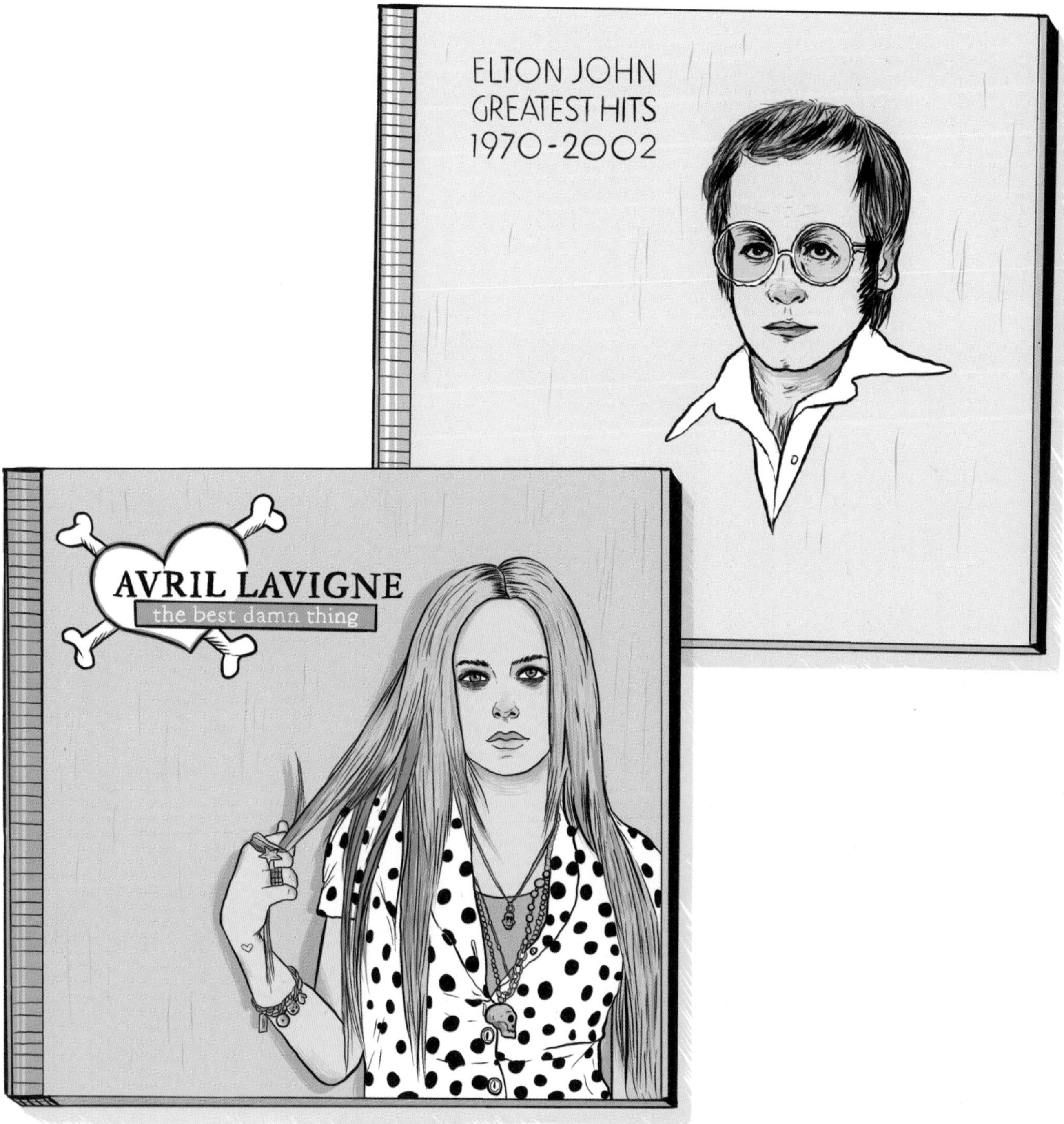

ELTON JOHN
GREATEST HITS
1970-2002
AVRIL LAVIGNE
the best damn thing

PART TWO

One of Those Girls

MY BODY IS BEGINNING TO CHANGE

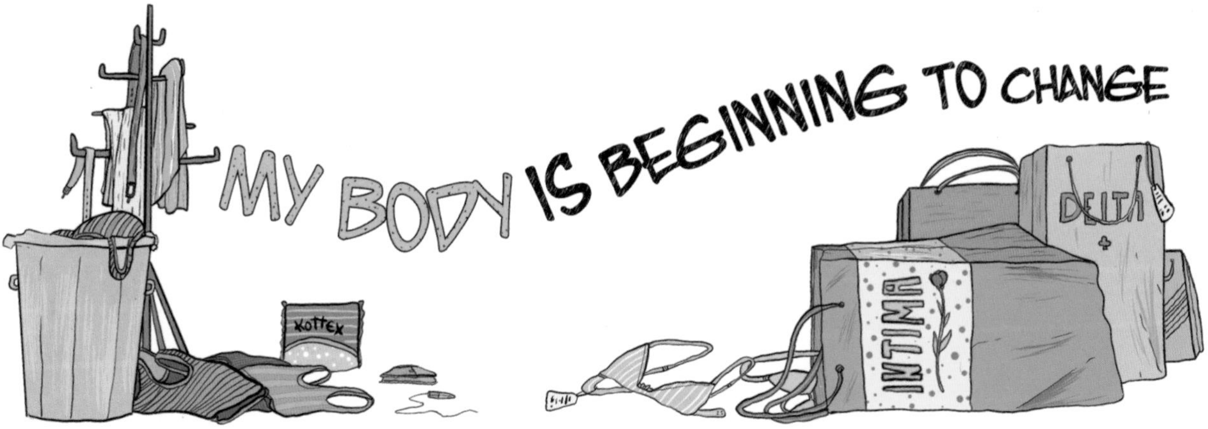
KOTTEX
INTIMA
DELTA

I had trouble understanding the changes. It bothered me, especially because I'd put on weight.

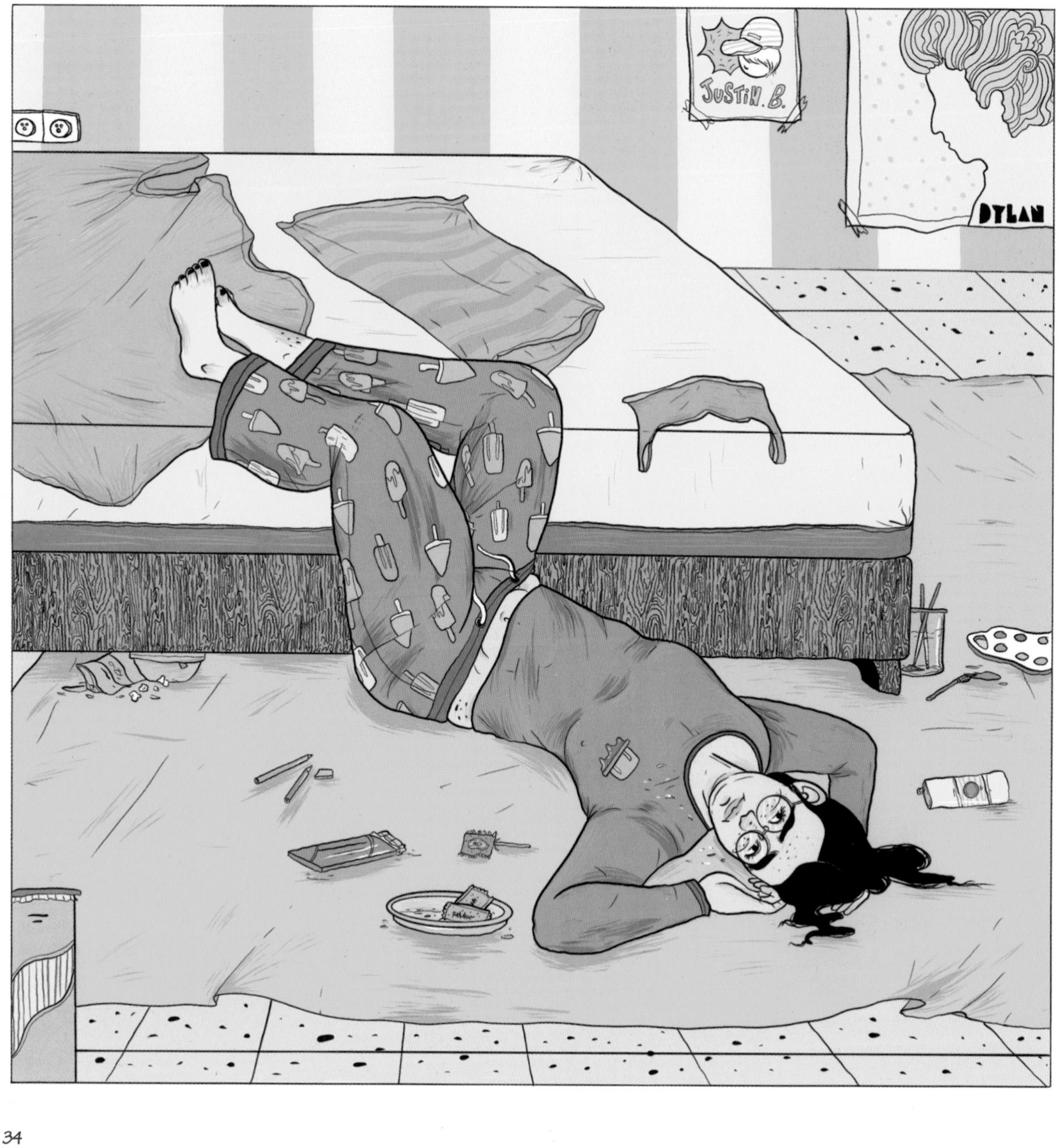
JUSTIN. B.
DYLAN

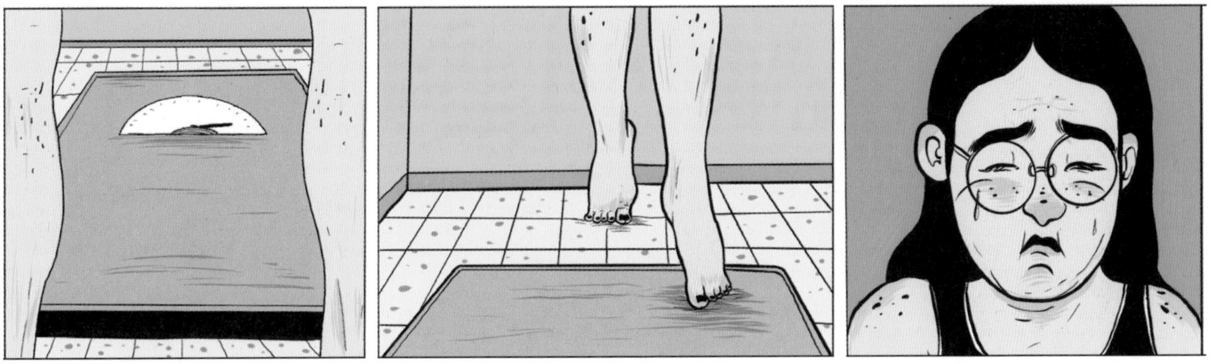

My mother suggested I see a nutritionist, who would help me monitor my weight, so I would feel better about myself.

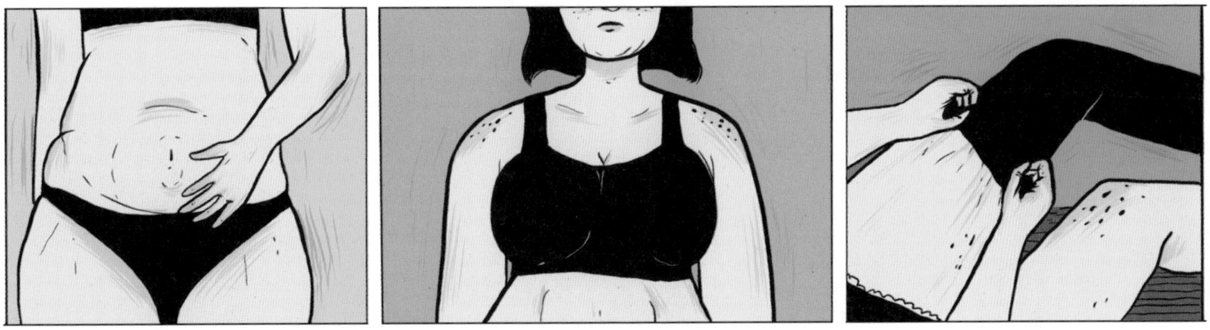

I kept it up for 6 months on a diet of cabbage and misery. And? Hooray! I lost 13 pounds.

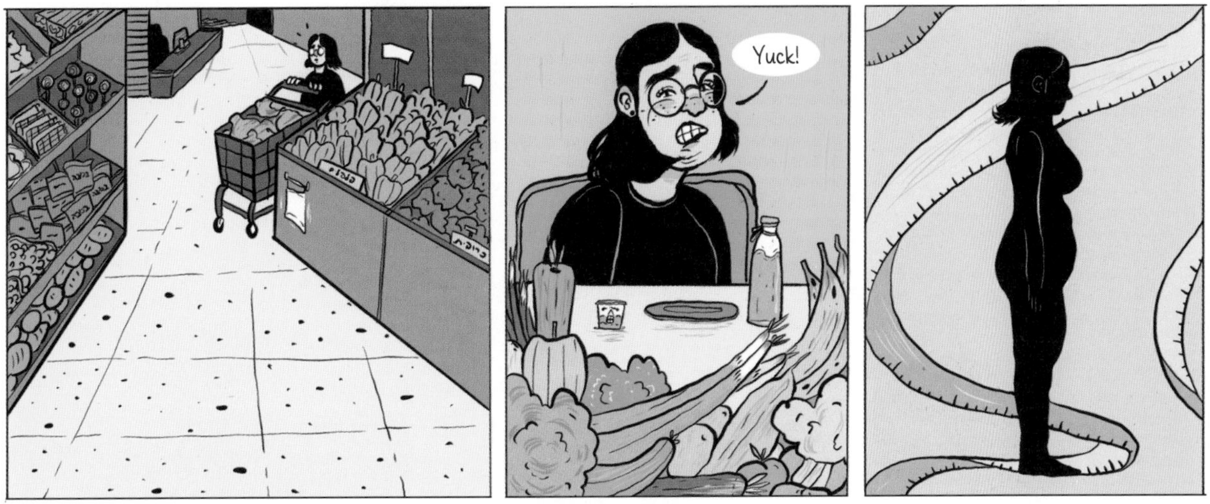
Yuck!

But I still felt fat. I had a big bust and my bra was a size bigger than my mother's.
Not to mention I was inches taller. I was like a foreign body among my brothers and sisters.

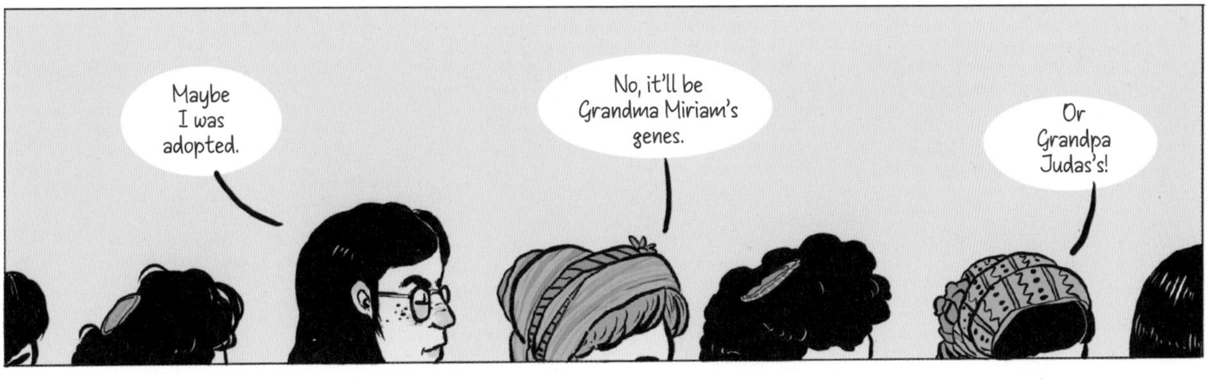
Maybe I was adopted.
No, it'll be Grandma Miriam's genes.
Or Grandpa Judas's!

I've always dreamt of being slim. All my sisters struggled with their weight, especially after their first pregnancies …
This body complex was familiar.

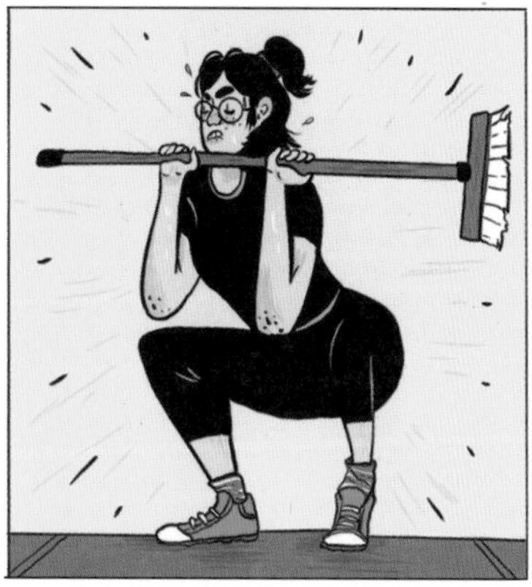

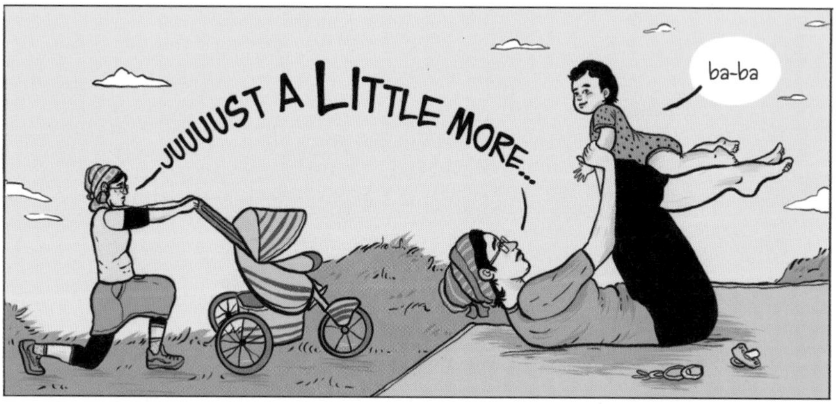
JUUUUST A LITTLE MORE…
ba-ba

At 16, I decided I was going to draw on my body and I was going to love it. During class, I rolled up my sleeves, and using all different colors of pen I decorated my hands and my legs, and even my friends. That way I added value to my body and others' bodies.

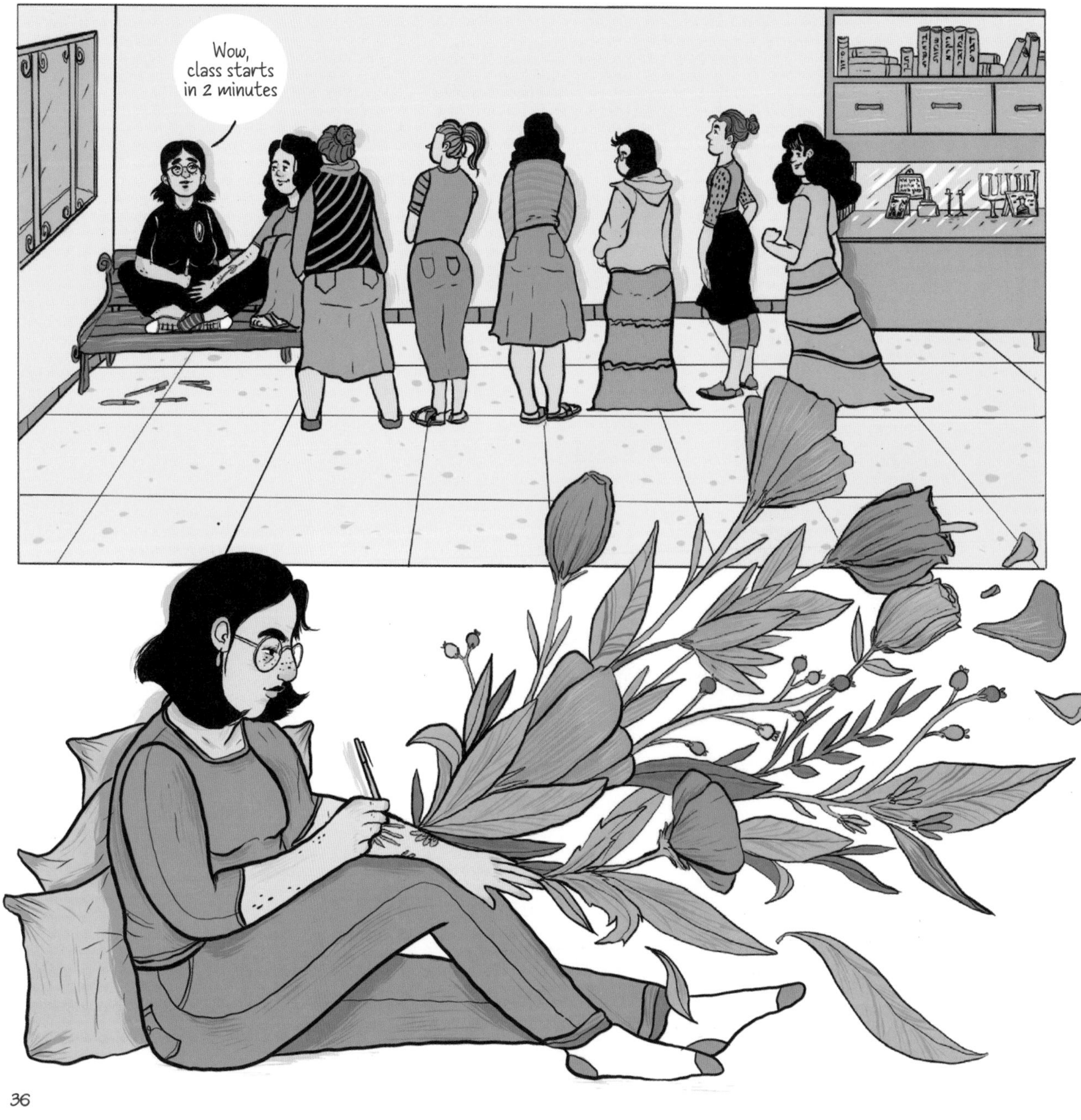
Wow, class starts in 2 minutes

When I got my first tattoo, I felt as if finally my body was giving back some of the love. And every new tattoo I've gotten since always reminds me of that elusive kind of love.

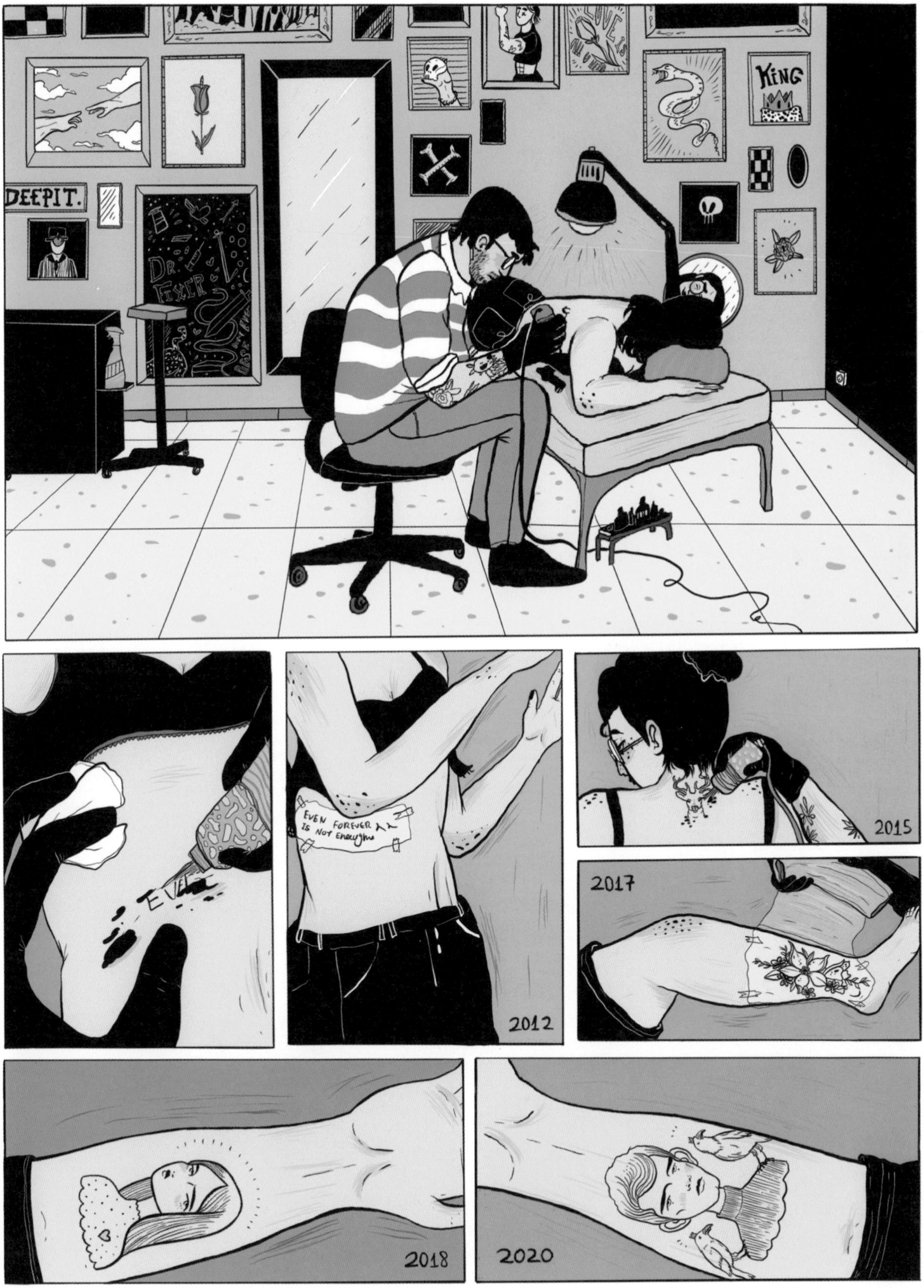
DEEPIT.
KING
EVEN FOREVER IS NOT ENOUGH
2012
2015
2017
2018
2020

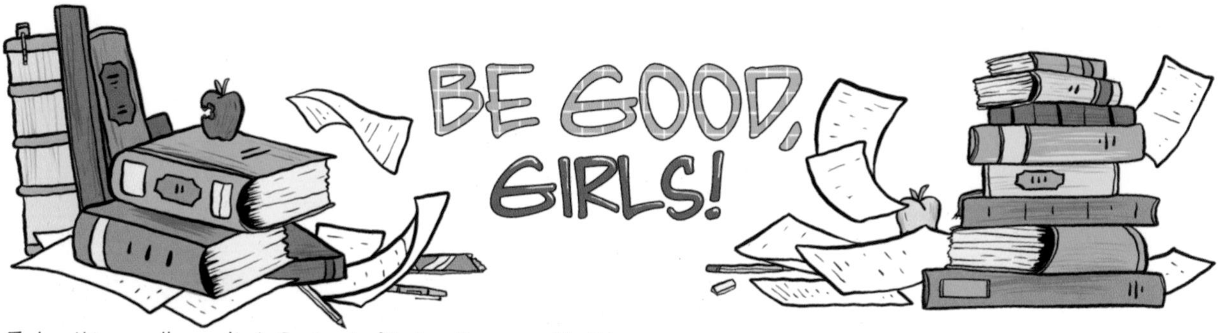
BE GOOD, GIRLS!

Today, things really aren't ok. I got out of bed on the wrong side this morning.
There's no one home, I'm all alone. I got my stuff and went down to the kitchen.

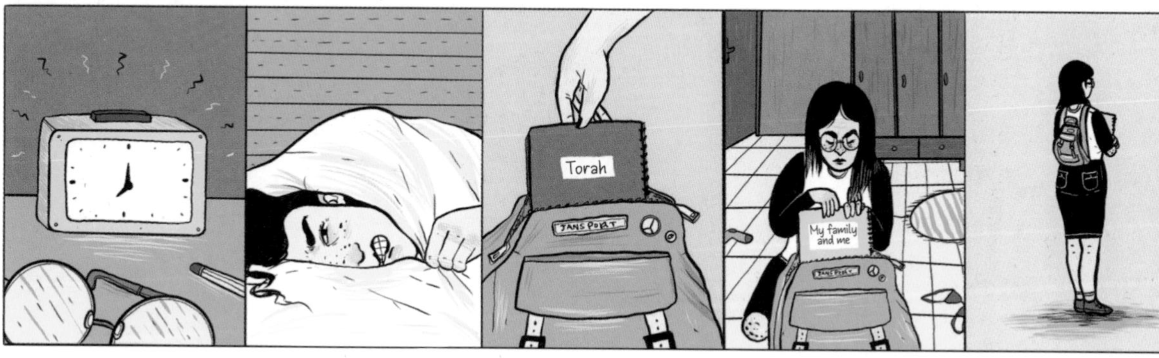
Torah
My family and me

I couldn't find anything to take for my lunch, apart from a frozen vegan meat patty that I stuffed into a pita, and off I went! Destination high school! It was a boiling-hot day, which made me even more cross. I was stifling in my school blouse, and walking quickly. If no car stopped to drop me off, I was going to miss the first class again. But I really had to get there in time because I'd worked all night writing a scathing critique of my family life.

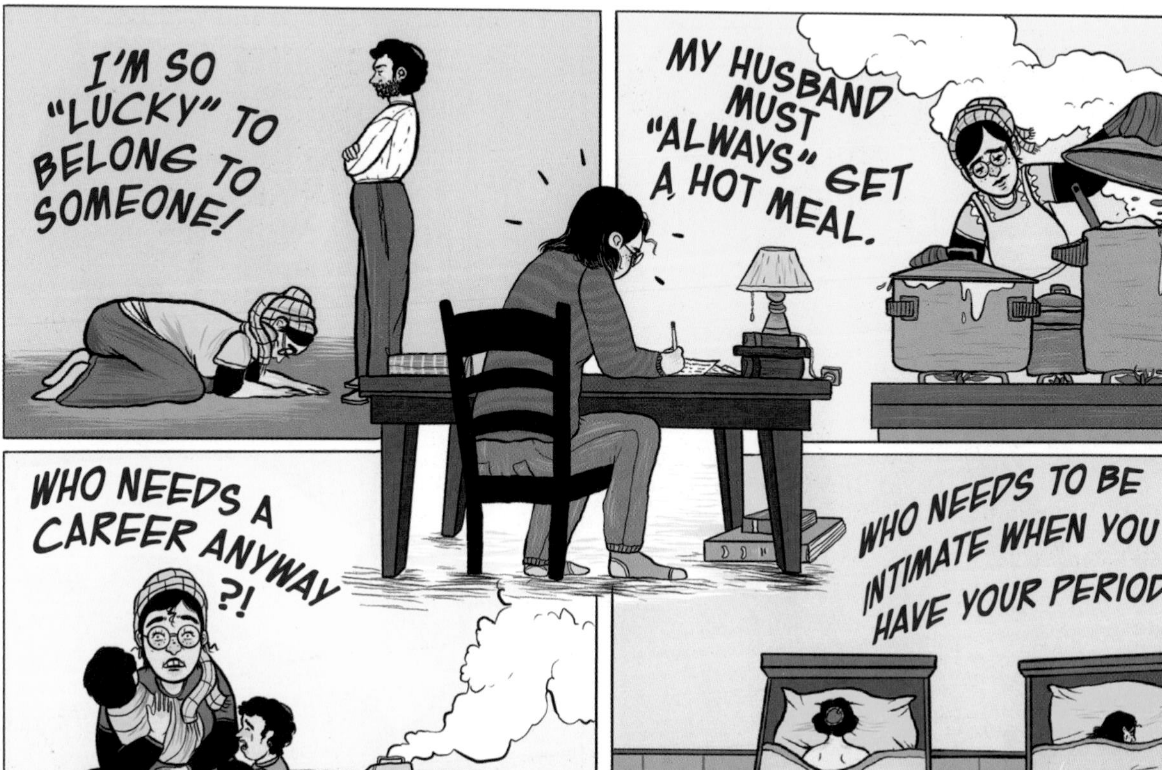
I'M SO "LUCKY" TO BELONG TO SOMEONE!
MY HUSBAND MUST "ALWAYS" GET A HOT MEAL.
WHO NEEDS A CAREER ANYWAY ?!
WHO NEEDS TO BE INTIMATE WHEN YOU HAVE YOUR PERIOD?

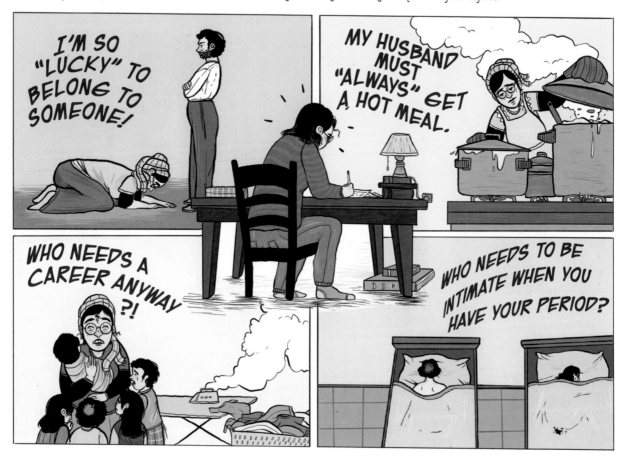

I got to the entrance of the Oulpena dripping with sweat after my long walk, and at the end of my rope.

Hmmm

Is everything ok, Vladi?

Sorry, but you can't come in like that!

Vladi, it's not up to you to decide if I can come in or not. Let me through, I'm late already.

It's the new rules. If there are any bare knees visible, I've been told not to let you in. Recently there have been too many indecent outfits. They want to change all that.

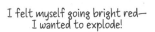

Seriously? You're there to look at young girls' knees? Do you hear yourself?

I felt myself going bright red—I wanted to explode!

I sat down on the pavement, furious, staring at my bare knees.

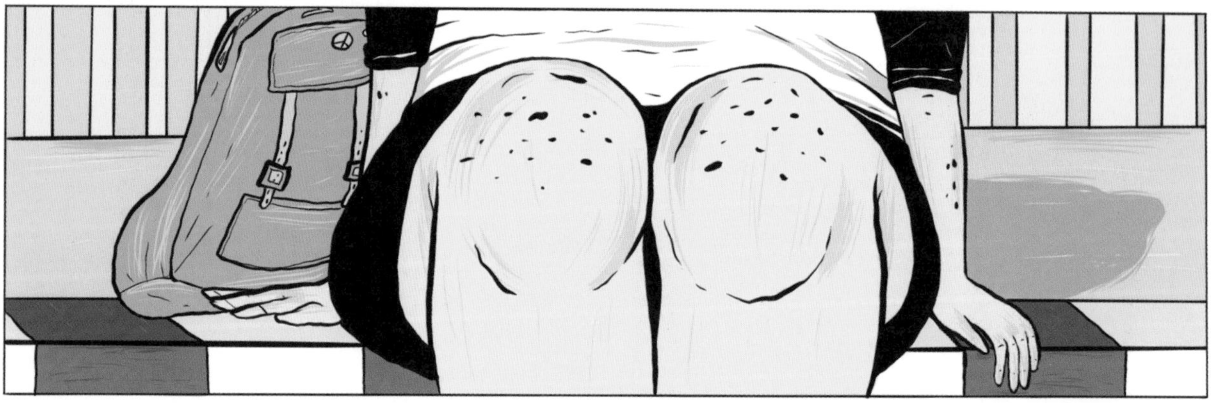

I thought about all the harsh truths I was going to come out with when I got back to class. I was facing another long walk back home.

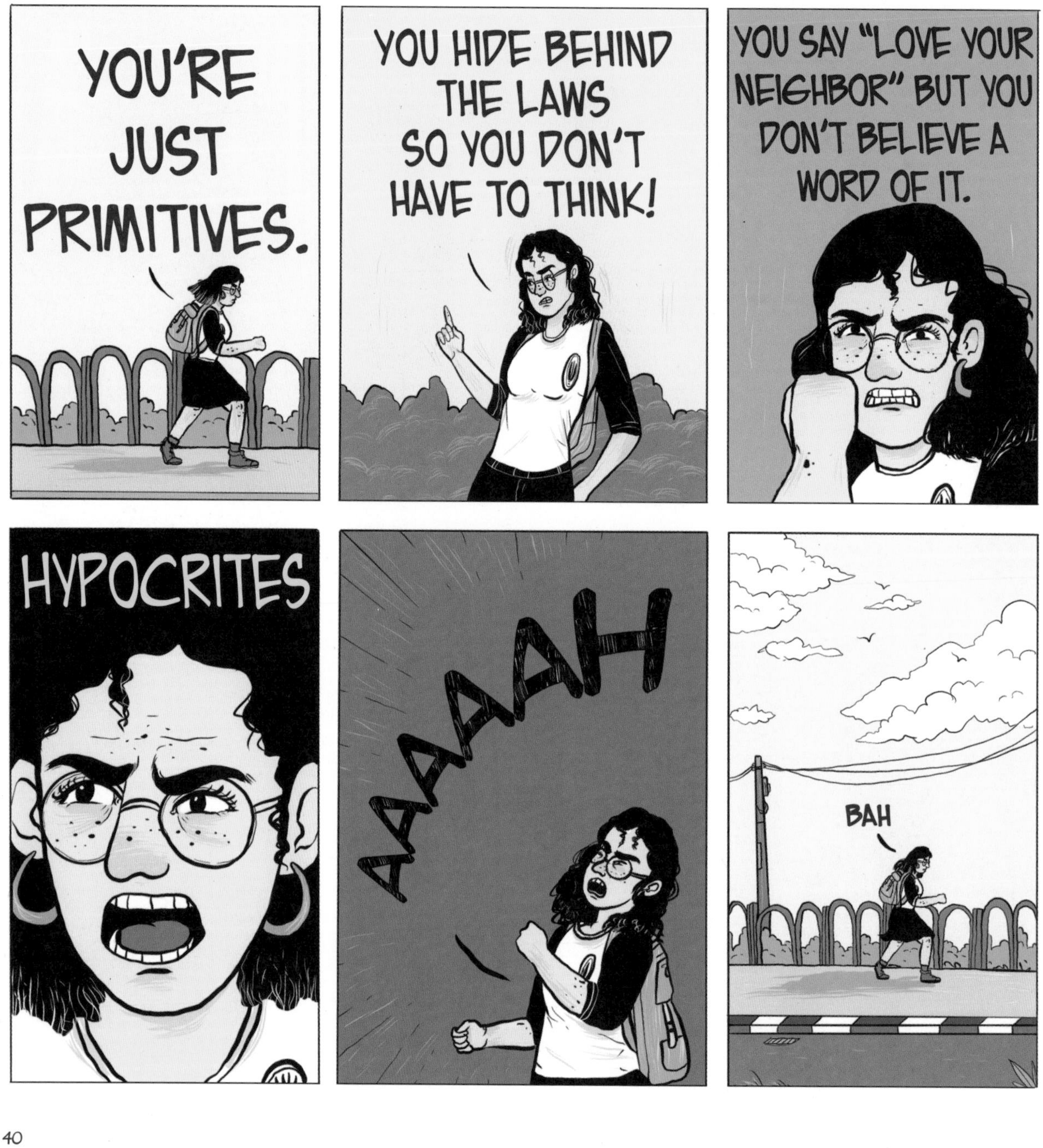

YOU'RE JUST PRIMITIVES.
YOU HIDE BEHIND THE LAWS SO YOU DON'T HAVE TO THINK!
YOU SAY "LOVE YOUR NEIGHBOR" BUT YOU DON'T BELIEVE A WORD OF IT.
HYPOCRITES
AAAAAH
BAH

At home, I put on my skirt that draggled along the ground. And I set off again, furiously, for the Oulpena.

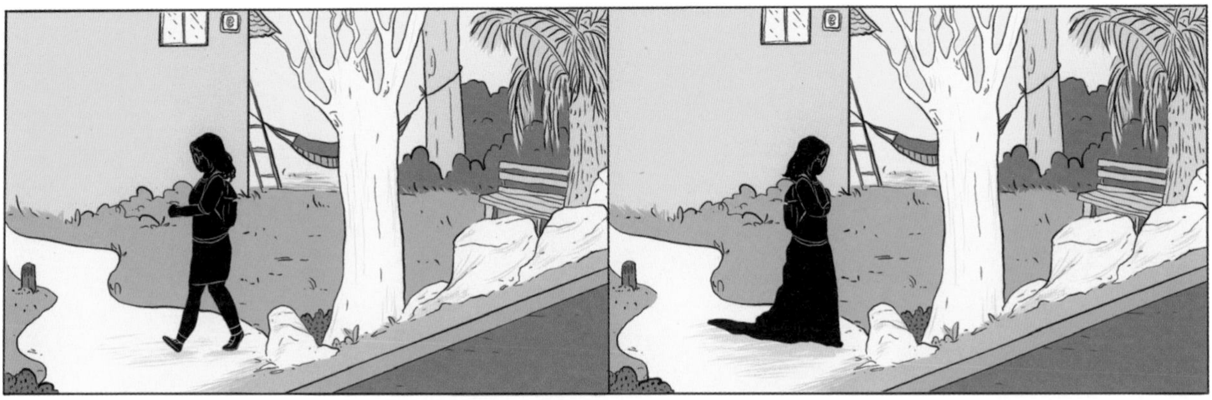

At school, I waited for the beginning of class, and I said nothing. I said nothing for three days, and no one even noticed.

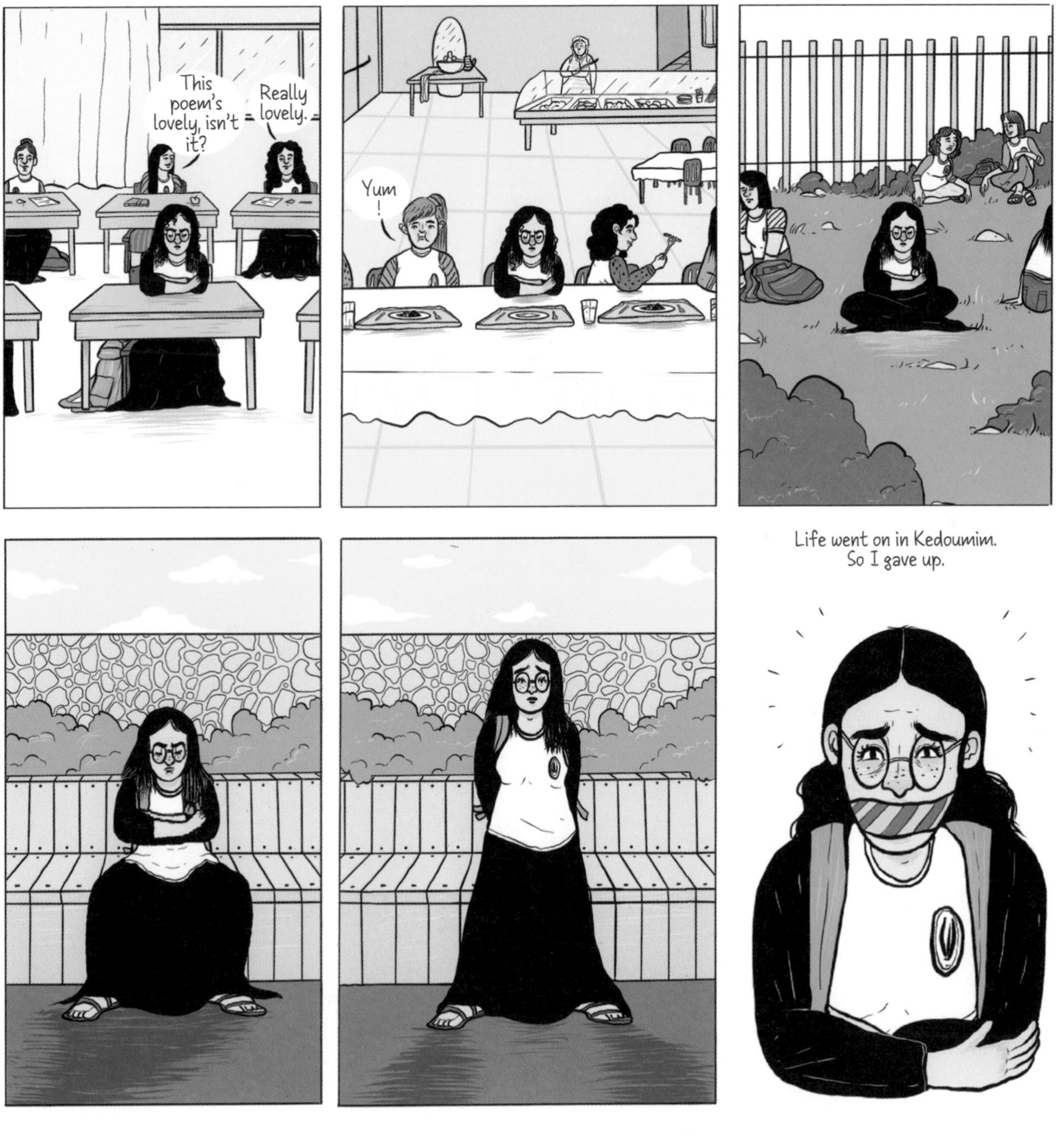
This poem's lovely, isn't it?
Really lovely.
Yum!
Life went on in Kedoumim.
So I gave up.

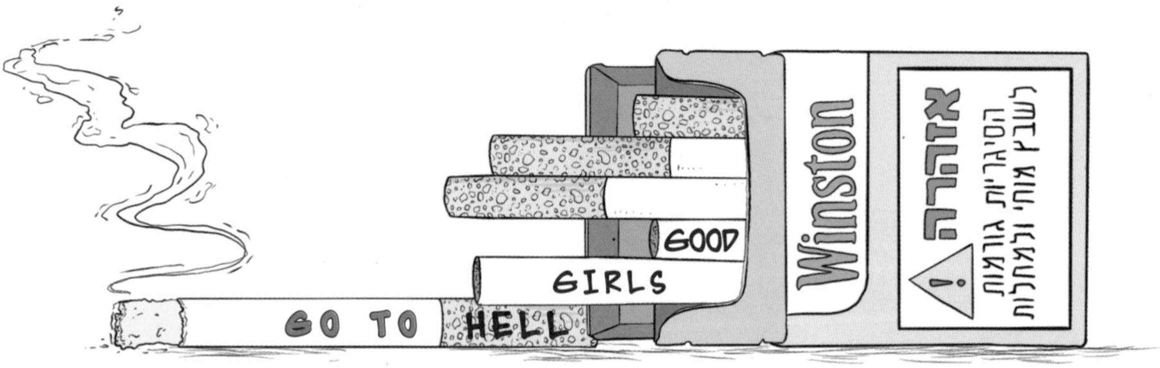
GOOD
GIRLS
GO TO HELL
Winston
אזהרה

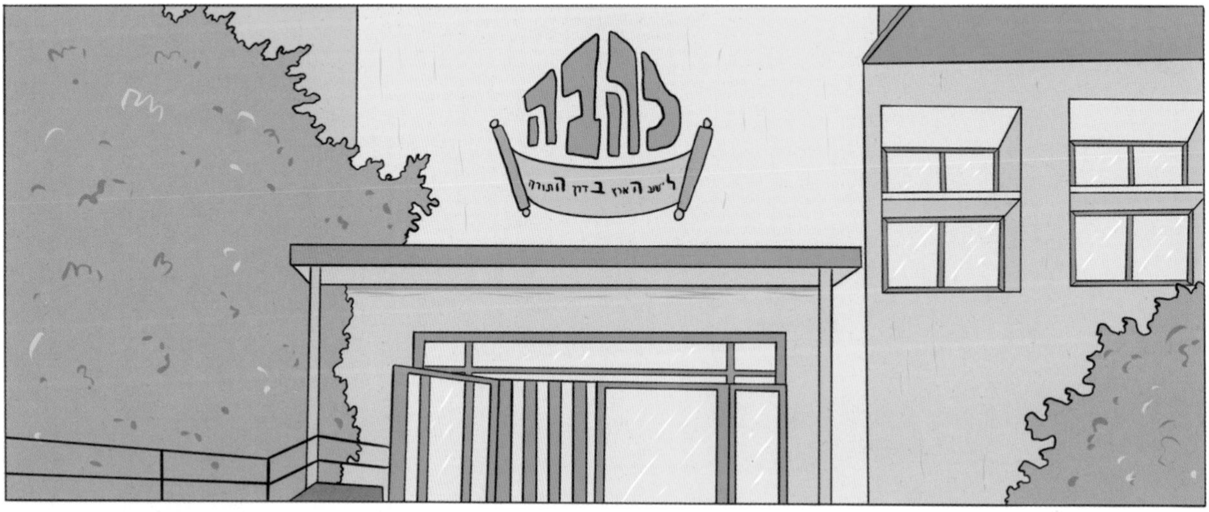
להבה

I met Eden on the steps of our Oulpena, "Lehava," as she was straightening her jet-black hair. There was a Beatles song playing. She was smiling broadly. That girl with her hair straightener, right in the middle of school, intrigued me.

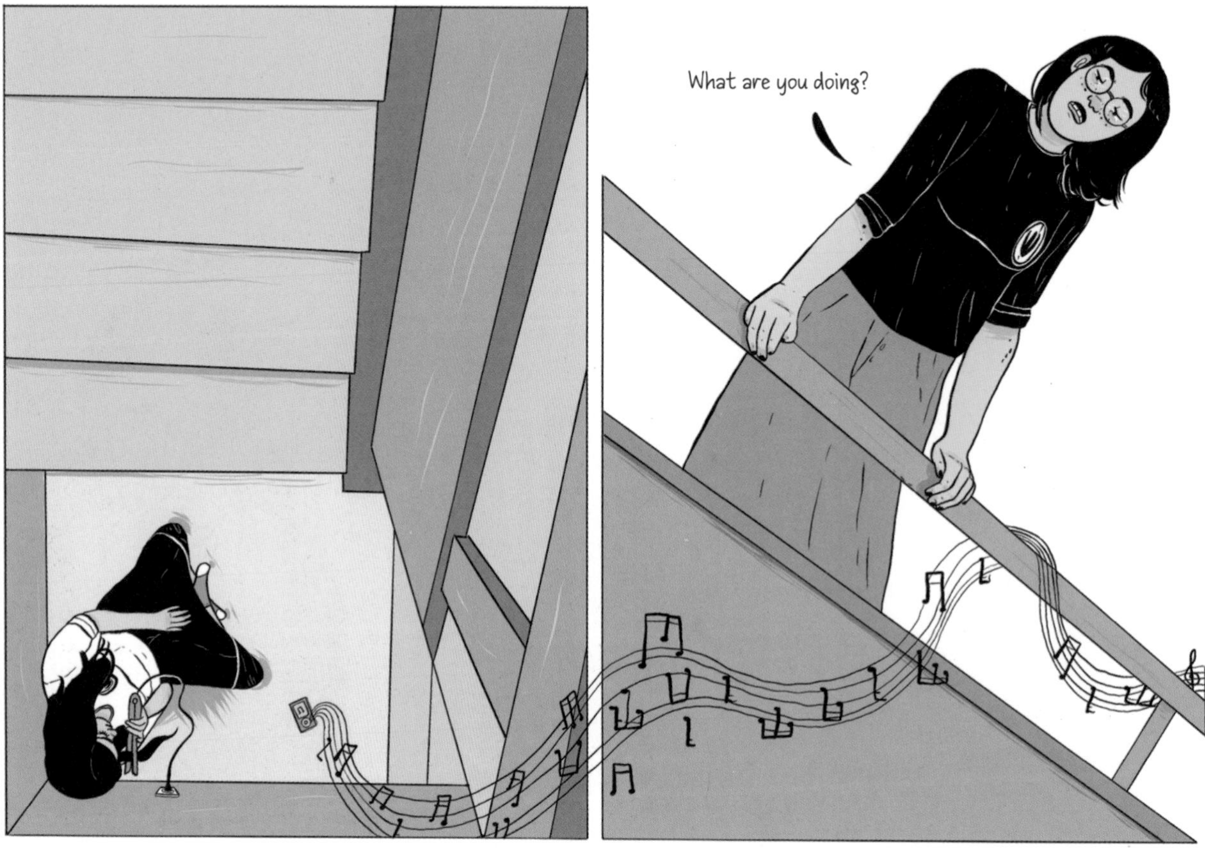
What are you doing?

It took her a few seconds to reply "I'm bored." Her calm, and her burst of laughter, made me sit down next to her. At first we didn't speak—she straightened her hair, and I was deep in thought, as usual. I don't remember exactly how we became friends, but that was our first meeting.

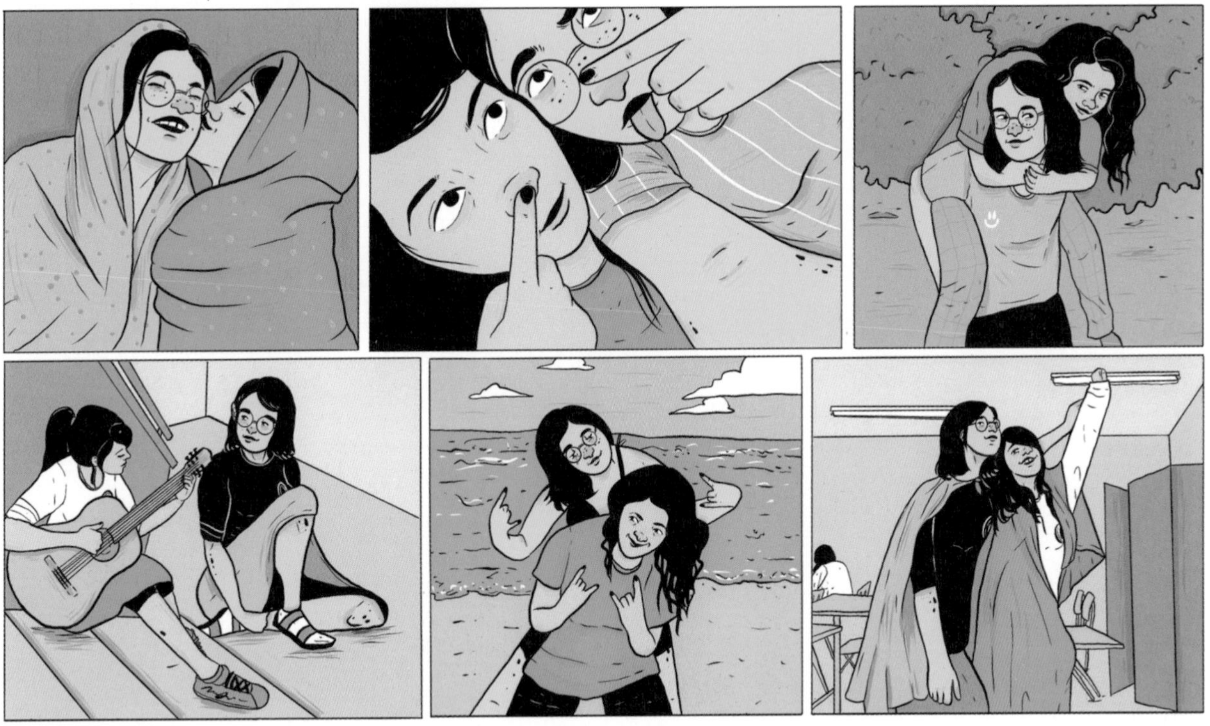

With her, you didn't need to make a big effort—she was a real friend, like in books. Then Zimratt joined us. They came into my life at a time when I'd given up wanting things: they were my life buoy, my lifeline.

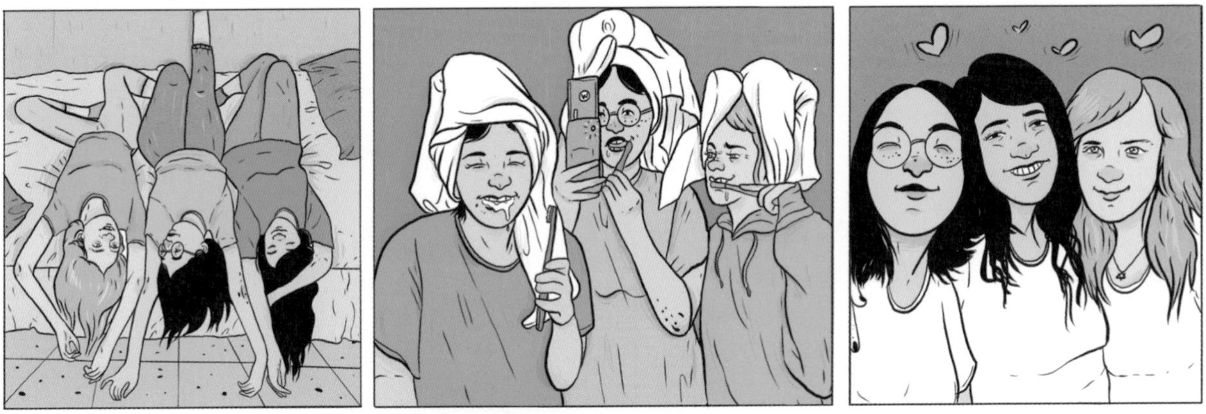

While Eden gave me her support, I was the shoulder for Zimratt to cry on.

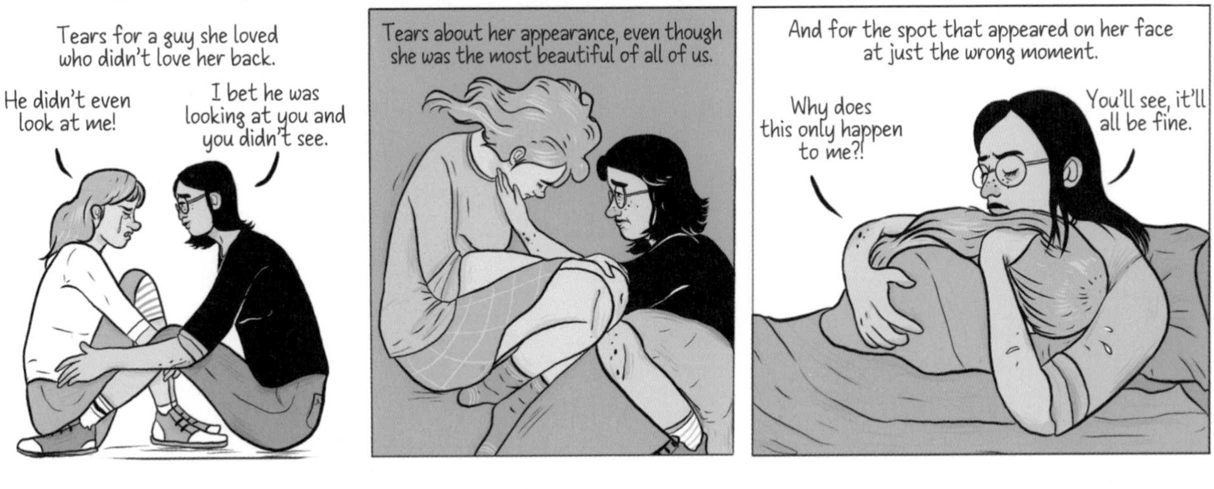

Tears for a guy she loved who didn't love her back.
He didn't even look at me!
I bet he was looking at you and you didn't see.
Tears about her appearance, even though she was the most beautiful of all of us.
And for the spot that appeared on her face at just the wrong moment.
Why does this only happen to me?!
You'll see, it'll all be fine.

We had nothing in common: the way we thought, acted, or even our size! But it worked well. An inseparable trio.
We lived through our firsts together, our first experiences.

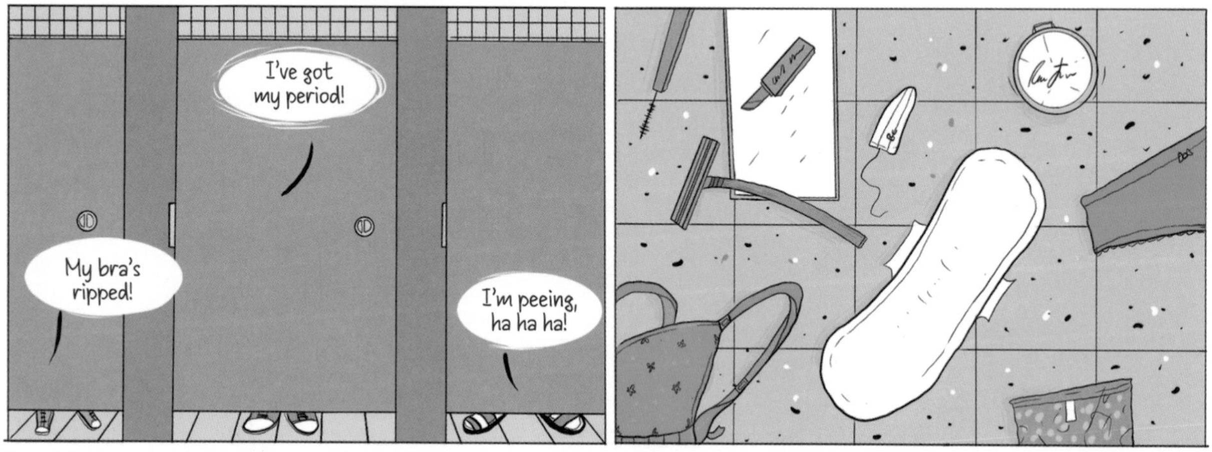
I've got my period!
My bra's ripped!
I'm peeing, ha ha ha!

One of these moments, an unforgettable one for me, was the evening they gave me my first cigarette!

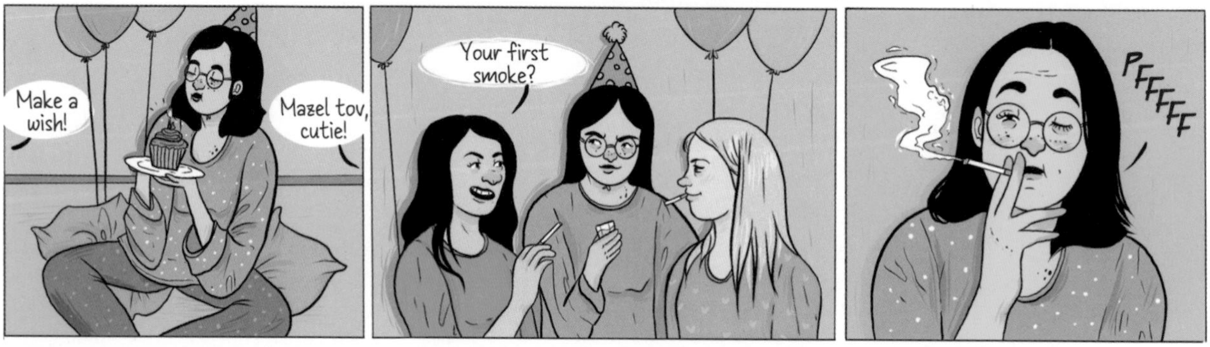
Make a wish!
Mazel tov, cutie!
Your first smoke?
PFFFFF

We were at my house. There was no one home, and I smoked it, sitting at the window, gazing over Kedoumim, experiencing the taste for the first time. That's when I realized that in fact I was fulfilling all the negative predictions everyone had of me, that I behaved badly, that I was a bad influence, deceitful, someone who trapped and dirtied everyone they touched.

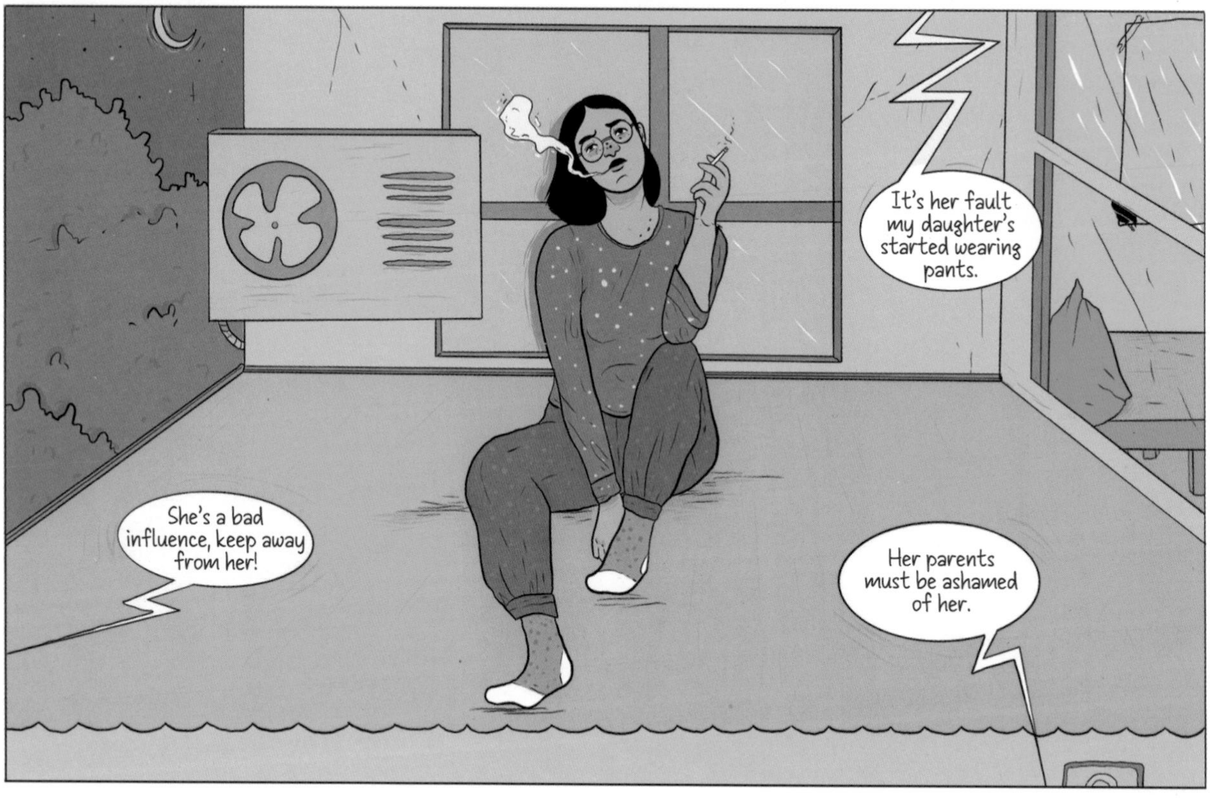
It's her fault my daughter's started wearing pants.
She's a bad influence, keep away from her!
Her parents must be ashamed of her.

And the irony of all that? It was those same people who had led me to that moment, that first cigarette.

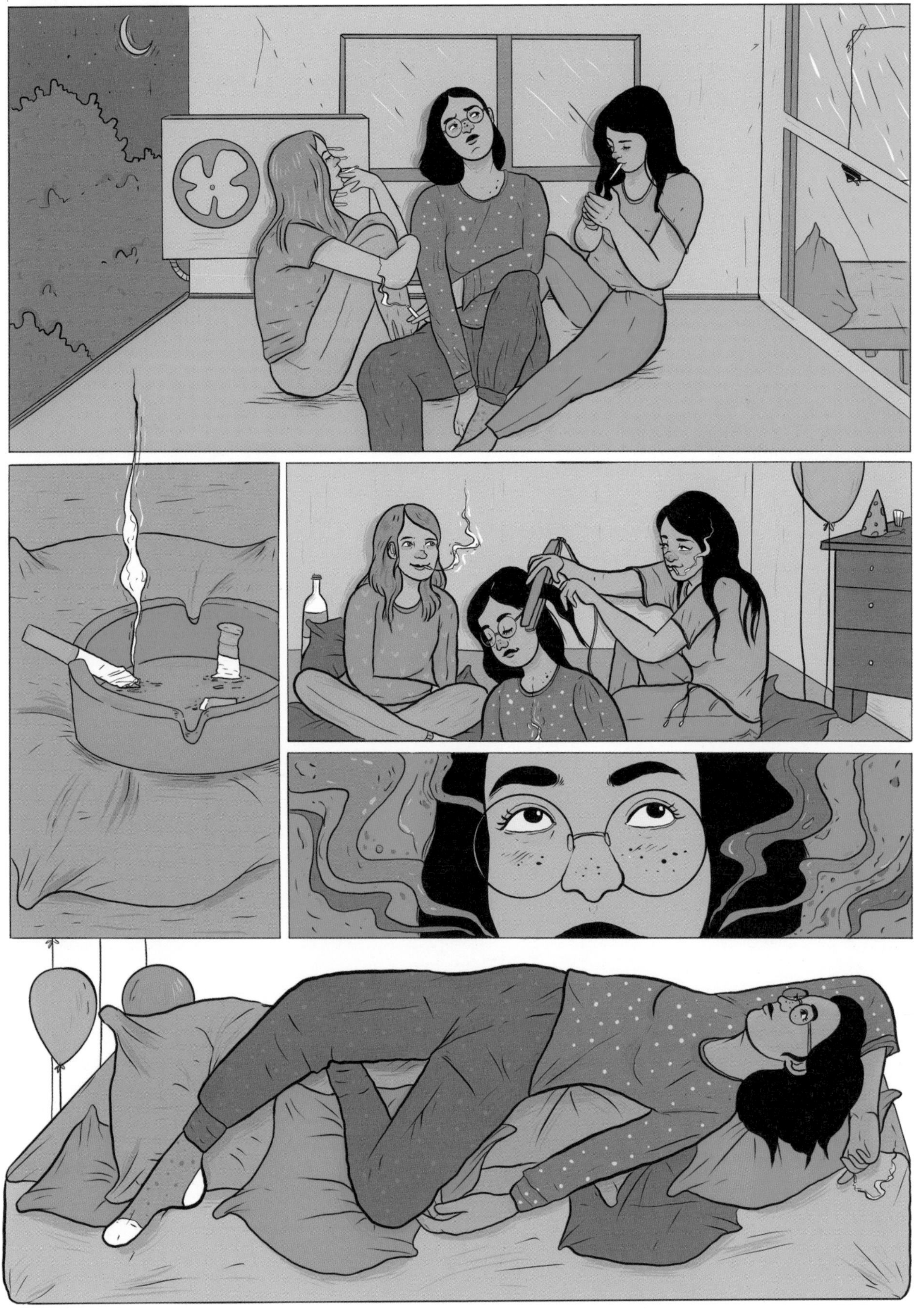

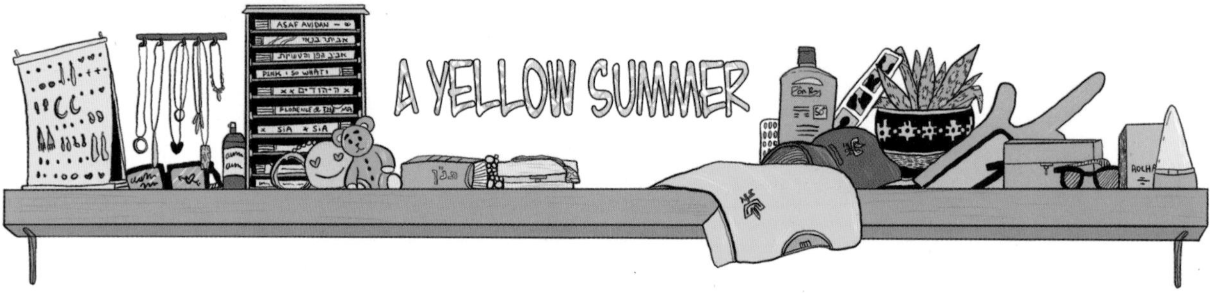
A YELLOW SUMMER
ASAF AVIDAN
PINK : SO WHAT
SIA

During the summer vacation between 9th and 10th grade, I looked for a job. All my friends were camp counselors in the Bnei Akiva movement, and obviously, given my situation, I'd been turned down. I had to fill the time.

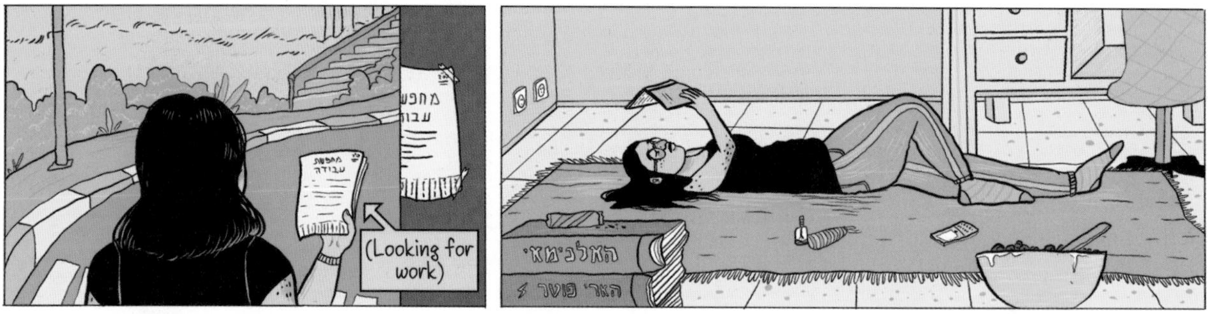
(Looking for work)

My sister Tiferett had moved to Tel Aviv. She had begun working with her husband, Nimrod, as leader of a holiday camp at Tel Aviv University.

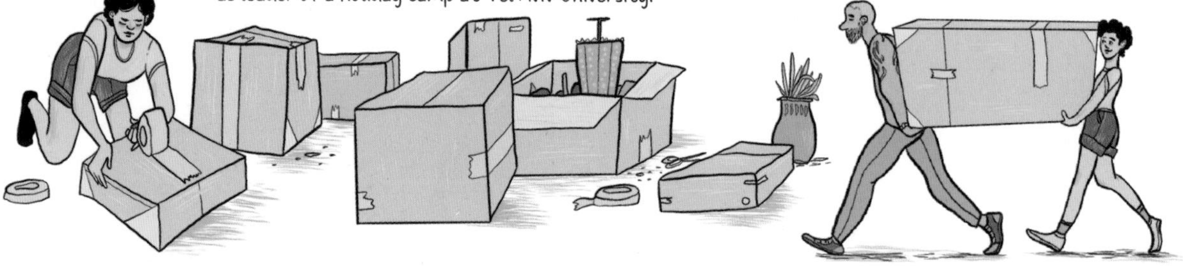

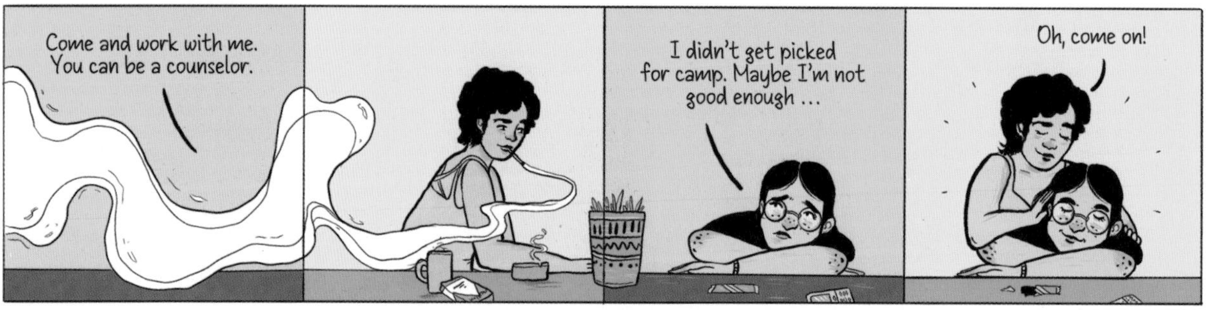
Come and work with me. You can be a counselor.
I didn't get picked for camp. Maybe I'm not good enough ...
Oh, come on!

So I went.
In the morning, my mother took me into Tel Aviv. She dropped me off at the main entrance to the university. I went up the stairs and then a green hillock to find the activity center.

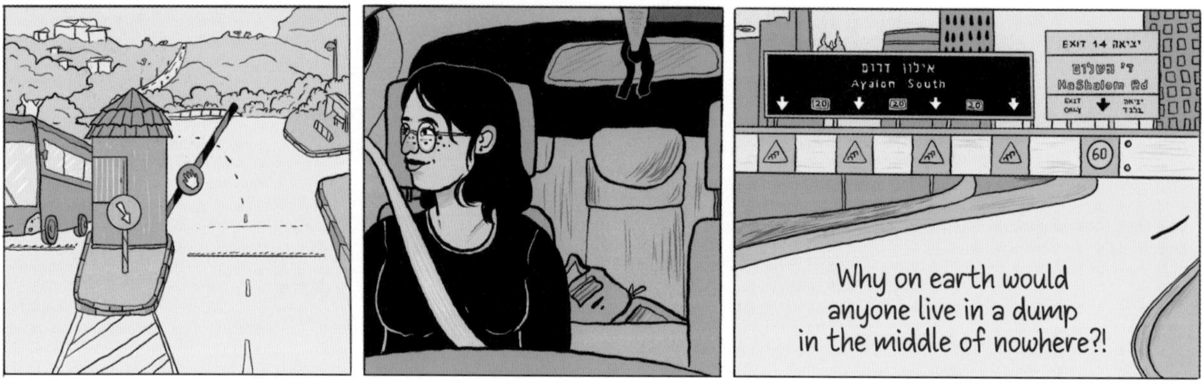
Ayalon South
EXIT 14
HaShalom Rd
60
Why on earth would anyone live in a dump in the middle of nowhere?!

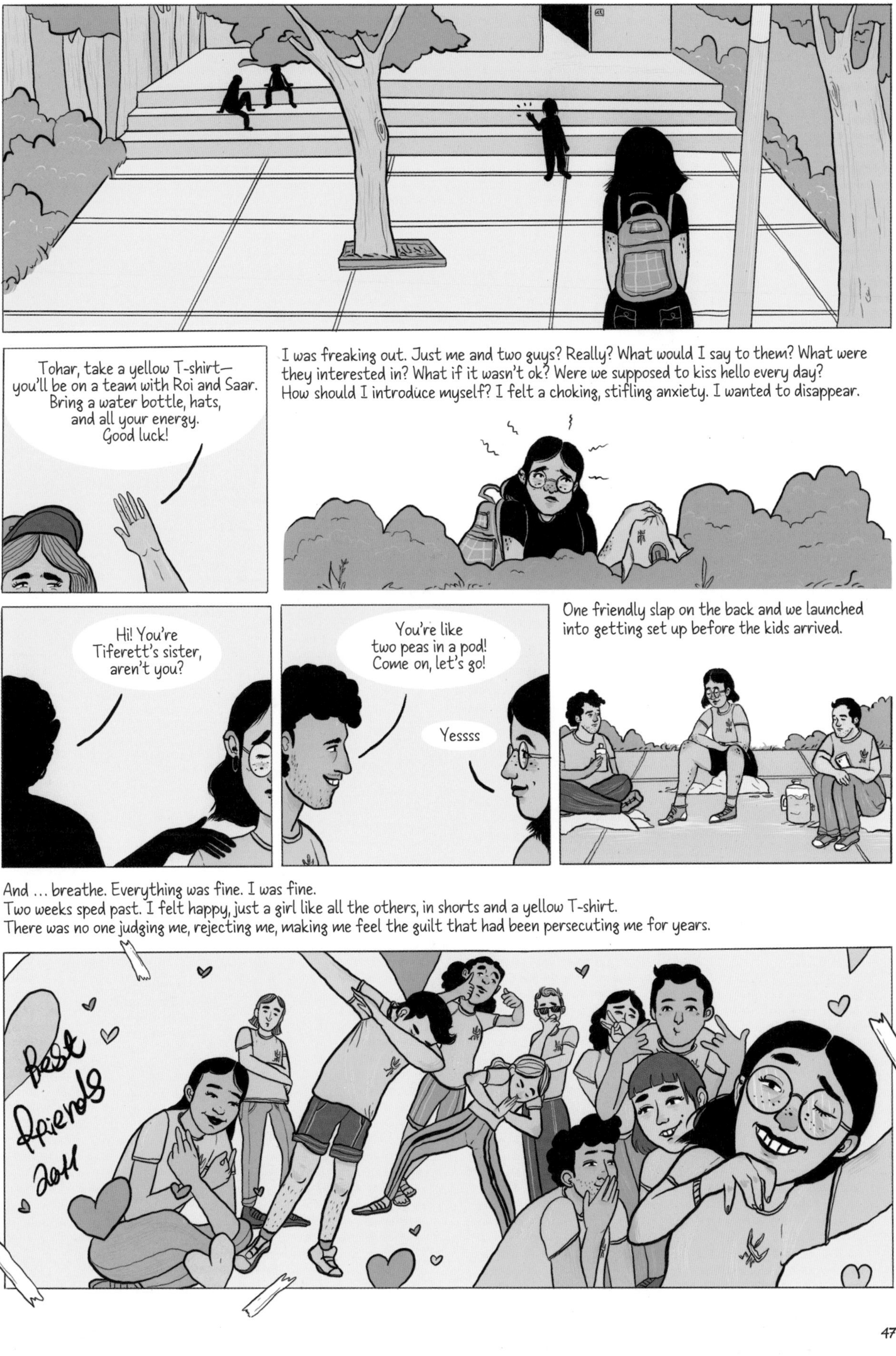
Tohar, take a yellow T-shirt—you'll be on a team with Roi and Saar. Bring a water bottle, hats, and all your energy. Good luck!
I was freaking out. Just me and two guys? Really? What would I say to them? What were they interested in? What if it wasn't ok? Were we supposed to kiss hello every day? How should I introduce myself? I felt a choking, stifling anxiety. I wanted to disappear.
Hi! You're Tiferett's sister, aren't you?
You're like two peas in a pod! Come on, let's go!
Yessss
One friendly slap on the back and we launched into getting set up before the kids arrived.
And … breathe. Everything was fine. I was fine.
Two weeks sped past. I felt happy, just a girl like all the others, in shorts and a yellow T-shirt.
There was no one judging me, rejecting me, making me feel the guilt that had been persecuting me for years.
Best Friends 2011

For the first time in my life, I was … me.

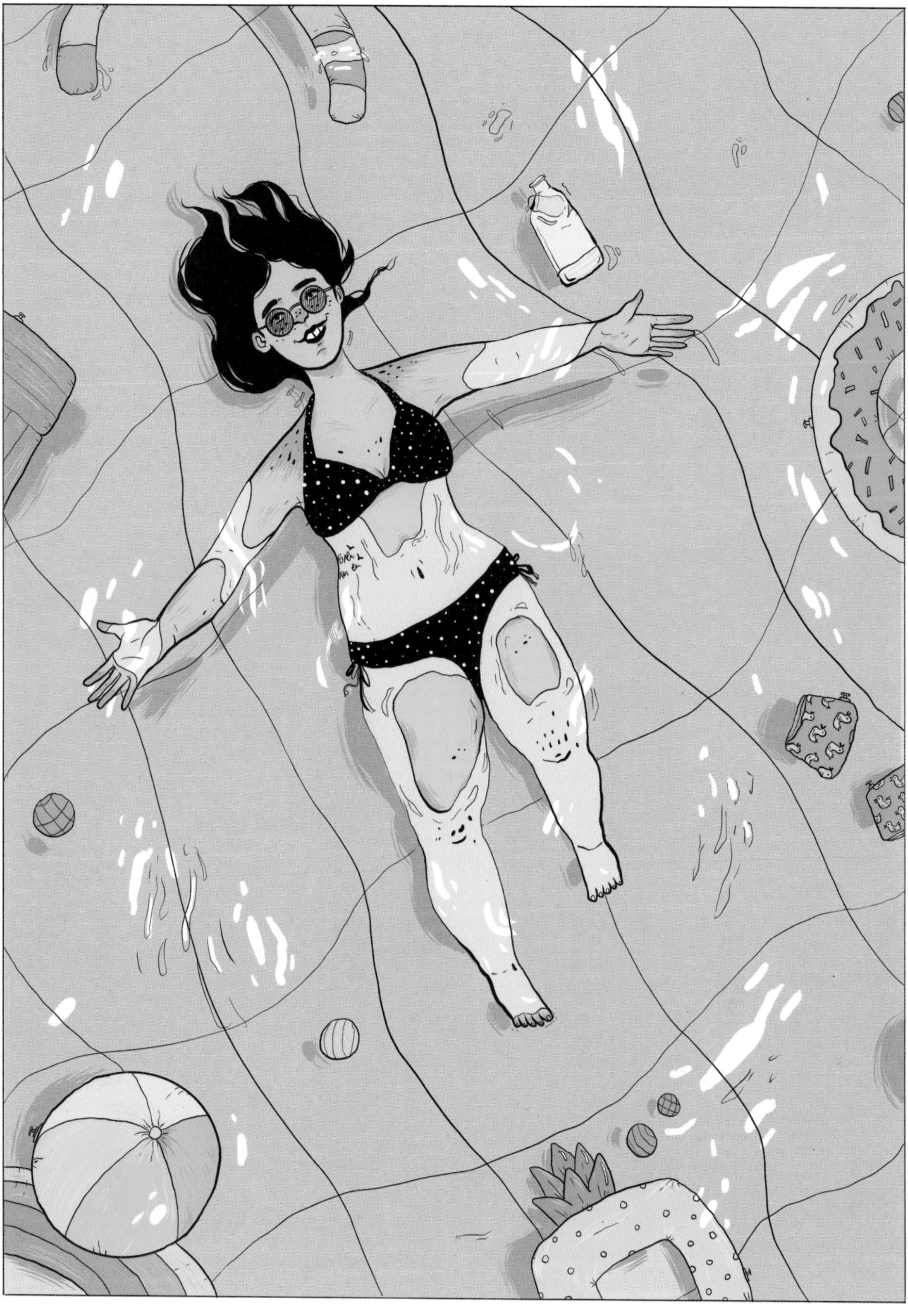

Three weeks later, during the break, I was sitting on a bench waiting for the kids and sketching.
A boy with long hair and a big smile came up to me.

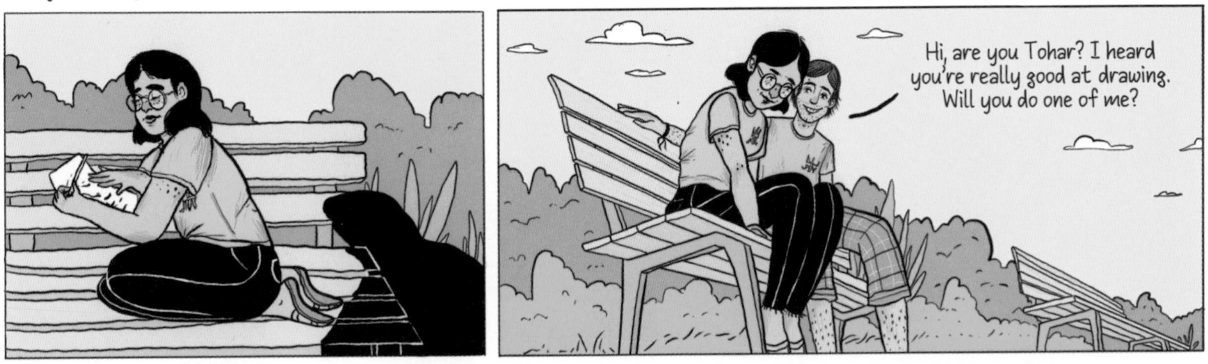
Hi, are you Tohar? I heard you're really good at drawing. Will you do one of me?

I pretended to ignore him, but I felt very comfortable with him. That summer, he became my other half, my best friend.

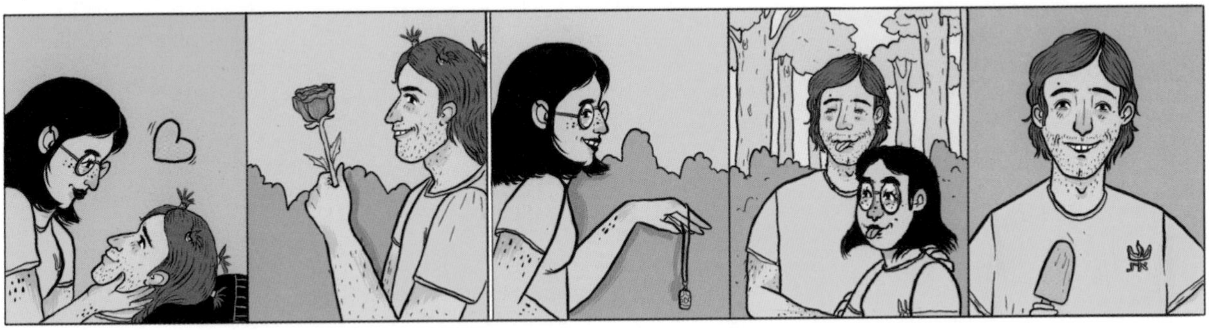

And that's how I met Daniel, or, as he's now known, my husband.

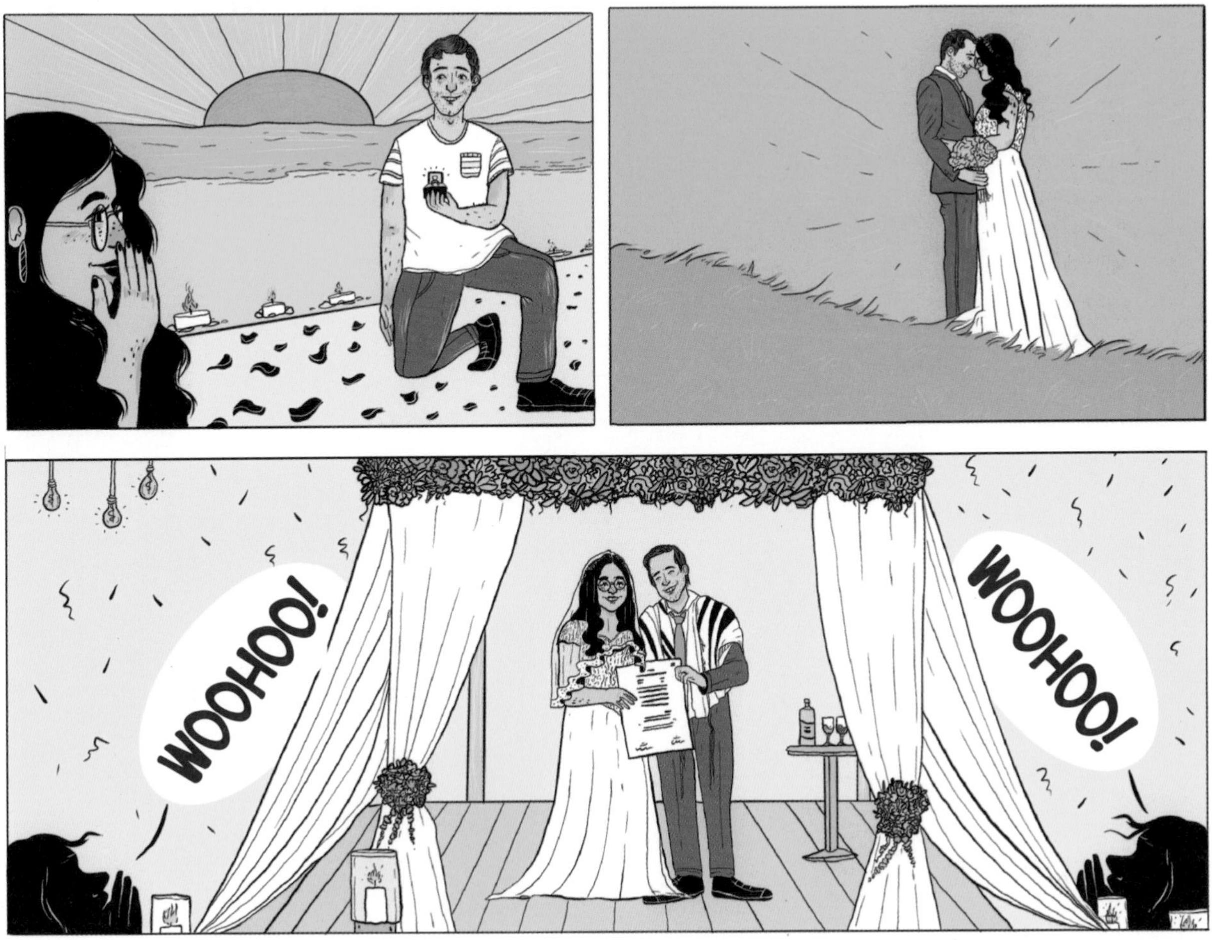
WOOHOO!
WOOHOO!

IS IT REALLY ... THAT BAD?

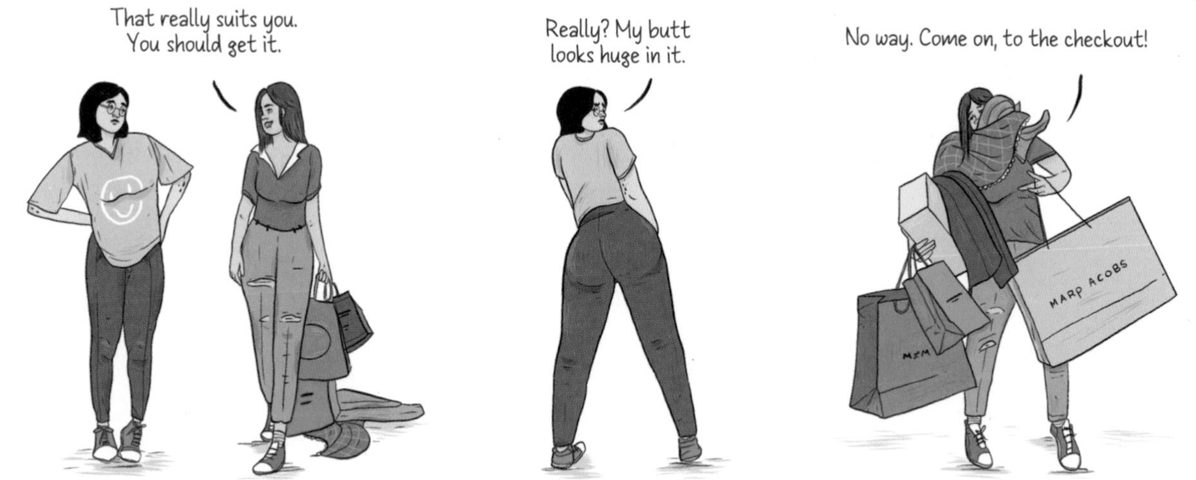
That really suits you. You should get it.
Really? My butt looks huge in it.
No way. Come on, to the checkout!
MARC JACOBS
MSM

Mika pushes me to the cash register. She always says the right thing at the right moment. Sometimes in life you feel like you'll never make any more new friends, that it takes too much effort—a real marketing campaign for yourself.

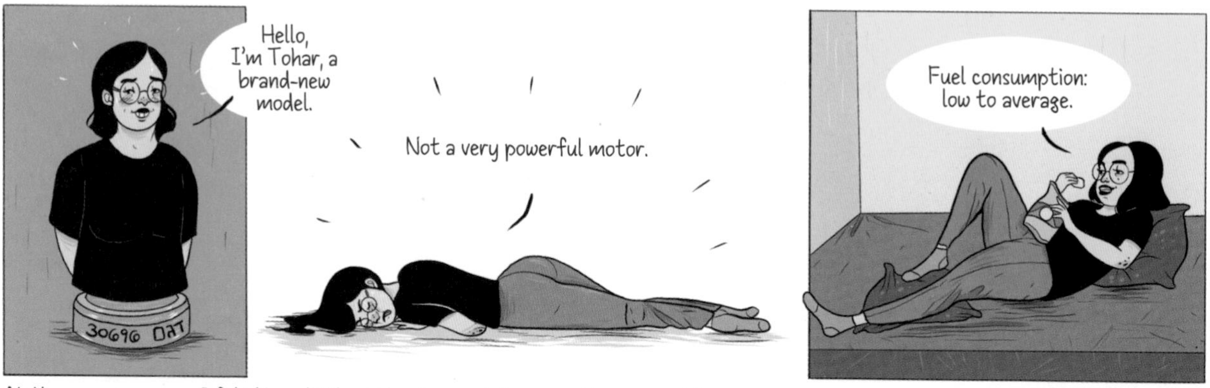
Hello, I'm Tohar, a brand-new model.
30696 DAT
Not a very powerful motor.
Fuel consumption: low to average.

At the summer camp, I felt like a little old beater next to some shiny powerful sports cars.

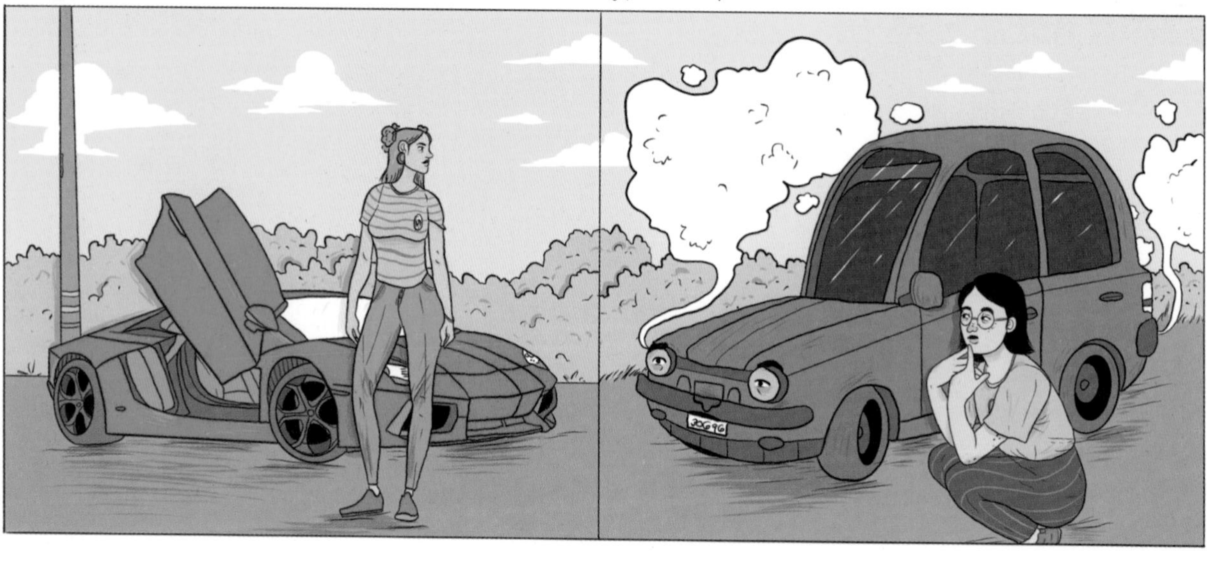
30696

When I met Mika, I couldn't imagine what she saw in me. Why would she make friends with me, living so far away? To get to my house, you have to take three buses, and the last one is armor-plated, bulletproof. But she had chosen me, and we were inseparable.

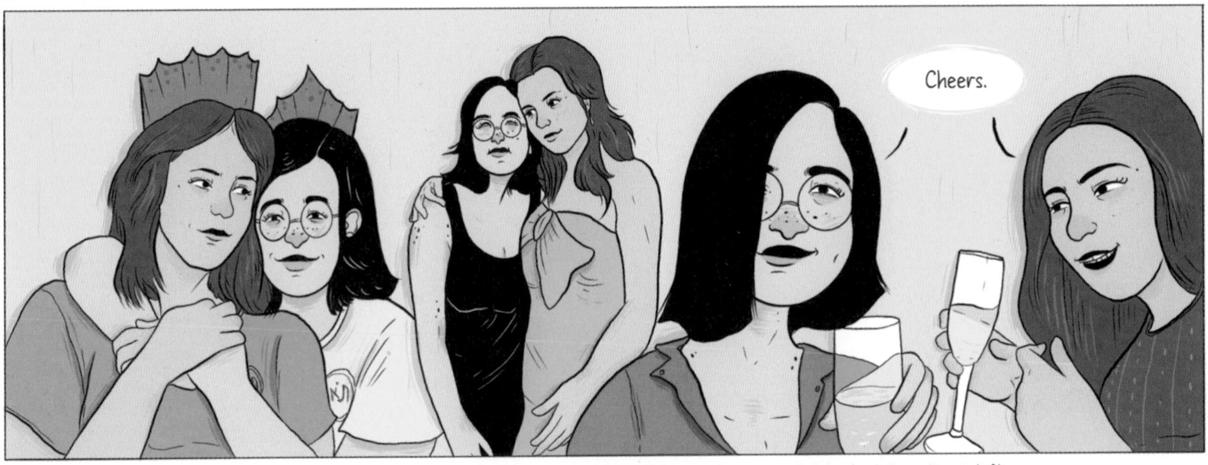
Cheers.

One day, she told me she liked Daniel. I was so happy for her. I thought they made a great couple. When Daniel flew to Los Angeles, we spent whole nights writing him messages together. And then he came back and it happened.

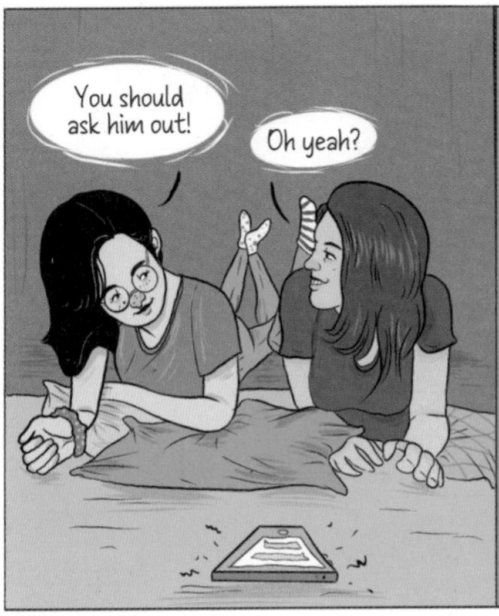
You should ask him out!
Oh yeah?

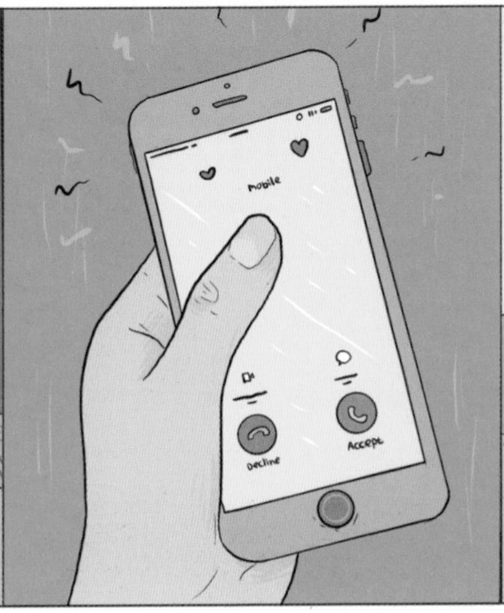

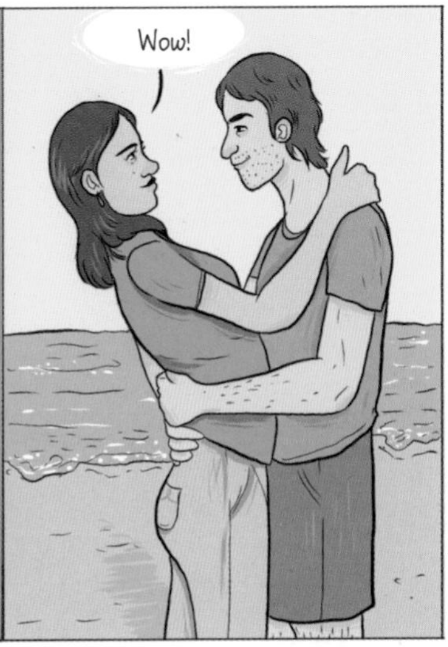
Wow!

They started going out, as a couple, and in groups, too ...

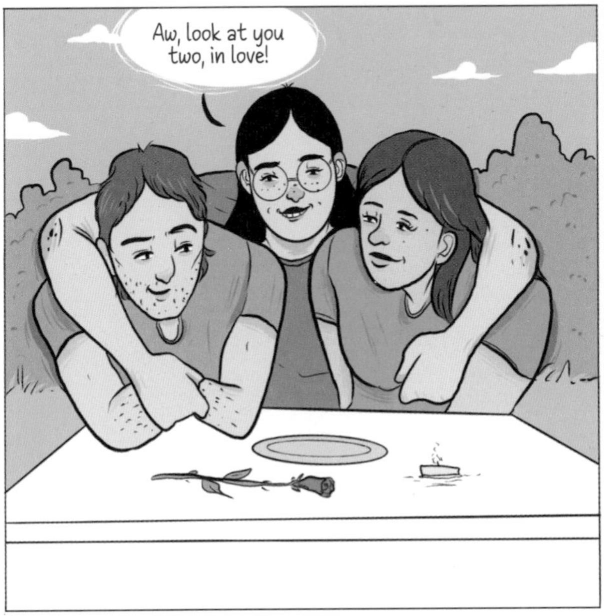
Aw, look at you two, in love!

I thought "one third of heaven"* was already earmarked for me.

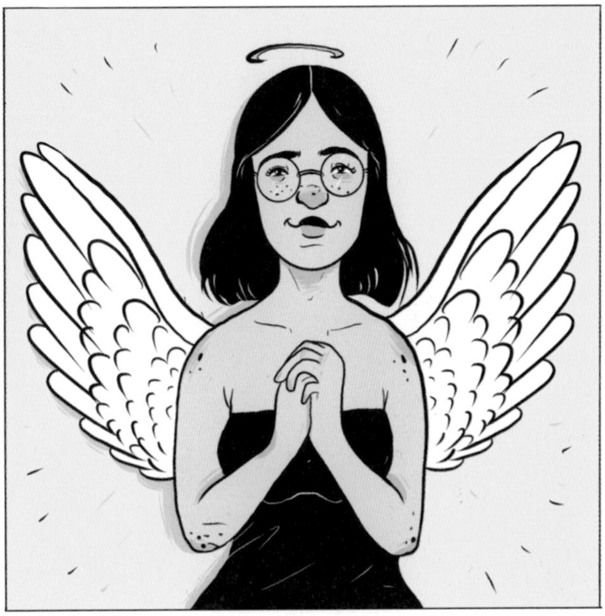

But they split up not long afterward.

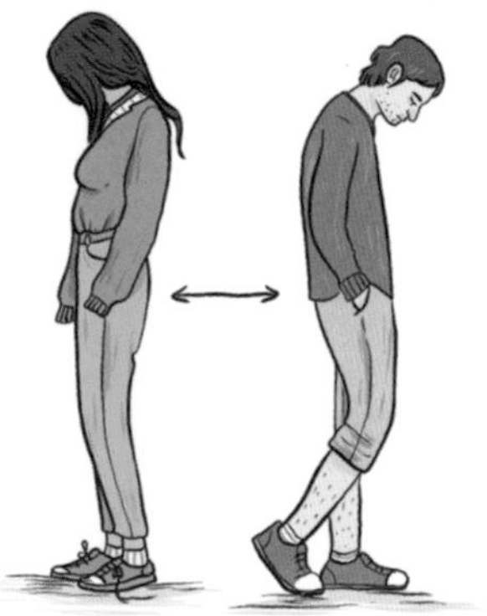

When we got together as a group, it had become tense and embarrassing.

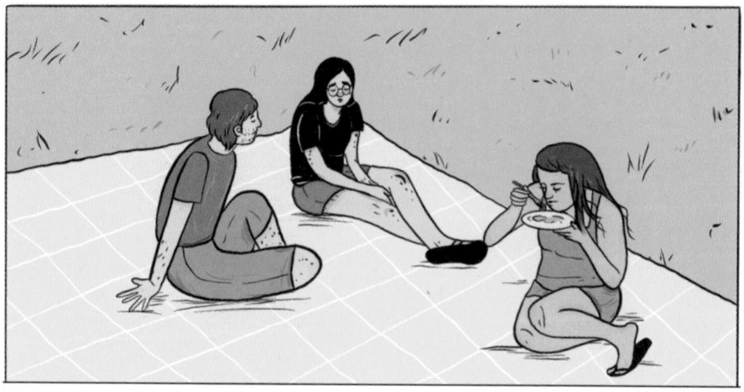

I wanted to know what had happened, why they ended it, but they didn't tell me anything.

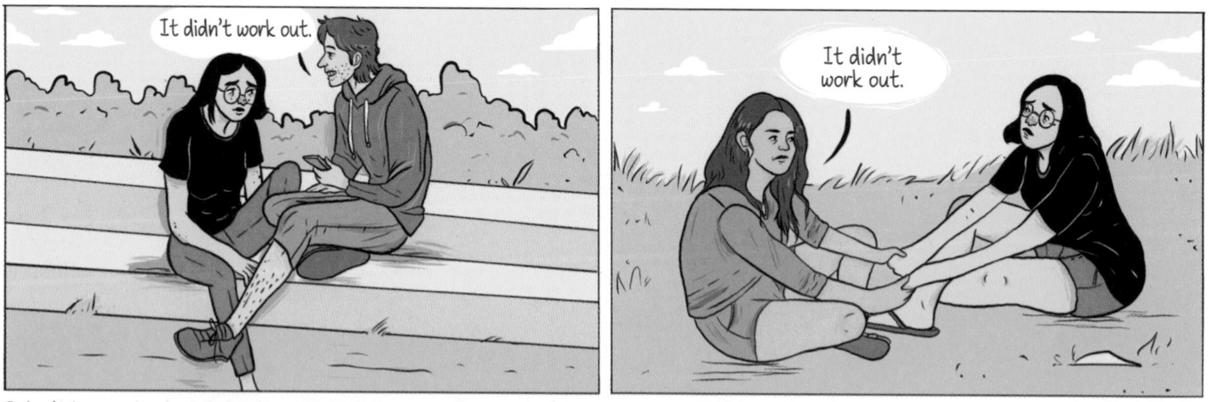
It didn't work out.
It didn't work out.

I don't know why, but I didn't really believe them. One day, Daniel arrived at Kfar-Saba to meet me.
Something was different about him, he was hesitant. He held out a letter to me.

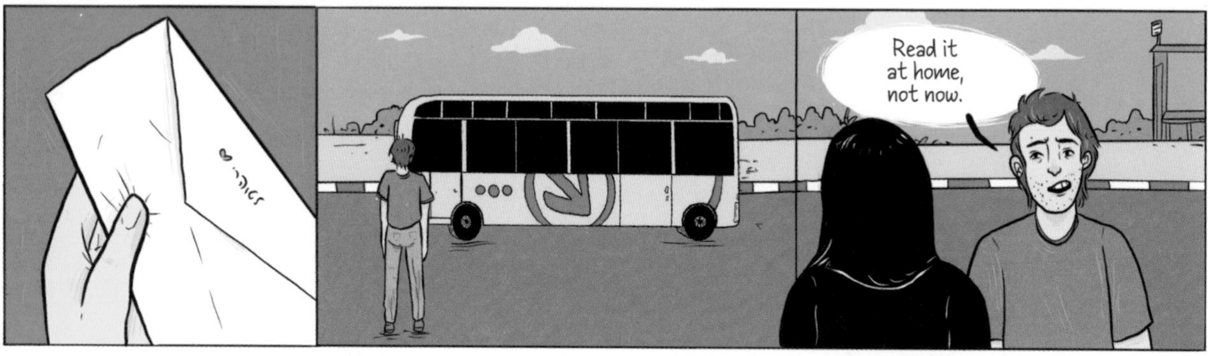
Read it at home, not now.

I didn't wait. I read it … on the bus.

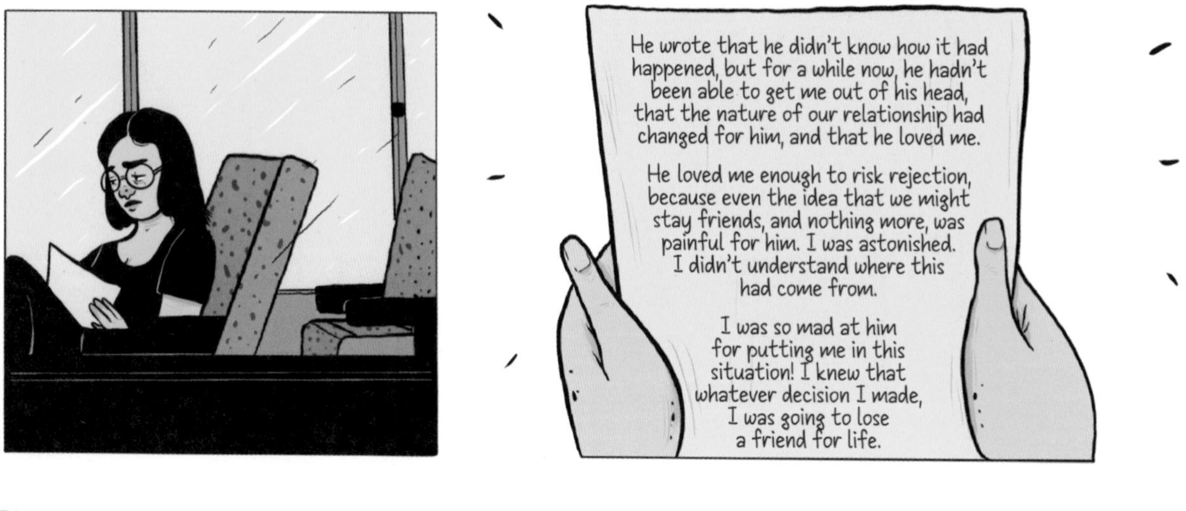
He wrote that he didn't know how it had happened, but for a while now, he hadn't been able to get me out of his head, that the nature of our relationship had changed for him, and that he loved me.
He loved me enough to risk rejection, because even the idea that we might stay friends, and nothing more, was painful for him. I was astonished. I didn't understand where this had come from.
I was so mad at him for putting me in this situation! I knew that whatever decision I made, I was going to lose a friend for life.

I tried to imagine us together, holding each other, touching each other, emotional.

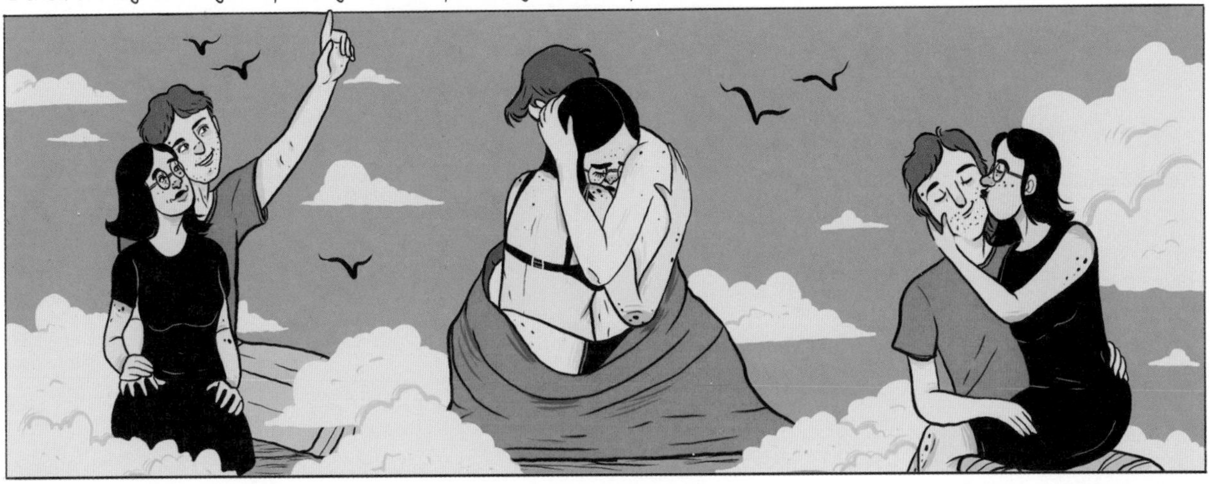

I couldn't see it. That evening at home, I decided to reply to him in writing, too.

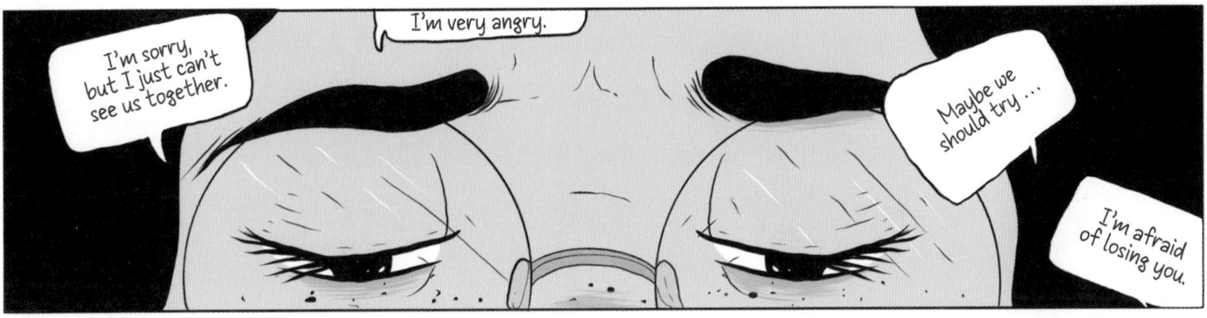

I'm sorry, but I just can't see us together.
I'm very angry.
Maybe we should try …
I'm afraid of losing you.

After many false starts and a great deal of hesitation, I took a deep breath and sent him a text.

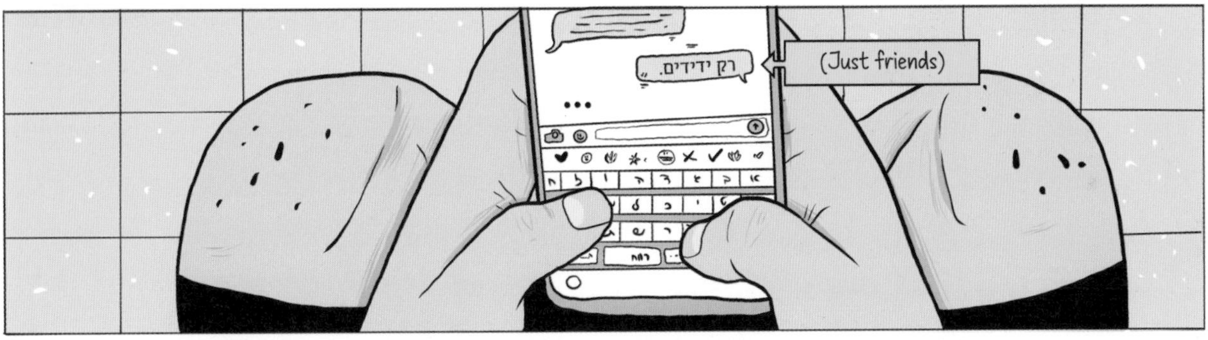

רק ידידים.
(Just friends)

That message was the beginning of the end of a relationship, but not the one with Daniel … the one with Mika.
Even if we didn't know it yet, for Daniel and me, this was the beginning of a beautiful love story.

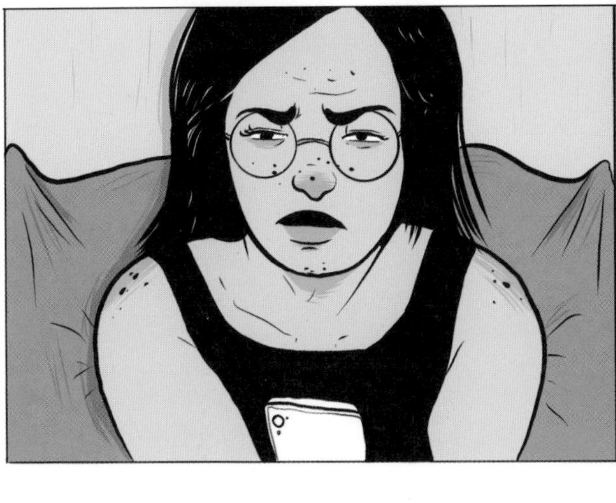

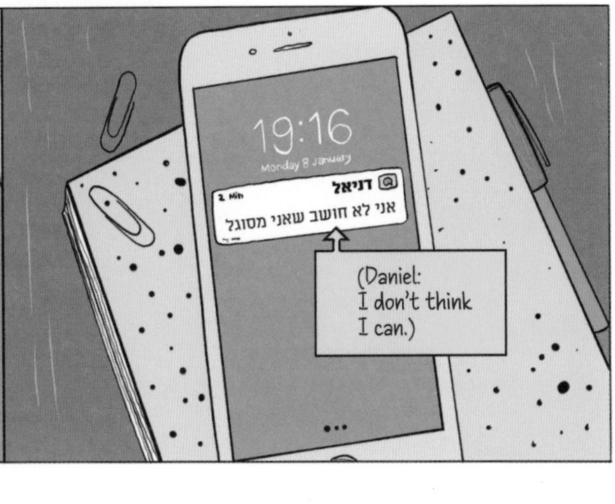

19:16
Monday 8 January
דניאל
אני לא חושב שאני מסוגל
(Daniel: I don't think I can.)

At the time, it was like a farewell. The days just passed me by, food had lost its taste.

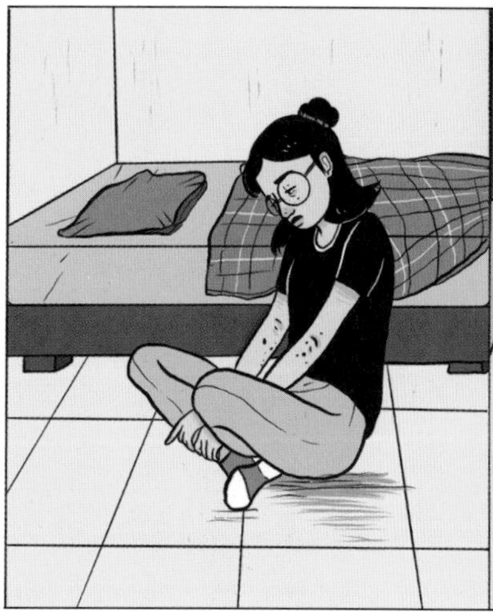

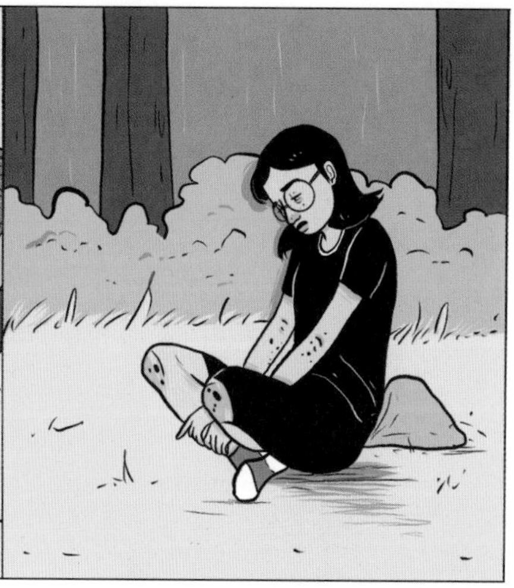

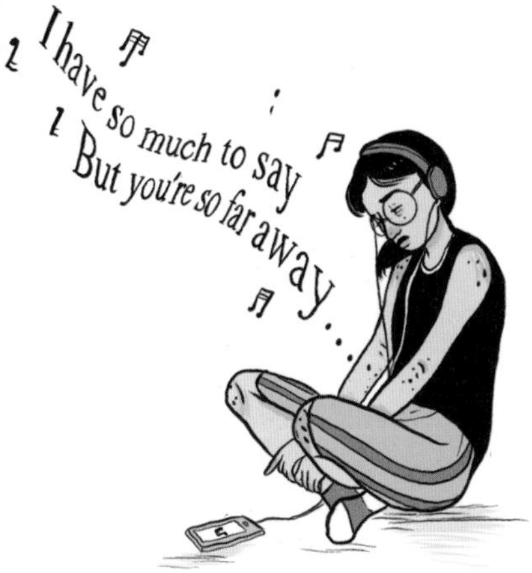
I have so much to say
But you're so far away...

Without me realizing, Daniel had become such an essential part of my life. His absence was like a presence in my life.

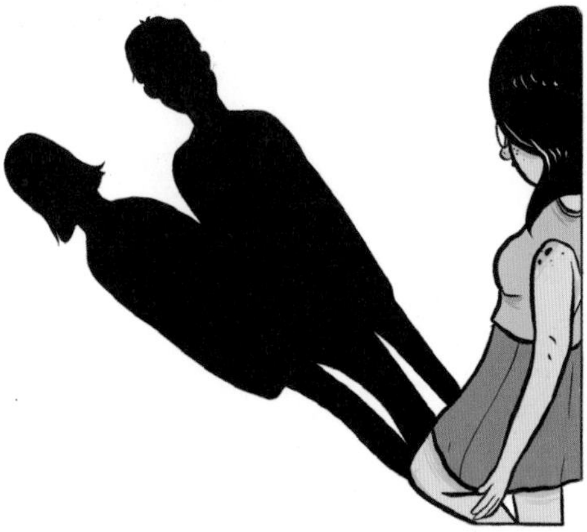

I tried to get through it, to go out with the summer camp gang. When we met up as a group, he completely ignored me. I stopped going. My heart was broken.

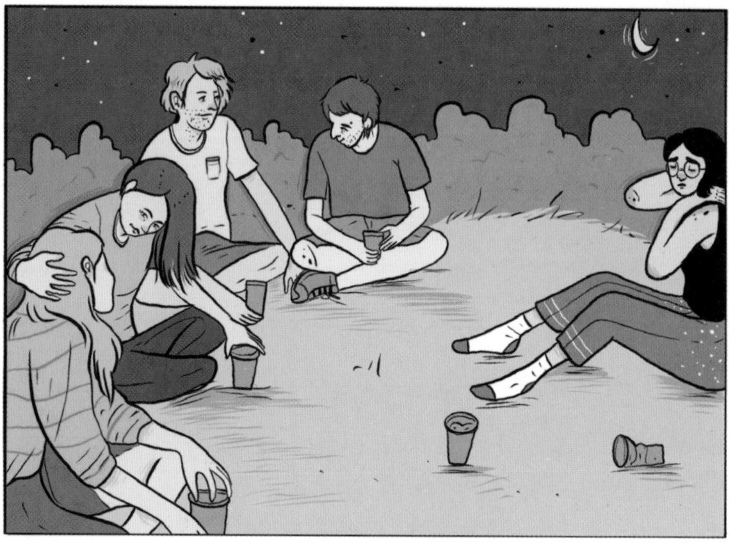

Mika didn't know why I was keeping my distance. She started to take it badly and tried to make me feel guilty.

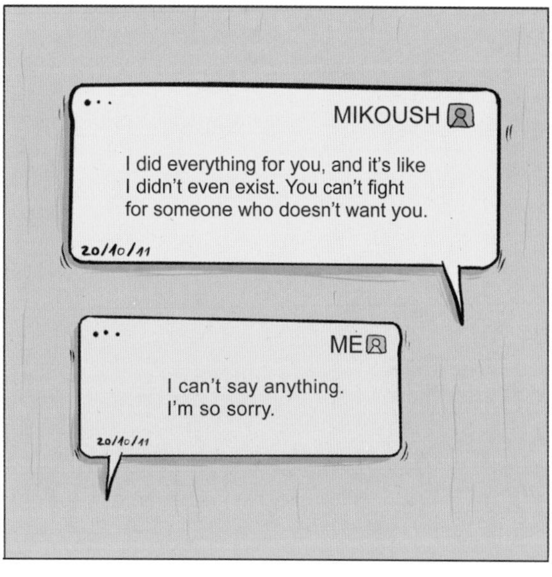
MIKOUSH
I did everything for you, and it's like I didn't even exist. You can't fight for someone who doesn't want you.
20/10/11
ME
I can't say anything. I'm so sorry.
20/10/11

It was too hard to explain, to her and to myself.
I had definitely made an unforgivable mistake.

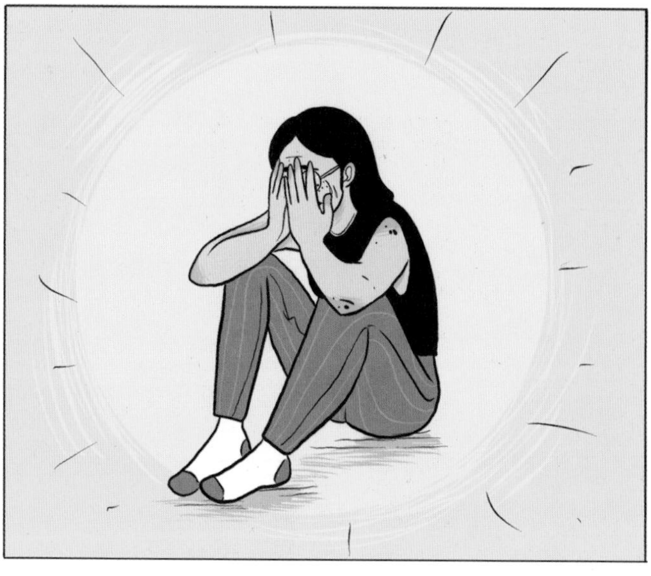

Then, after three months, I said to myself, "That's it!" I've lost both of them. What am I doing?! My heart had made the choice for me.

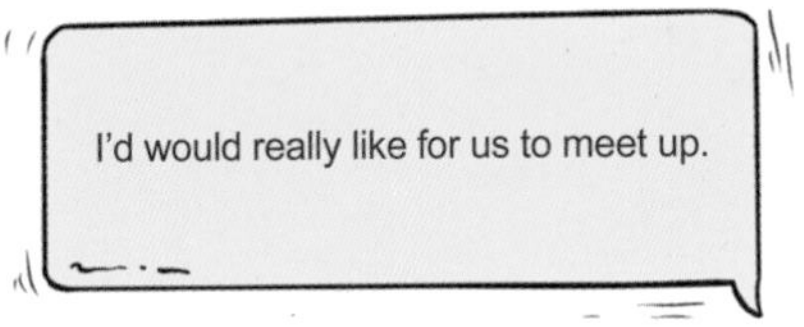
I'd would really like for us to meet up.

I wrote to him. When we met up, I felt the air rush back into my lungs—I could breathe again. The friendship was already there, love would come with time, I told myself. And it did come, in full force.

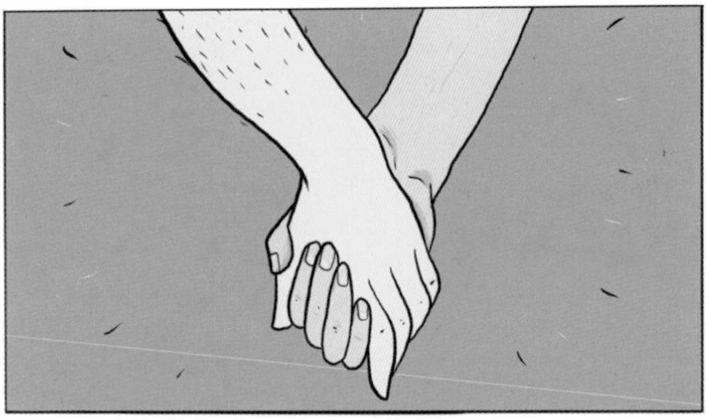

The closer Daniel and I became, the more distant Mika became. A few phone calls, some texts, then … nothing.

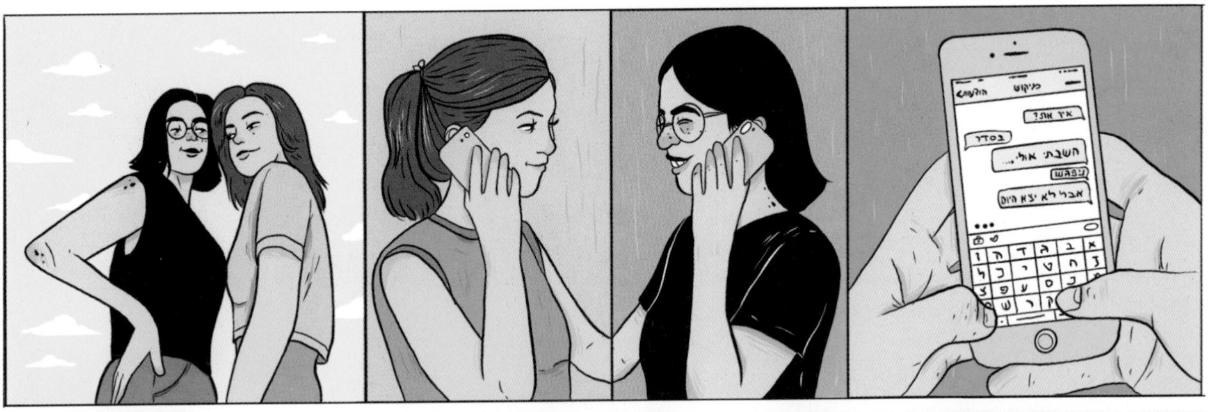

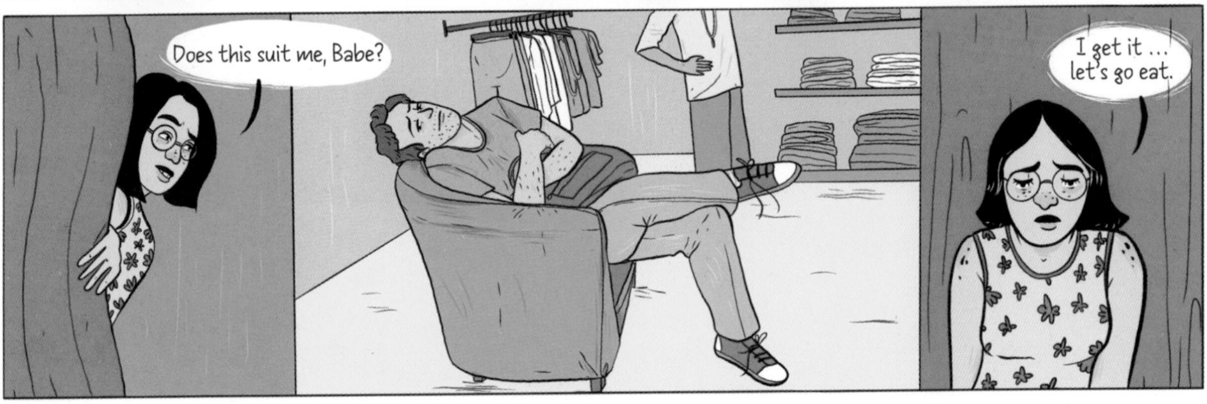
Does this suit me, Babe?
I get it … let's go eat.

I thought about Mika, who would be standing there with her warm smile. Did I miss her? Or maybe she still had a part of me?

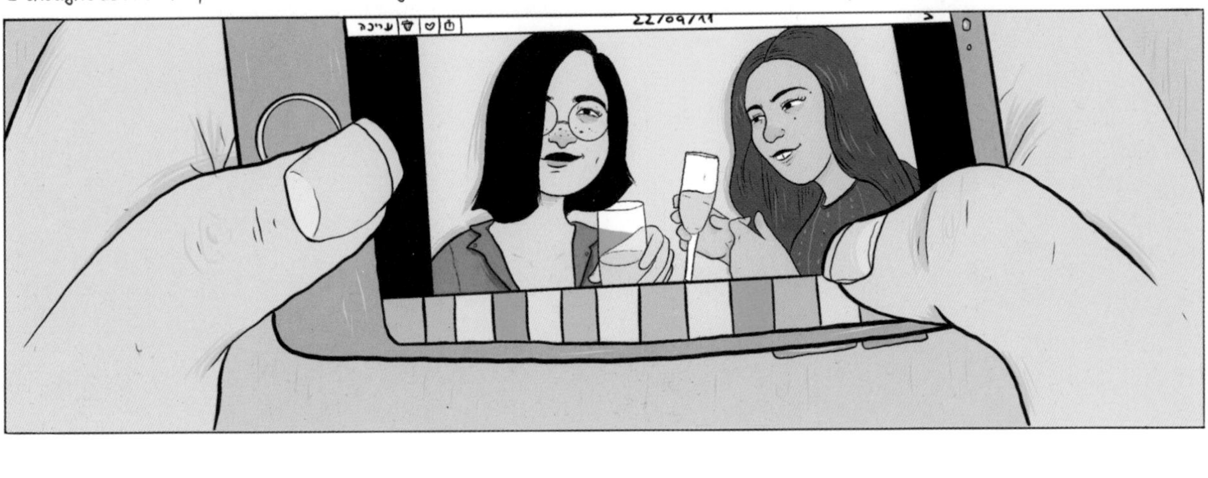
22/09/11

LITTLE LIES

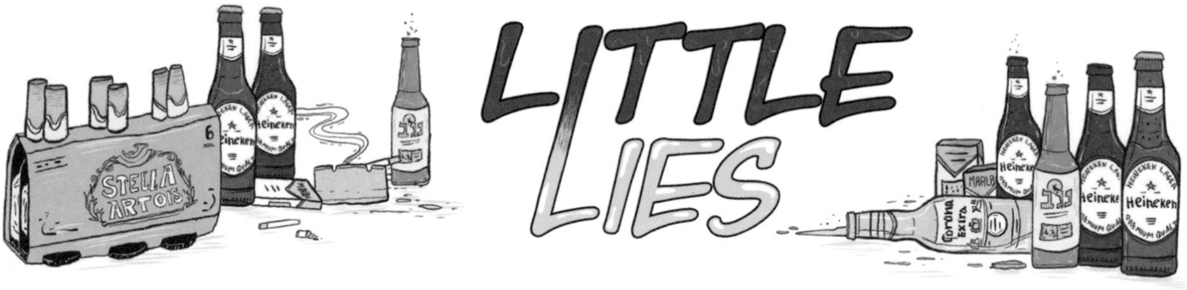

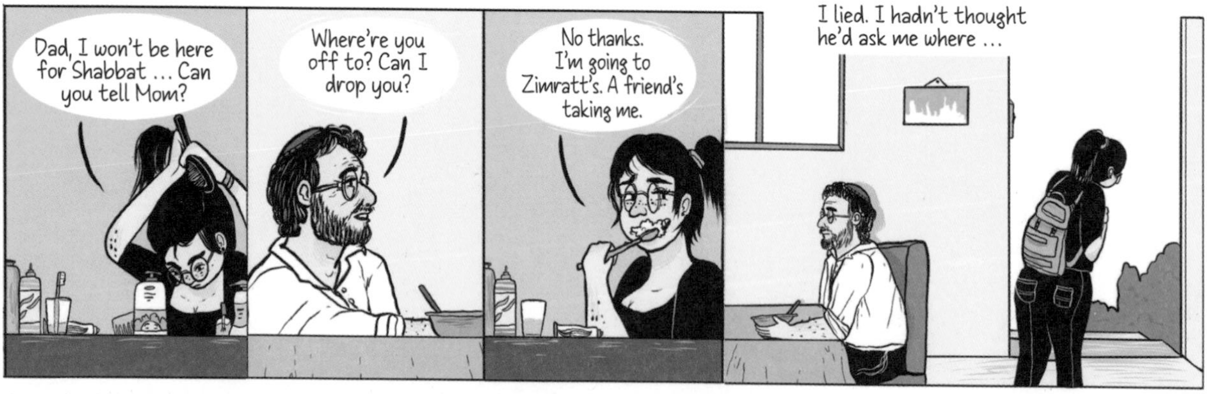

Dad, I won't be here for Shabbat … Can you tell Mom?
Where're you off to? Can I drop you?
No thanks. I'm going to Zimratt's. A friend's taking me.
I lied. I hadn't thought he'd ask me where …

A tiny little lie, that was all. Because it was true that I was going out, but not to Zimratt's …
My parents had always trusted me. I was sure there wouldn't be a problem—that they wouldn't start nitpicking.
And as far as I was concerned, what they didn't know … couldn't hurt them. I took my stuff and headed to the bus station.
During the ride to Tel Aviv, I felt sick. My first Shabbat away from home.

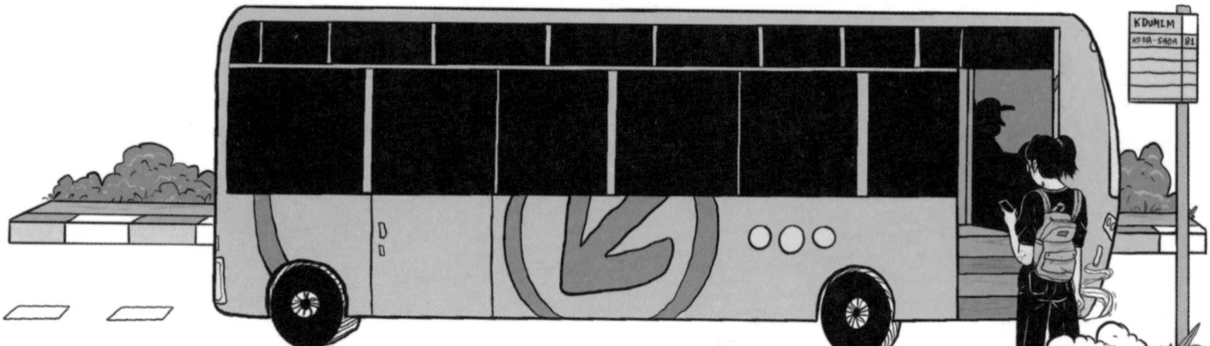

I'd never spent a Shabbat alone, away from the house. A hot wind beat across my face.
I felt like I was melting away in the heat.

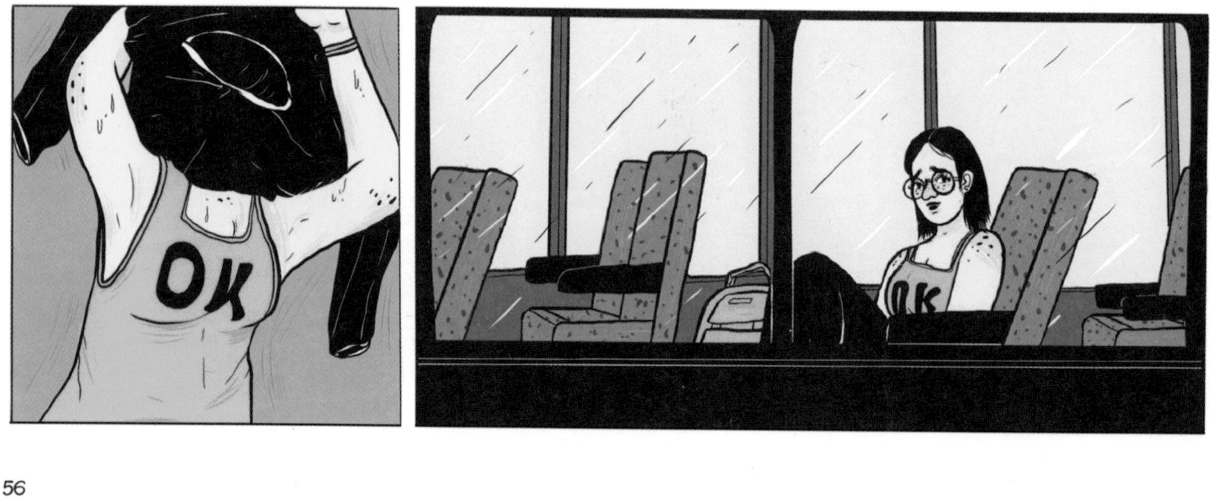

Daniel came to pick me up in his car. I was going to meet all his friends. It was my first summer with non-Orthodox friends. We had planned to go camping. When Daniel suggested I come, I said yes right away. I hadn't thought about how complicated it would be, and how I was going to explain it to my parents. We met up with the group. Some of them had already put their tents up. The butterflies in my stomach refused to fly away.

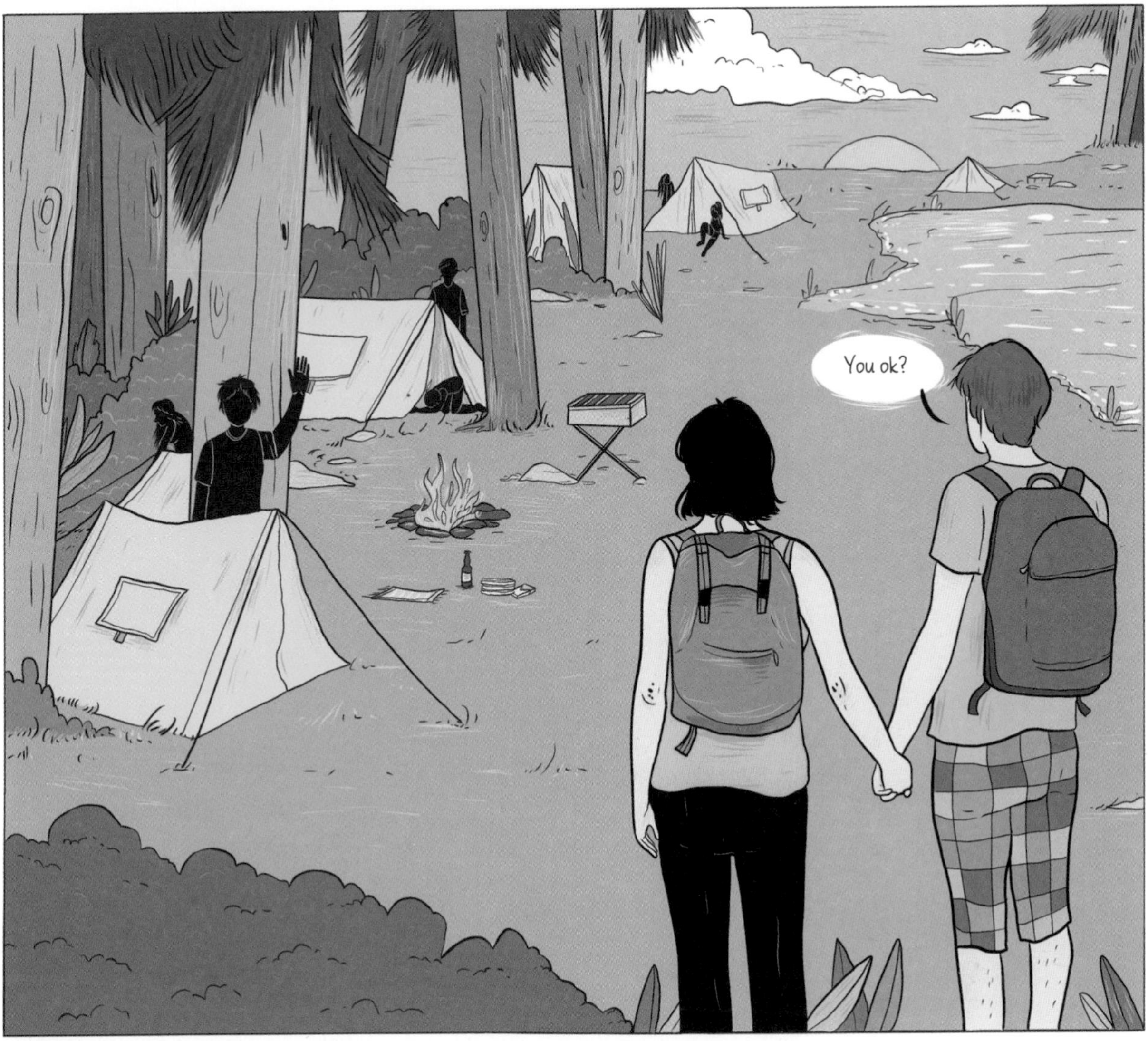
You ok?

We had just opened some beers when … my phone rang. When I saw the name on the screen, I nearly choked. I walked away from the group, took a deep breath … and answered.

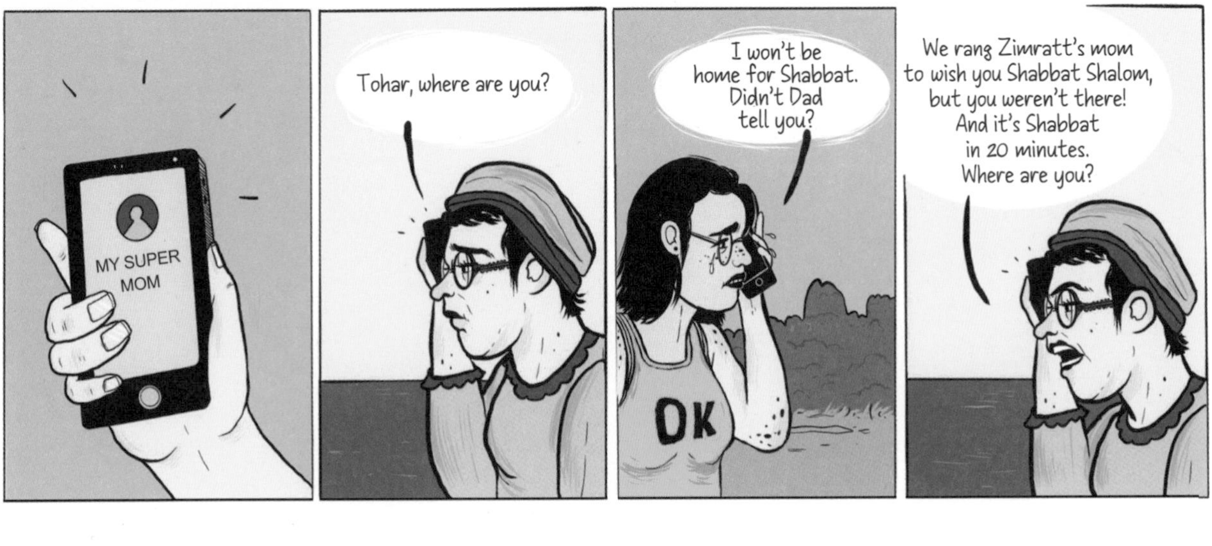
MY SUPER MOM
Tohar, where are you?
I won't be home for Shabbat. Didn't Dad tell you?
OK
We rang Zimratt's mom to wish you Shabbat Shalom, but you weren't there! And it's Shabbat in 20 minutes. Where are you?

My mother hardly ever gets angry, but when she starts making these barely audible noises, that means it's serious.
And that's how it was for me right then.

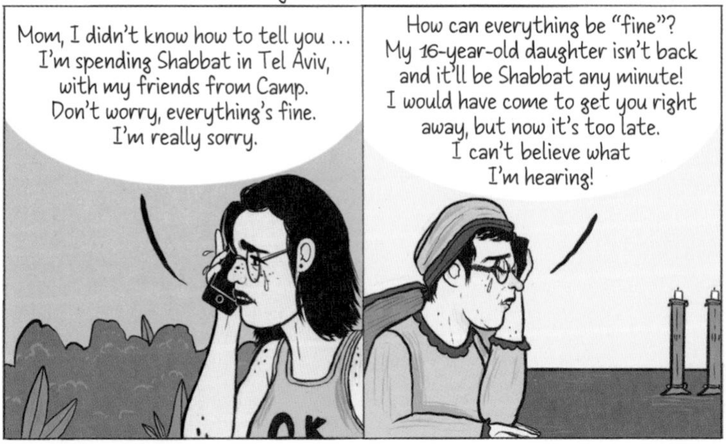
Mom, I didn't know how to tell you … I'm spending Shabbat in Tel Aviv, with my friends from Camp. Don't worry, everything's fine. I'm really sorry.
How can everything be "fine"? My 16-year-old daughter isn't back and it'll be Shabbat any minute! I would have come to get you right away, but now it's too late. I can't believe what I'm hearing!
OK

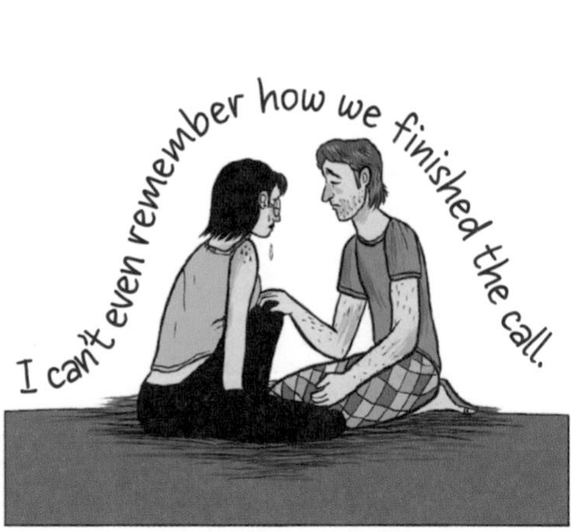
I can't even remember how we finished the call.

I spent the rest of the evening moping around.
Everyone seemed to be having fun, laughing, and I felt bad, like a con artist in an American movie, the one everyone hates.
Daniel came to sit with me. He tried to make me laugh, and it worked. I accepted one smoke from a friend, then another.

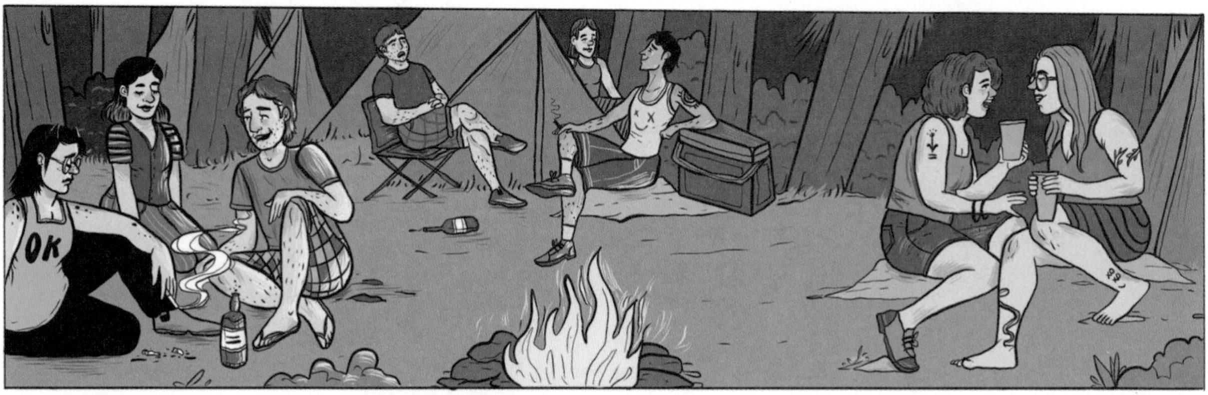
OK

When I'd de-stressed a bit, I told myself that it was ok, that I had the right to make mistakes, try stuff out …
Yes, I had the right. We drank, played cards, played guitar …

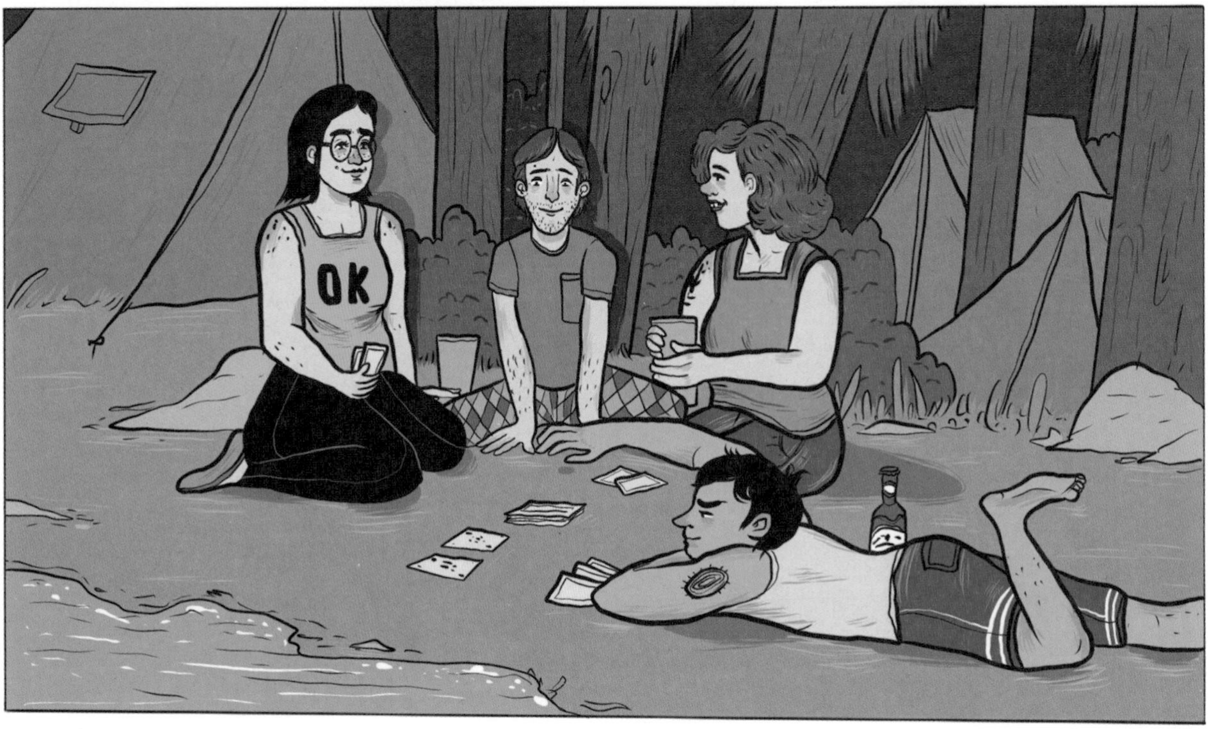
OK

I gazed at the stars all night, and I said to Daniel: "If that hadn't gone so wrong, this would have been the most beautiful weekend of my whole life."

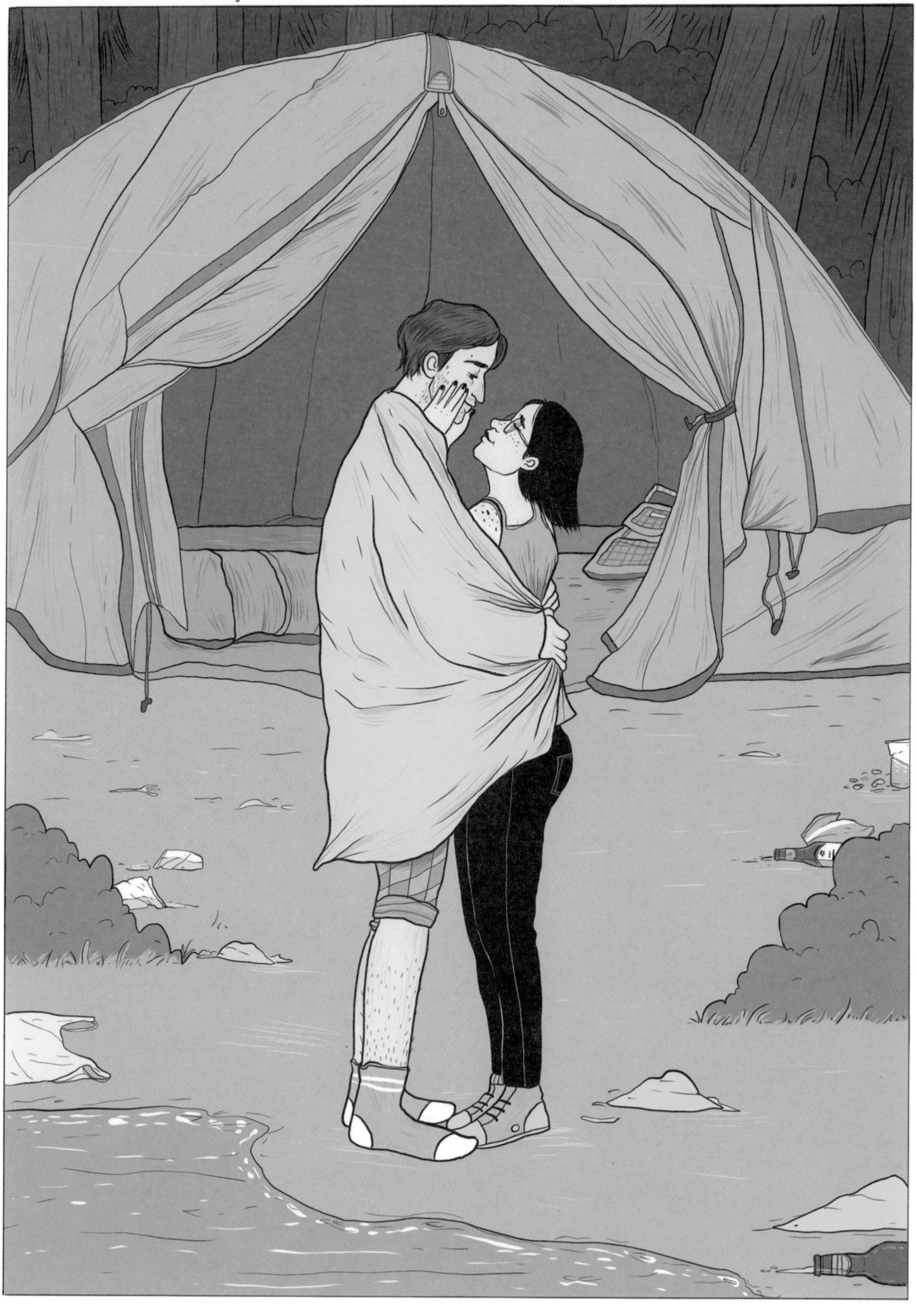

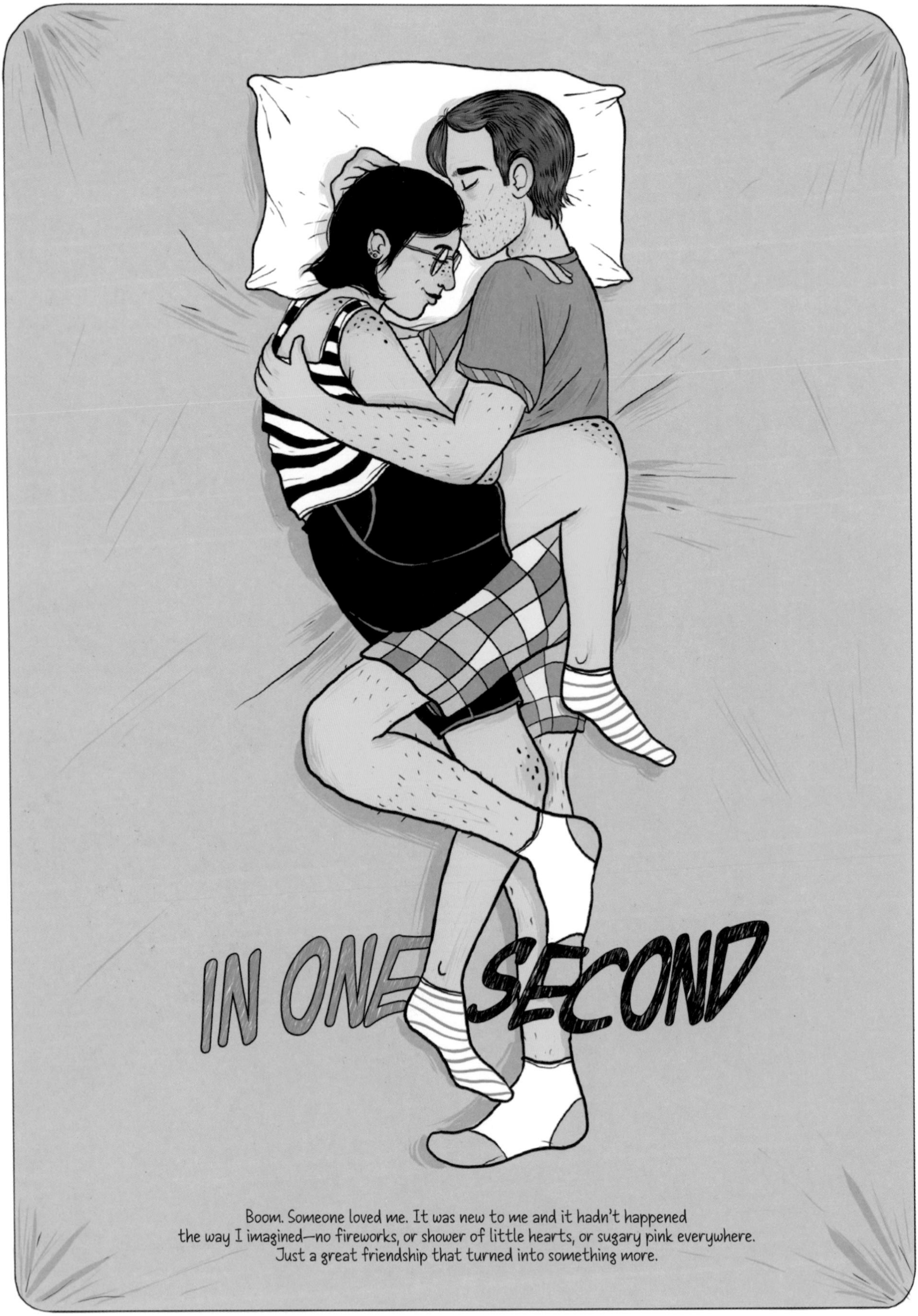
IN ONE SECOND
Boom. Someone loved me. It was new to me and it hadn't happened
the way I imagined—no fireworks, or shower of little hearts, or sugary pink everywhere.
Just a great friendship that turned into something more.

When did I know I was in love with him? One day, we were together at the hospital in Tel Aviv, in the Internal Medicine department, sharing the same hospital chair. The beeping of the drip connected to Daniel's vein was making me lose the thread of our conversation, and we fell into a long silence.

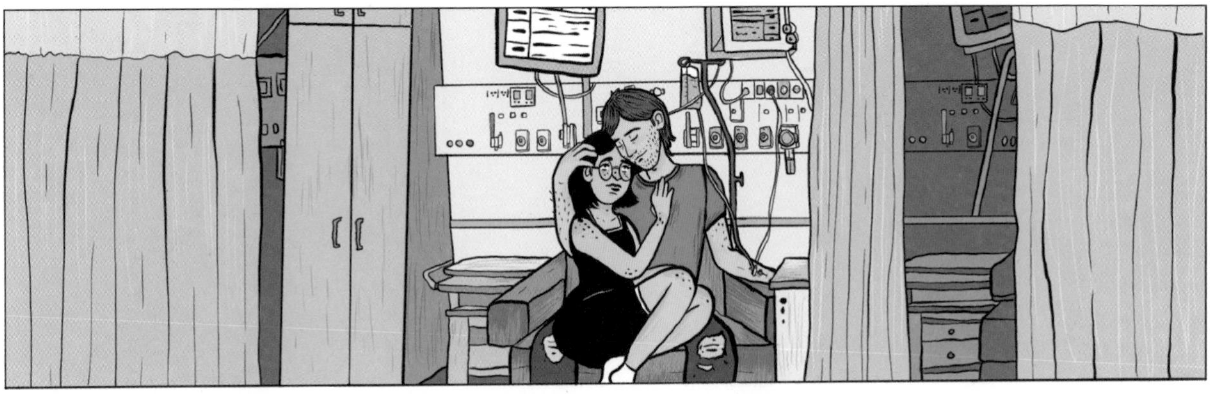

"I'm a bit hungry ... " I said to him. He murmured something, and I realized he'd fallen asleep. Suddenly, it happened. It hadn't been so obvious before. We'd experienced so many things together! We had known each other for two years, we had been going out for eight months, and it was only now that I understood.

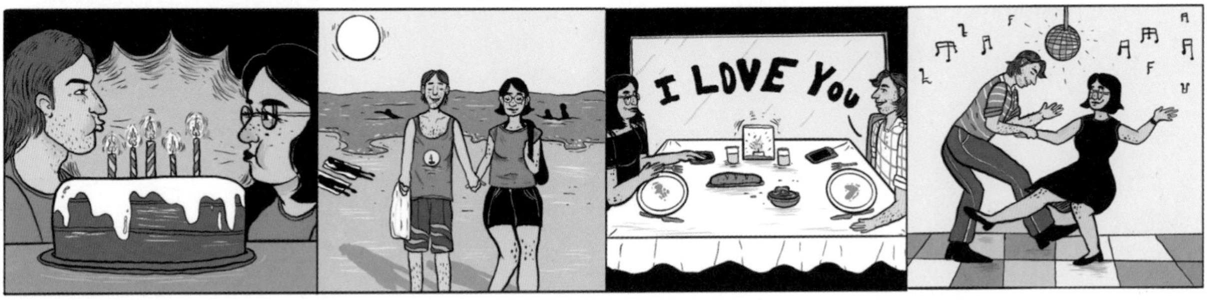
I LOVE You

I got up carefully so as not to wake him and left the room. Suddenly I felt a kind of emptiness inside. I didn't have the right words anymore to describe that feeling of love. A new feeling.

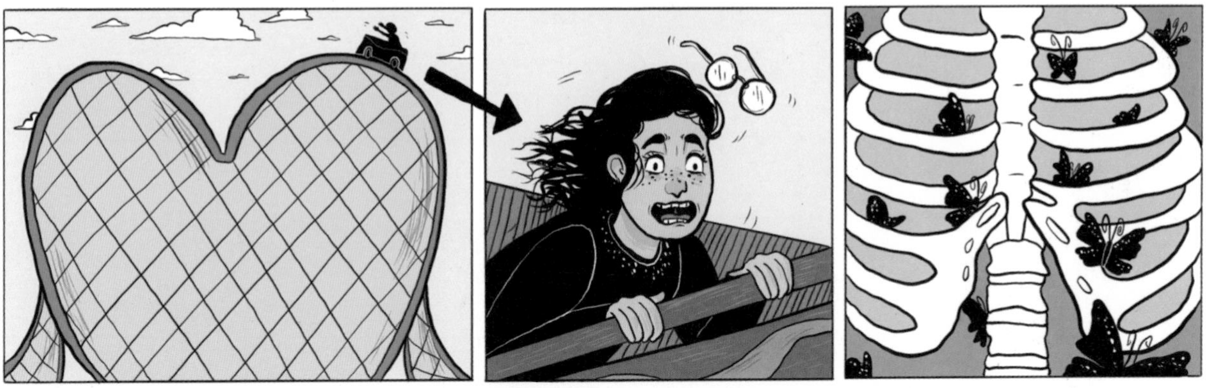

I tiptoed back to sit down by him and wait for him to wake up. I had forgotten what it was to really want something. I still had trouble opening my heart. But I thought I would get there if I kept at it.

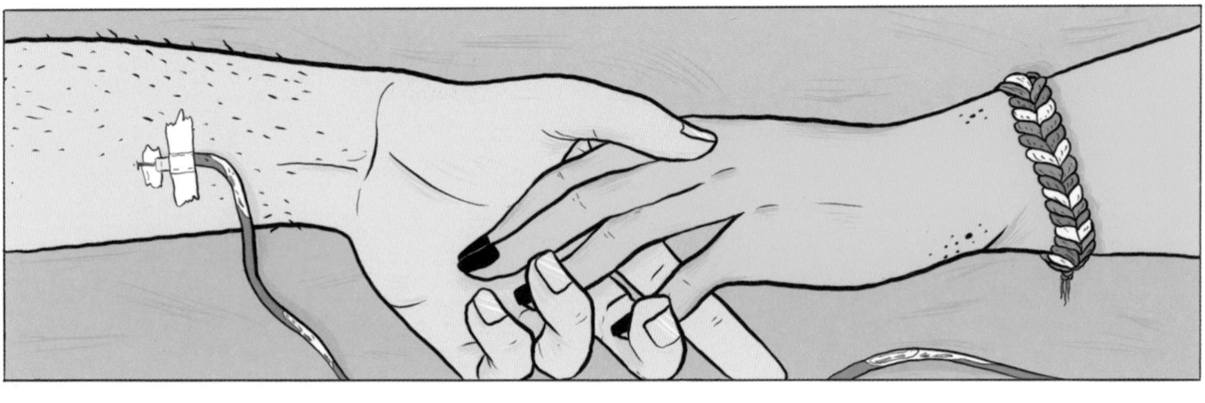

WE FREAK OUT!

Is there a problem?

Are you kidding me?
Go home!

The bouncer was looking at me contemptuously. I tried the nice approach.

Don't you think my photo looks pretty then?

I was trying to lighten the mood, but instead of replying he just cut my card up with a pair of scissors! I was furious!

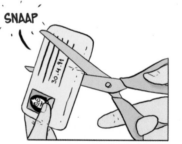

SNAAP

I wanted to respond, but Daniel pulled me away.

Better not!

I felt guilty. He turned 18 today, and because his girlfriend was underage, he couldn't party! I felt the disappointed looks of his friends like daggers in my back.

But it's your birthday, Babe!

The most important thing is that we're together.

Everyone was looking forward to a crazy night, the kind you'd forget the next day.

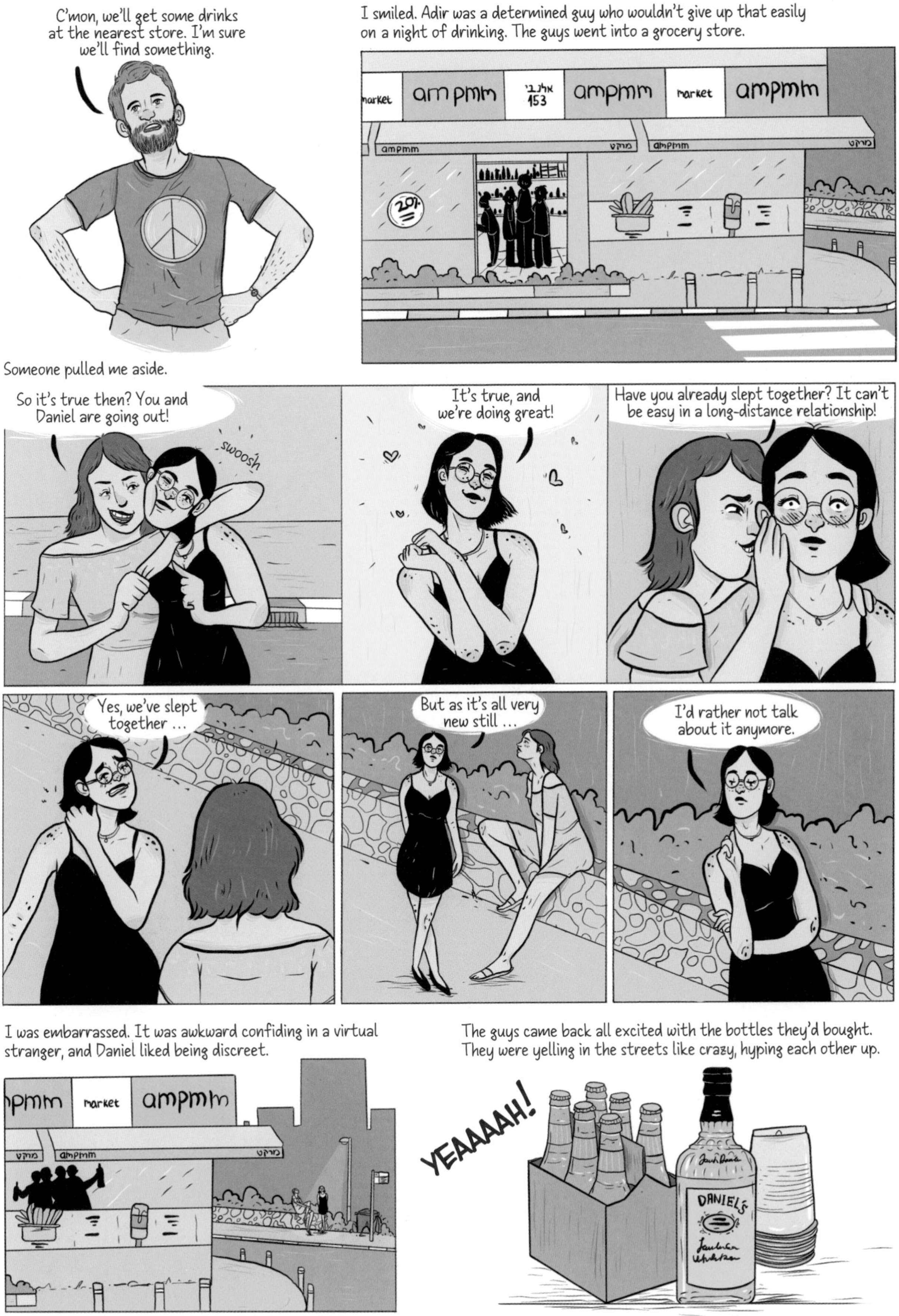

C'mon, we'll get some drinks at the nearest store. I'm sure we'll find something.
I smiled. Adir was a determined guy who wouldn't give up that easily on a night of drinking. The guys went into a grocery store.
market
ampmm
אלנבי 153
ampmm
market
ampmm
Someone pulled me aside.
So it's true then? You and Daniel are going out!
swoosh
It's true, and we're doing great!
Have you already slept together? It can't be easy in a long-distance relationship!
Yes, we've slept together …
But as it's all very new still …
I'd rather not talk about it anymore.
I was embarrassed. It was awkward confiding in a virtual stranger, and Daniel liked being discreet.
The guys came back all excited with the bottles they'd bought. They were yelling in the streets like crazy, hyping each other up.
YEAAAAH!
DANIEL'S

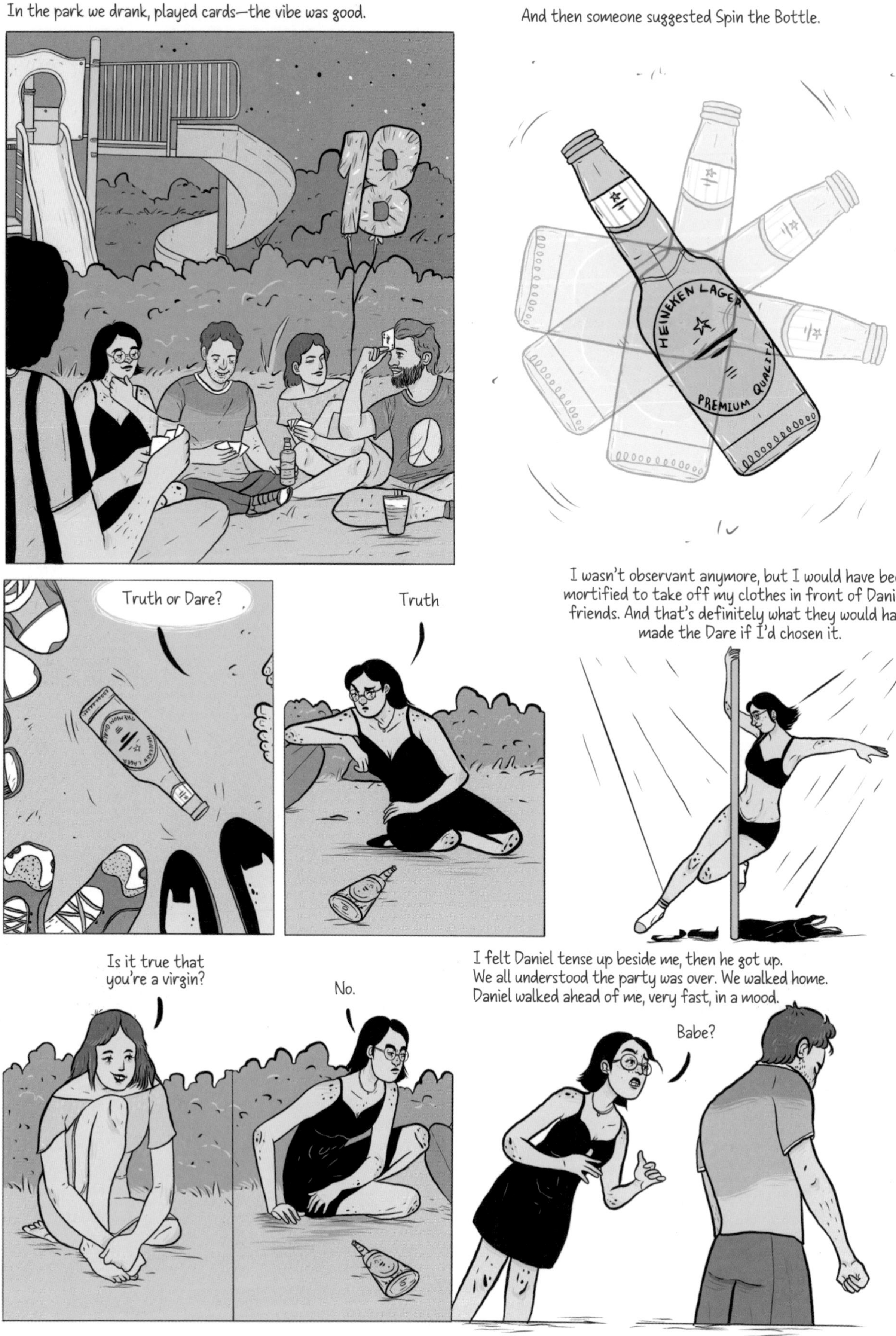

In the park we drank, played cards—the vibe was good.
18
And then someone suggested Spin the Bottle.
HEINEKEN LAGER
PREMIUM QUALITY
Truth or Dare?
Truth
I wasn't observant anymore, but I would have been mortified to take off my clothes in front of Daniel's friends. And that's definitely what they would have made the Dare if I'd chosen it.
Is it true that you're a virgin?
No.
I felt Daniel tense up beside me, then he got up.
We all understood the party was over. We walked home.
Daniel walked ahead of me, very fast, in a mood.
Babe?

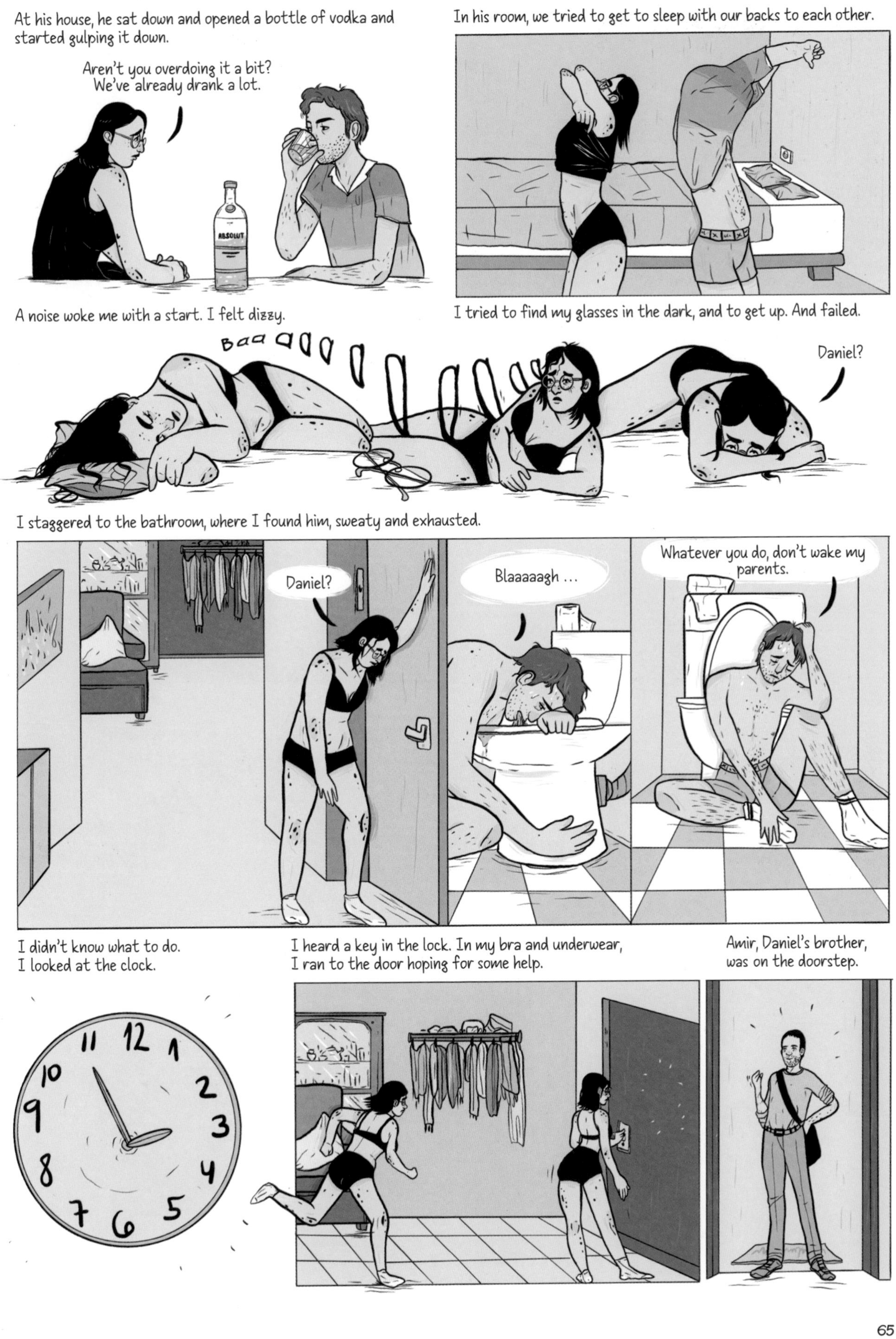
At his house, he sat down and opened a bottle of vodka and started gulping it down.
Aren't you overdoing it a bit? We've already drank a lot.
ABSOLUT
In his room, we tried to get to sleep with our backs to each other.
A noise woke me with a start. I felt dizzy.
I tried to find my glasses in the dark, and to get up. And failed.
Baaaaaaaaaaa
Daniel?
I staggered to the bathroom, where I found him, sweaty and exhausted.
Daniel?
Blaaaaagh …
Whatever you do, don't wake my parents.
I didn't know what to do. I looked at the clock.
I heard a key in the lock. In my bra and underwear, I ran to the door hoping for some help.
Amir, Daniel's brother, was on the doorstep.

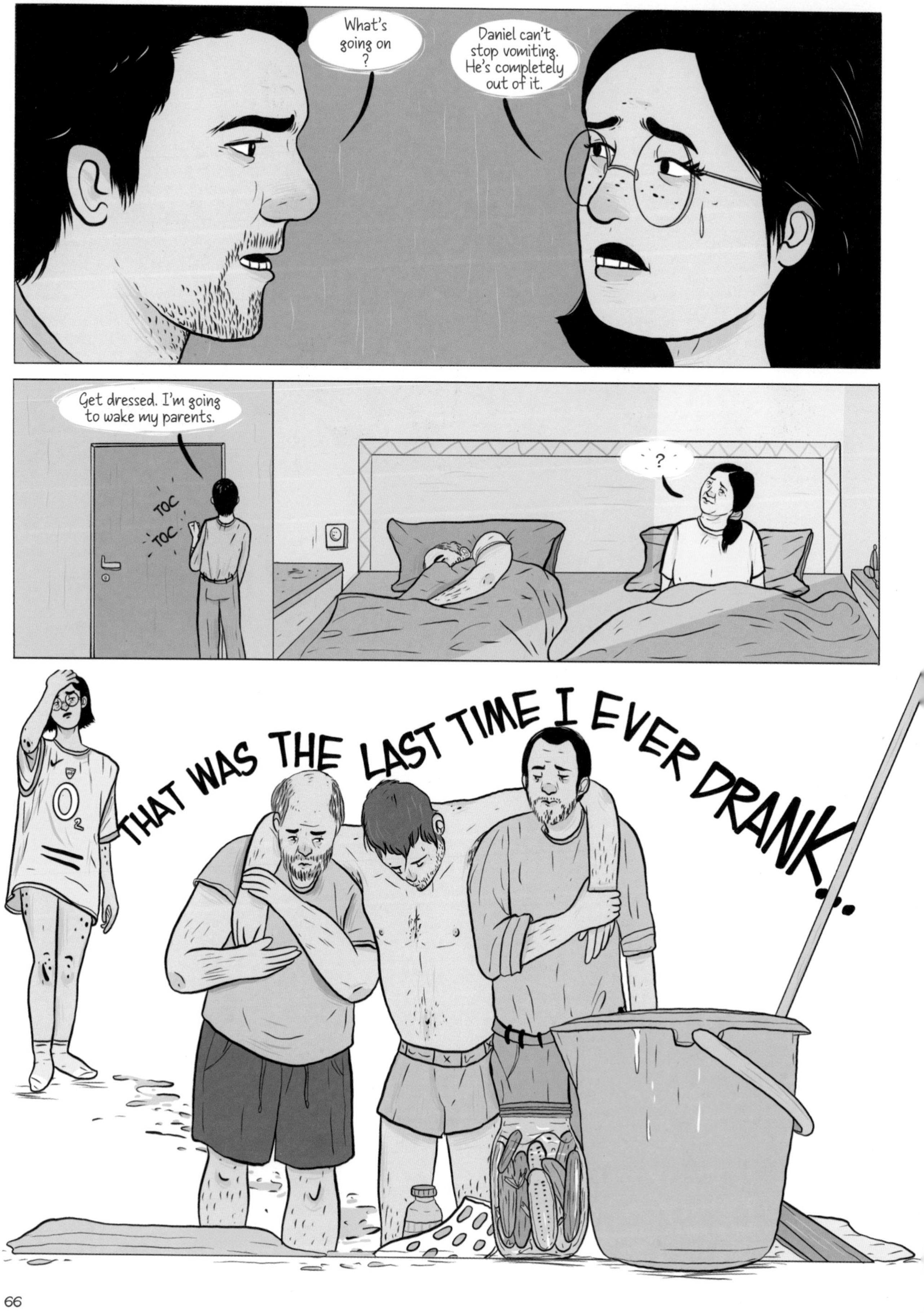
What's going on ?
Daniel can't stop vomiting. He's completely out of it.
Get dressed. I'm going to wake my parents.
TOC TOC
?
THAT WAS THE LAST TIME I EVER DRANK...

We got back into bed, exhausted, barely awake. "You shouldn't have told them," he said.
"I know, but you shouldn't have freaked out," I replied, wondering how long it would take us to heal this rift.

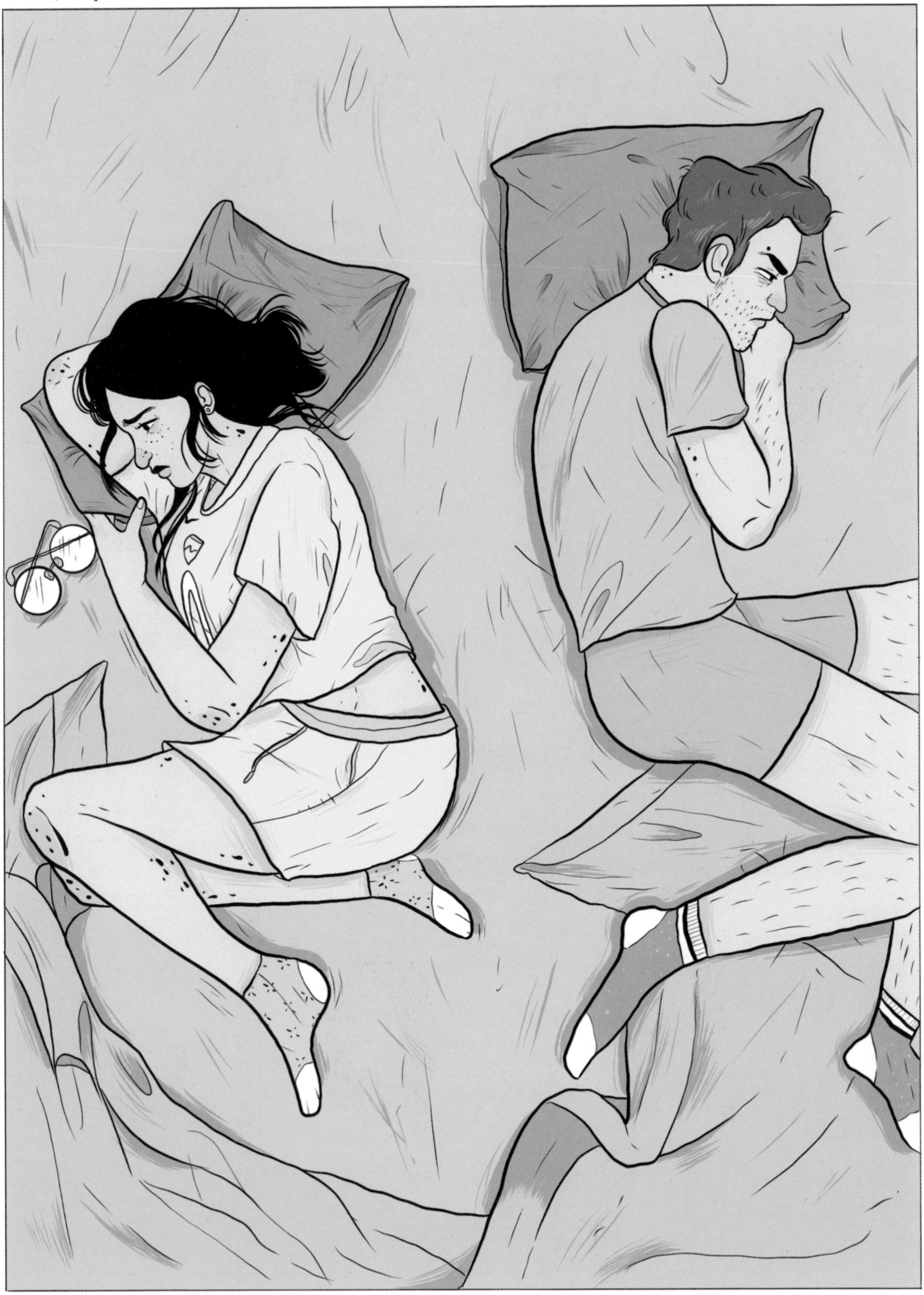

BEHIND THE SCENES

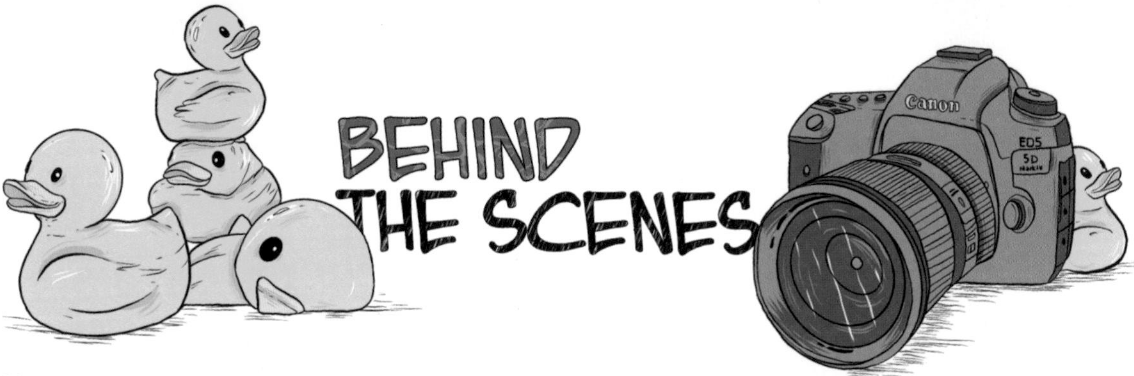

Canon
EOS
5D

Seeing Tiferett and Nimrod together always made me uneasy, the way he gripped her when he talked to her.

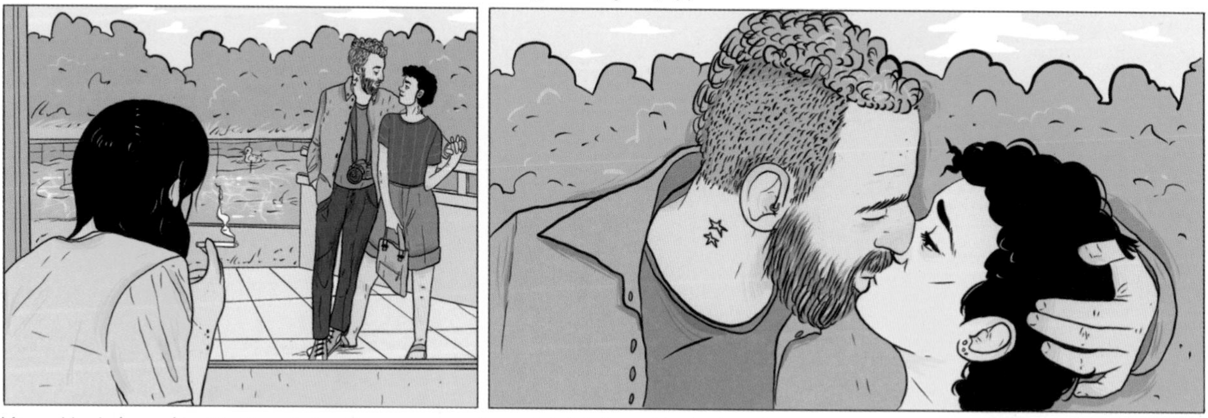

Nimrod had always liked taking photos, from every angle, and it didn't matter to him if it suited anyone else or not—he never asked. Anyway, no one would ever have dared refuse.

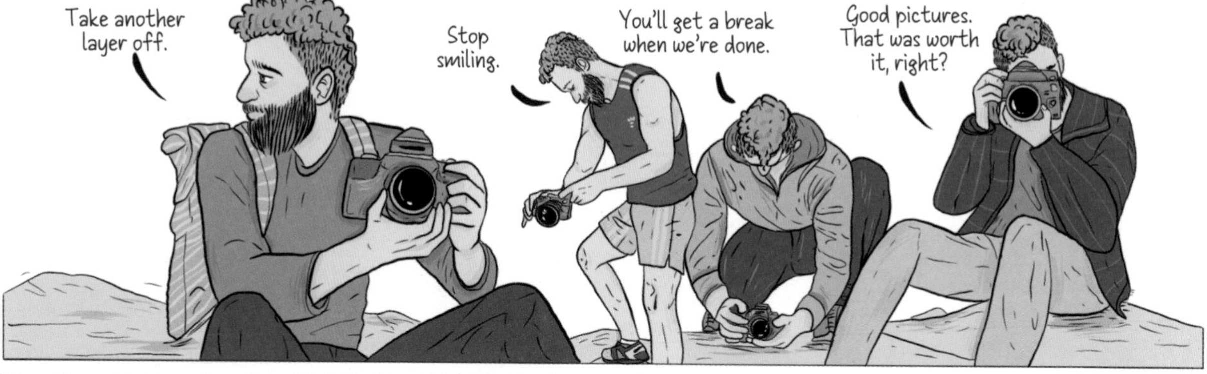

Take another layer off.
Stop smiling.
You'll get a break when we're done.
Good pictures. That was worth it, right?

When Nimrod told me I was beautiful, I believed him. Whether he wanted to photograph me for an exhibition or just for fun, I said yes without hesitation. In front of the camera, I felt like a model. I forgot all the flaws I was so familiar with.

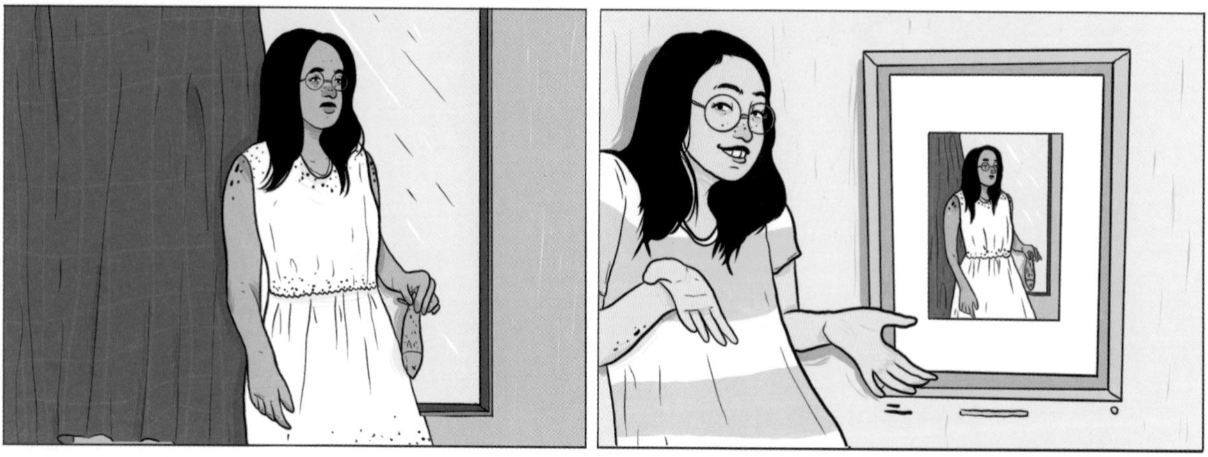

When he photographed me, his expression had that same disturbing intimacy I saw between him and my sister.

One day Nimrod wanted to photograph us both, me and Daniel, in swimwear. I didn't think it through, and I said yes. While I tried to put on the swimsuit he'd brought me, I heard my sister through the door.

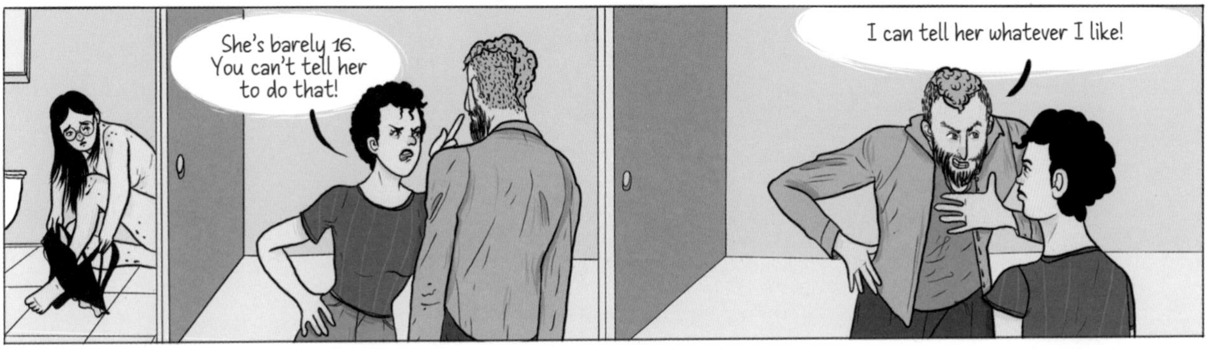
She's barely 16. You can't tell her to do that!
I can tell her whatever I like!

I came downstairs in my suit, embarrassed to be baring my skin like that.

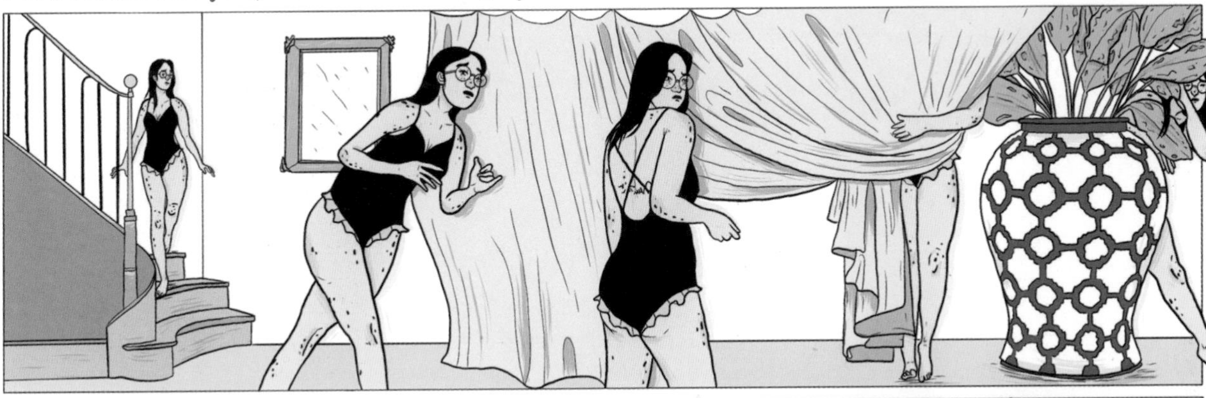

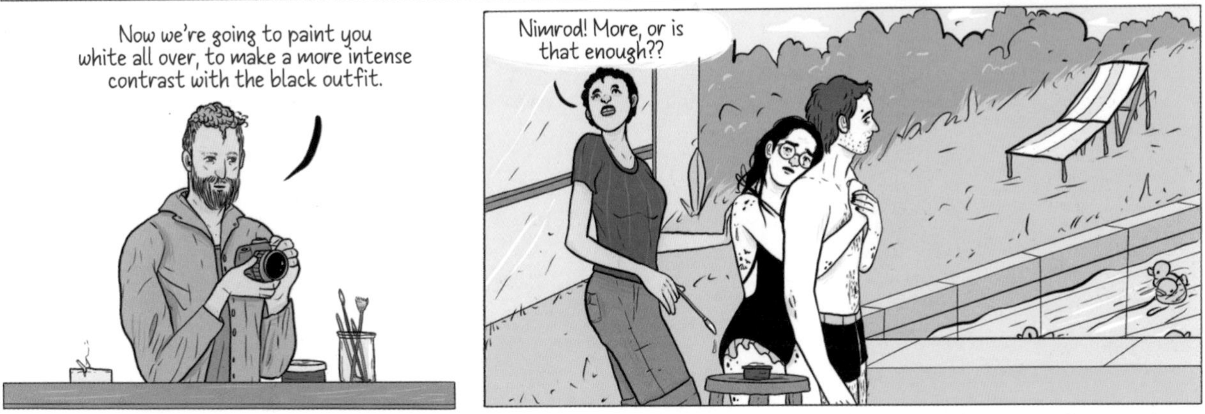
Now we're going to paint you white all over, to make a more intense contrast with the black outfit.
Nimrod! More, or is that enough??

My body painted white, I looked at the pool: plastic ducks were strewn round it like a memory of my childhood that was fast receding.

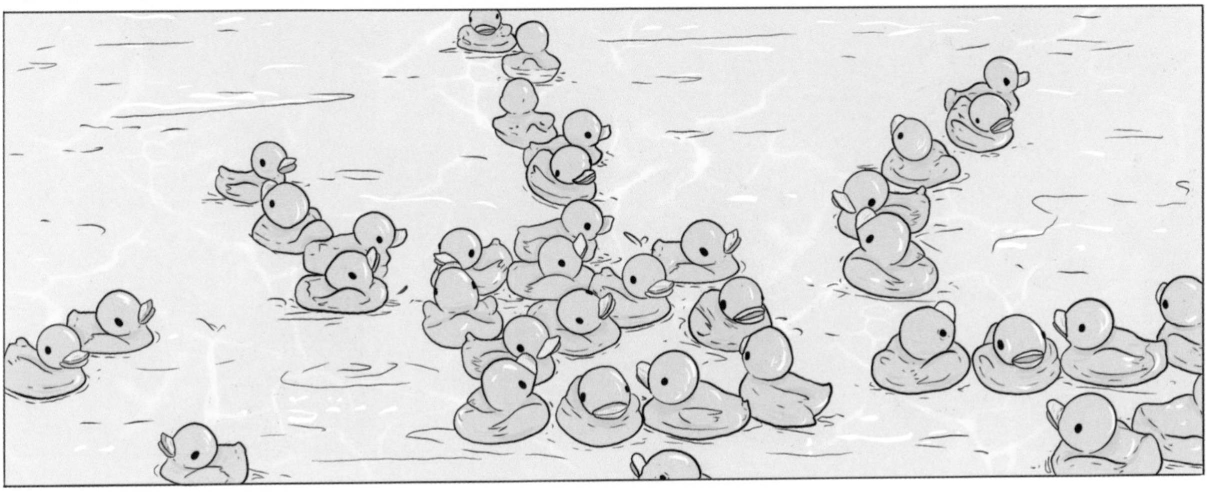

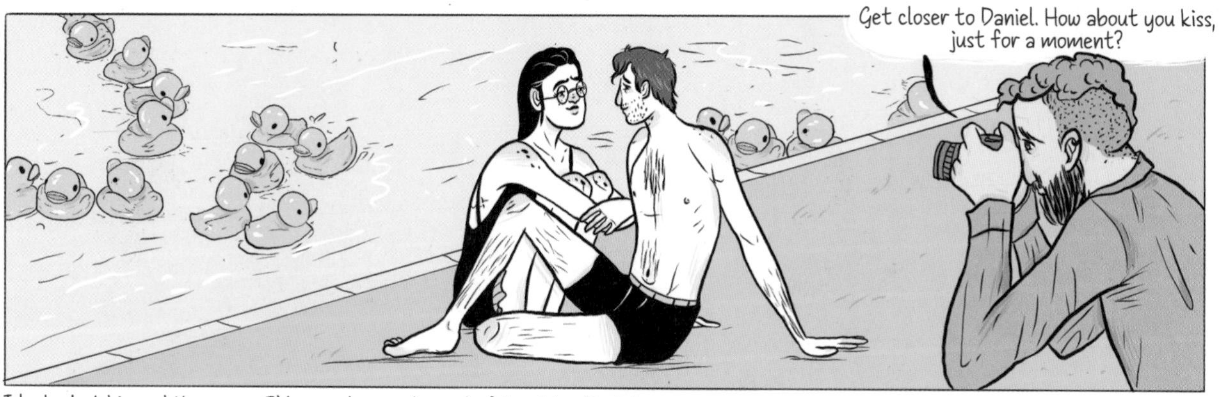
Get closer to Daniel. How about you kiss, just for a moment?

I looked at him, a bit uneasy. I'd never been ashamed of touching Daniel, but something in the atmosphere was too intense. But I did it.

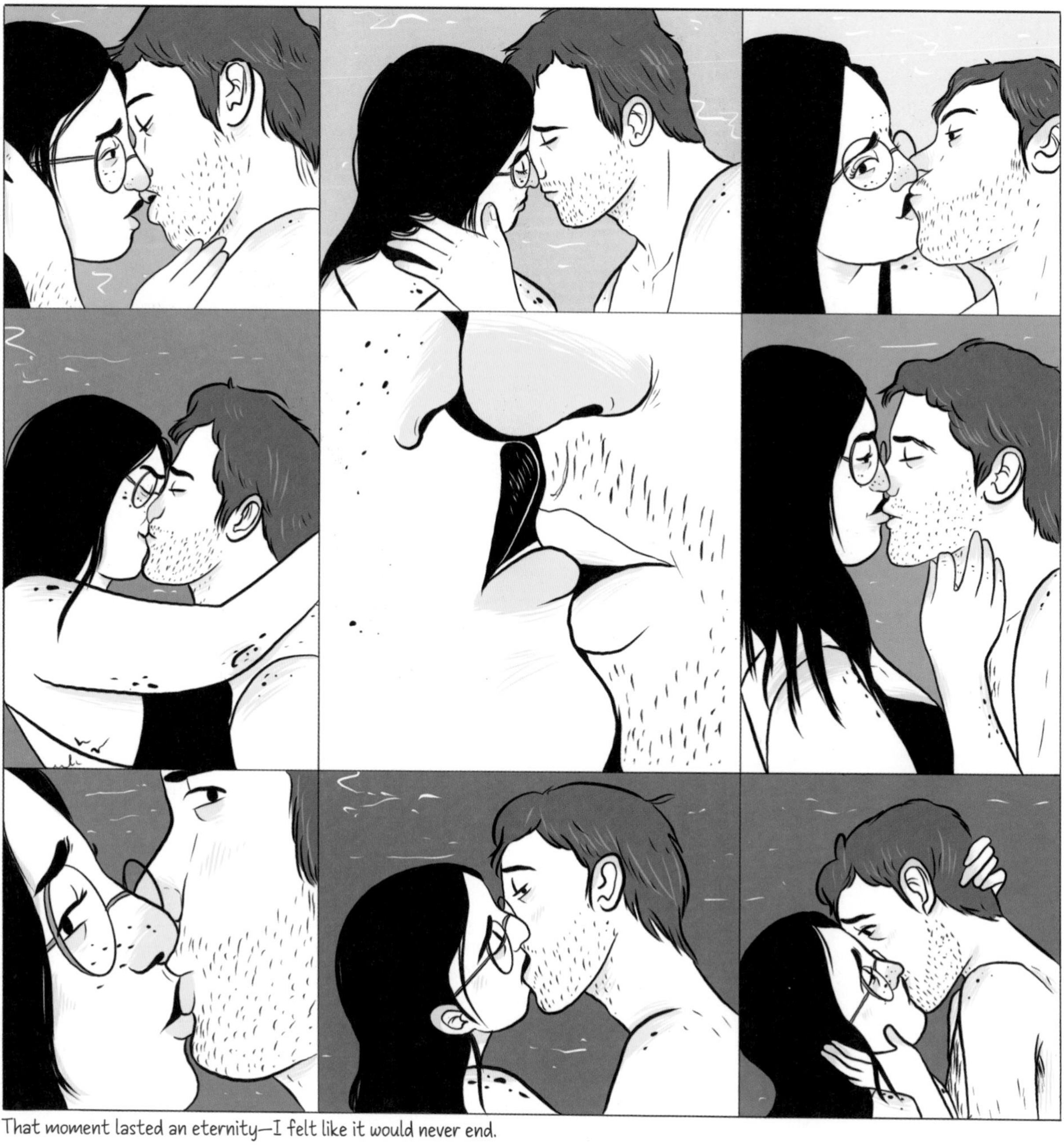

That moment lasted an eternity—I felt like it would never end.

While we were getting dressed and washing off the layers of white paint, I looked over to Nimrod at the other end of the garden, and behind him, I saw my sister's look, a look that was both sad and pitiful.

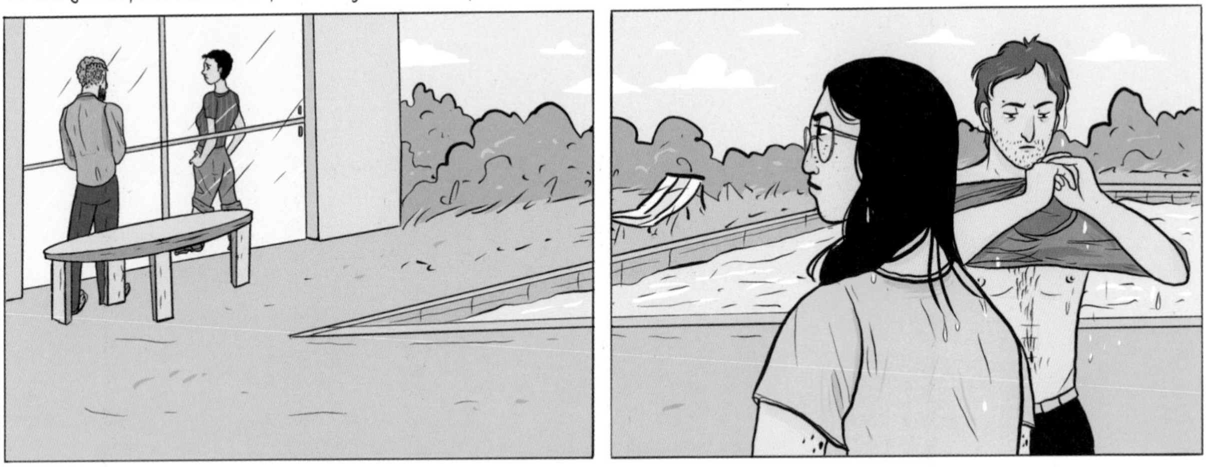

I don't know how many times he'd humiliated her. But that day she began to be wrapped in her unhappiness, a color that darkened day by day. If only I'd known …

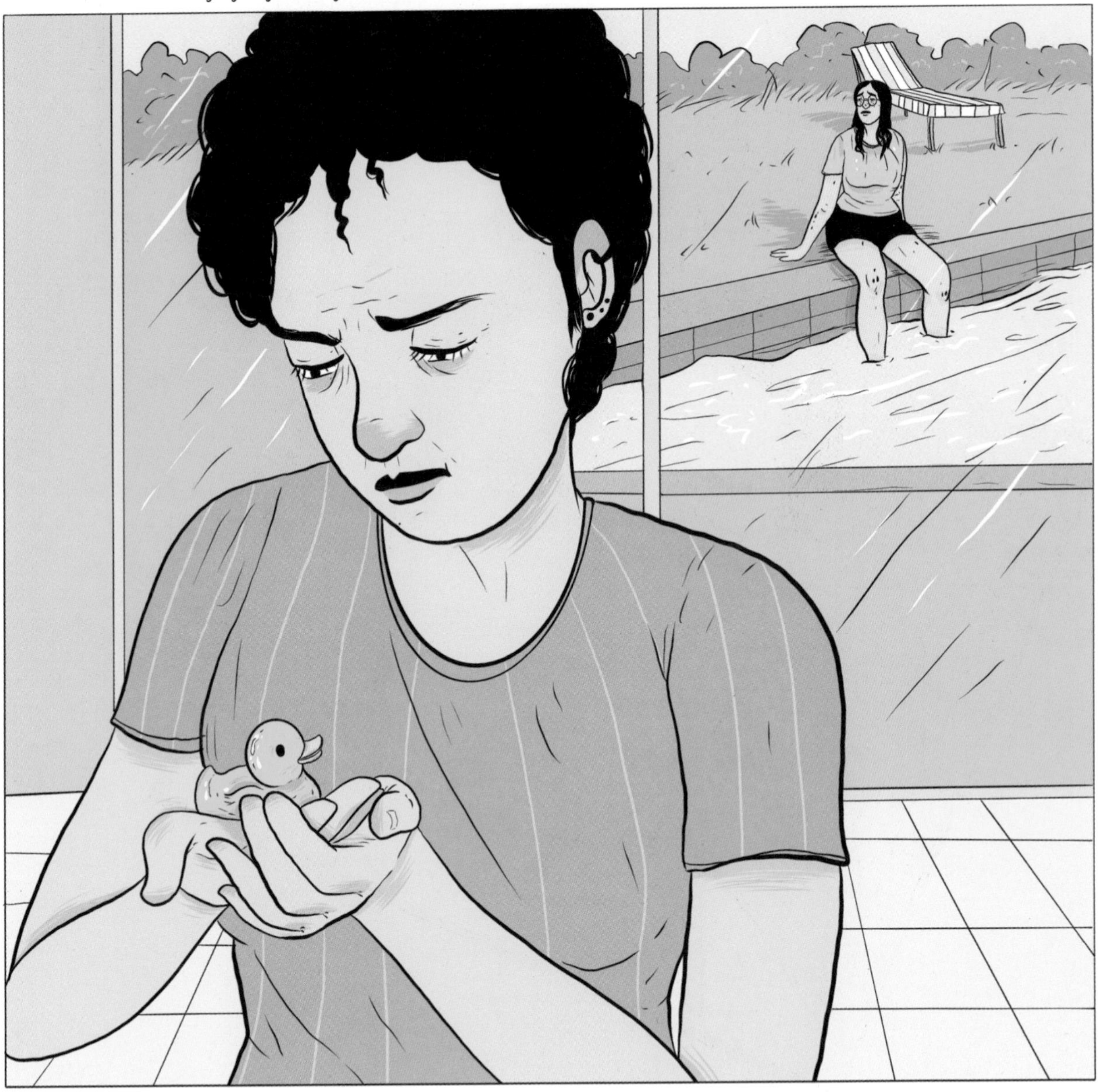

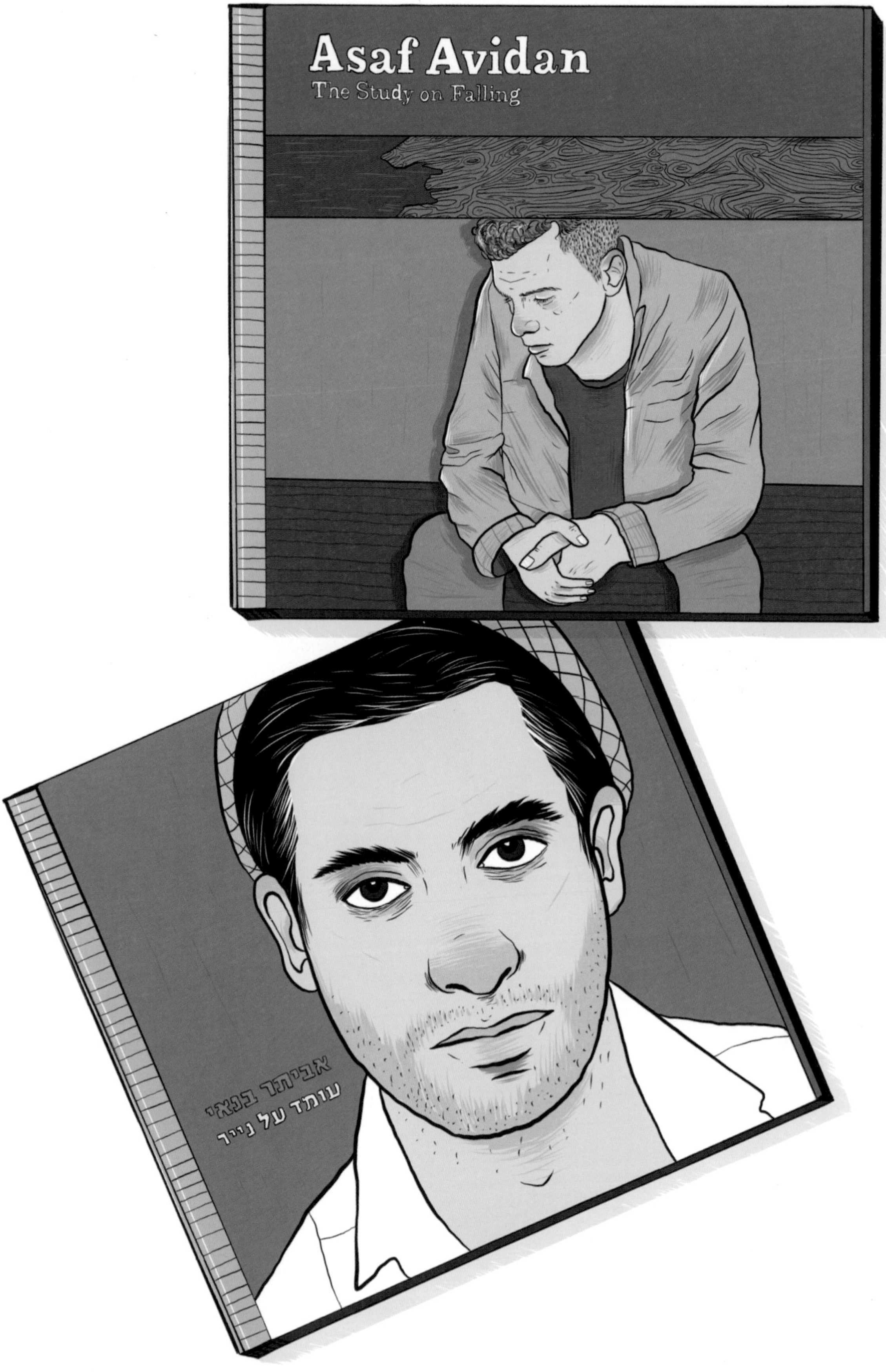
Asaf Avidan
The Study on Falling
אביתר בנאי
עומד על נייר

PART THREE

Learning to Fall

TWO RED LINES

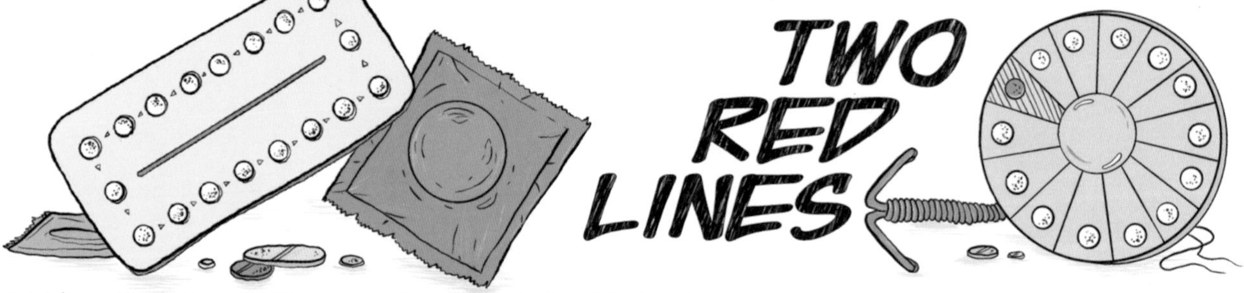

I didn't need to do the test—I knew deep inside me already. Something had changed.
For a few days my chest had been aching, I didn't feel like myself.

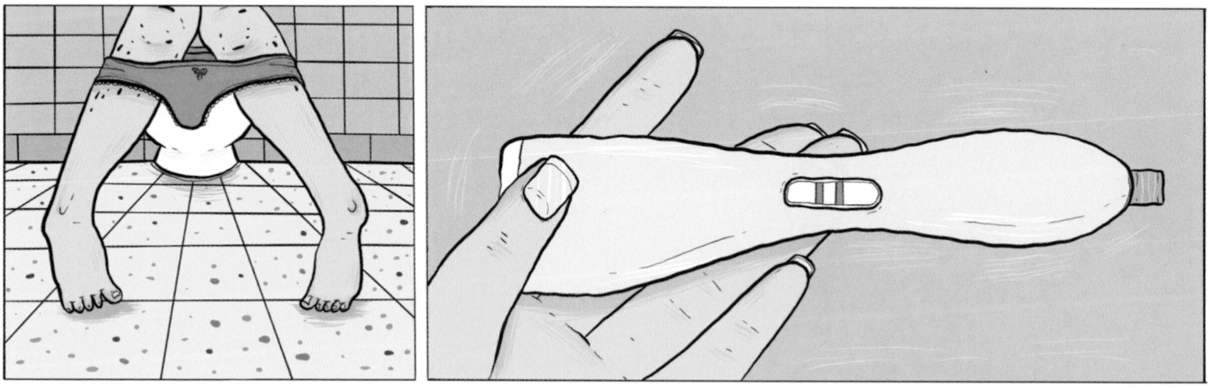

When I came out, it was obvious. Daniel just couldn't stand still. You could see the thoughts going round and round in his head.

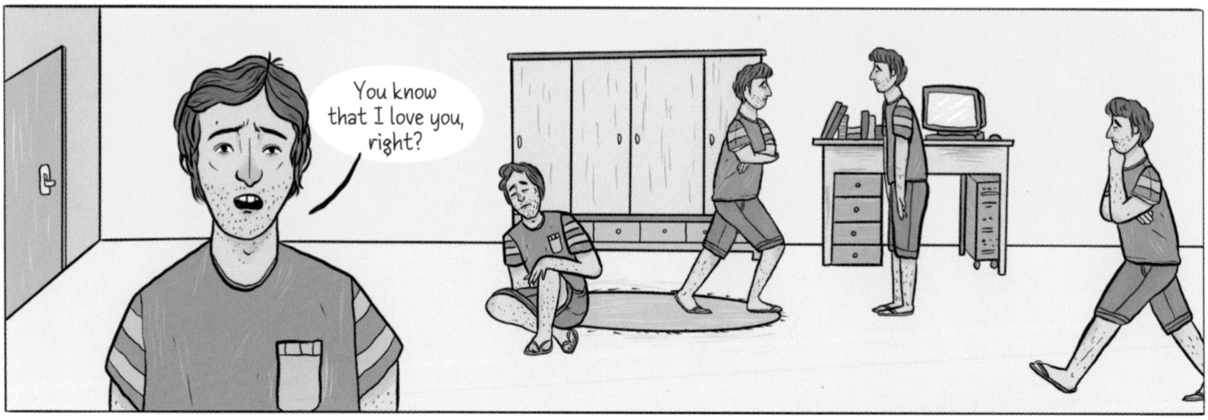

You know that I love you, right?

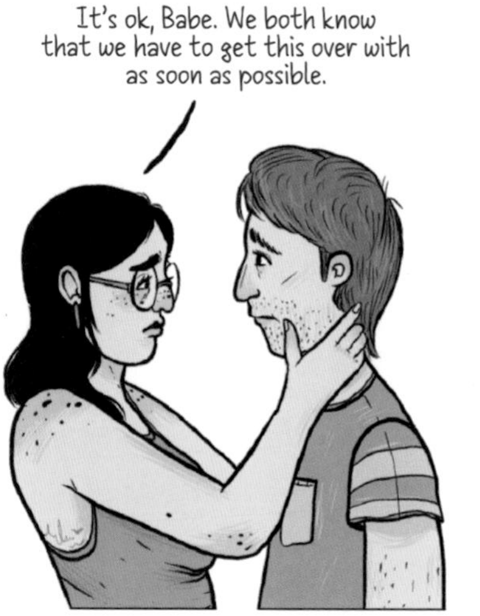

It's ok, Babe. We both know that we have to get this over with as soon as possible.

I heard a shattering noise. Tiferett had thrown down one of my porcelain dolls.

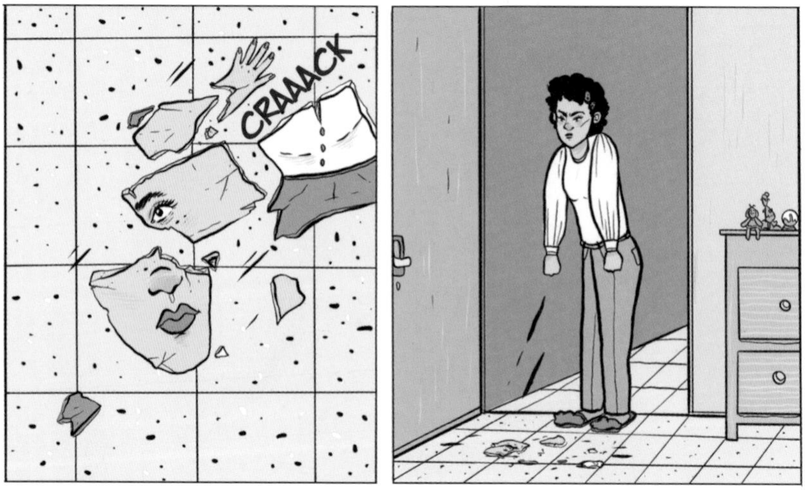

CRAAACK

The head of the doll was almost undamaged, while its whole body had shattered into a thousand pieces—how ironic.

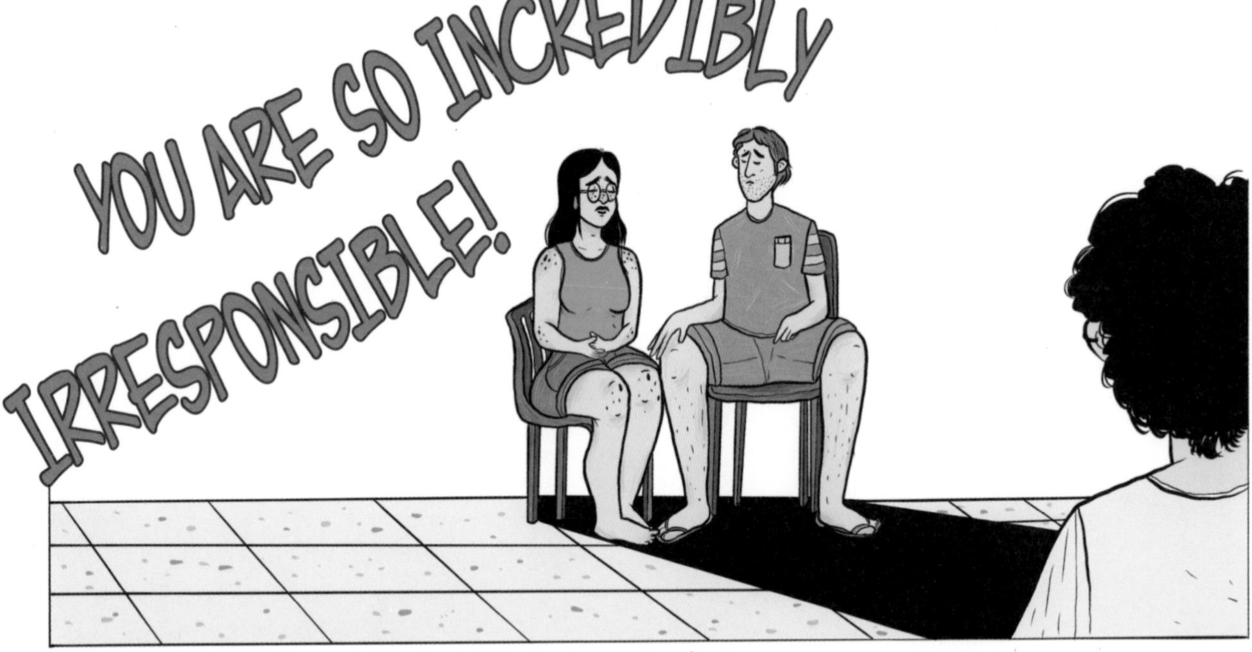
YOU ARE SO INCREDIBLY IRRESPONSIBLE!

I felt her vocal cords tensing up, and she shouted for about a quarter of an hour, before moving on to pity, tears, and "It will be ok"

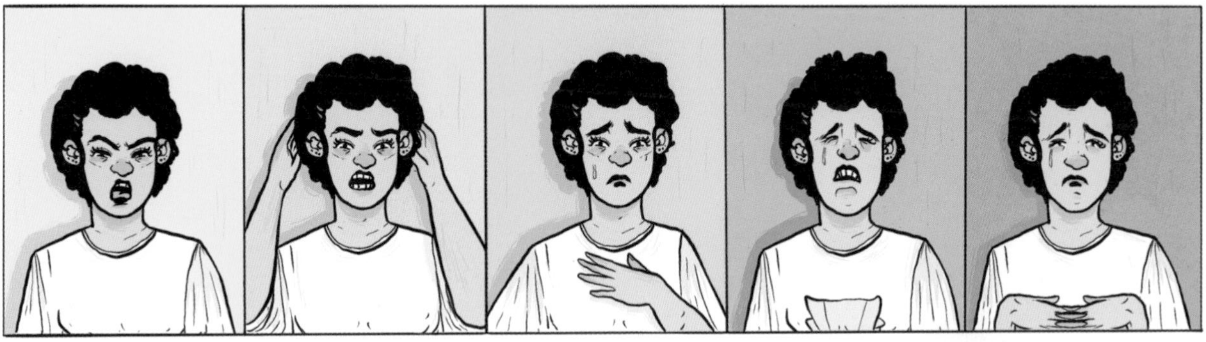

I'd never seen Daniel so silent.
Well, there's a first time for everything. At any rate, I decided to never confide in my sister again.

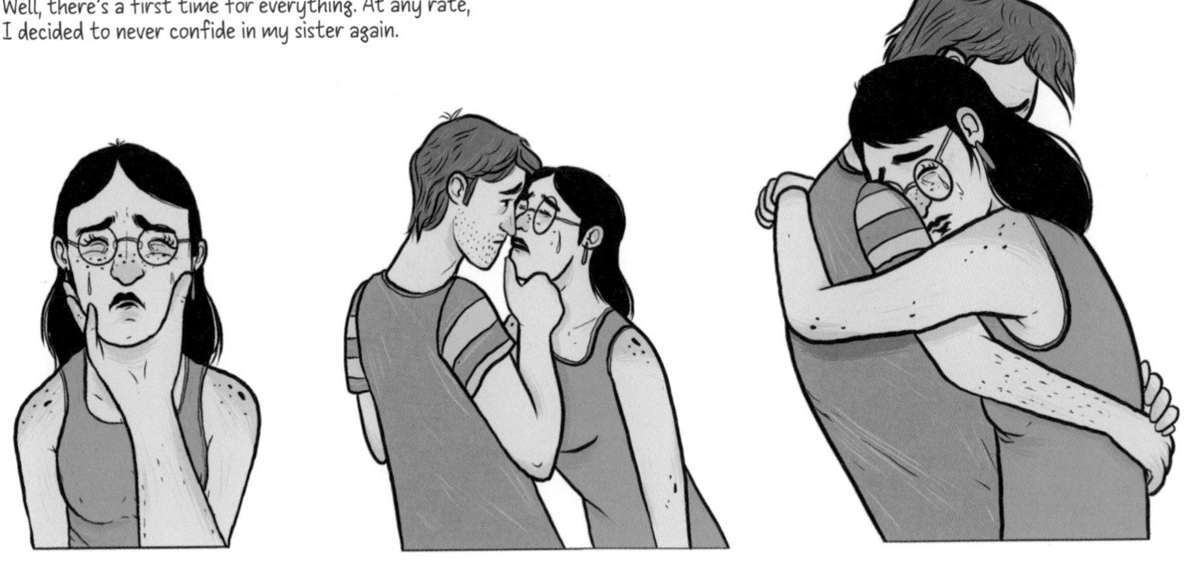

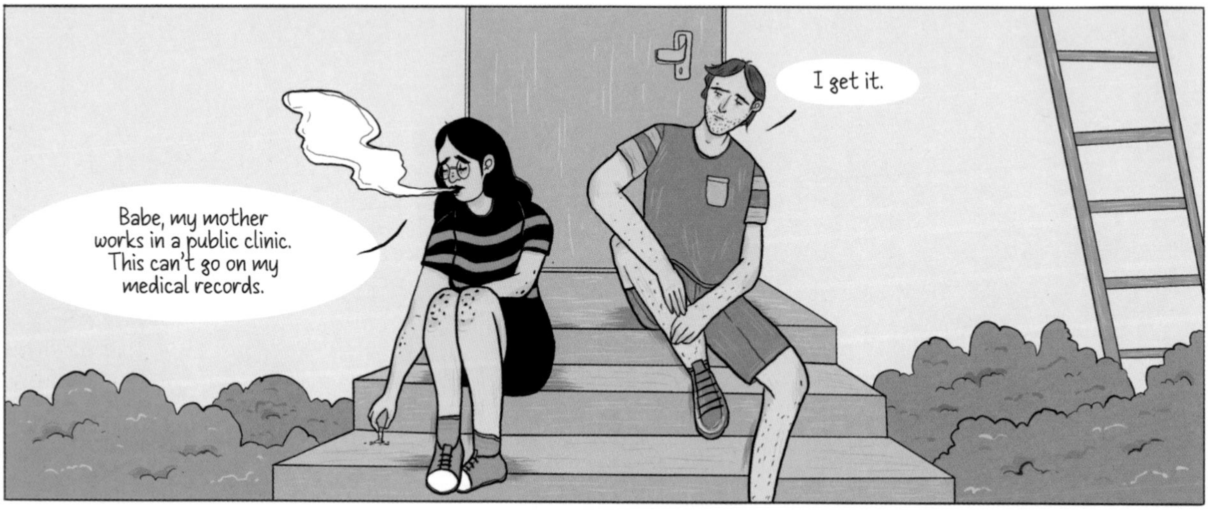
I get it.
Babe, my mother works in a public clinic. This can't go on my medical records.

One of my skills is planning everything, finding solutions … And yet this was happening to me! The girl who is self-sufficient, sensible, arranges everything down to the last detail, the one you come to in order to mend broken hearts.
But we are young, I thought, and this relationship won't last. Luckily my sister helped us. She got us an appointment in a private clinic.

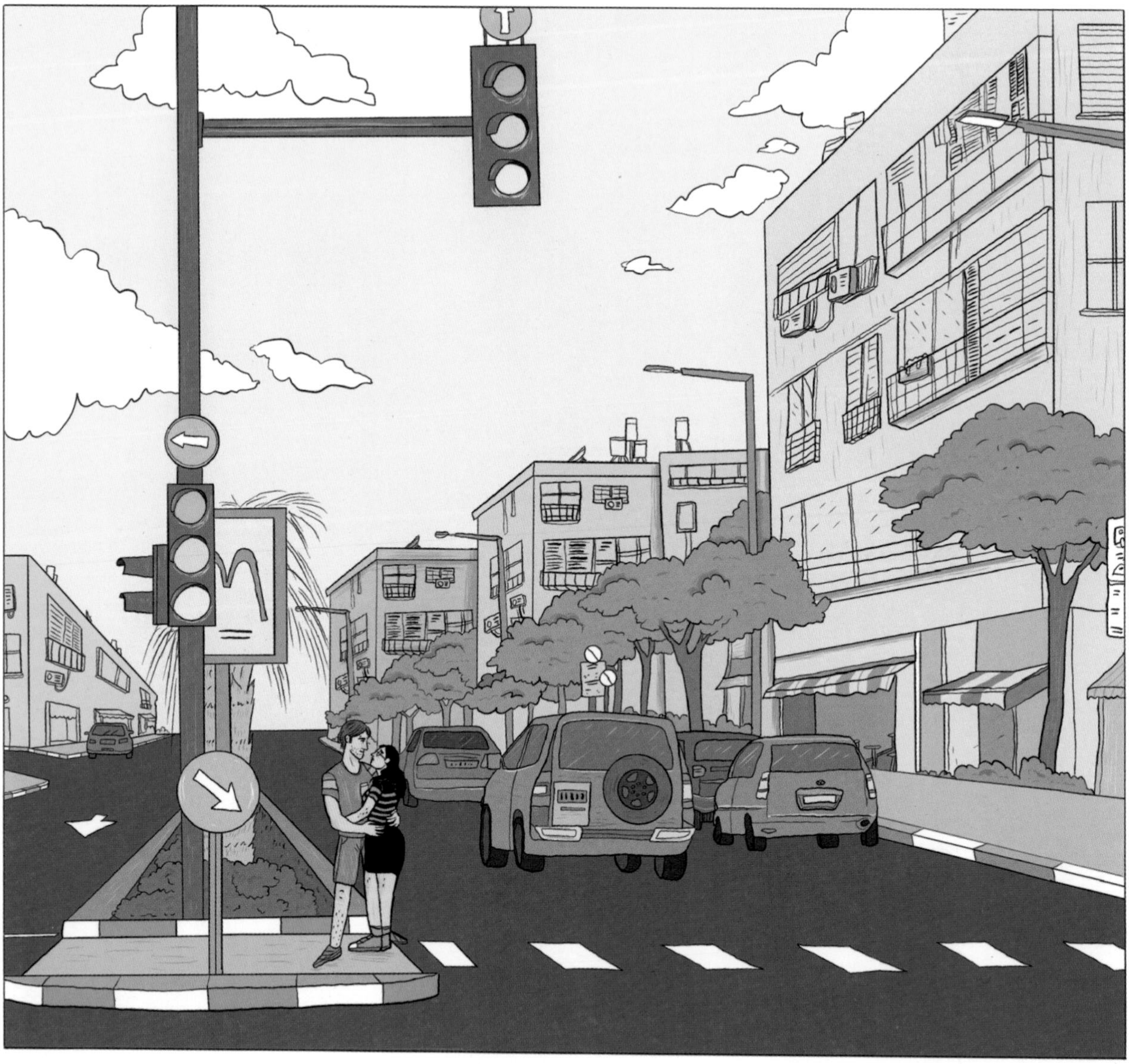

Why do you want an abortion? How old are you? Why aren't you going through your health insurance? Do you know that the Torah forbids this kind of procedure? Who are your parents? Your father's a rabbi? Well, I never!

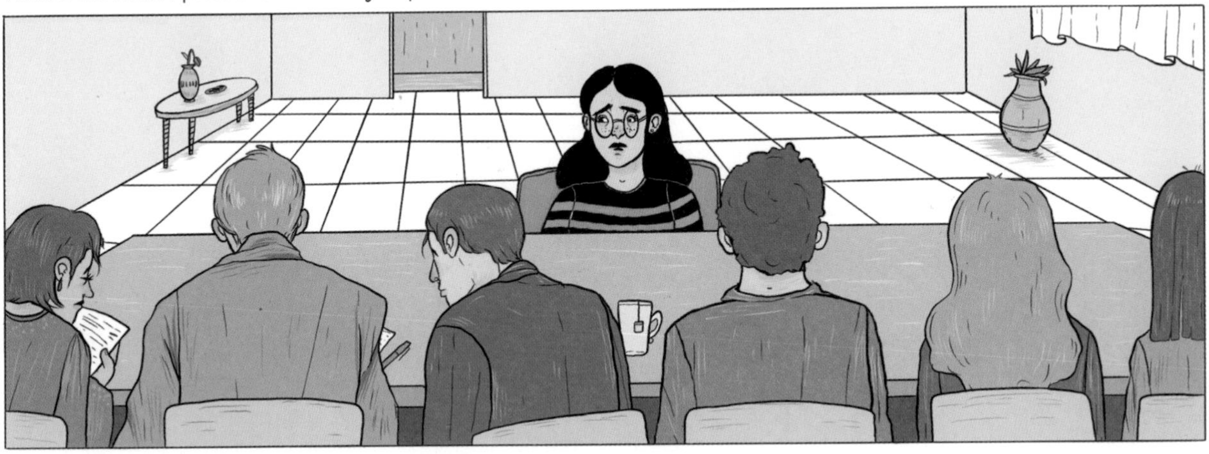

One little pill and it was done.

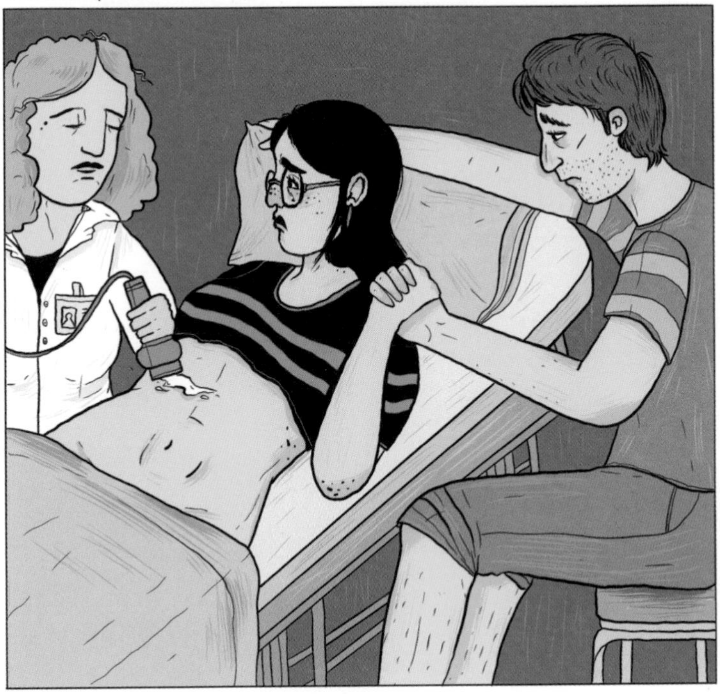

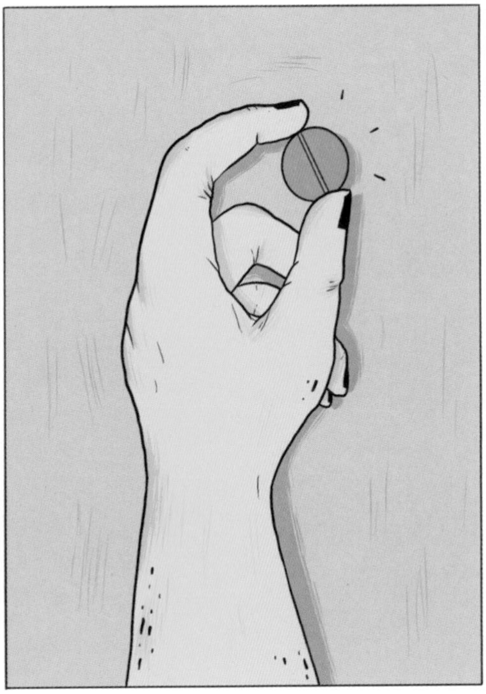

I started to bleed. It was as though my body was trying to push out all the pus and heal the wound.

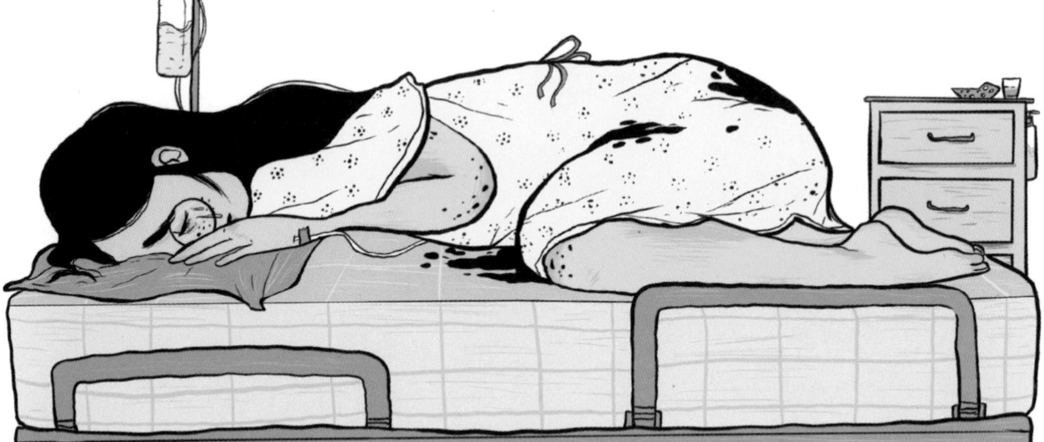

Six months went by, and the relationship survived. There were good times, tough times, a lot of thinking, lots of dates. But mostly we wanted to forget the trauma. Until the trip to the Nazi concentration camps in Poland.

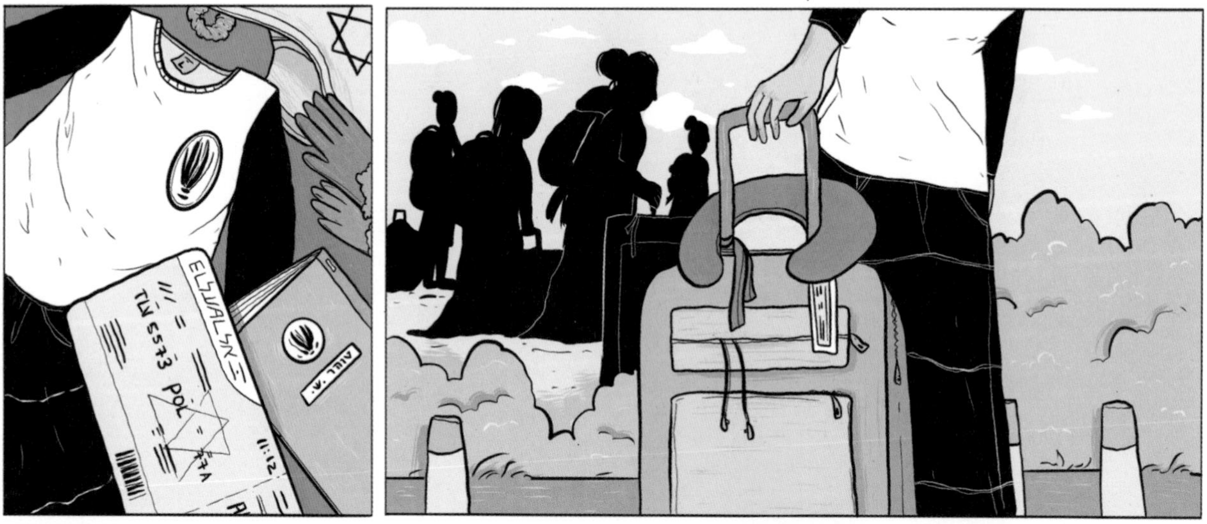

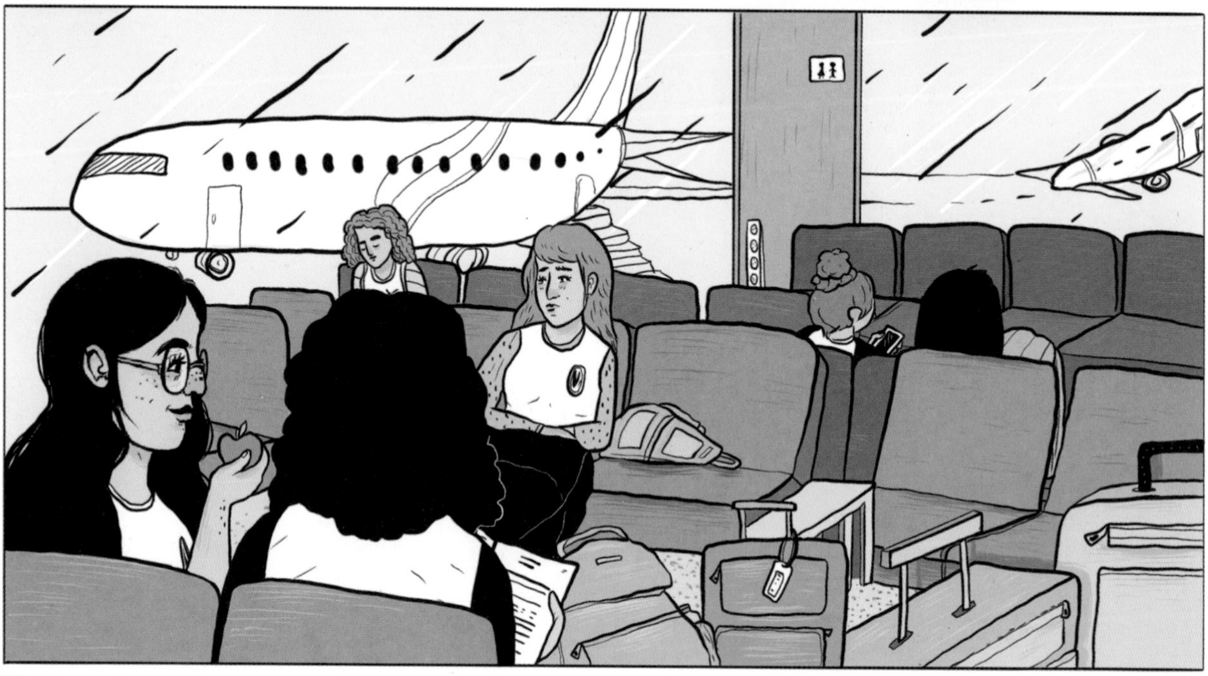

The Tarnow forest with its thousands of massacred Jewish children. I felt completely empty.

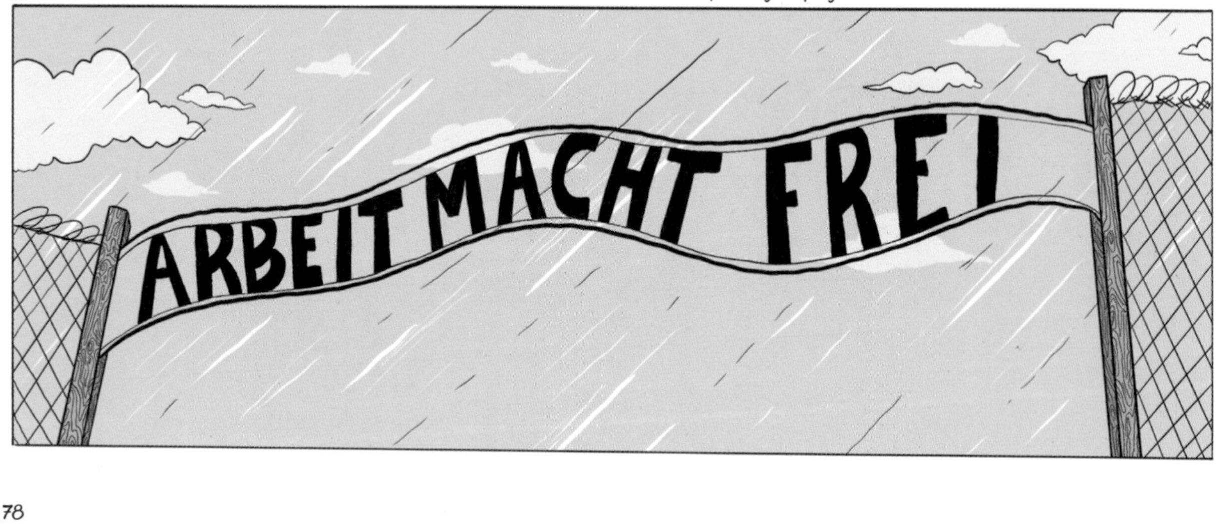
ARBEIT MACHT FREI

Swathed in layers that hugged me instead of arms, I remember the feeling of responsibility that I had felt six months previously. I spoke at the ceremony in the Children's Forest. Writing, reading, and crying. I try not to think about them, or about the cruelty in the world, or about the thing that was and then was not. And most of all, I try not to think about myself.

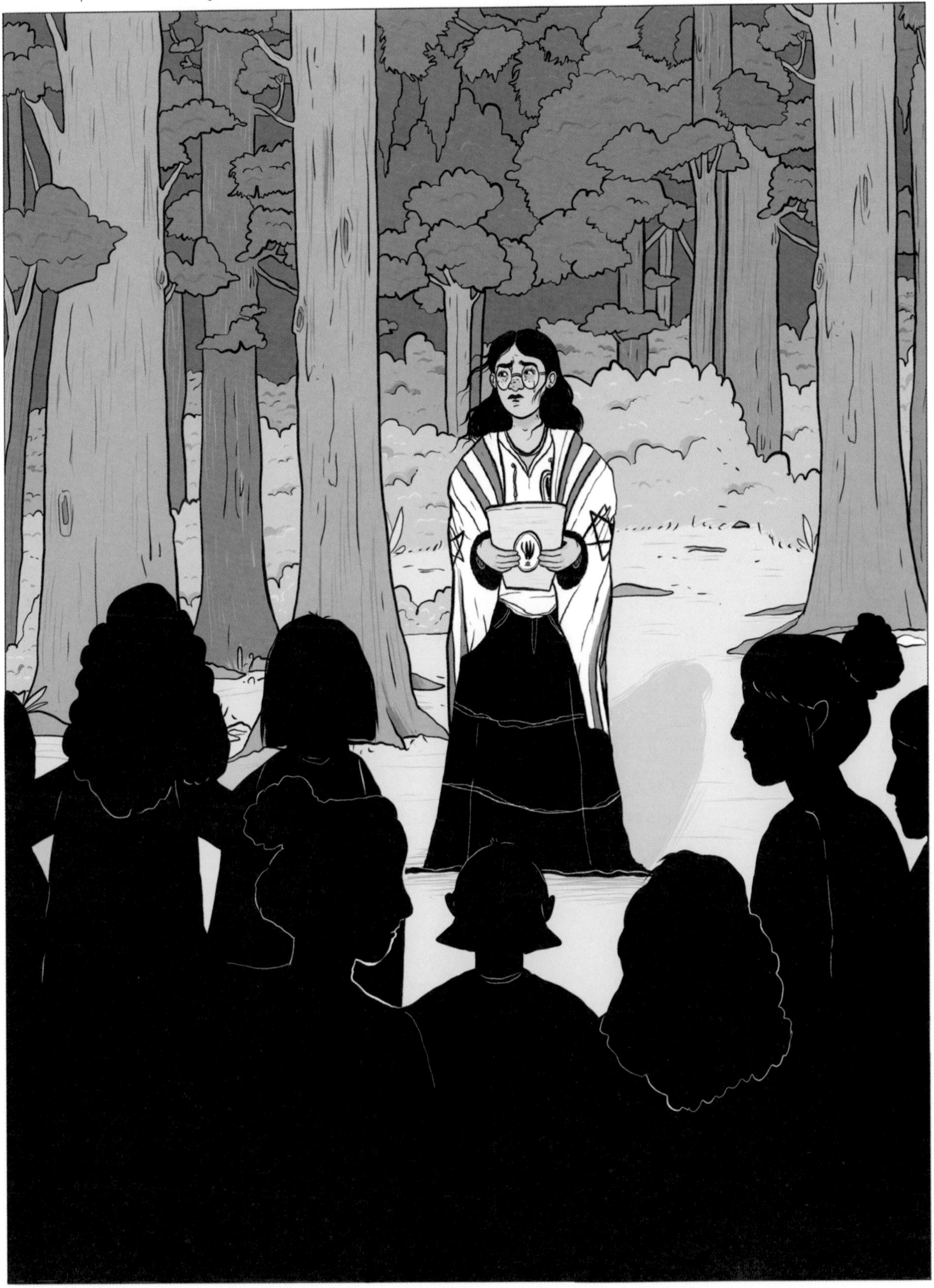

LIVING IN PEACE

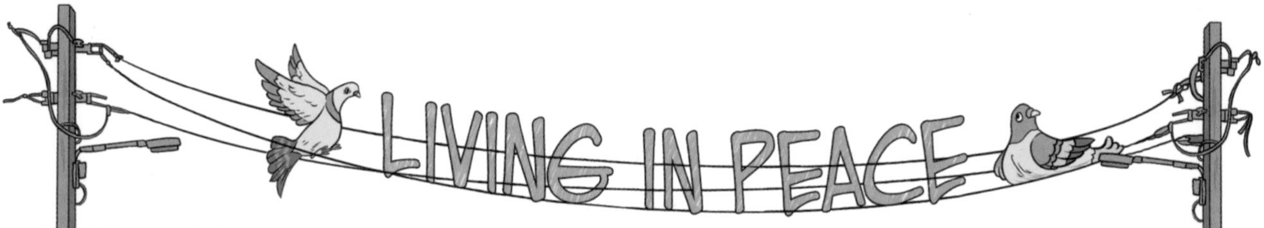

Life in the Kedoumim settlement goes along at a much slower pace than the rest of the world.

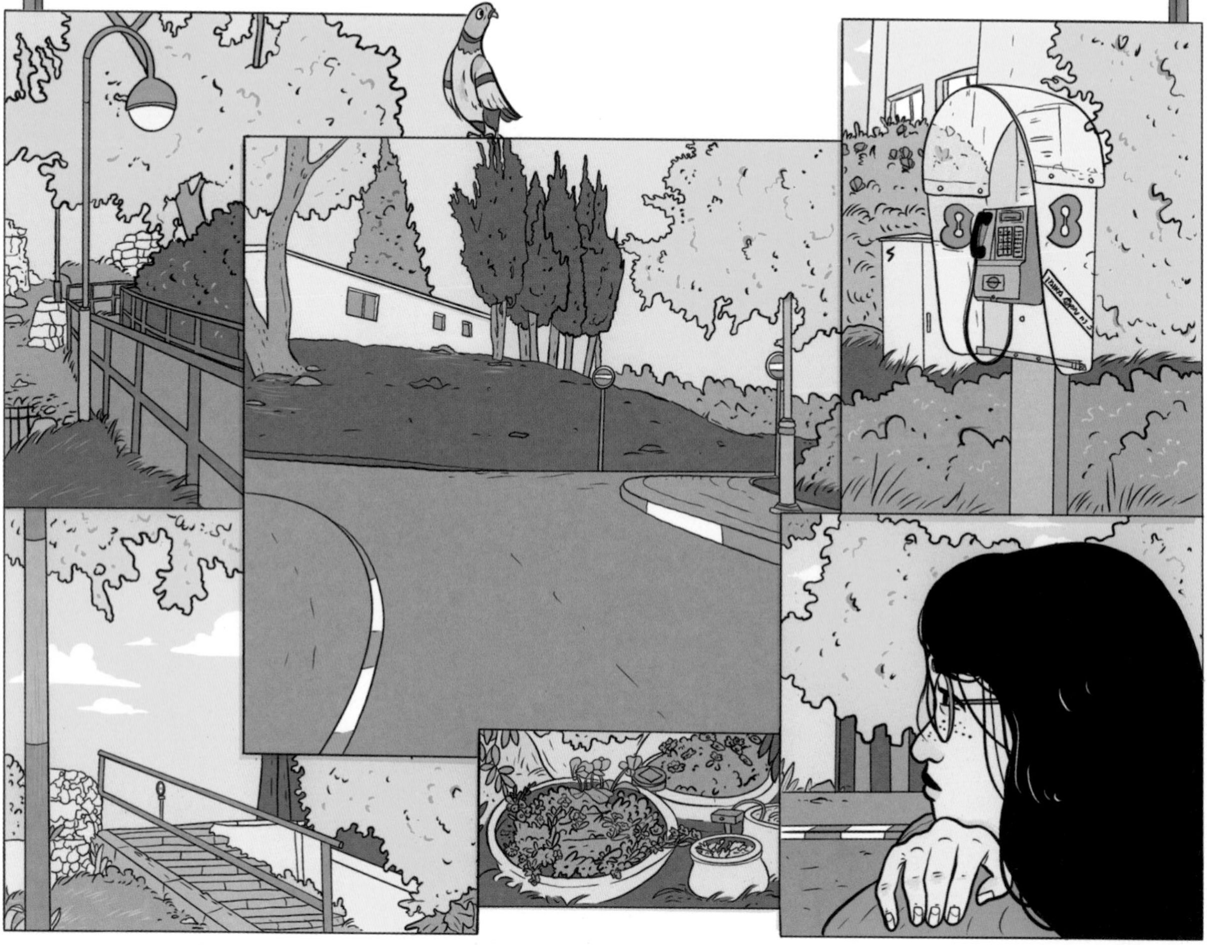

One day, coming back from school, I looked around. The road is often empty, apart from a few kids cycling around merrily. I wondered what it would be like to live in a city, to wander about incognito. I could imagine the noise of the cars, the horns, and the smell of exhaust fumes.

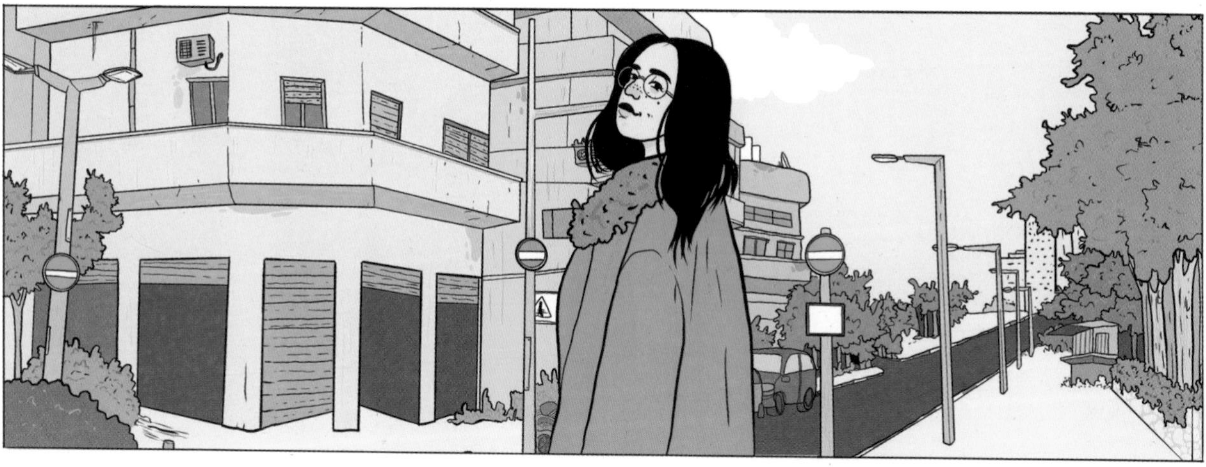

I hate the silence here. It was 9 p.m., and there was not a soul to be seen outside.
The only sound was the call of the muezzin—too bad I couldn't understand what it meant ...

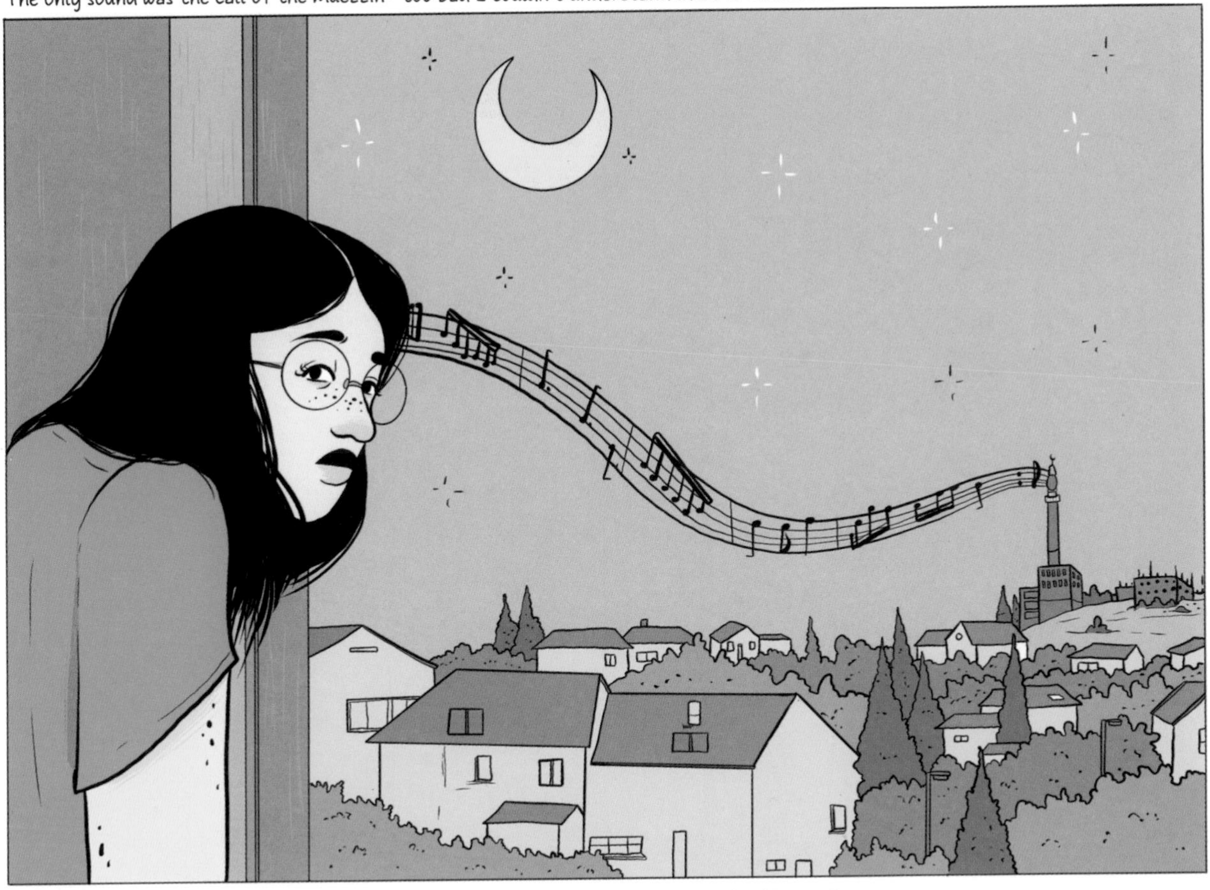

Hills covered with olive groves surround the settlement, as if to show that peace should reign here and that we're far from having achieved the goal.

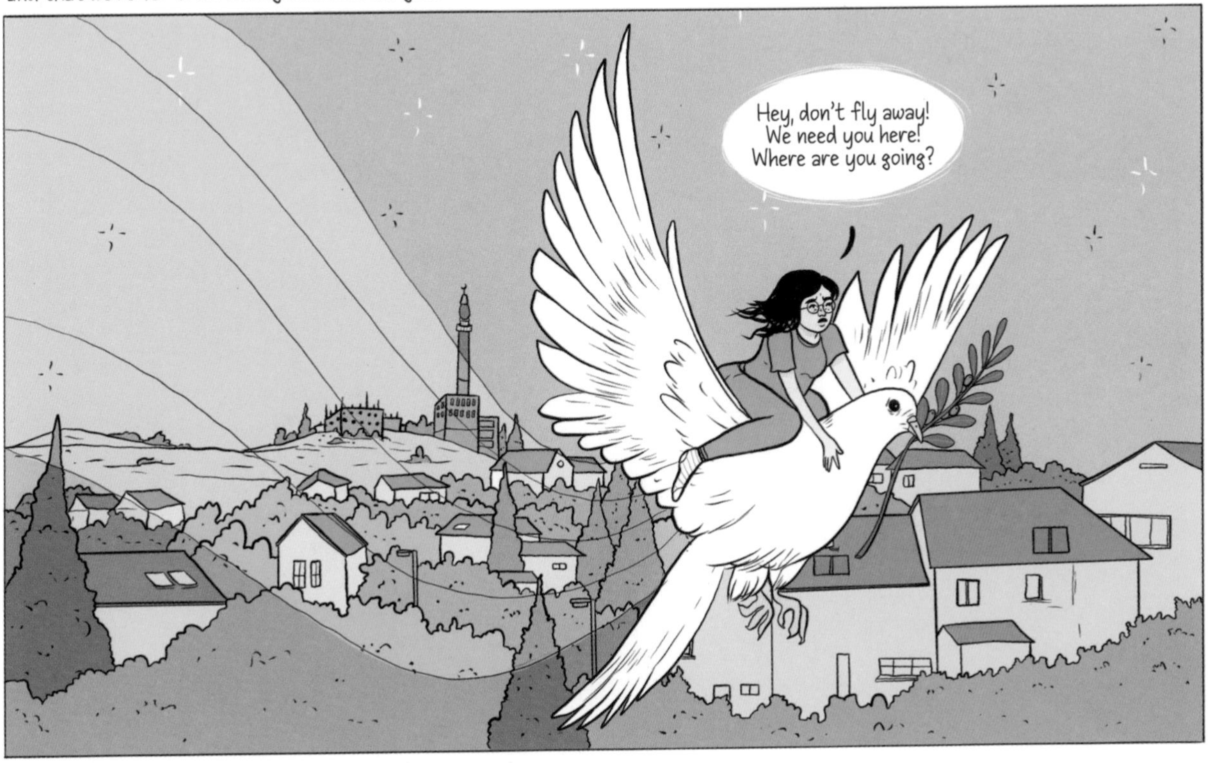
Hey, don't fly away! We need you here! Where are you going?

The quiet of Kedoumim is part of me. When I learned to drive in the city, I realized I don't cope well with noise.

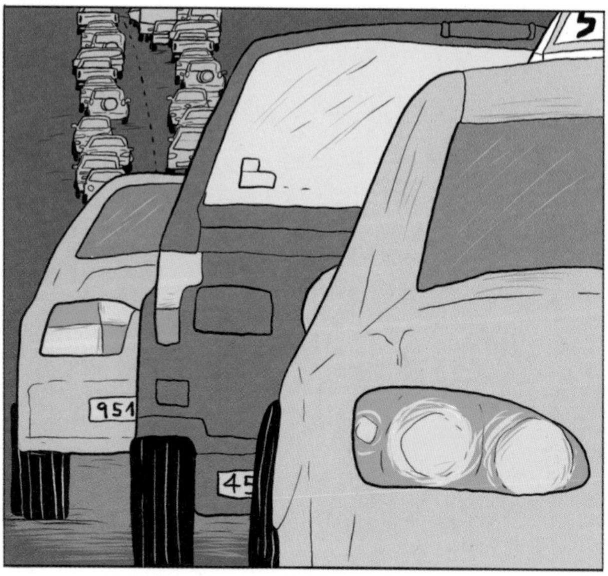

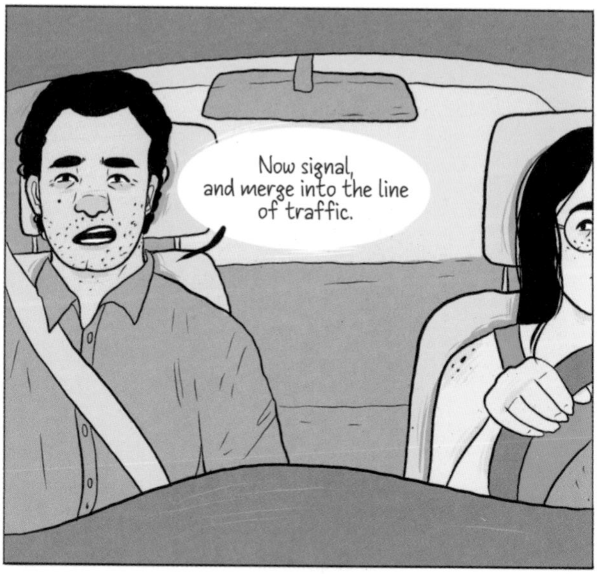
Now signal,
and merge into the line
of traffic.

I think my driving instructor hates me.

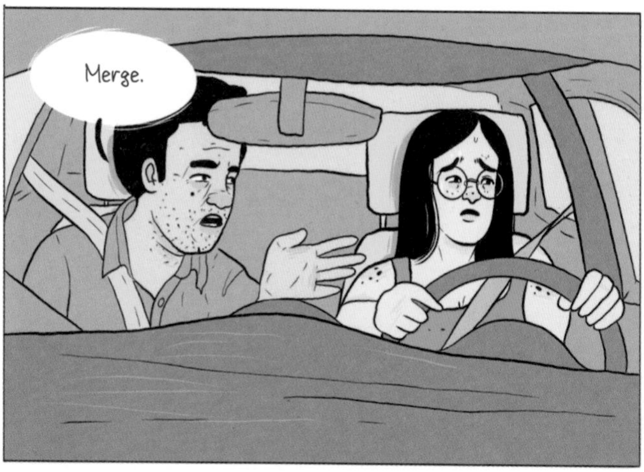
Merge.

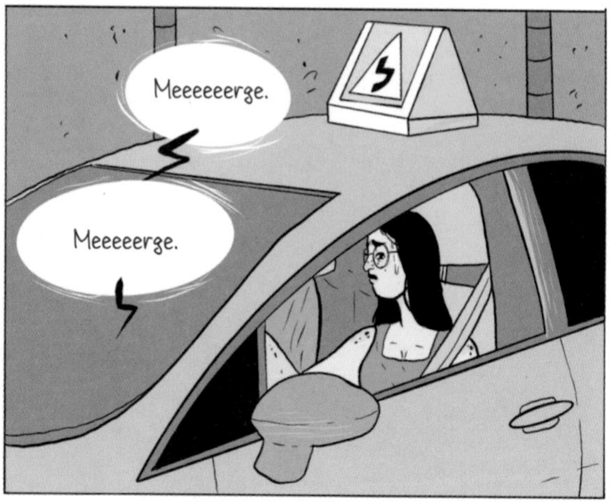
Meeeeeerge.
Meeeeerge.

When I got out of the car, I was relieved to think that I wasn't going to have to drive all the way home, and I headed quickly over to the bus stop. The sign showed that the number 81 wasn't going to arrive for at least another half hour. I sighed despairingly and walked to the junction to hitch a ride.

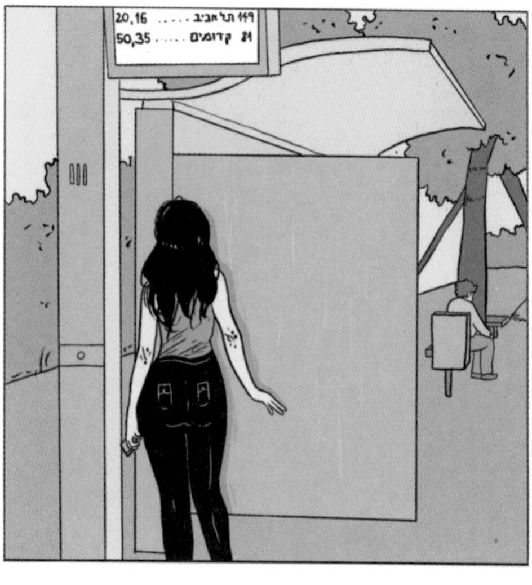

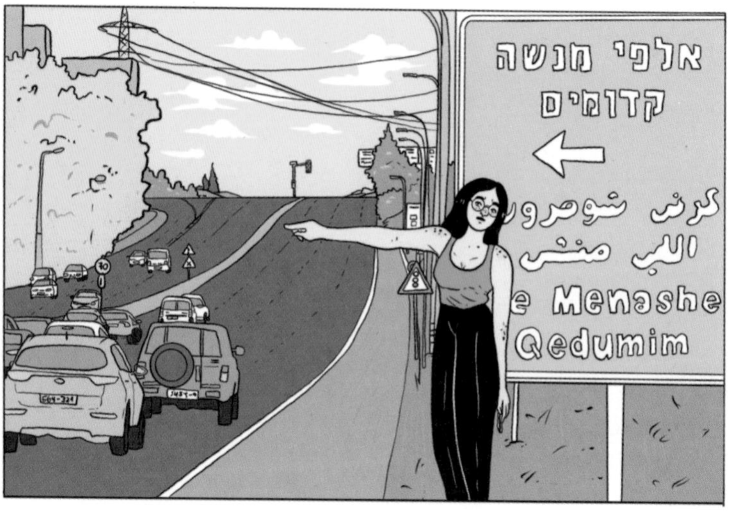
אלפי מנשה
קדומים
e Menashe
Qedumim

A gray car pulled up next to me, and the driver rolled down his window.

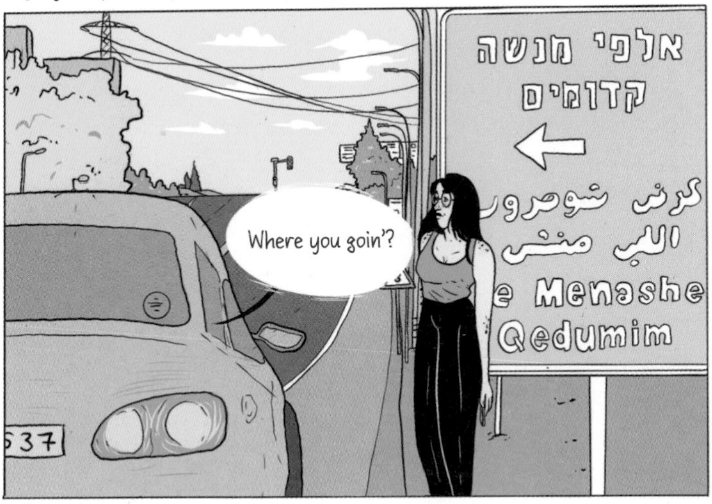

אלפי מנשה
קדומים
e Menashe
Qedumim
Where you goin'?

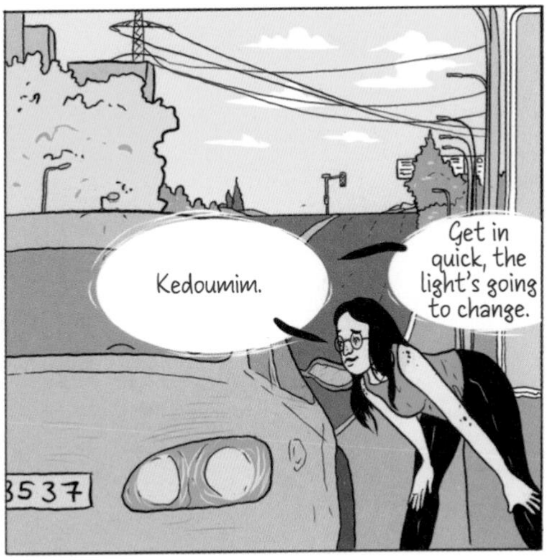

Kedoumim.
Get in quick, the light's going to change.

I got in hurriedly. All through those years when I was hitchhiking, for safety I had gotten into the habit of noting down all the details of the journey, to send it to a friend. So I started jotting everything down.

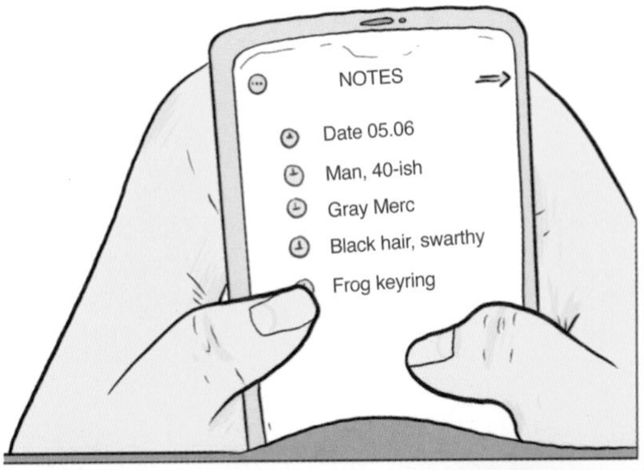

NOTES
Date 05.06
Man, 40-ish
Gray Merc
Black hair, swarthy
Frog keyring

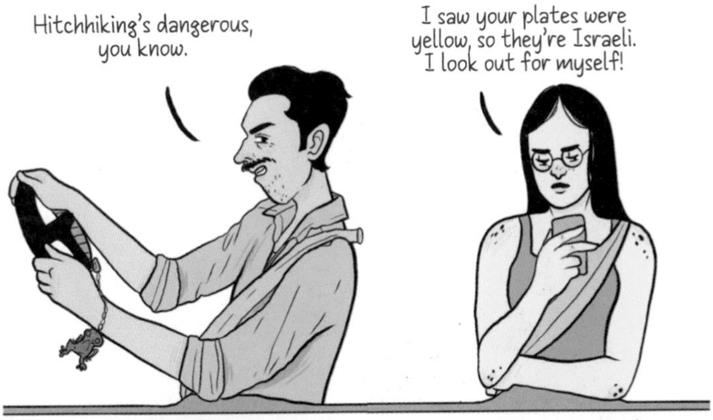

Hitchhiking's dangerous, you know.
I saw your plates were yellow, so they're Israeli. I look out for myself!

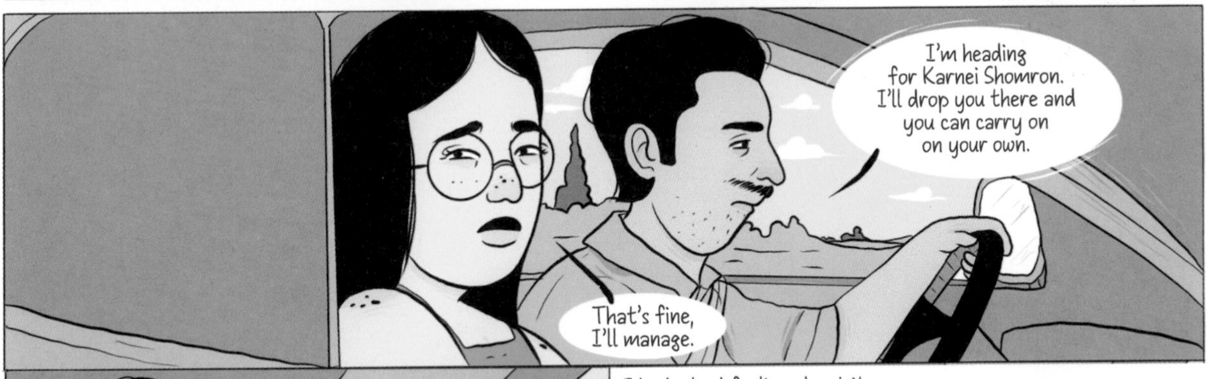

I'm heading for Karnei Shomron. I'll drop you there and you can carry on on your own.
That's fine, I'll manage.

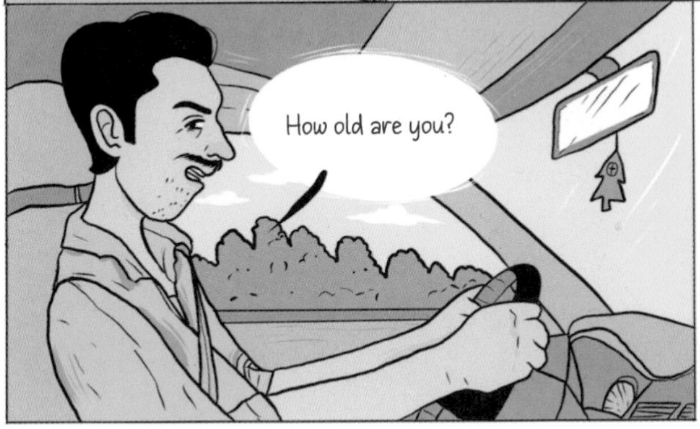

How old are you?

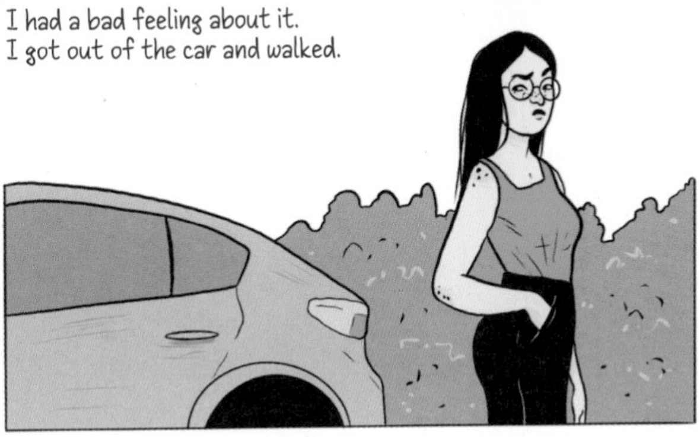

I had a bad feeling about it.
I got out of the car and walked.

People in the city surely don't let their kids get into cars with strangers.
In the settlements, it's a normal thing. Did my parents worry about it? I don't know.
It seemed so ordinary to hitchhike. When the 81 bus finally arrived, I got on.

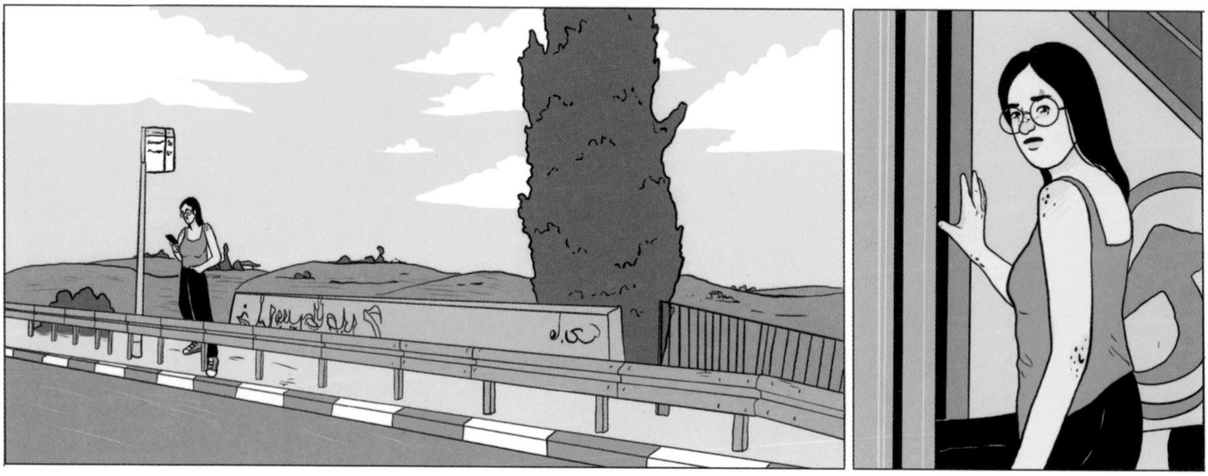

From behind the bulletproof glass, I looked at the trees, spotted an election poster or the name of the neighborhood we were going through. Since I was little, I'd been told over and over there are areas where you absolutely shouldn't venture.

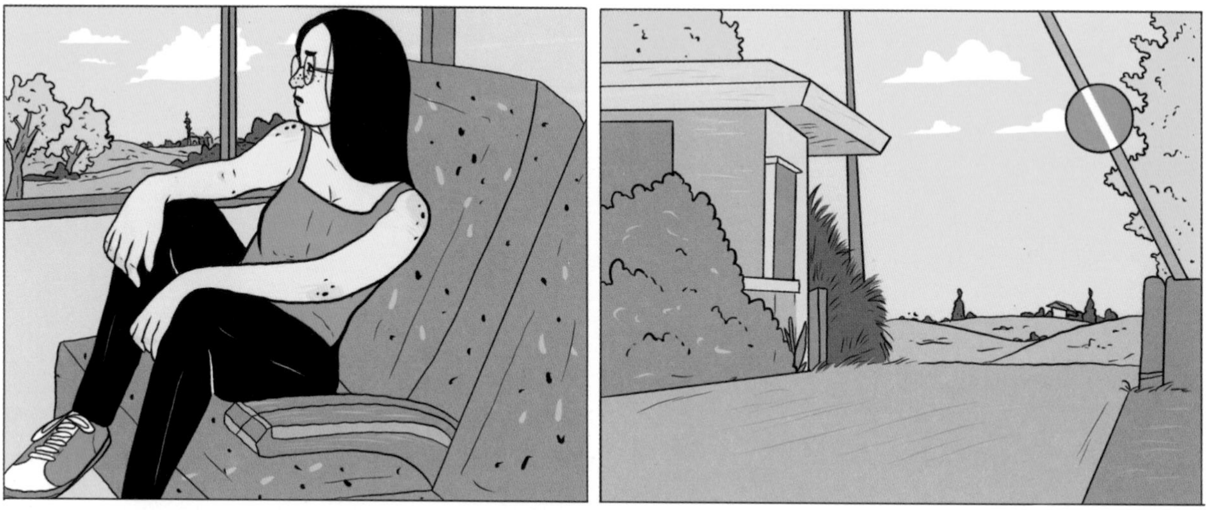

Even if it was possible, you go there at your own risk. Someone from my settlement went there once to buy vegetables and he was lynched. And yet, I never thought of Kedoumim as dangerous.

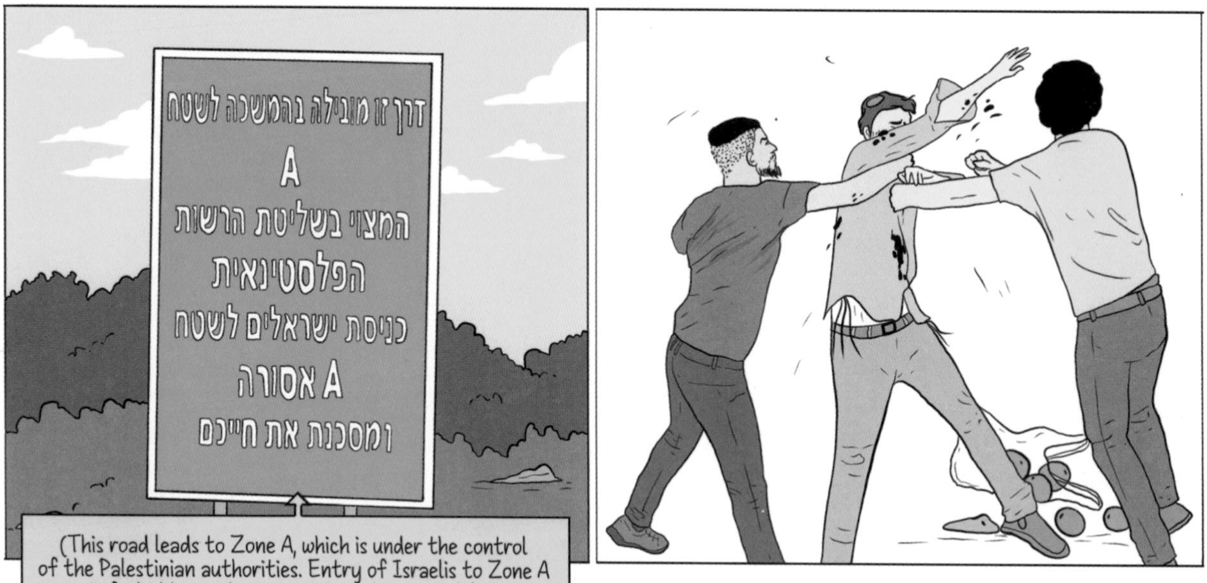
דרך זו מובילה בהמשכה לשטח
A
המצוי בשליטת הרשות
הפלסטינאית
כניסת ישראלים לשטח
A אסורה
ומסכנת את חייכם
(This road leads to Zone A, which is under the control of the Palestinian authorities. Entry of Israelis to Zone A is forbidden and carries risk of danger to life.)

It's 9:30 p.m. I went out in my slippers to get some fresh air, and the muezzin's call was still going strong.
So quiet. At least that ensures a good night's sleep.

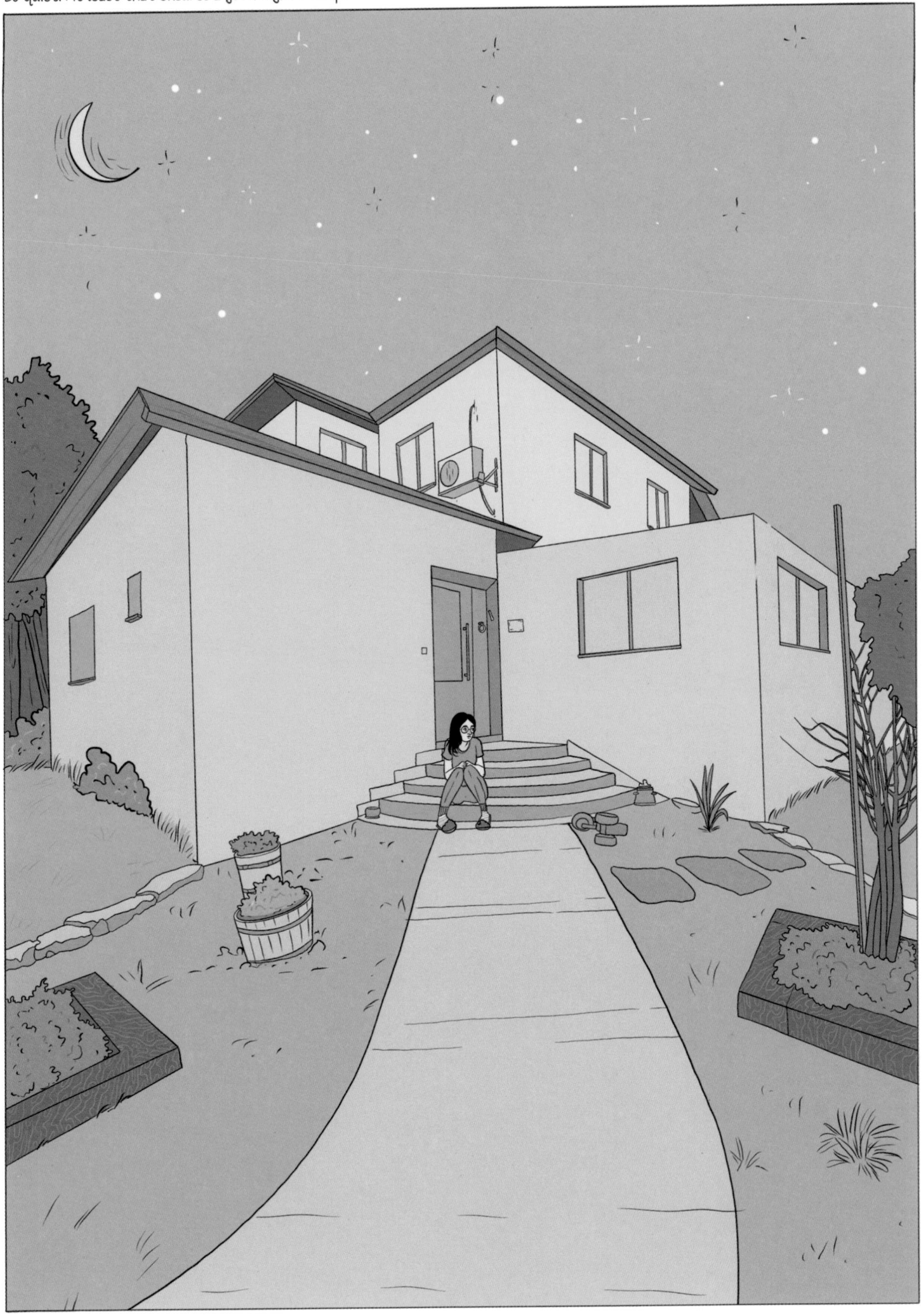

THE SMELL OF RAIN

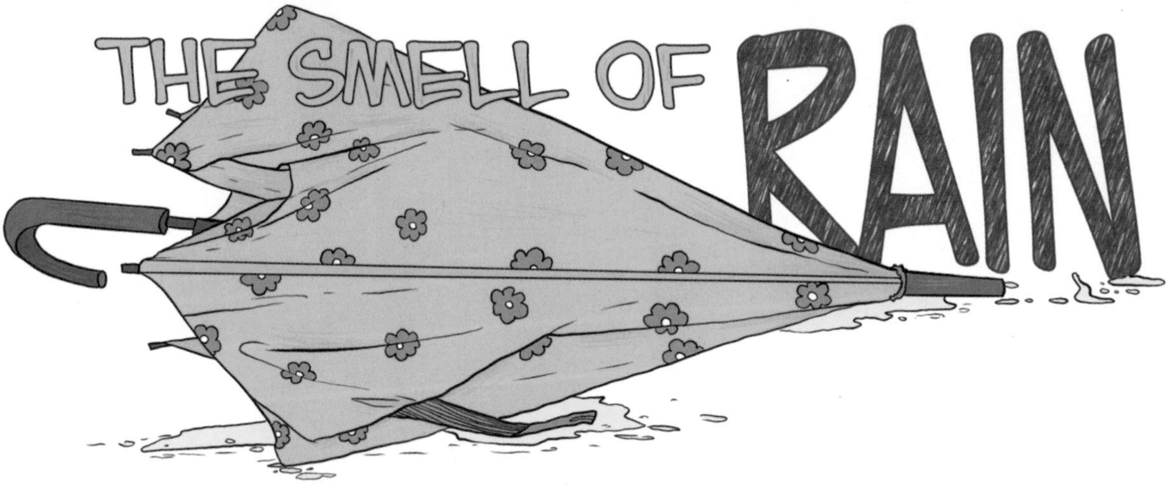

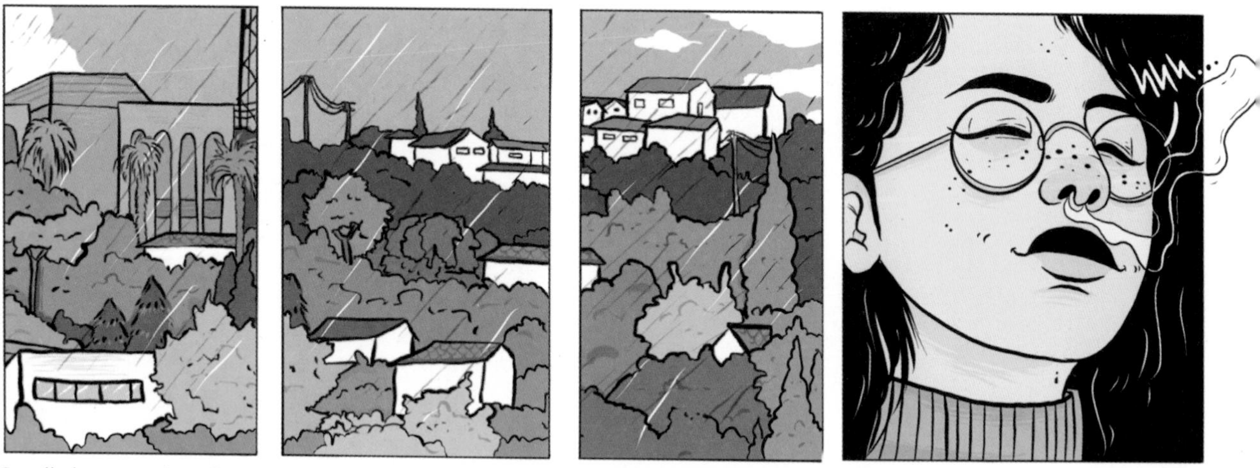
hhh...

I really love gray days. I take a deep breath in, and breathe out. The vapor from my mouth looks like smoke.
When my big brother was in the army, we visited him on his base.
The smell of rain mingled with the lingering scent of polish and cigarette smoke.

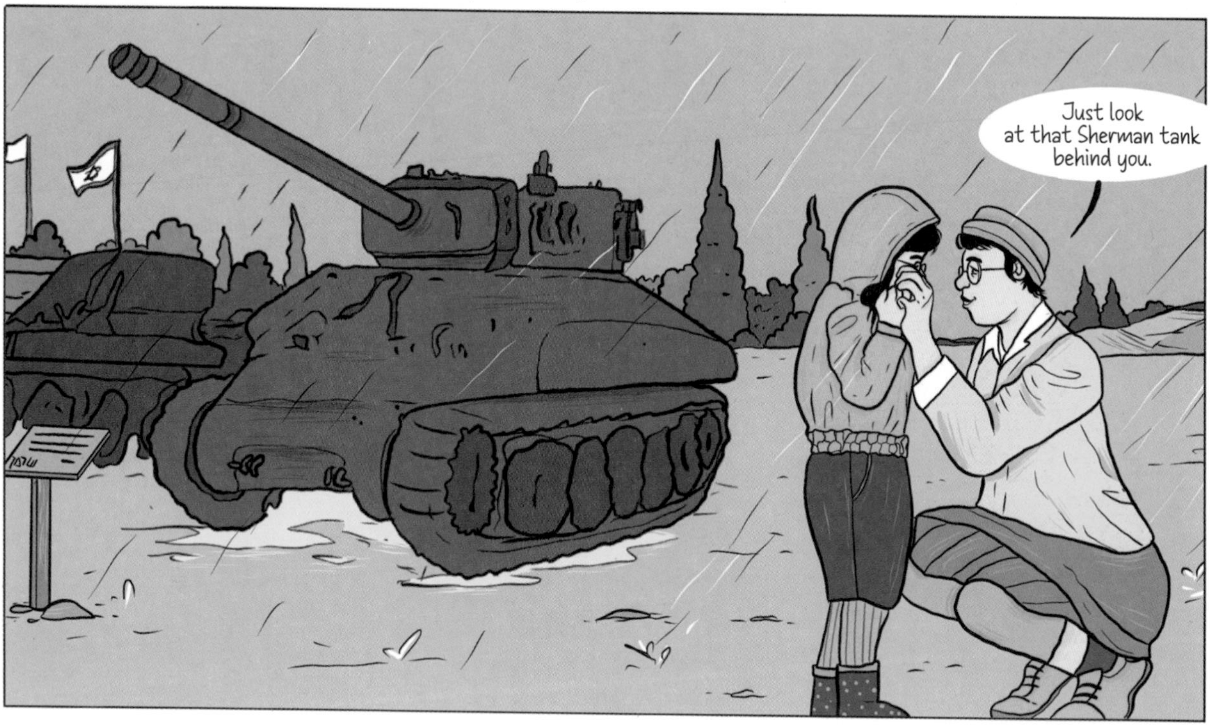
Just look at that Sherman tank behind you.

I imagined my brother sitting in that mountain of steel—hunched up and squashed in that tight space, feeling like he was suffocating.

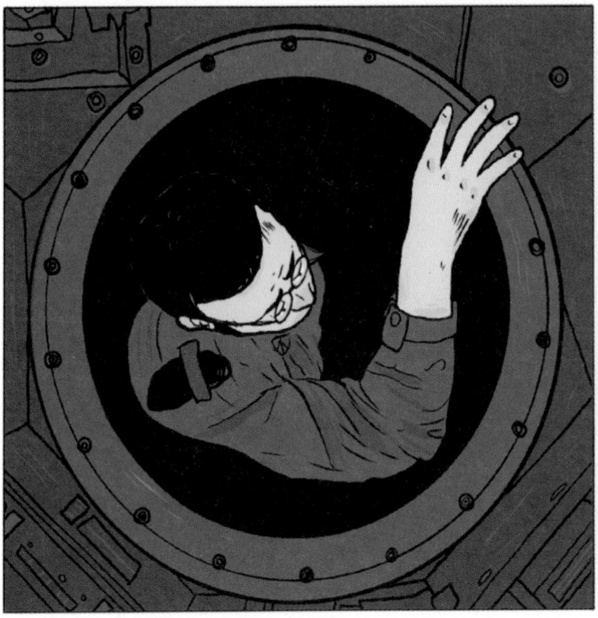

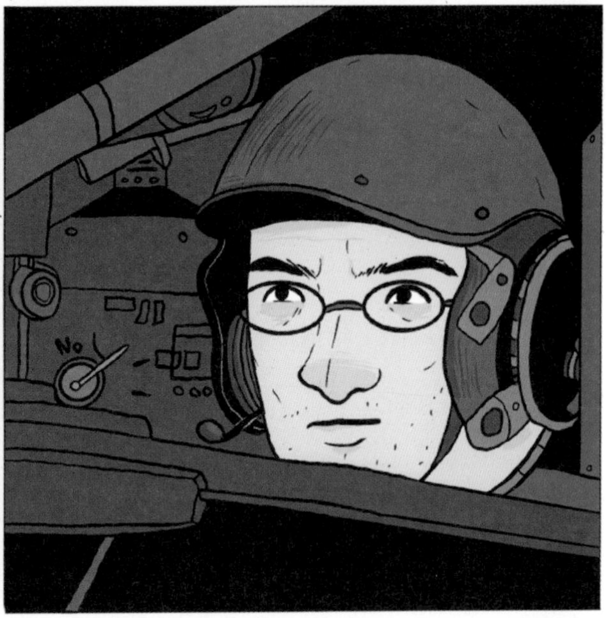
No

When I saw him, I ran to him and tried to dissolve into him, inside his rain-soaked army fatigues. When I finally let him go, I looked at him and thought to myself that I'd like to do military service, too, and be a soldier.

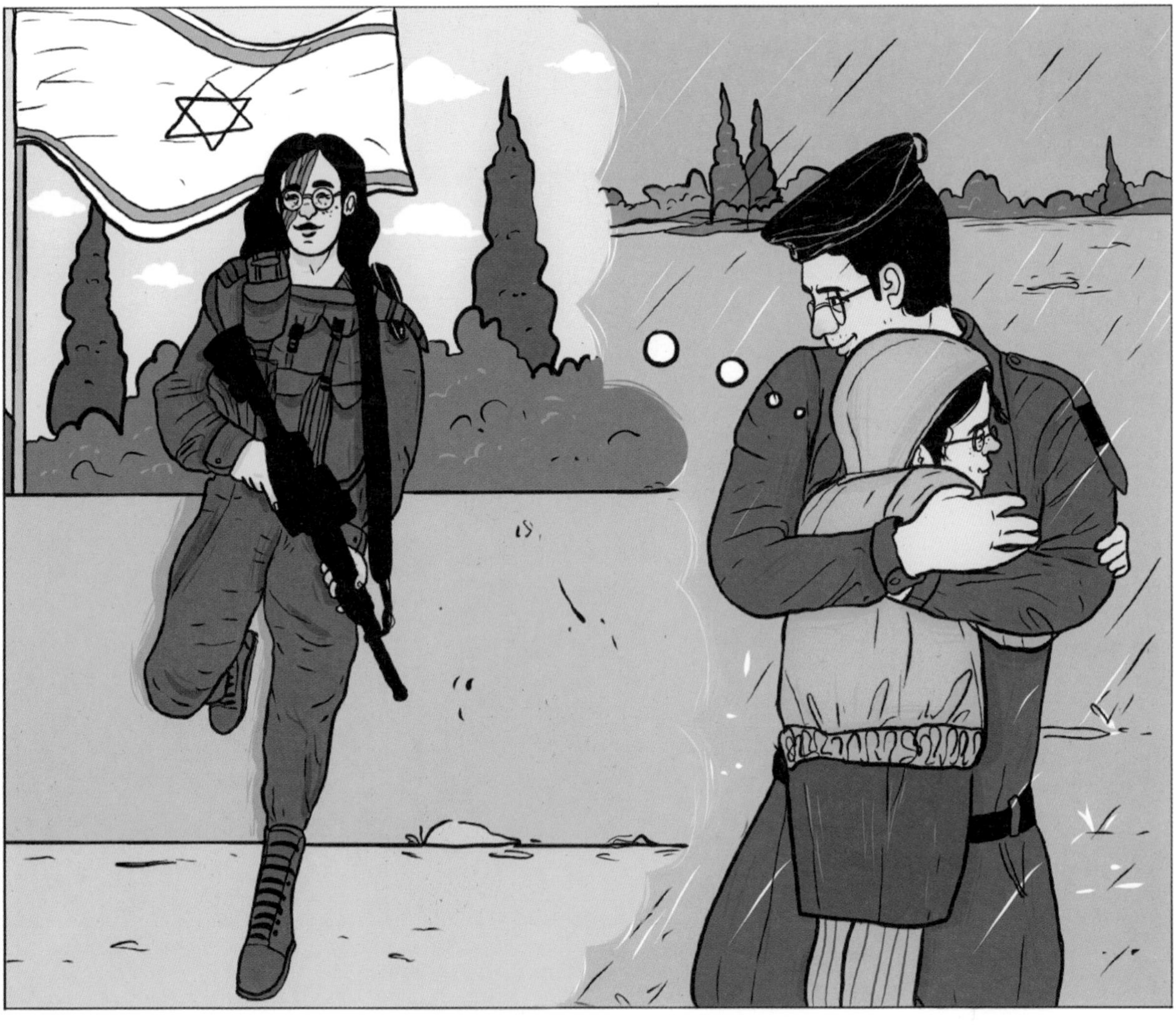

During senior year, the girls at the Oulpena had to choose where they were going to do their national service (instead of military service in the army). The school corridors were turned into a big fair where we could find out all the options for national service.

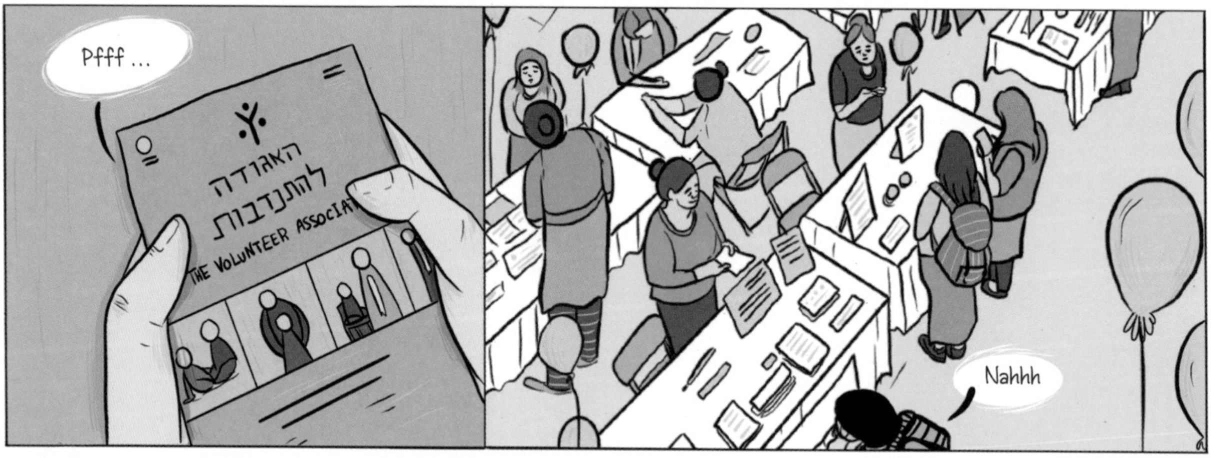
Pfff ...
האגודה להתנדבות
THE VOLUNTEER ASSOCIAT
Nahhh

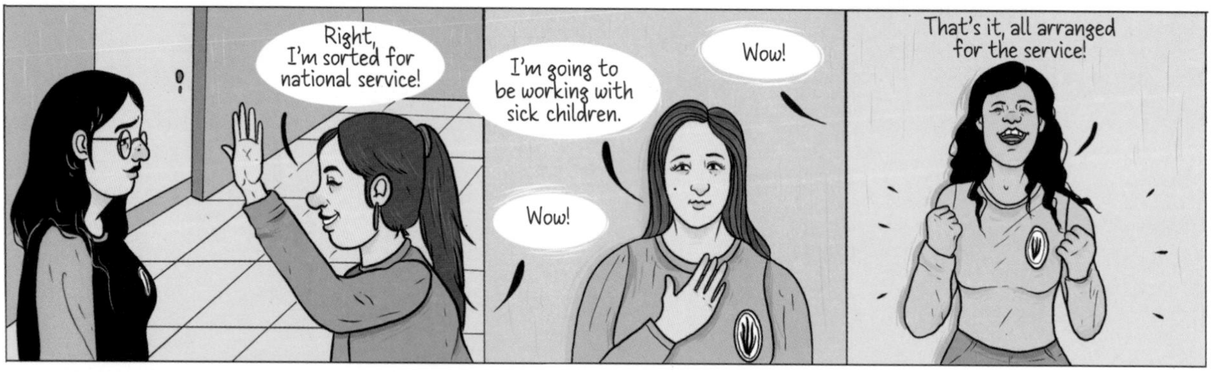
Right, I'm sorted for national service!
I'm going to be working with sick children.
Wow!
Wow!
That's it, all arranged for the service!

And me? All I was thinking about was the uniform. I was convinced that I was going to be a soldier in the army.
A panel of girls, former Oulpena pupils, came to talk about the national service they'd chosen.
I was waiting impatiently for the ones who would be talking about their military experience!

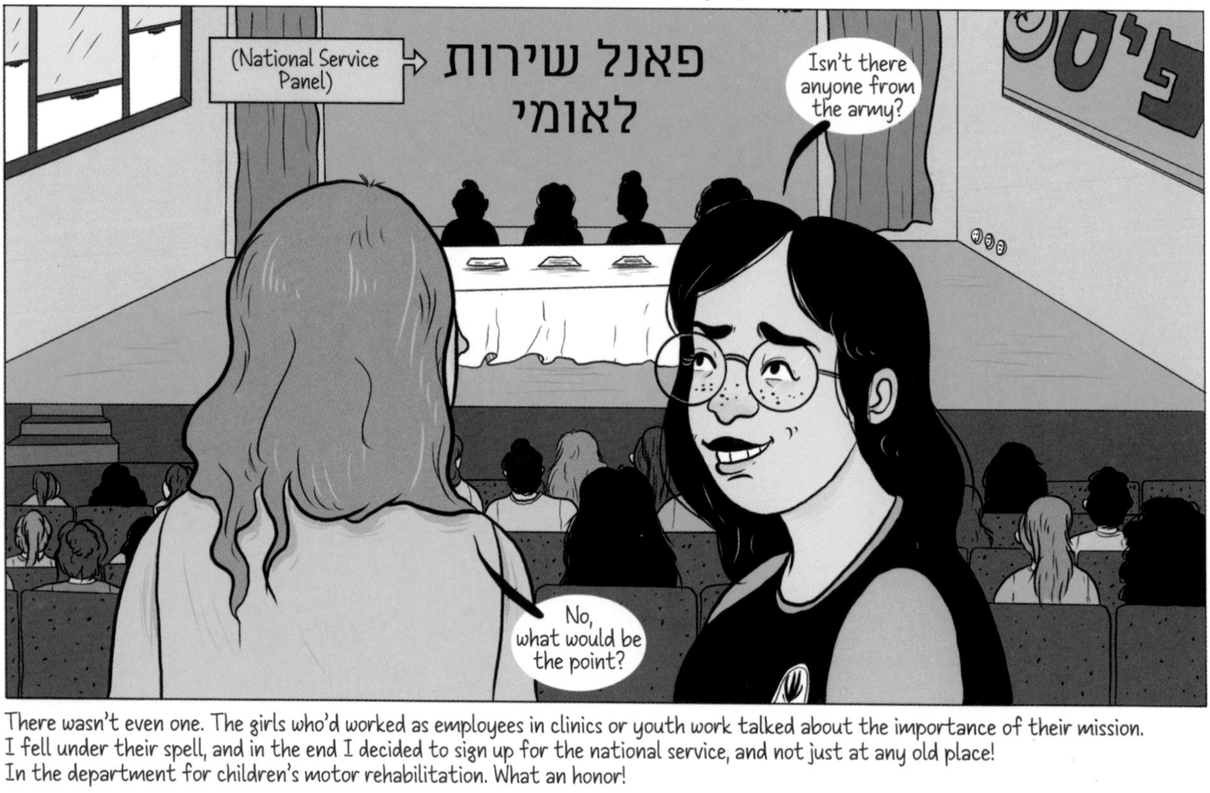
(National Service Panel)
פאנל שירות לאומי
Isn't there anyone from the army?
No, what would be the point?

There wasn't even one. The girls who'd worked as employees in clinics or youth work talked about the importance of their mission.
I fell under their spell, and in the end I decided to sign up for the national service, and not just at any old place!
In the department for children's motor rehabilitation. What an honor!

A year later, in the little apartment shared by girls in the national service in Raanana, I saw gray clouds through the window, and I took a deep breath. The little girl who dreamt of becoming a soldier had popped up again. I felt her inside me, disappointed.

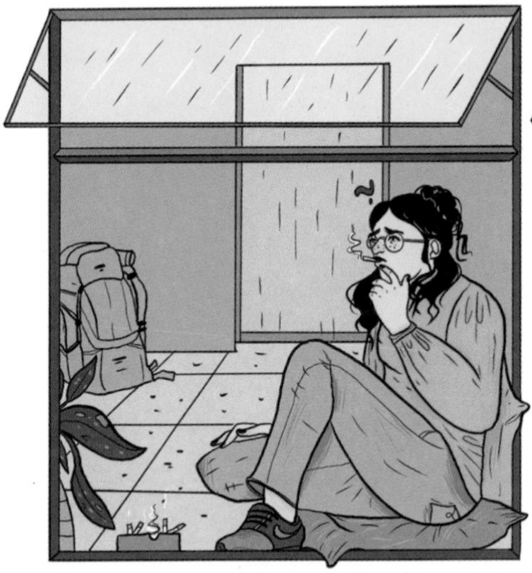

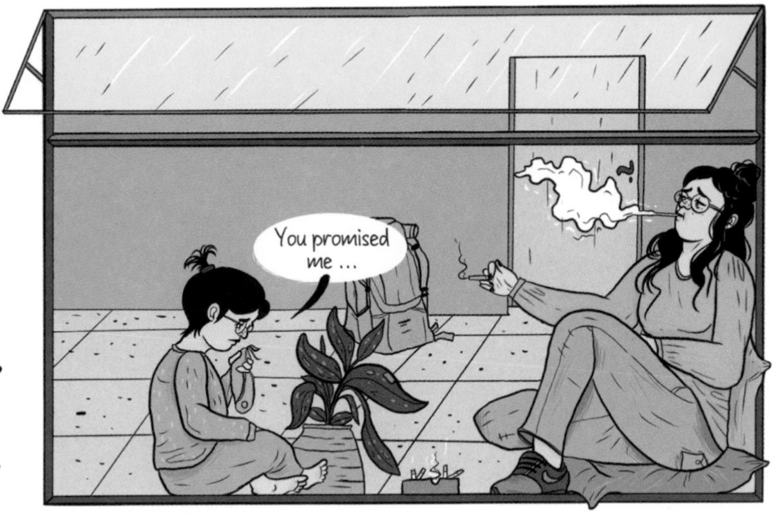
You promised me …

I'd grown up since, telling myself that my choice, national service instead of military service, was more meaningful. What would I have done in the army, anyway? I tried to convince myself with all my might.

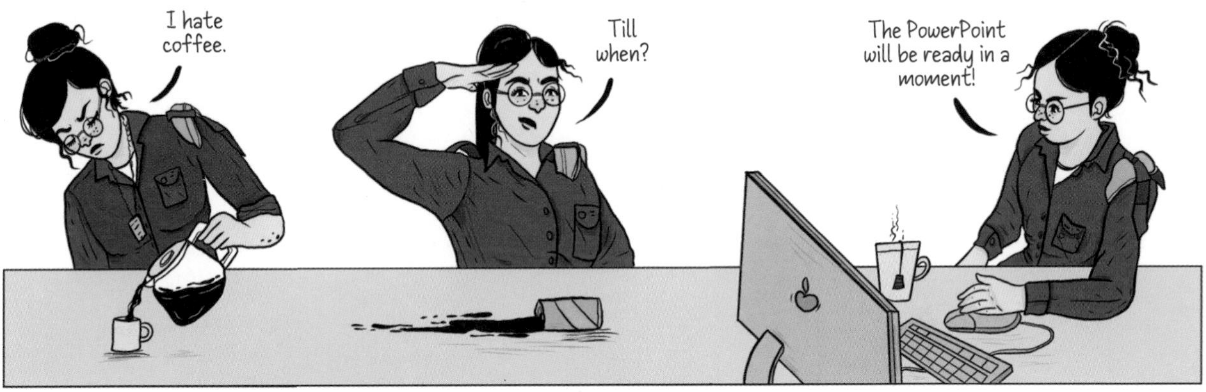
I hate coffee.
Till when?
The PowerPoint will be ready in a moment!

But the little girl sitting on my shoulders was pricking my conscience. My conscience, which had slunk away. *I smell rain*, I thought, blowing smoke rings into the cold winter air.

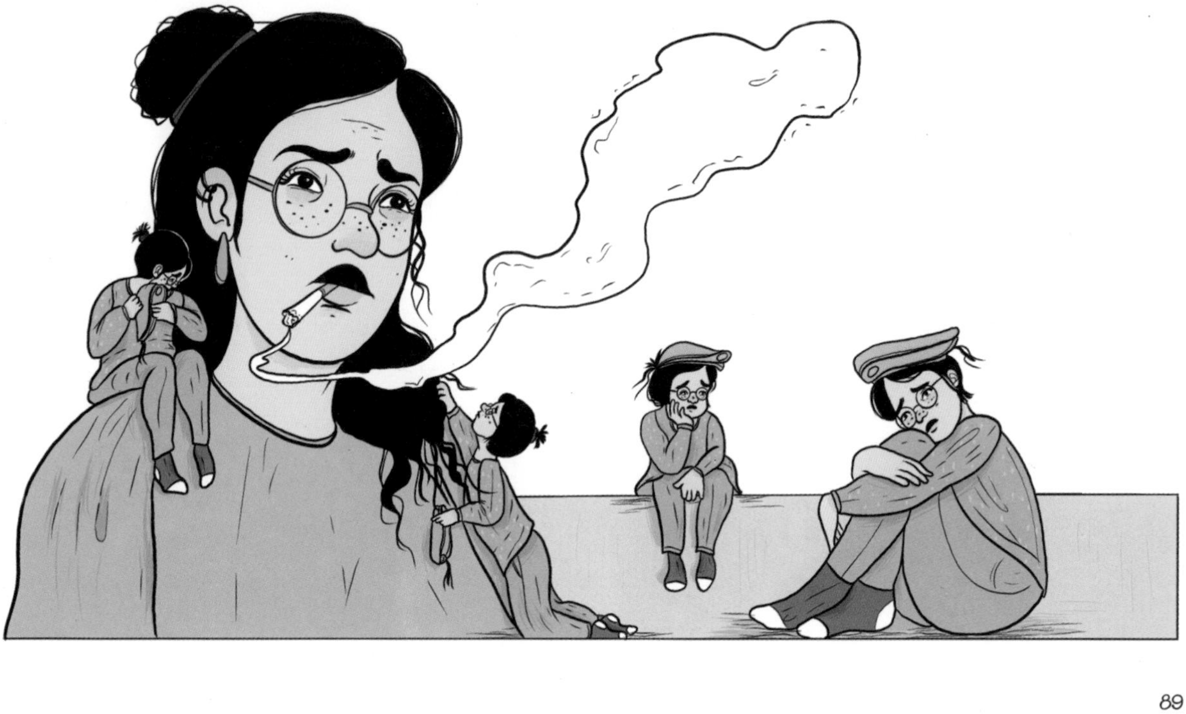

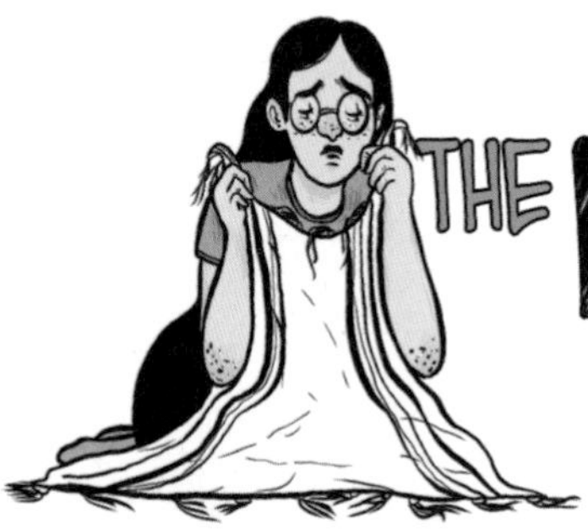

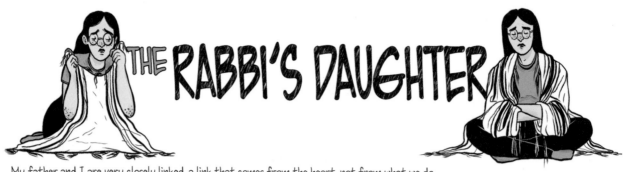

THE RABBI'S DAUGHTER

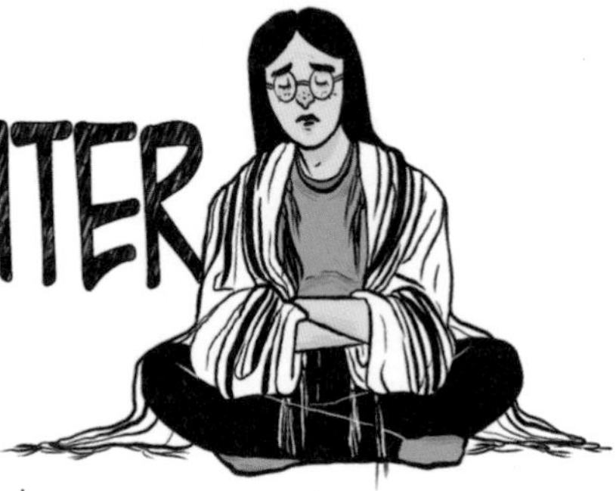

My father and I are very closely linked, a link that comes from the heart, not from what we do.

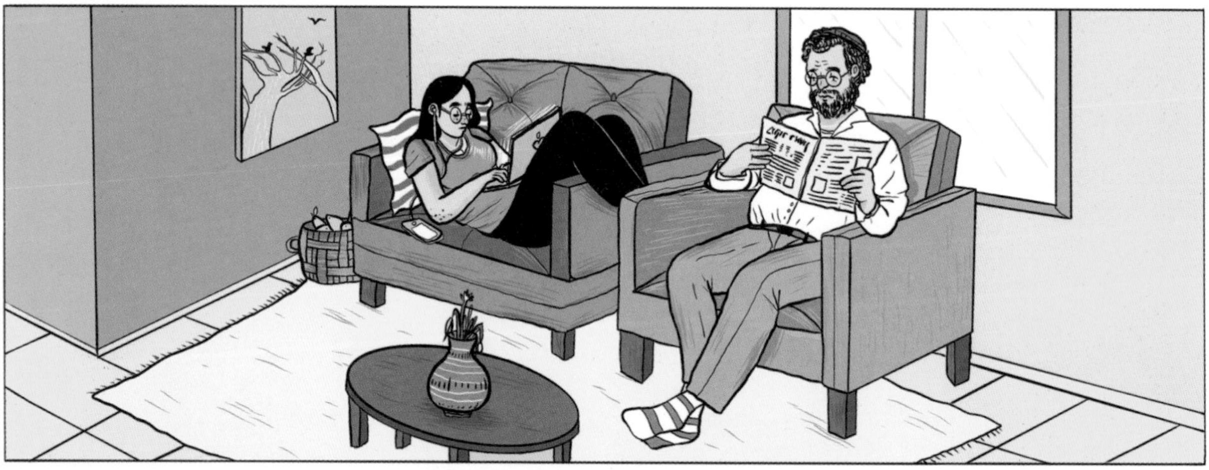

When I was a kid, the expression "the Rabbi's daughter" made me feel uneasy and like I didn't belong.

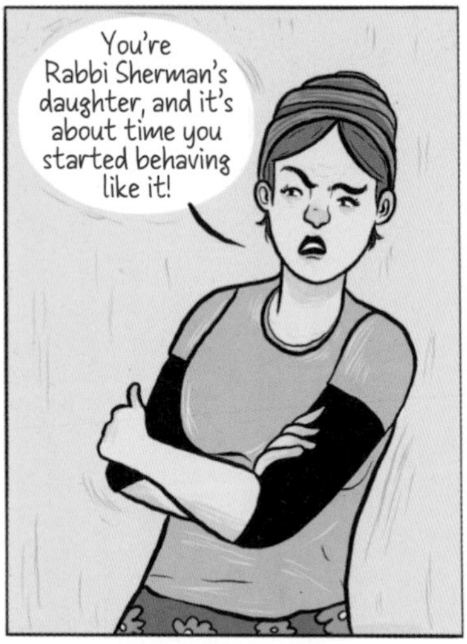
You're Rabbi Sherman's daughter, and it's about time you started behaving like it!

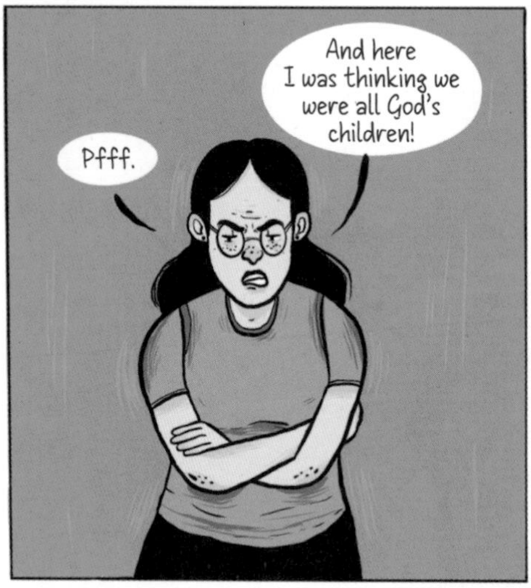
Pfff.
And here I was thinking we were all God's children!

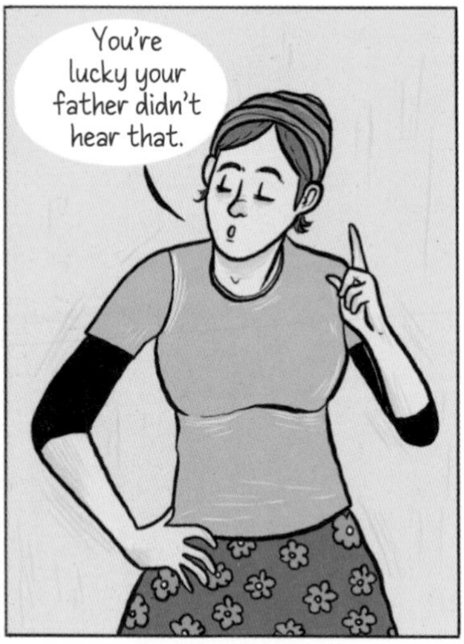
You're lucky your father didn't hear that.

The respect that was demanded limited contact between us, as well as our discussions, which essentially centered on Jewish thought.

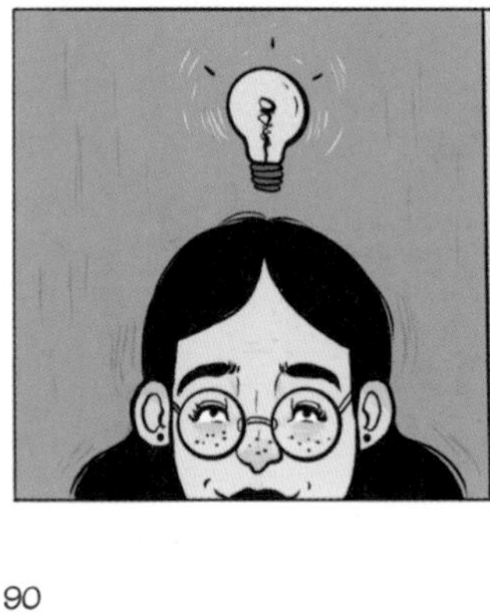

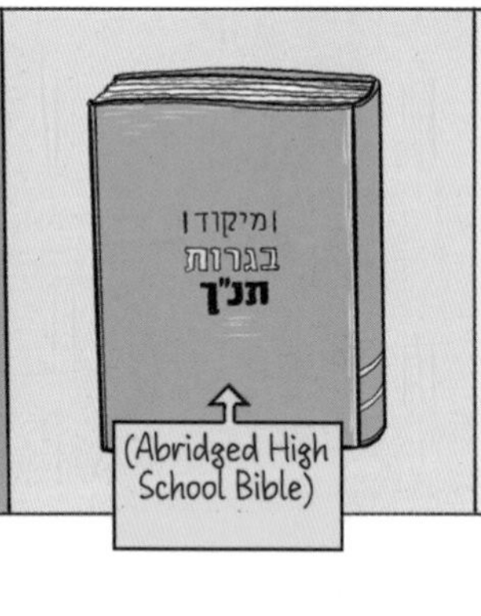
| מיקוד |
בגרות
תנ"ך
(Abridged High School Bible)

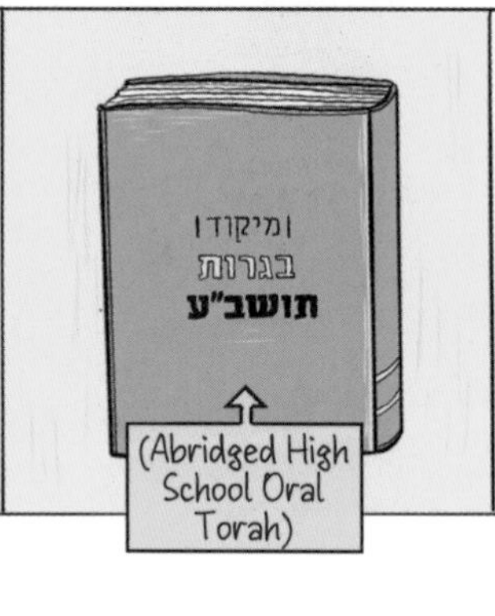
| מיקוד |
בגרות
תושב"ע
(Abridged High School Oral Torah)

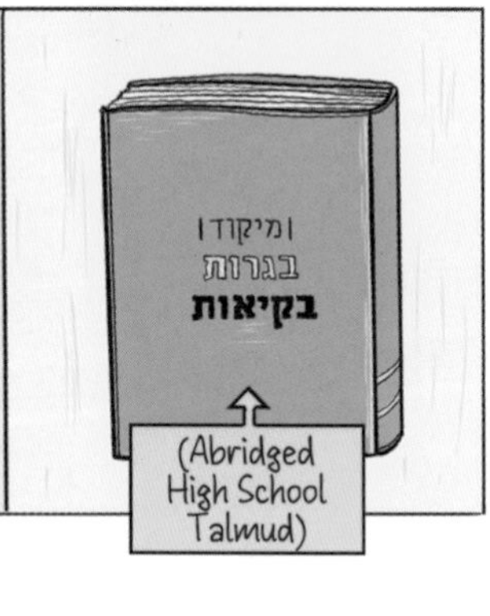
| מיקוד |
בגרות
בקיאות
(Abridged High School Talmud)

I was sad for him that I was his daughter, that I was what I was.

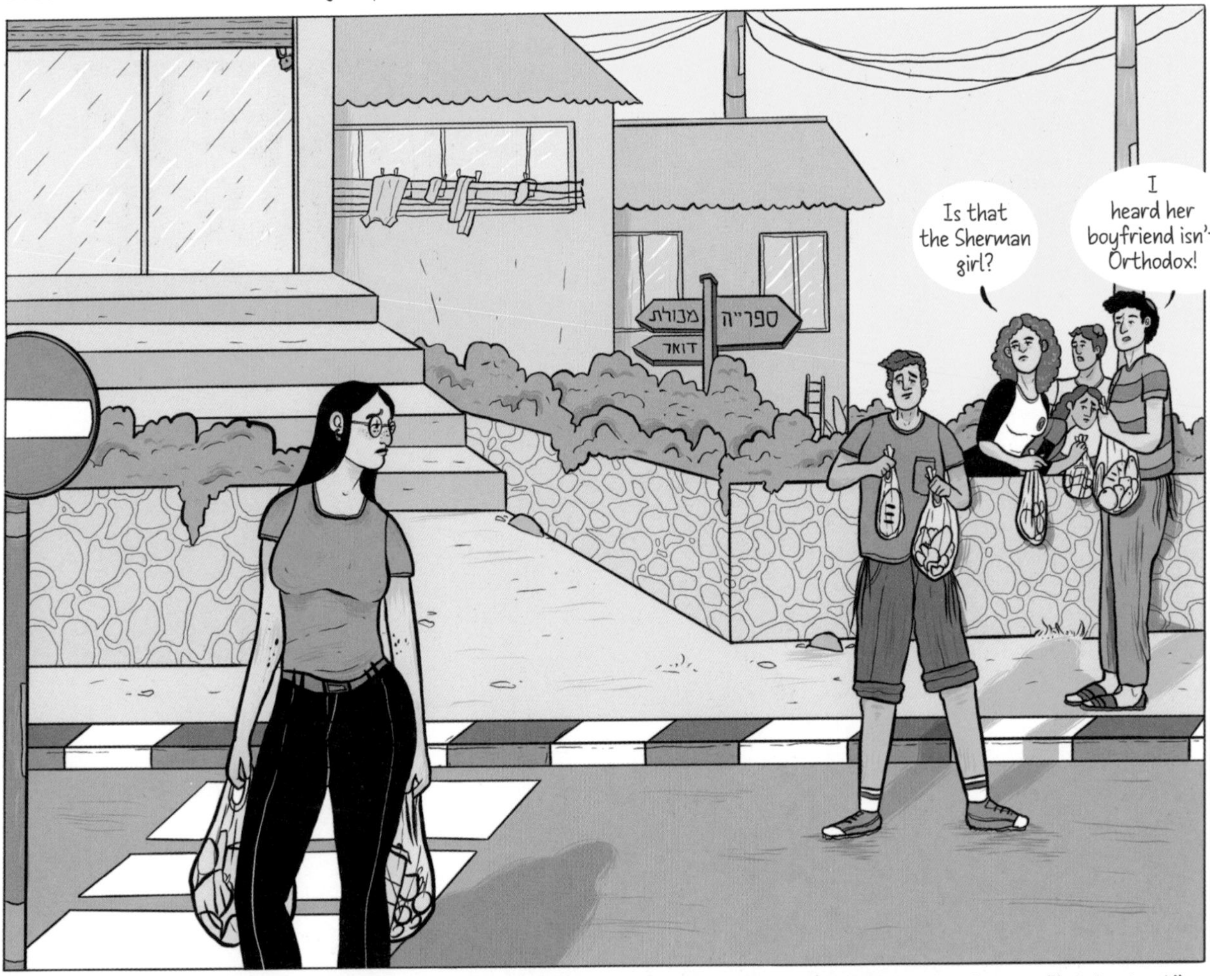
ספרי"ה
מכולת
דואר
Is that the Sherman girl?
I heard her boyfriend isn't Orthodox!

When I told him that I wasn't religious anymore, I remember that he fell silent. His look said, "When you're older, you'll understand."

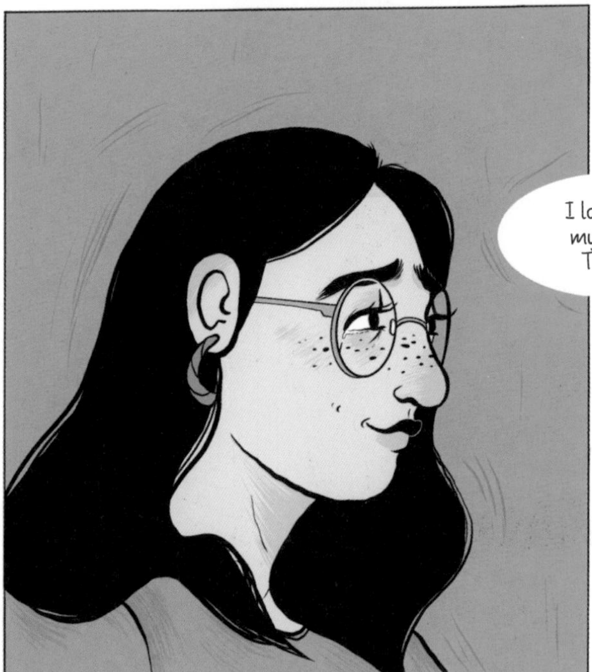

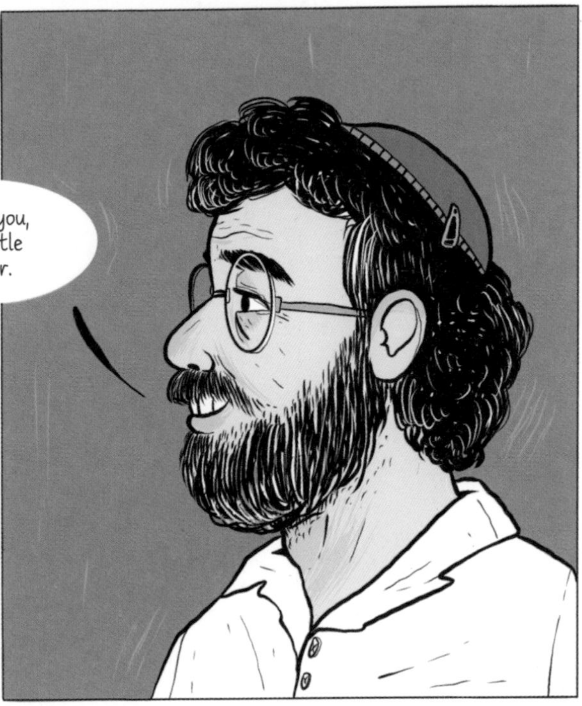
I love you, my little Tohar.

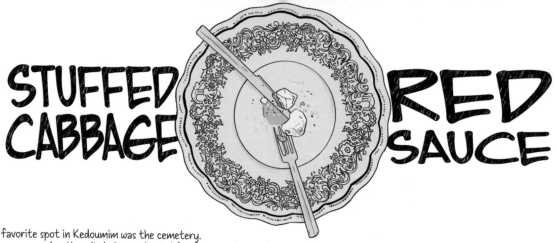

STUFFED CABBAGE RED SAUCE

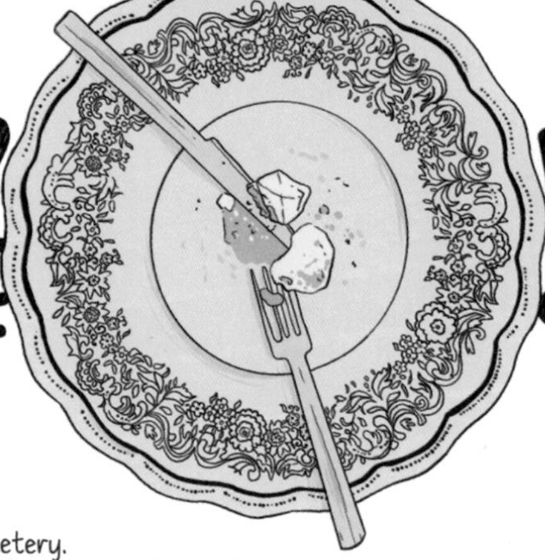

My favorite spot in Kedoumim was the cemetery.
When my grandmother died, she was buried far from our home. So whenever I wanted to speak to her, the only thing I could do was meditate in our cemetery, even if her grave wasn't there.

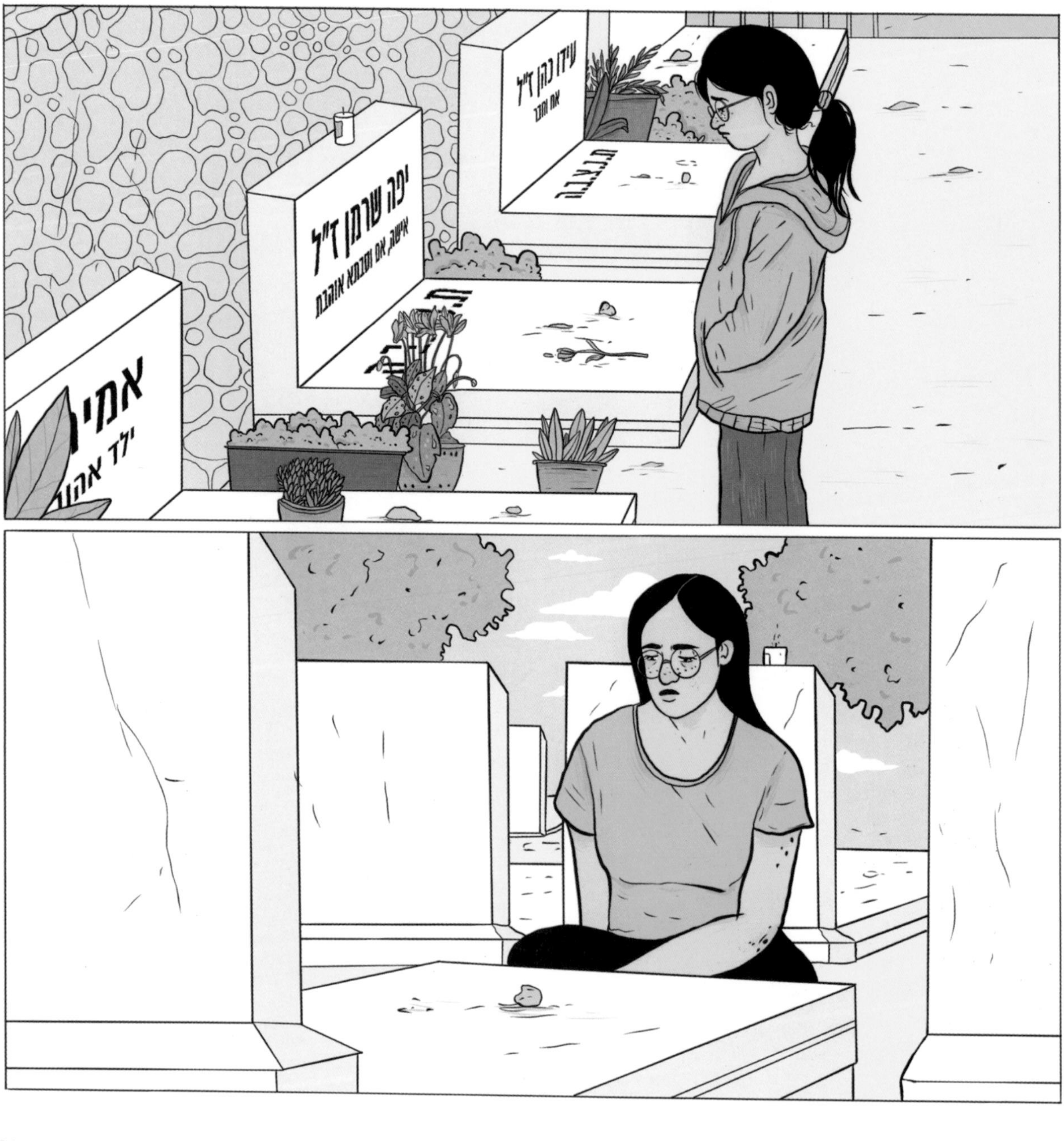

עידו כהן ז"ל
יפה שרמן ז"ל
אישה, אם וסבתא אוהבת

As I grew up, my memories of her gradually faded. First her voice, then her laugh and our conversations.

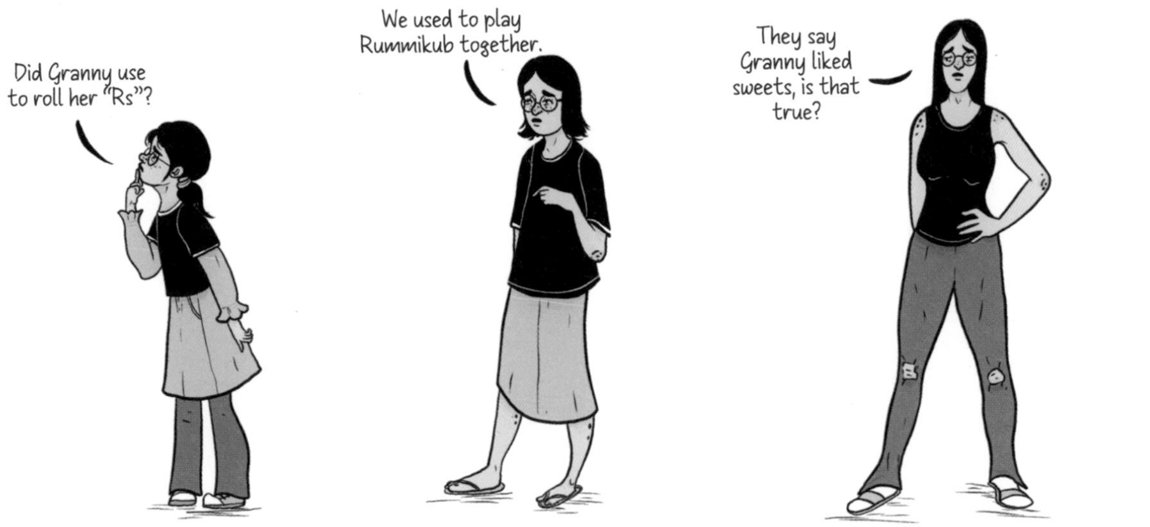
Did Granny use to roll her "Rs"?
We used to play Rummikub together.
They say Granny liked sweets, is that true?

Piece by piece, like a jigsaw puzzle in reverse, other details disappeared, and only her recipes stayed with me.

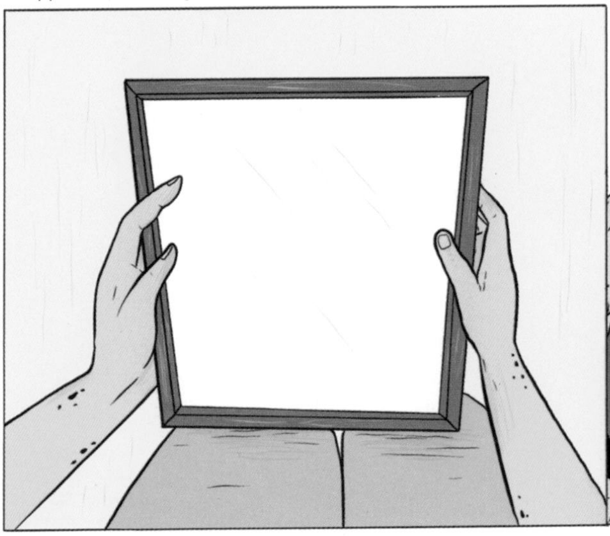

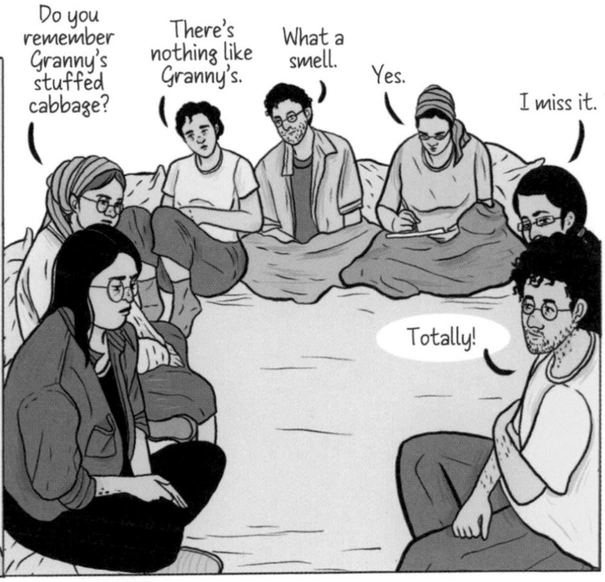
Do you remember Granny's stuffed cabbage?
There's nothing like Granny's.
What a smell.
Yes.
I miss it.
Totally!

One day, I decided to make her stuffed cabbage. I followed her recipe to the letter.

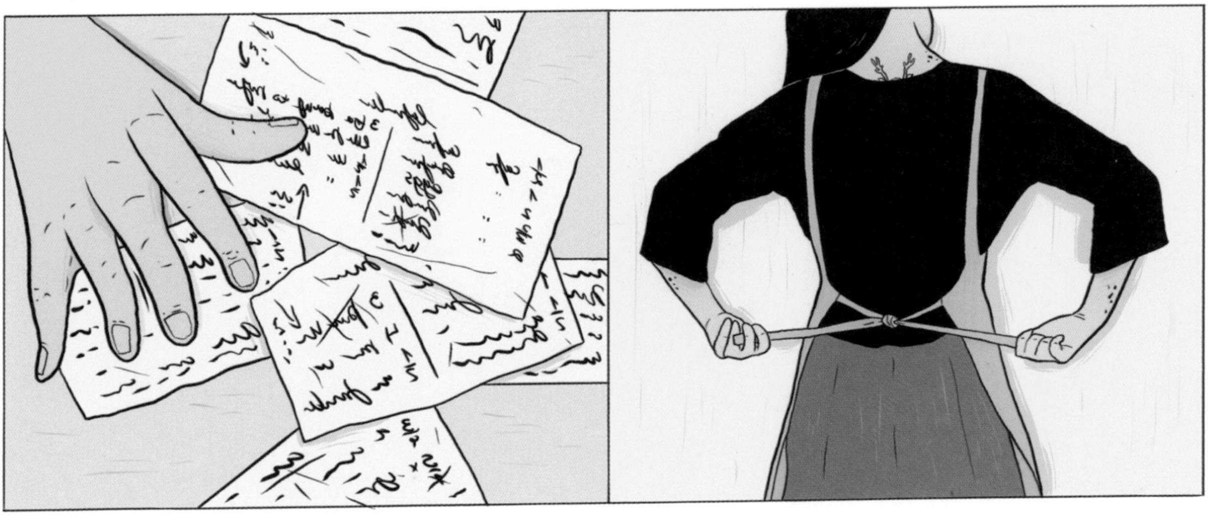

I carefully unrolled the cabbage leaves, put the stuffing in, and folded up the stuffed leaves before putting the pot on the stove.

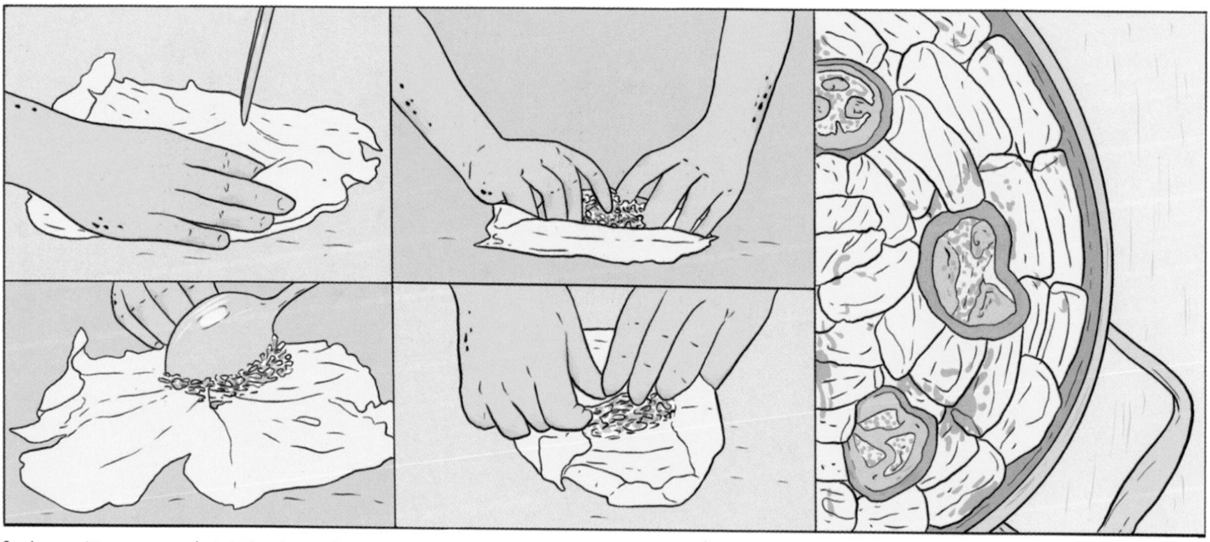

Such emotion on my plate! The taste, her taste, was going to be a dive into memories. I so wanted to remember her.

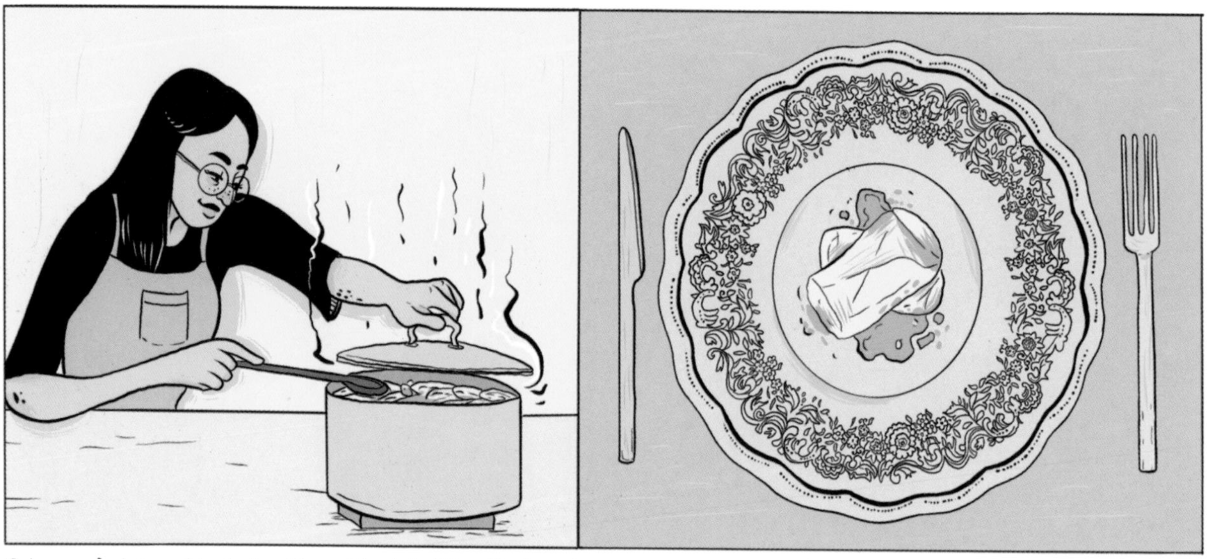

I dug my fork in and tasted ... It was bland. And I suddenly understood that she was so far away from me.
I ate, and I cried. I especially cried for myself. She had had a whole life, and I only remembered crumbs of it.

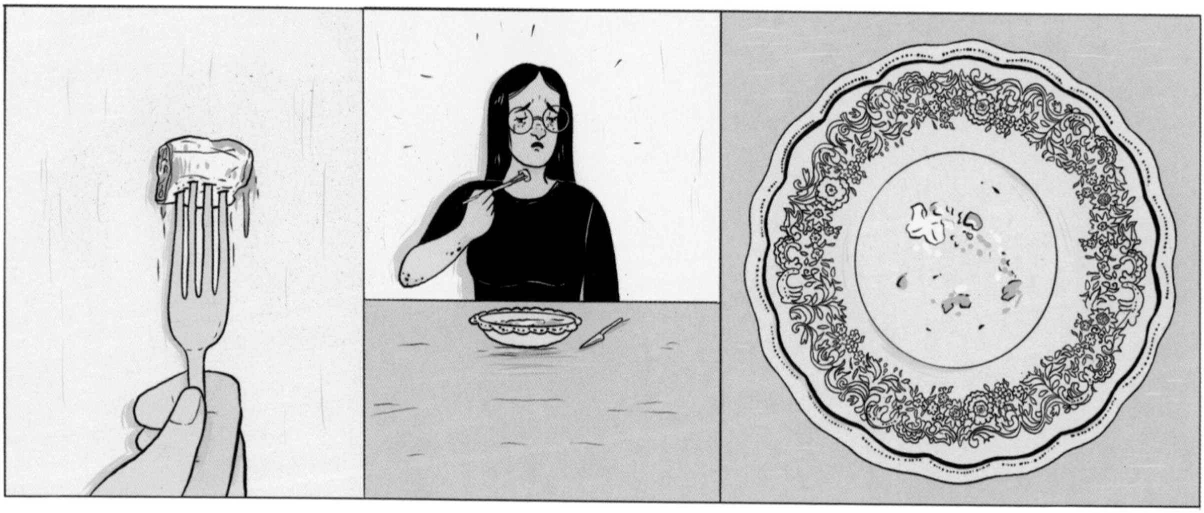

I went out, down the path toward the hitchhiking stop, and past the pizza stand. Every step made me feel a little better.

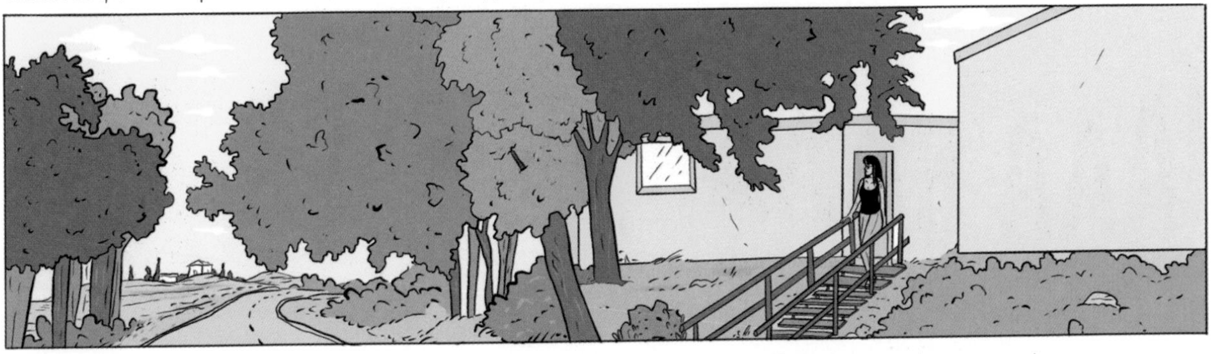

I went to the woods at the edge of the village. Between the trees, the setting sun was fading away, and so were my tears.

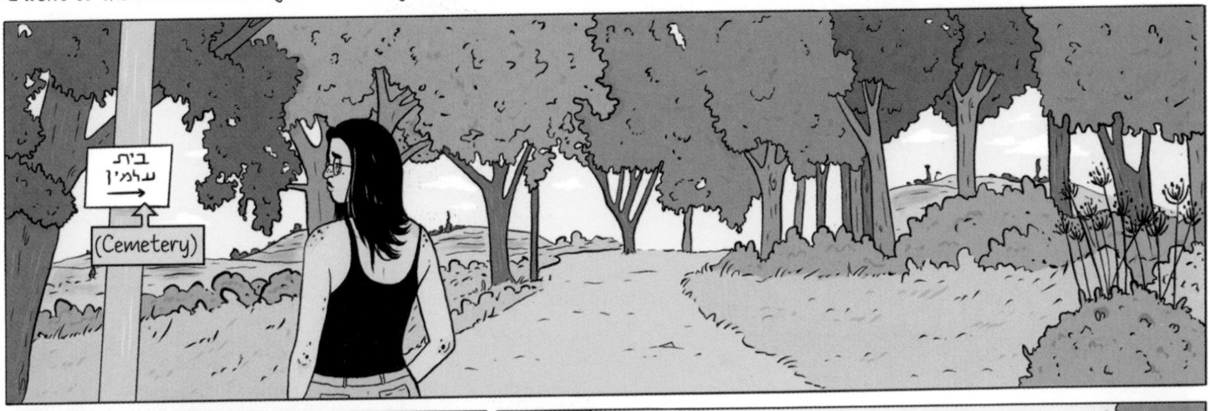

בית
עלמין
(Cemetery)

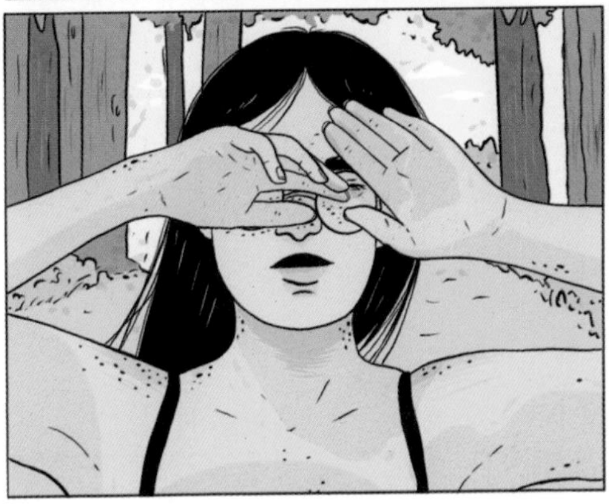

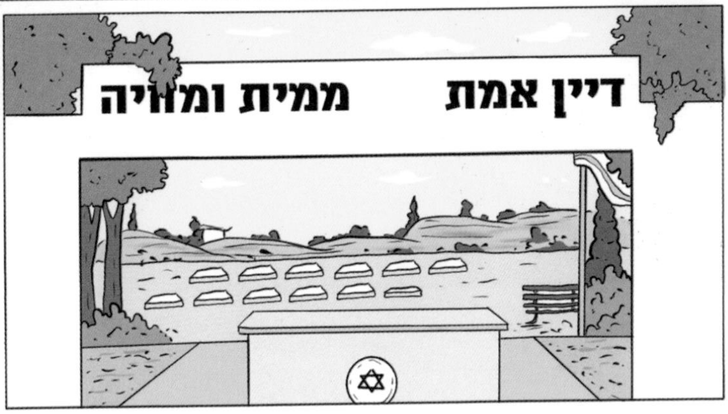

דיין אמת
ממית ומחיה

When I got to Kedoumim cemetery, I sat down on a white stone, and I began to talk.
I told her about my cabbage fail, and how much I loved ketchup, or "catchoop," as she used to call it.

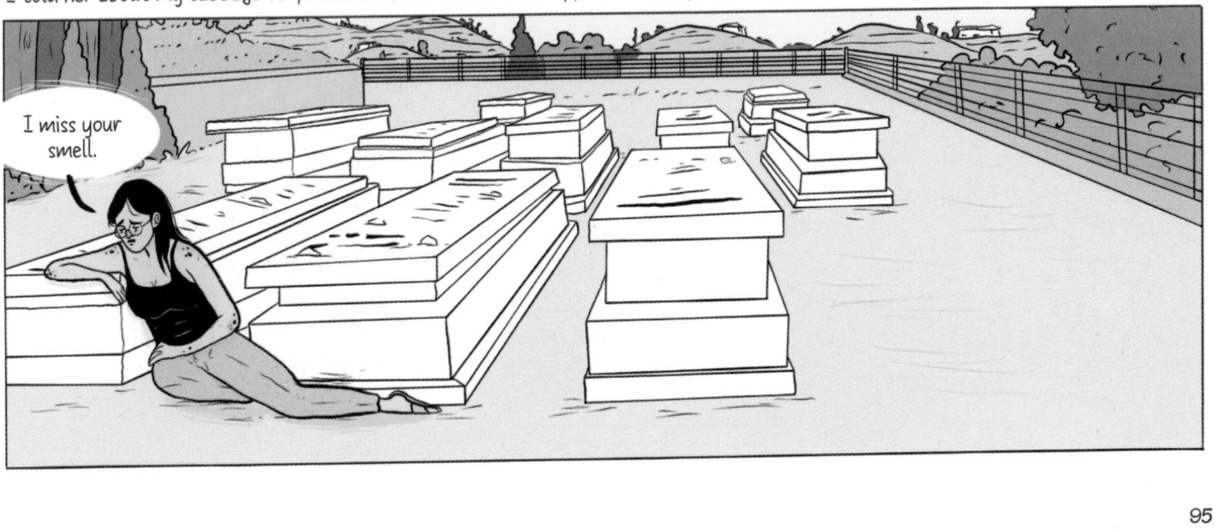

I miss your smell.

At that very moment, I could have sworn I heard her laugh, a wavering burst of laughter, a bit hoarse and so comforting.

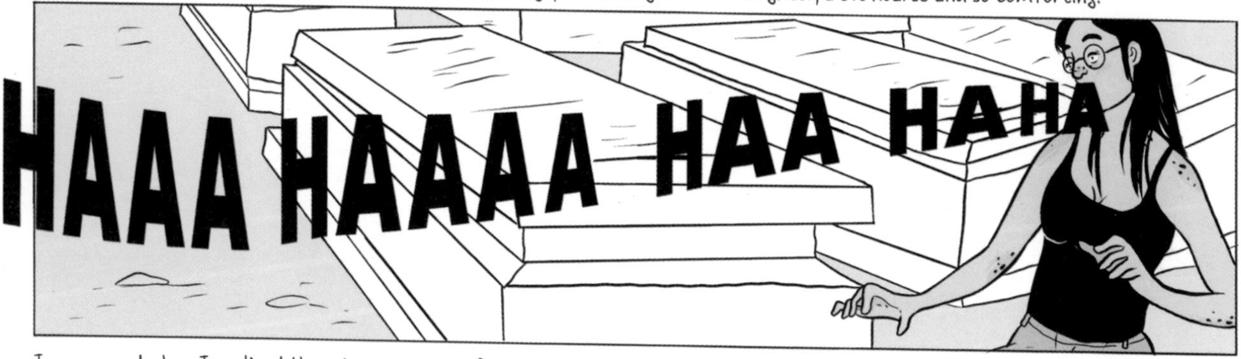
HAAA HAAAA HAA HAHA

I was scared when I realized the voice was coming from me, like a reflex my body had imposed on me, the body that knew that she was inside me. I tried to laugh again, a desperate attempt to reach the part of me that remembered, but the new laugh that came out was completely different, and the disappointment set off tears that flowed all the way down to my mouth. The salty taste and the fake laughs reminded me that I'd never really properly separated from her.

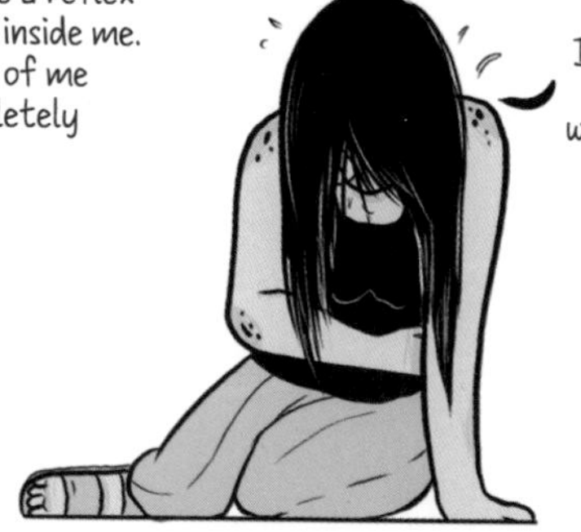

I'm sorry that I never learned to know you, sorry to end up without thousands of memories of you, and not to have been able to show you what I've become.

The next day I set off with a pot of stuffed cabbage, to visit my grandmother's real grave.

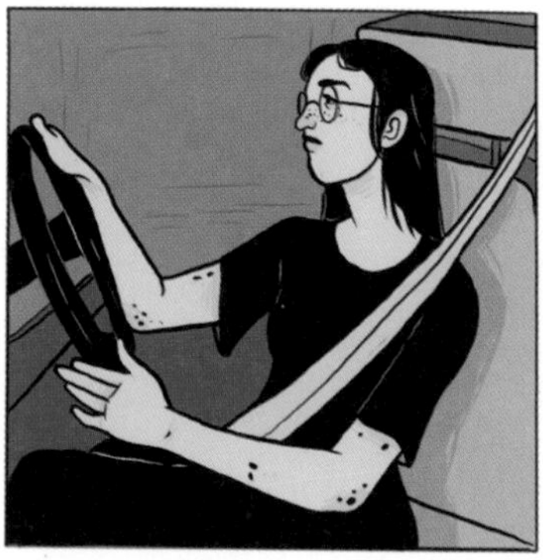

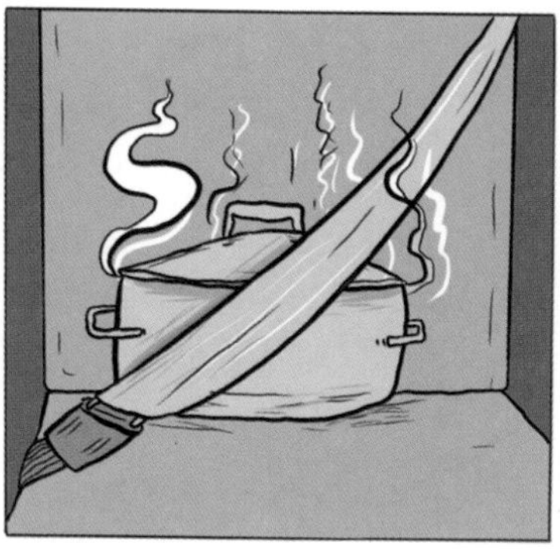

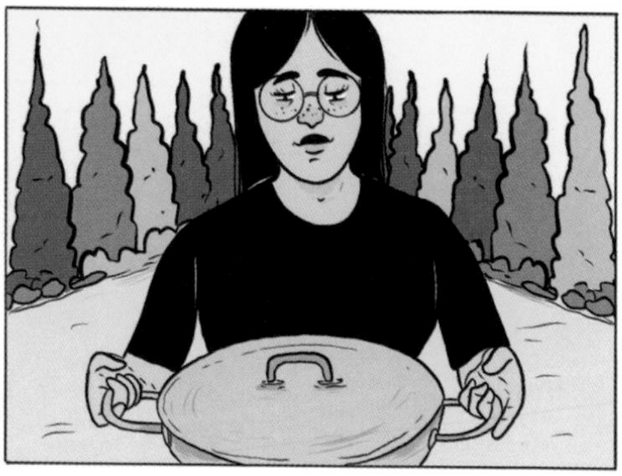

It was a long time since I'd been there, and being near her grave gave me some comfort. I ran my fingers over the words on her tombstone and decided never to make stuffed cabbage in red sauce ever again.

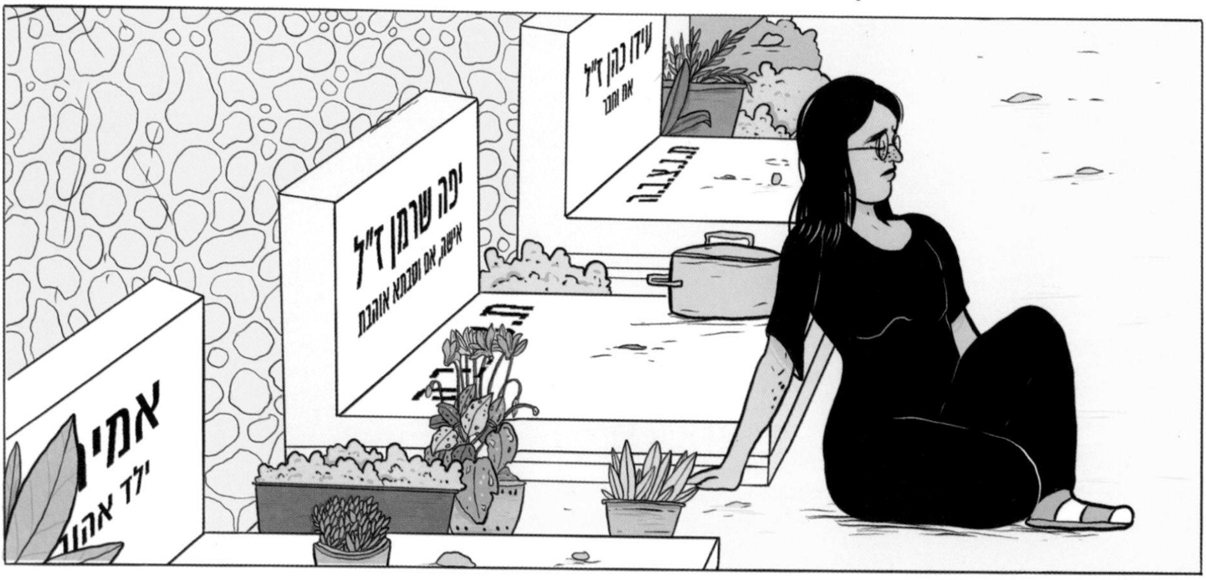
עידו כהן ז"ל
יפה שרמן ז"ל
אישה, אם וסבתא אוהבת

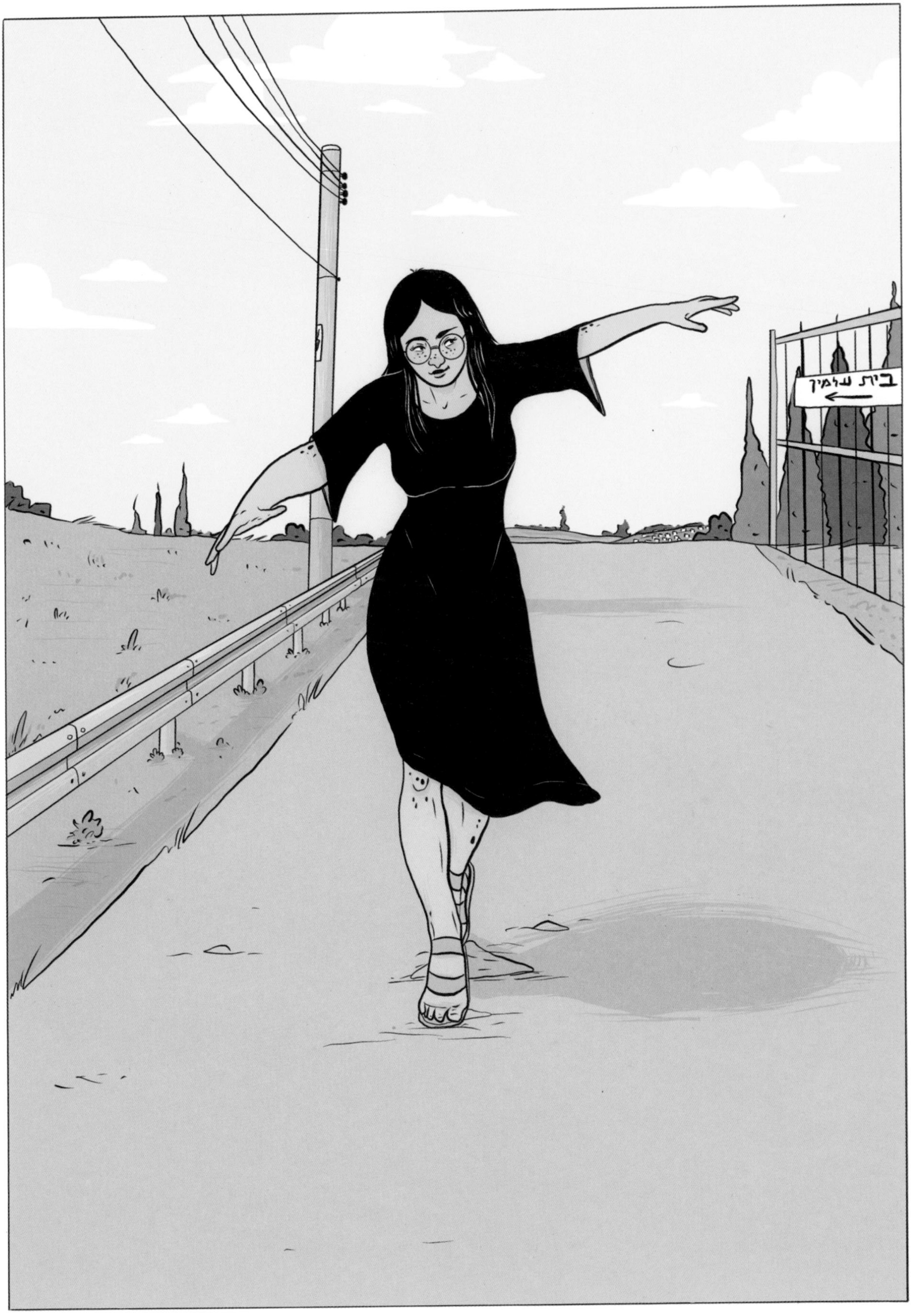
בית עלמין

LOSING CONTROL

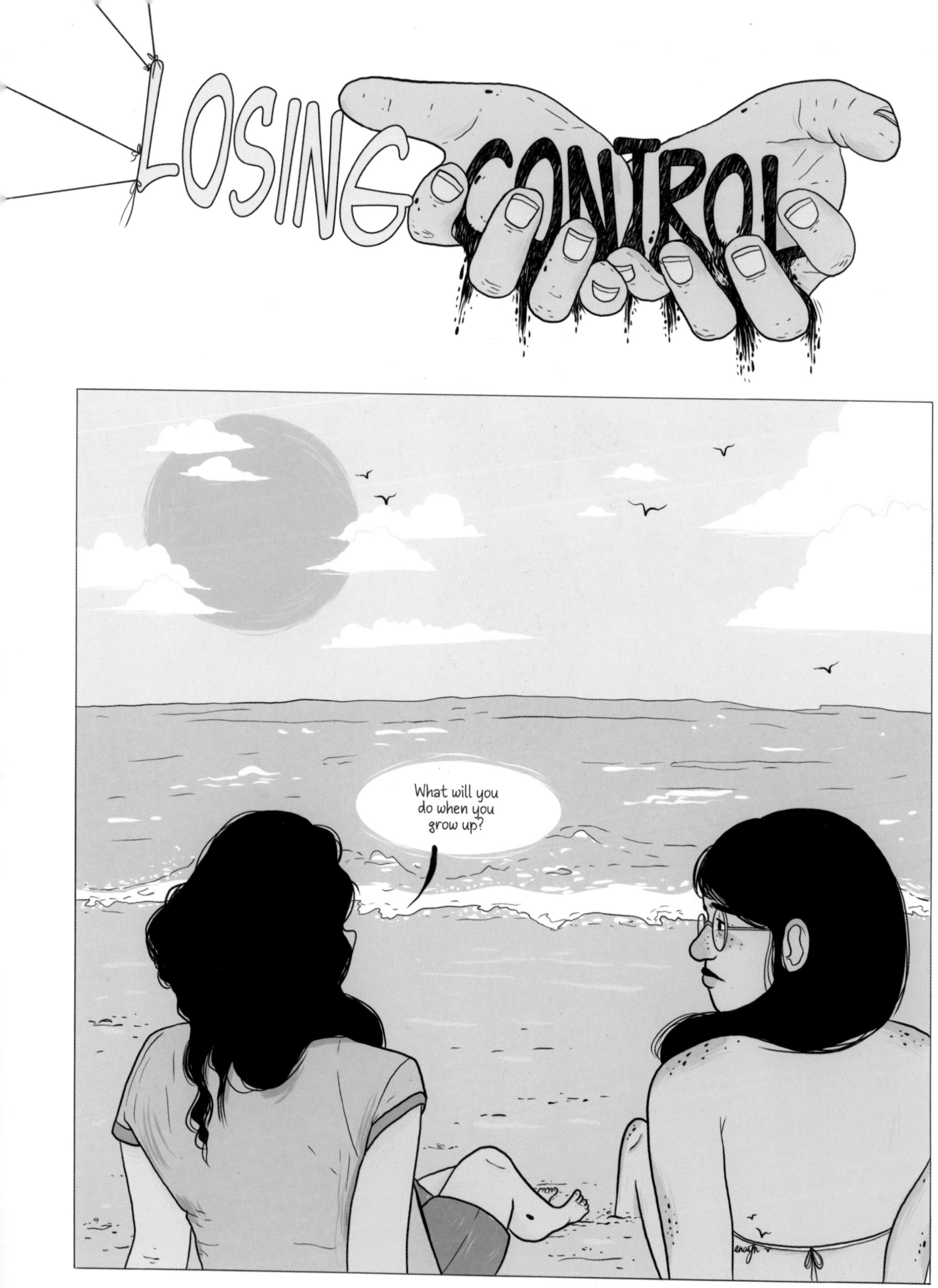
What will you do when you grow up?

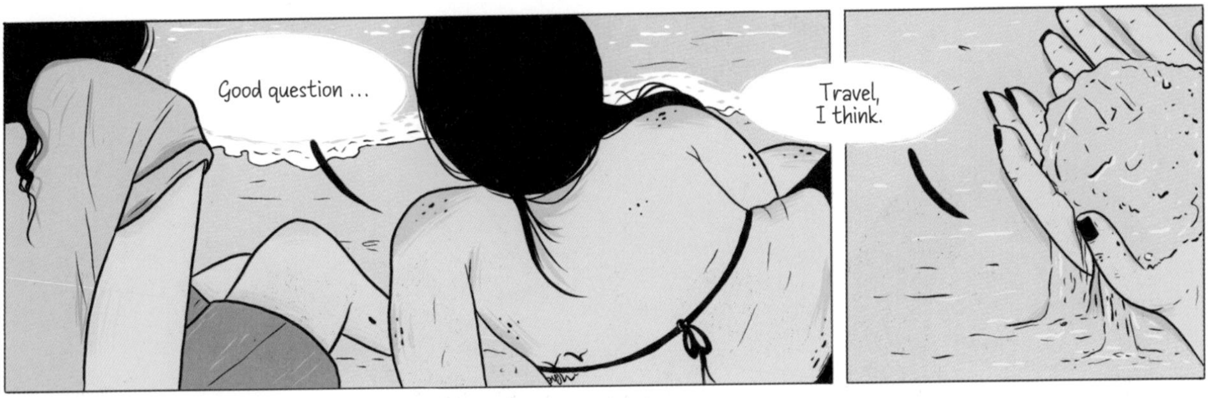
Good question ...
Travel, I think.

The sun was blinding me, and I lay down on my front. She burst out laughing. I looked at her teeth as she laughed, a row of tidy little white squares.

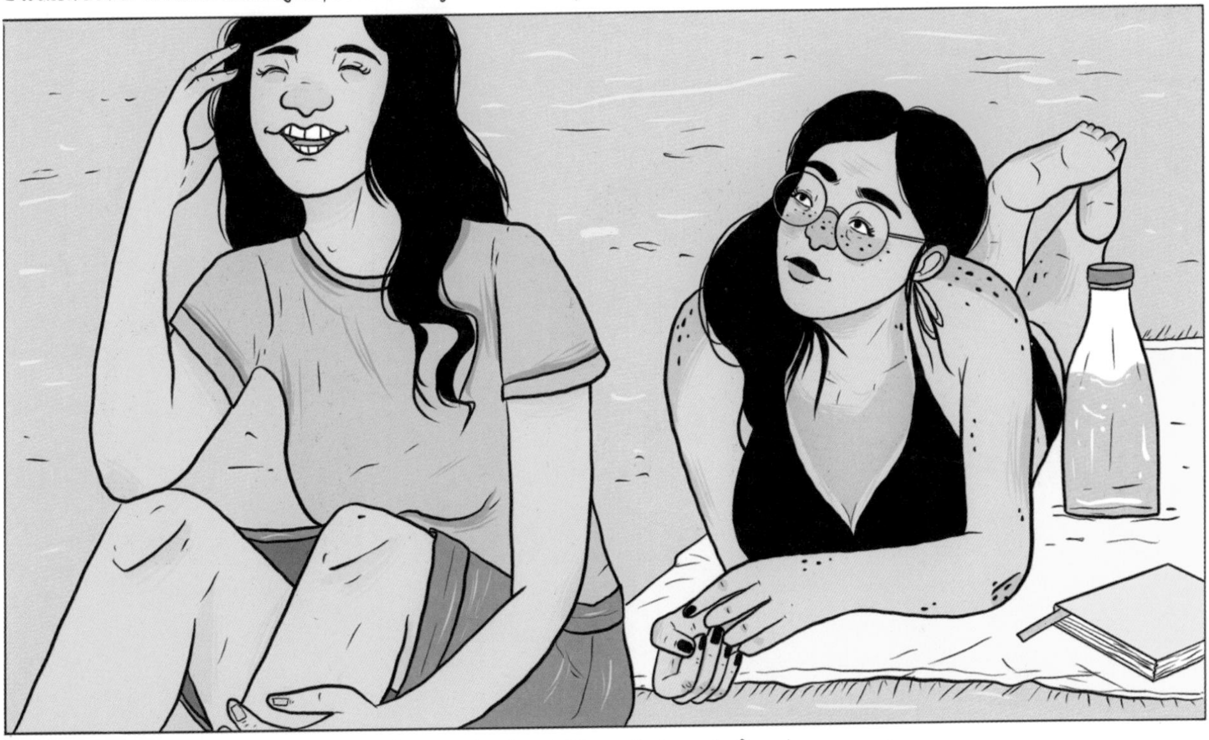

Since I was really young, my teeth were really spaced out, and I knew that most of my teenage years were going to be accompanied by those awful hooks on my teeth. Over time, I learned to live with them.

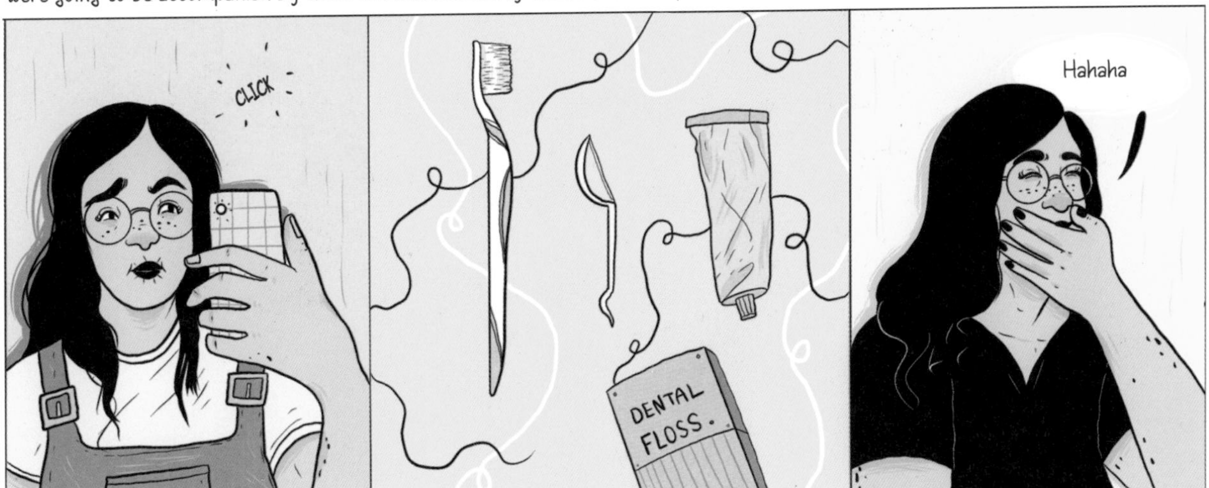
CLICK
DENTAL FLOSS.
Hahaha

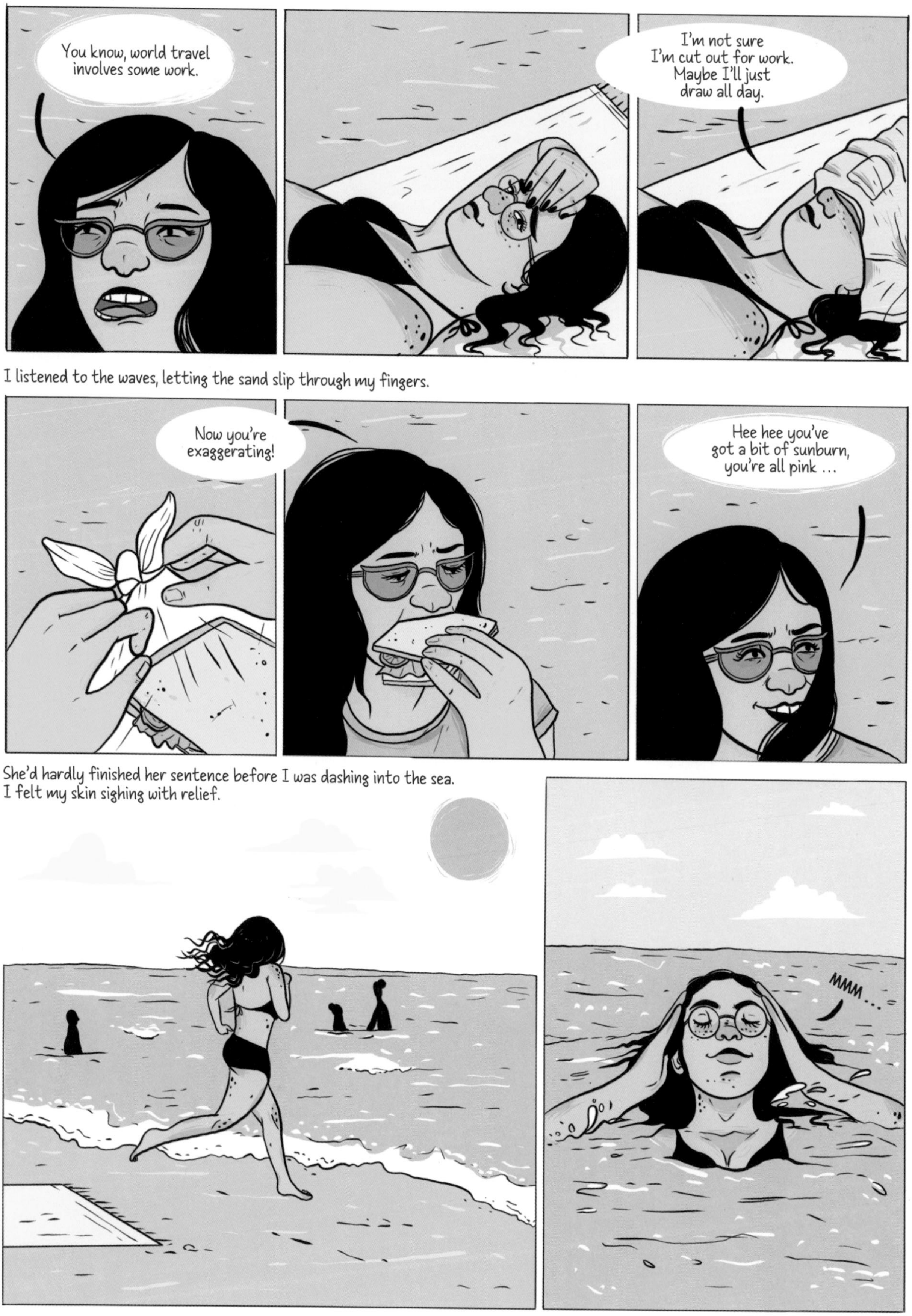
You know, world travel involves some work.
I'm not sure I'm cut out for work. Maybe I'll just draw all day.
I listened to the waves, letting the sand slip through my fingers.
Now you're exaggerating!
Hee hee you've got a bit of sunburn, you're all pink …
She'd hardly finished her sentence before I was dashing into the sea.
I felt my skin sighing with relief.
MMM…

On the way back I examined my face in the rearview mirror. Dozens of new freckles had appeared. My mother would say that freckles are like kisses from the sun. It was a nice way of saying that they weren't a skin rash.

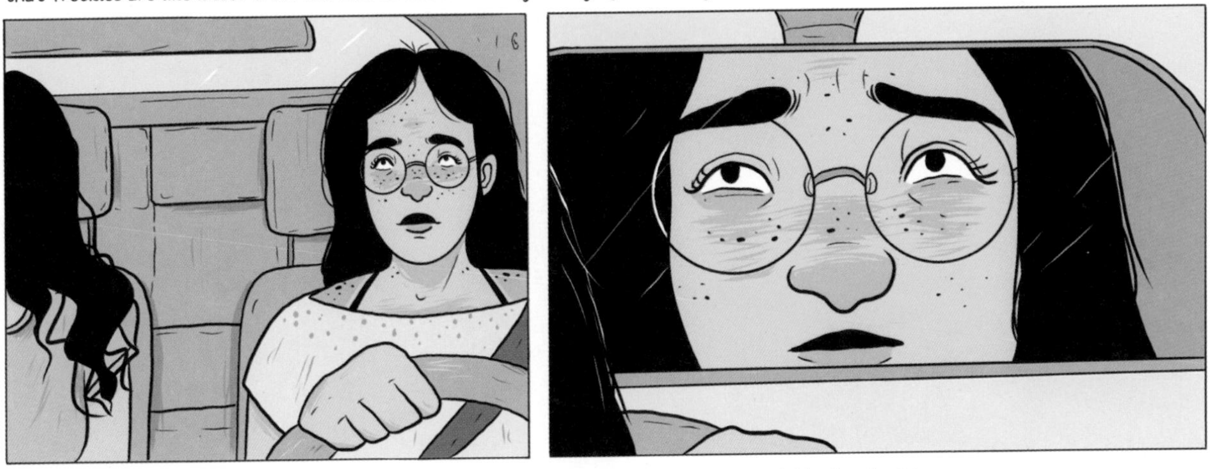

My mother was diagnosed with Parkinson's. The first sign was a tremor in her right hand. Her handwriting had started to change, and when I looked at her carefully I got the impression she couldn't control her hand.

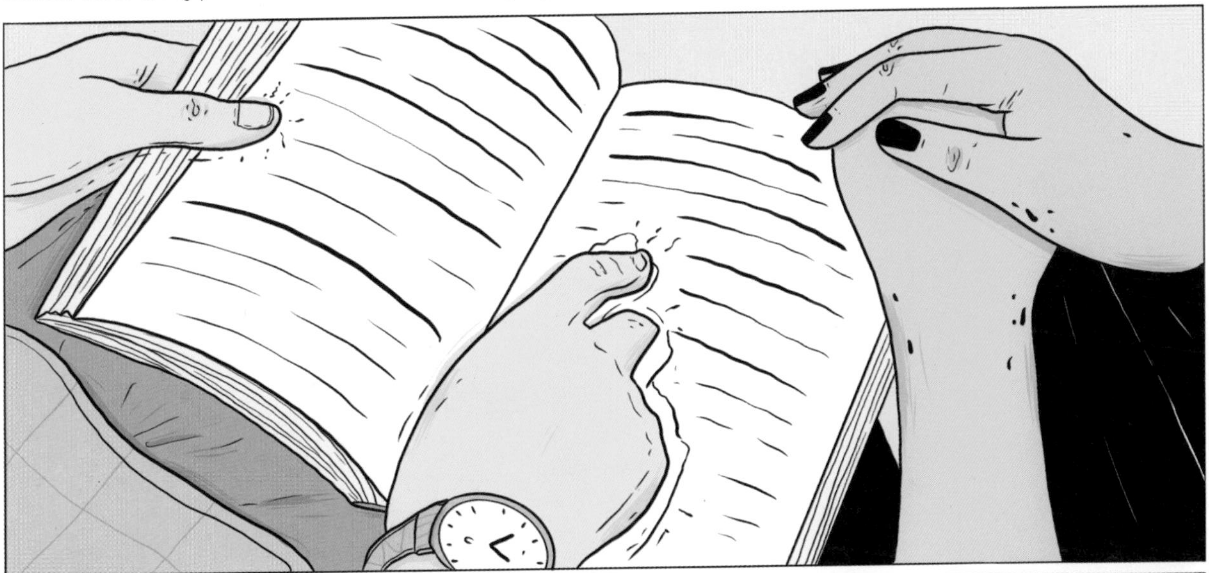

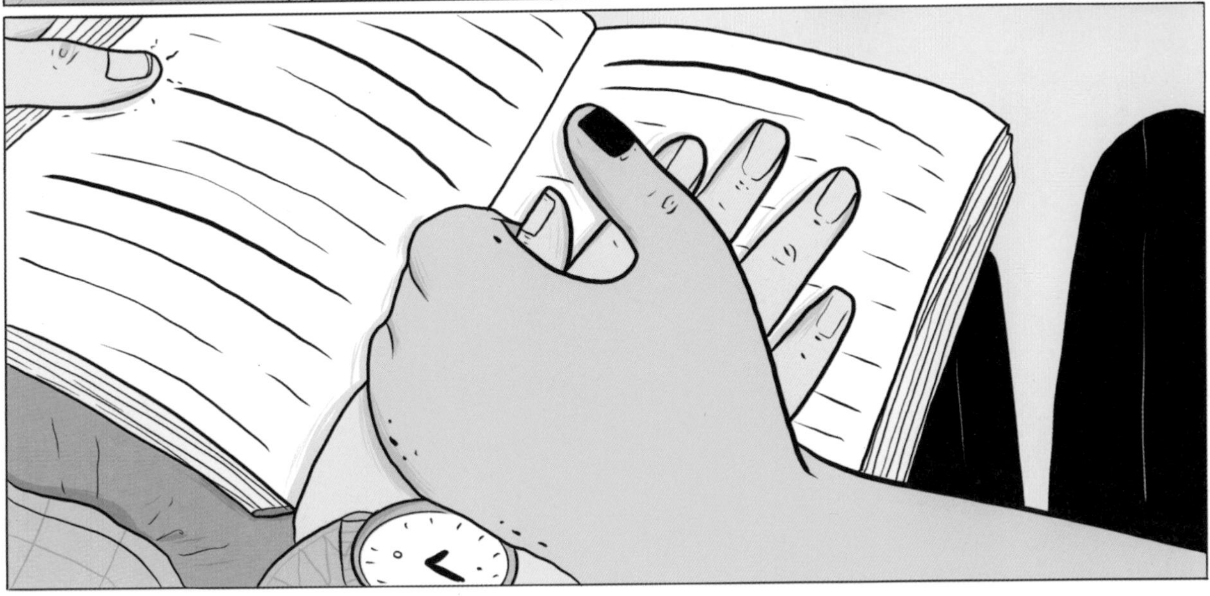

I remembered that conversation on the beach, and I looked at my hands. I felt a sudden wave of anxiety. What would they become? I realized how much they were a part of me, of my identity.

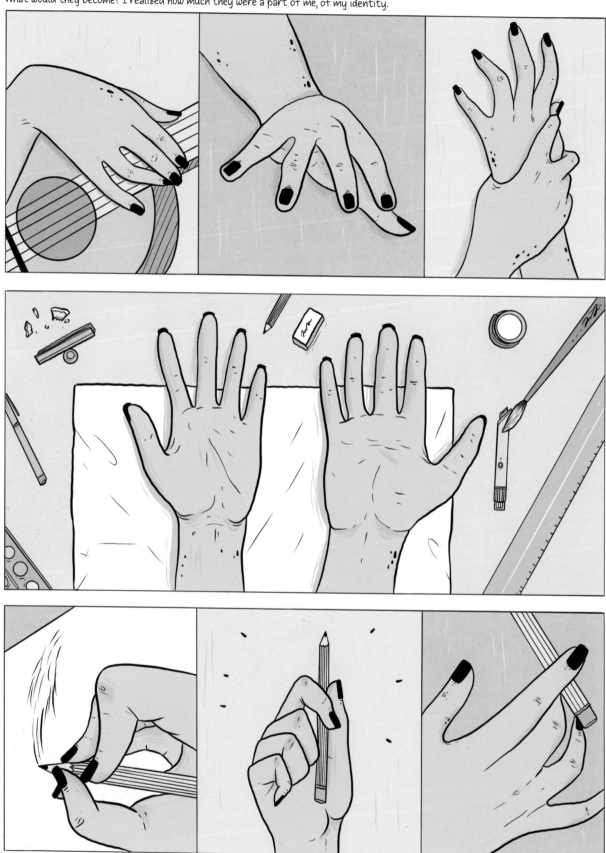

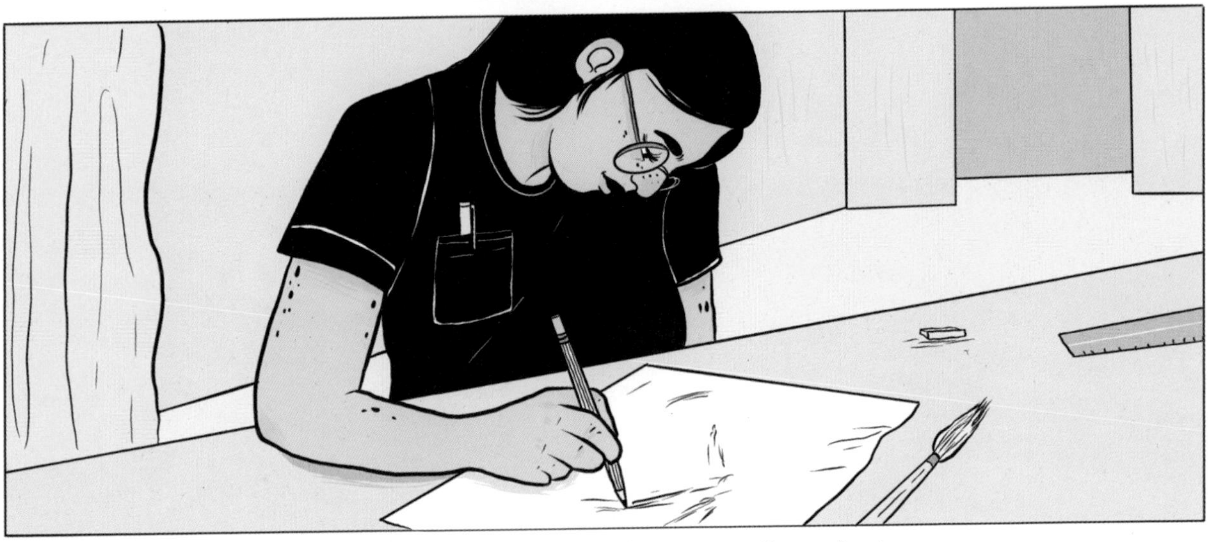

When I began to draw that evening, with every stroke of the pencil I felt the strength in my hand.
I looked at the drawing I was working on. I looked at myself, creating, and I knew.
I knew what I wanted to do when I grew up. I only had to hope my body would let me.

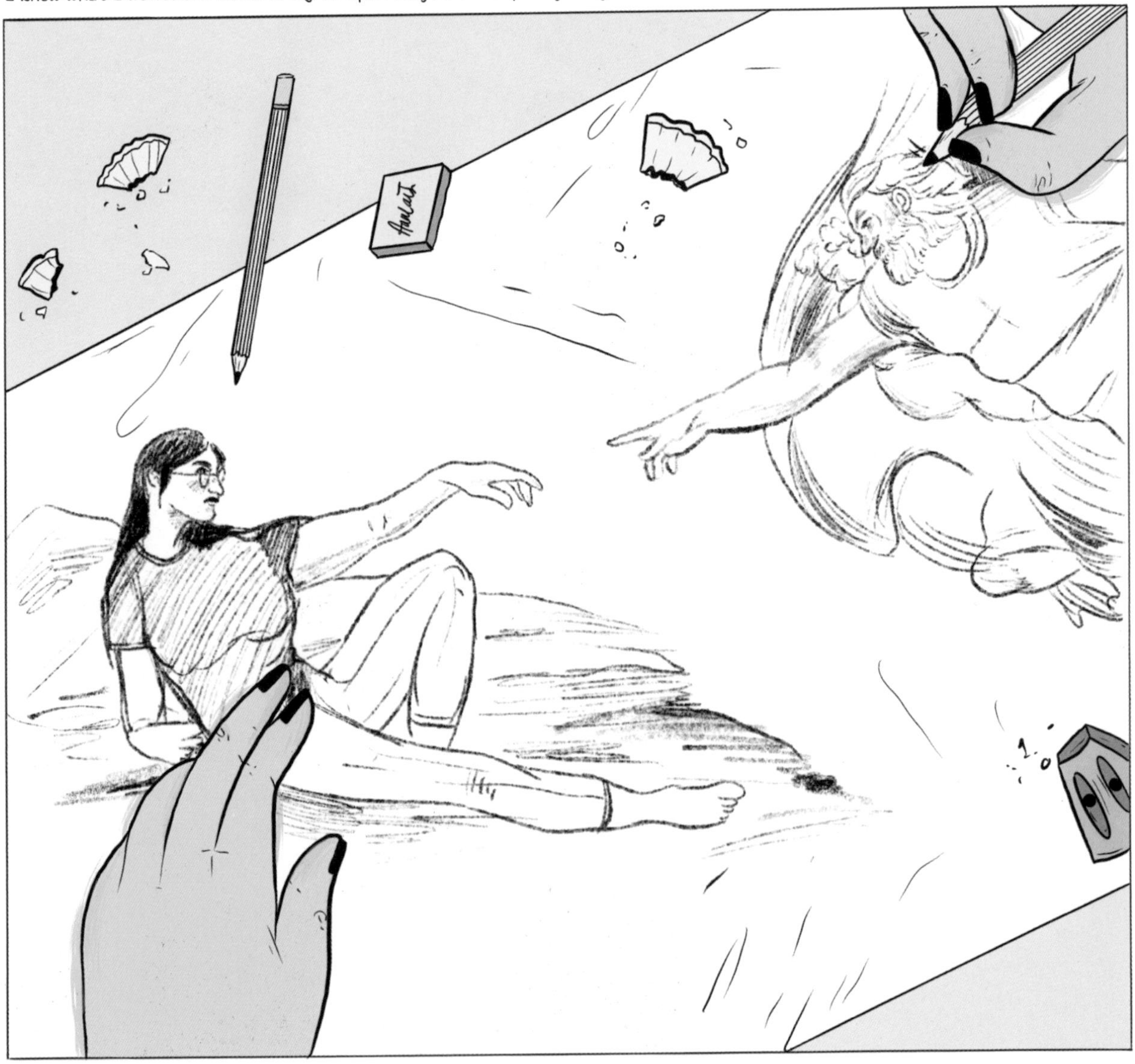

DOUBTS

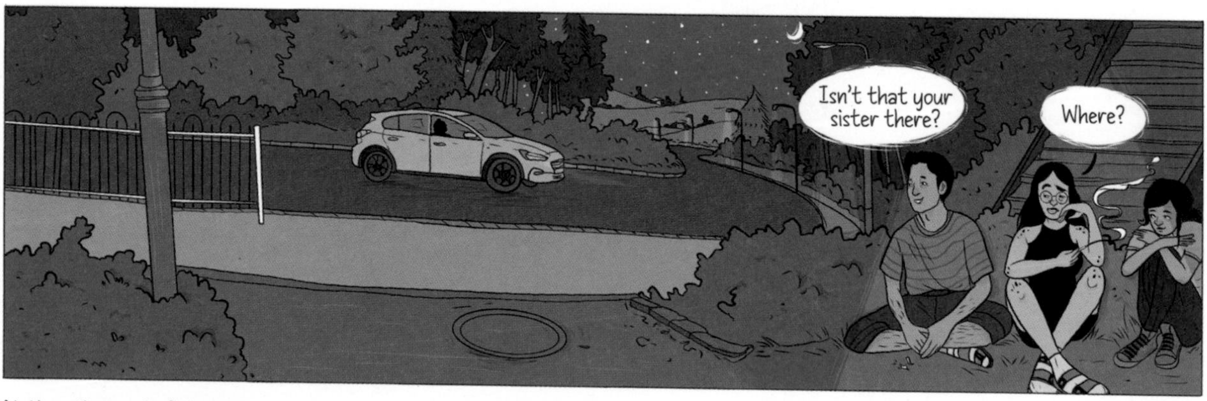
Isn't that your sister there?
Where?

At the other end of the park, I saw my mother's car but didn't recognize who was at the wheel. Squinting a bit I recognized Tiferett and waved at her.

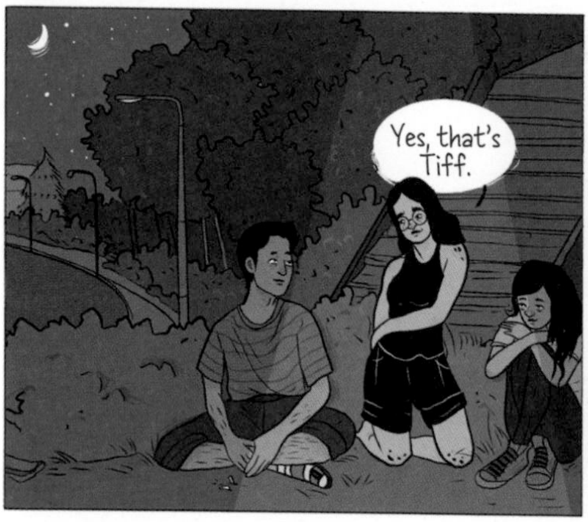
Yes, that's Tiff.

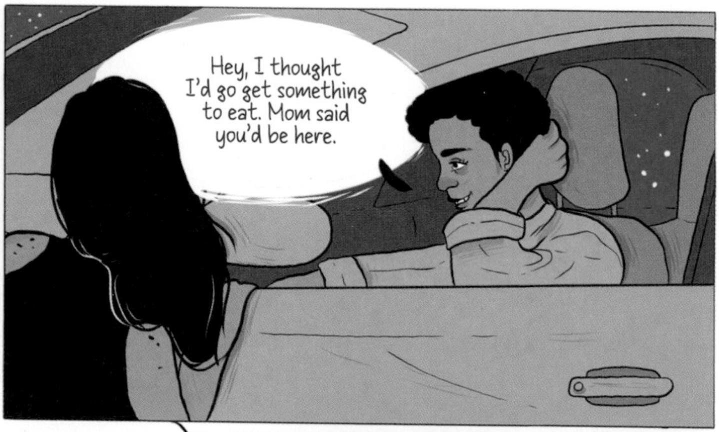
Hey, I thought I'd go get something to eat. Mom said you'd be here.

I heard my stomach rumbling. One of the things I liked doing since I'd been hanging around in Tel Aviv was getting takeout. In Kedoumim there was only pizza. Any other snack cravings had to be quashed in short order because no one wanted to deliver to the settlements.

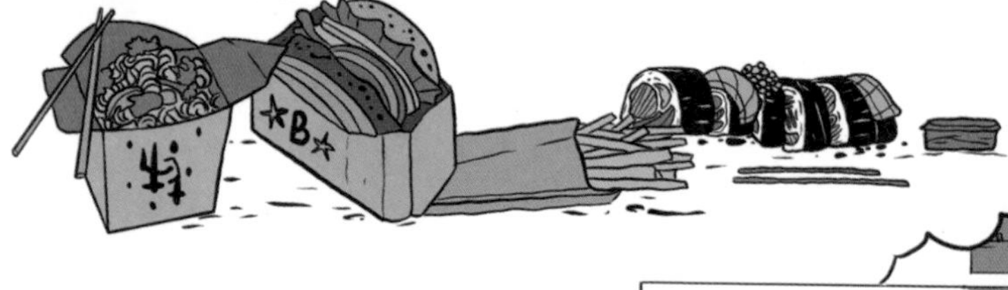

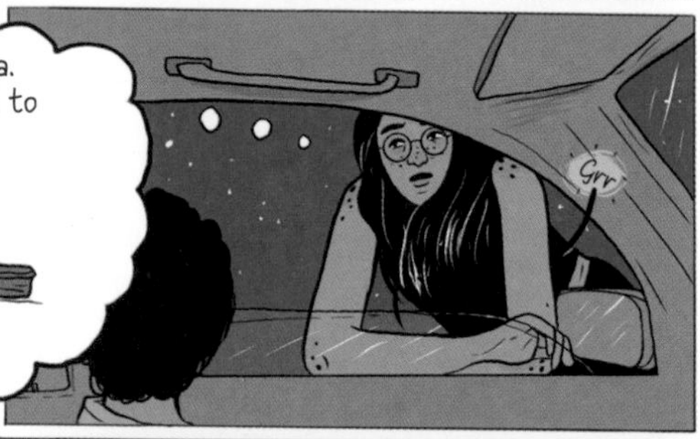
Grr

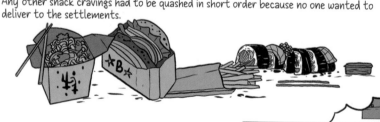

Lately I'd been spending most of my time with Daniel, and my childhood friends had been feeling a bit hurt …
For once we were all together, and I didn't really want to drop them and head off.

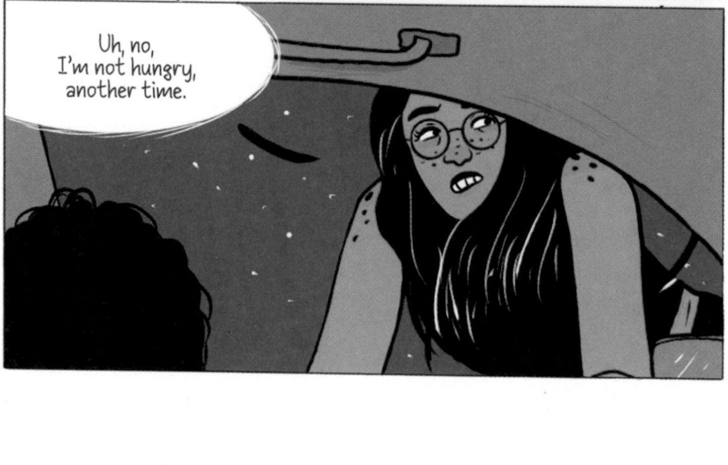
Uh, no, I'm not hungry, another time.

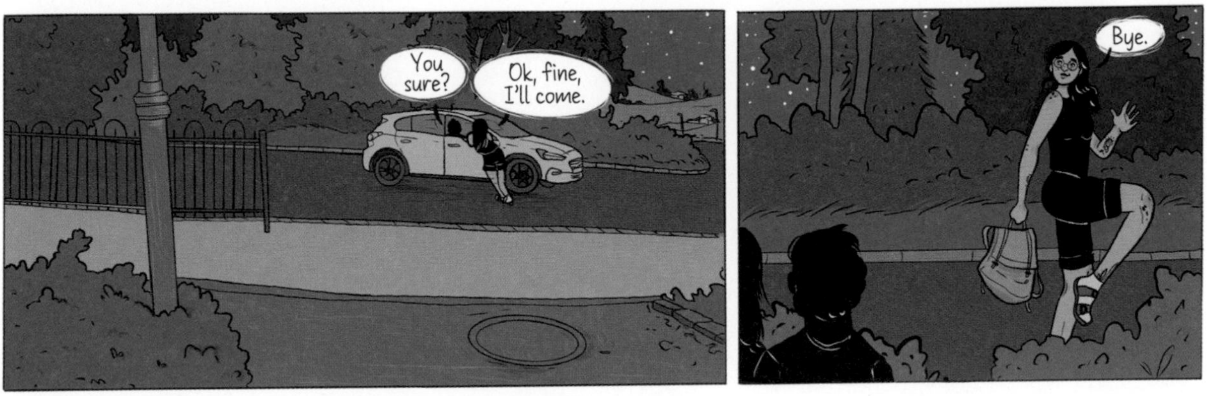
You sure?
Ok, fine, I'll come.
Bye.

After I'd said goodbye, I got in the car and put my seat belt on.
It had been a long time since the two of us had gotten together.
I felt her emotion, but I also felt bad for missing the date with my friends.

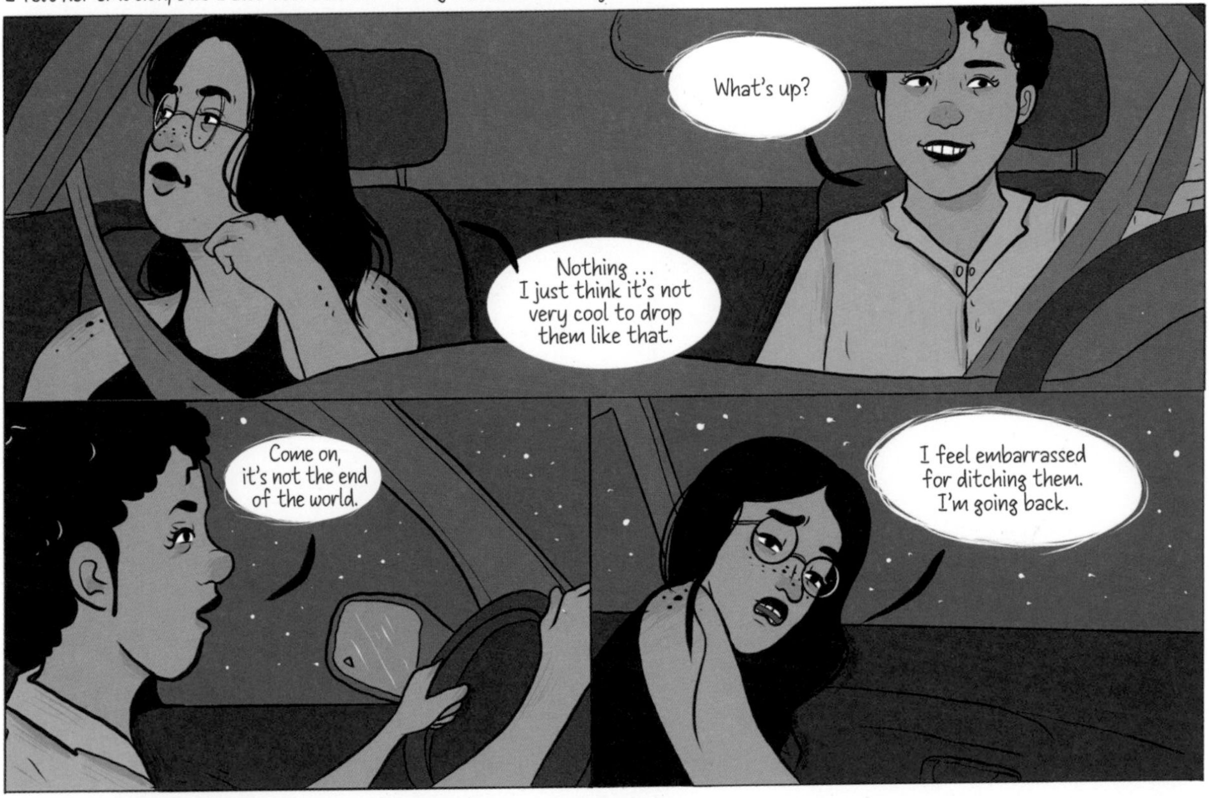
What's up?
Nothing ... I just think it's not very cool to drop them like that.
Come on, it's not the end of the world.
I feel embarrassed for ditching them. I'm going back.

She gave me a disappointed look, and I got out of the car.
I was sure she wouldn't talk to me for days. As I walked back to see my friends,
I reassured myself that at least she'd be eating something nice tonight.

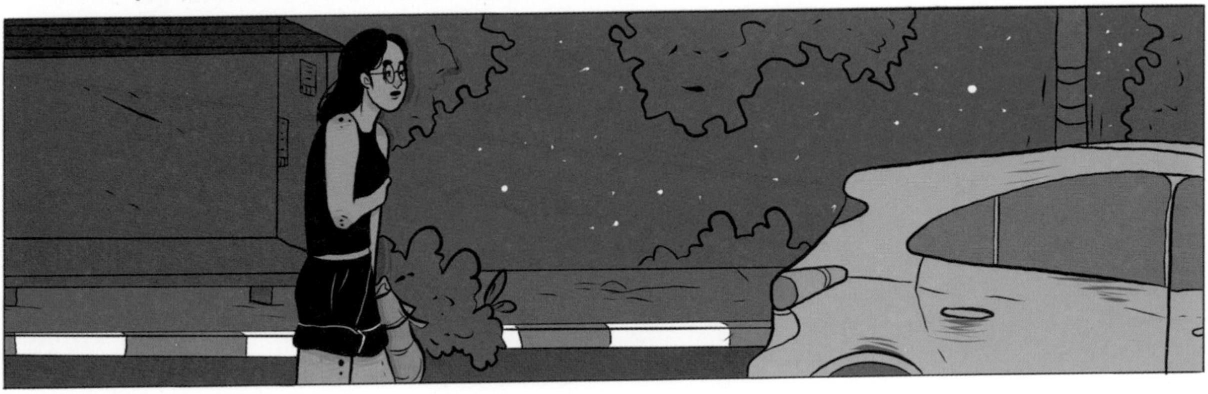

At about 2 a.m. I tiptoed into the house so as not to wake anyone.

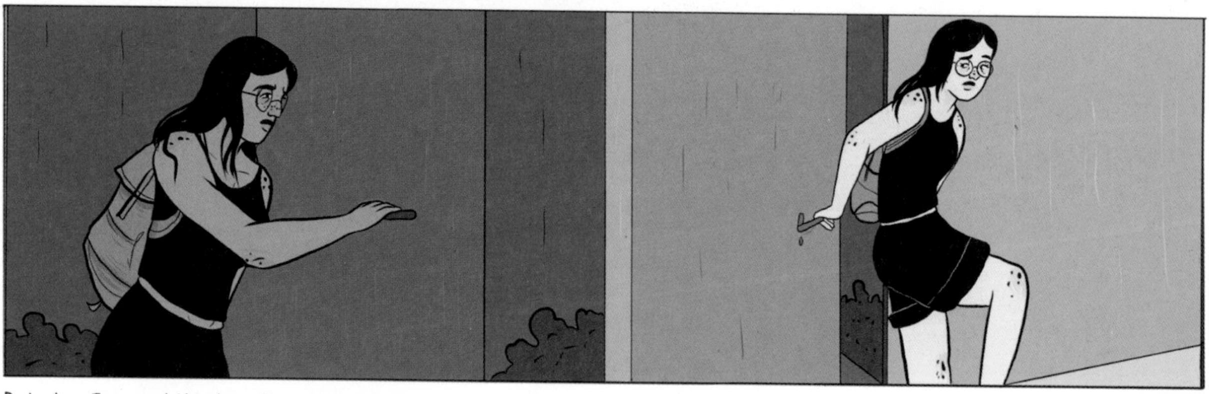

But when I opened the door, I was surprised to see my parents and Tiferett in the sitting room.

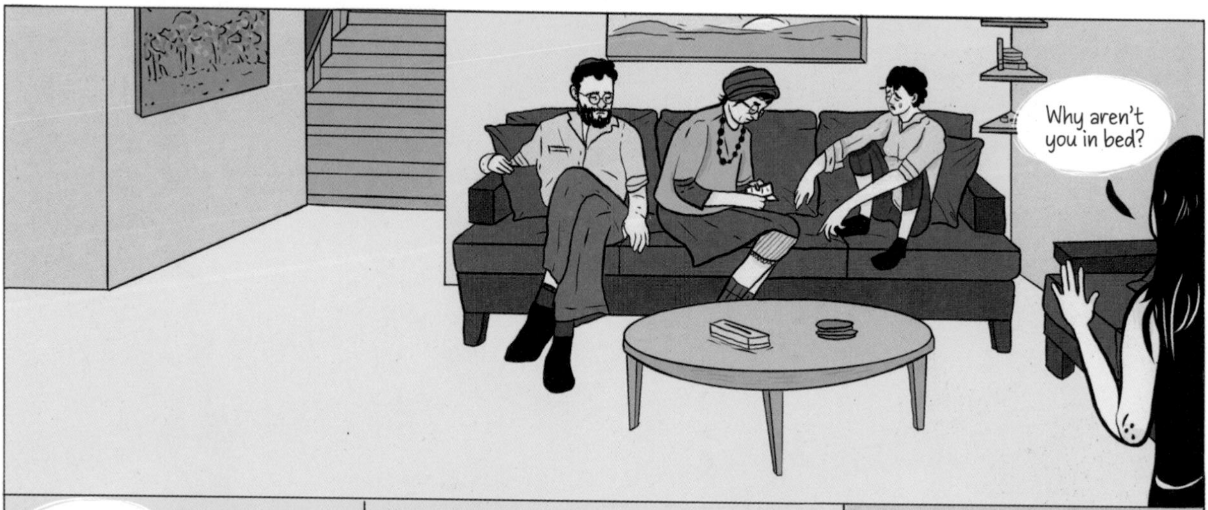
Why aren't you in bed?

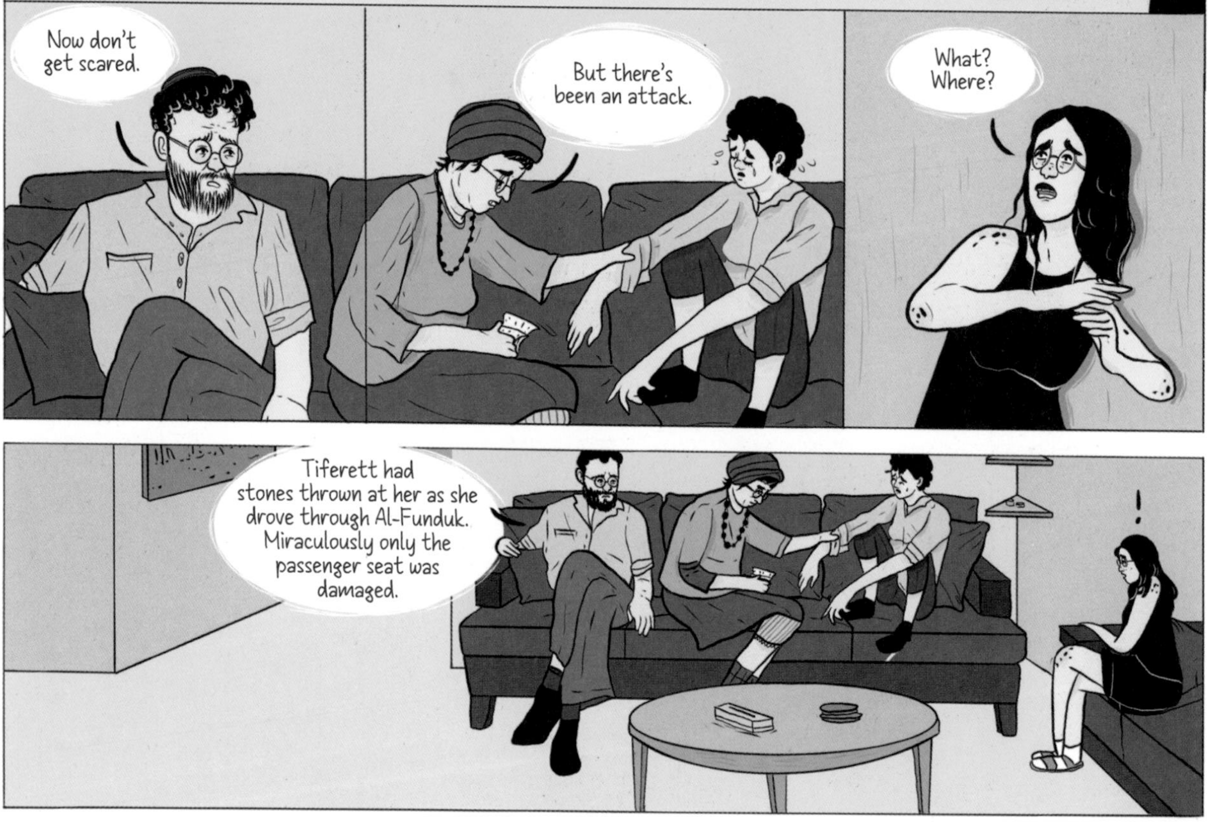
Now don't get scared.
But there's been an attack.
What? Where?
Tiferett had stones thrown at her as she drove through Al-Funduk. Miraculously only the passenger seat was damaged.
!

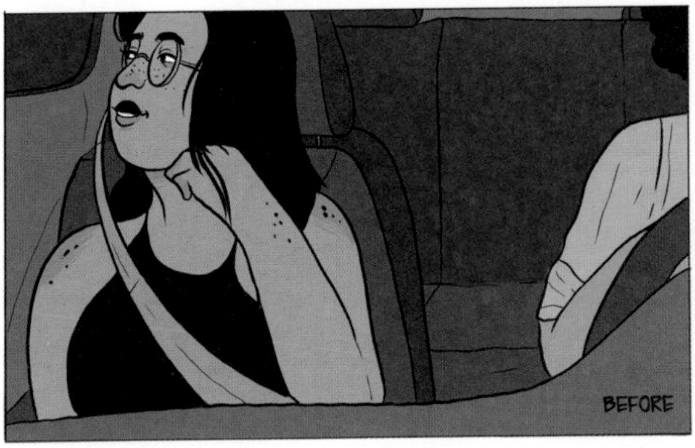
BEFORE

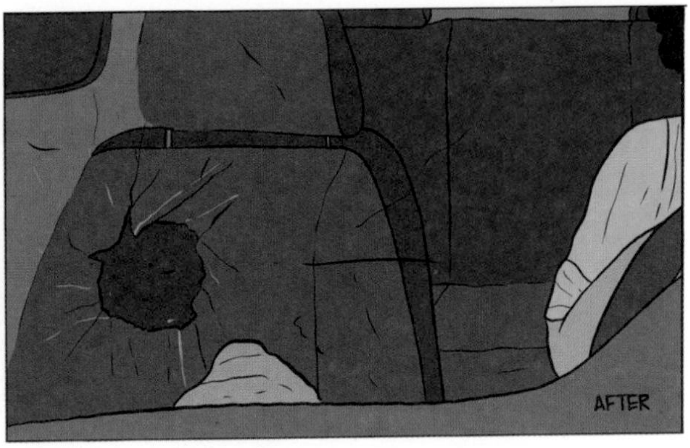
AFTER

I couldn't believe my ears. Just a few hours ago that had been *my* seat. For the next few days I kept on thanking heaven. The firm foundations of my new secular life were wobbling and everyone was talking about a miracle.

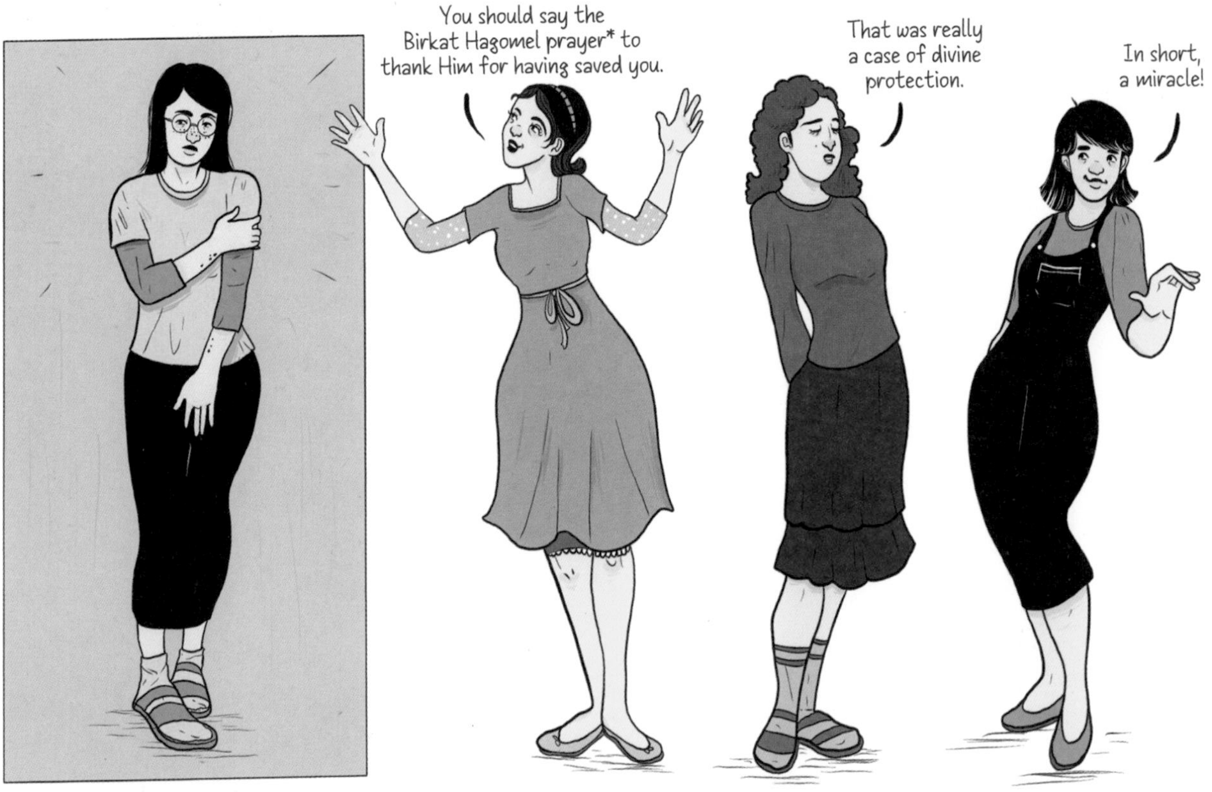
You should say the Birkat Hagomel prayer* to thank Him for having saved you.
That was really a case of divine protection.
In short, a miracle!

Blessing, fate, miracle, these were words I'd been very keen to erase from my mind and my heart. I felt ungrateful for the first time in my life. If there was a God, he was giving me a nod from up there: "I've shown her that I exist, and that it's only thanks to Me that she exists." The seeds of doubt were back.

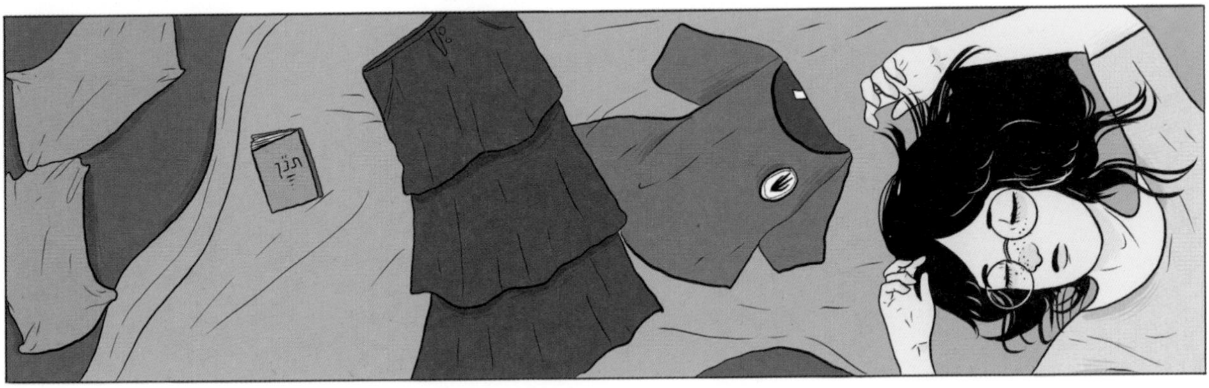

A little while afterward, lying down in my room, I heard the news on my phone.

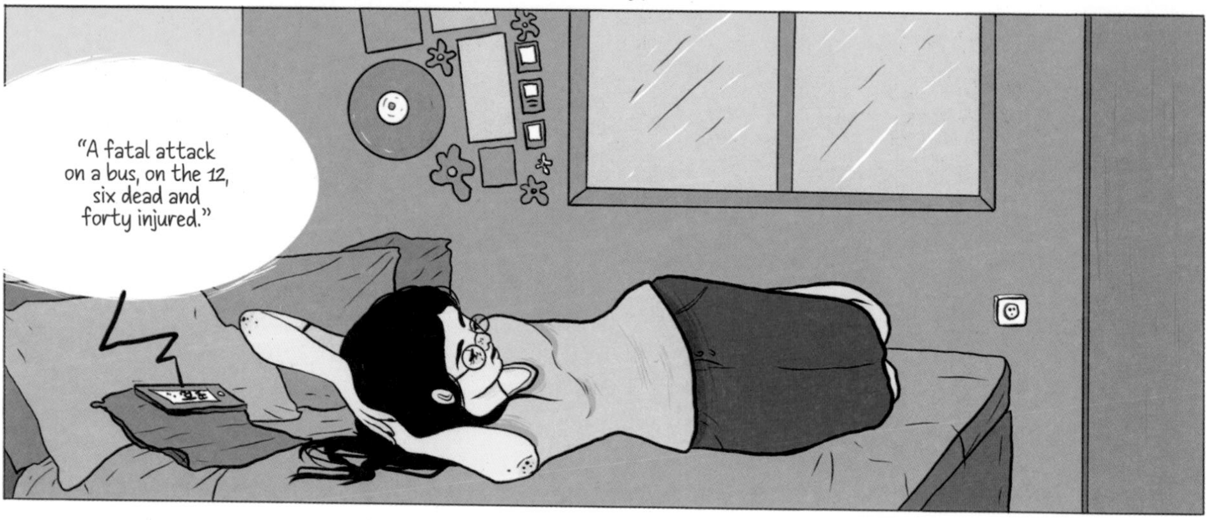
"A fatal attack on a bus, on the 12, six dead and forty injured."

The reporter kept talking, but I wasn't listening anymore.
I felt the Sacred Terror slipping away. How could there be a god when everyone was dying round here?
One "could have been" didn't make up for all the others.

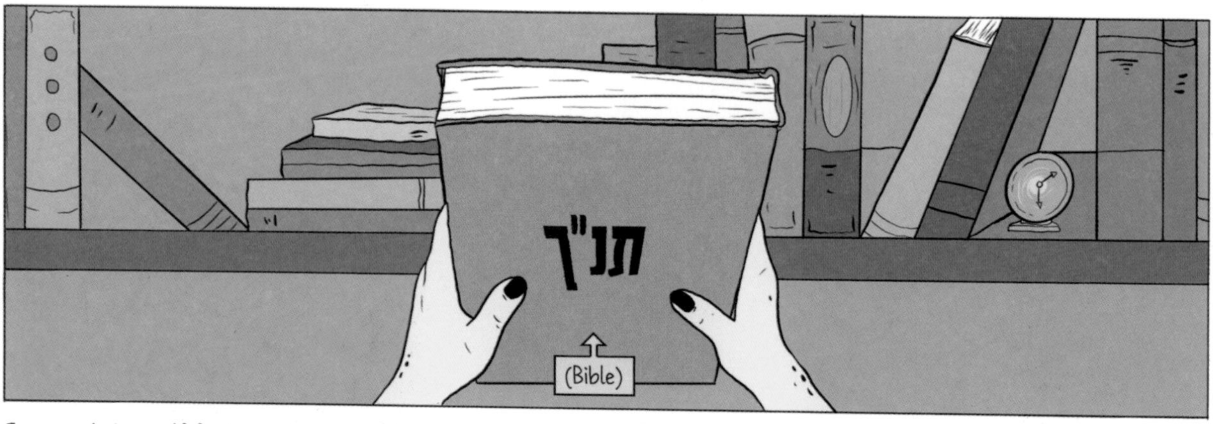
תנ"ך
(Bible)

I was mad at myself for having lost my identity, my way. How could I, on a whim, almost have joined the millions of people muttering psalms, eyes closed, or deep in religious texts, looking for signs?

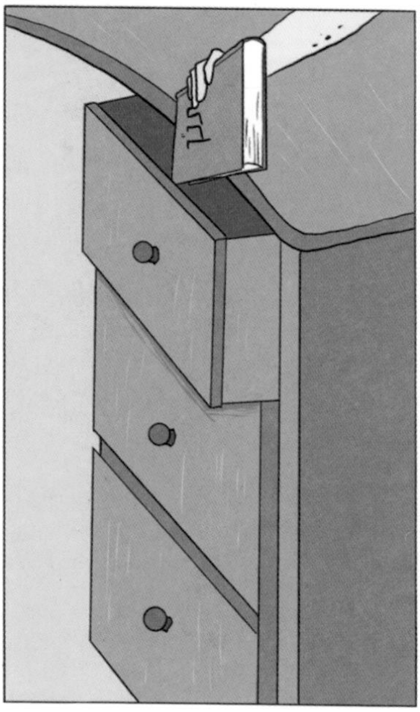

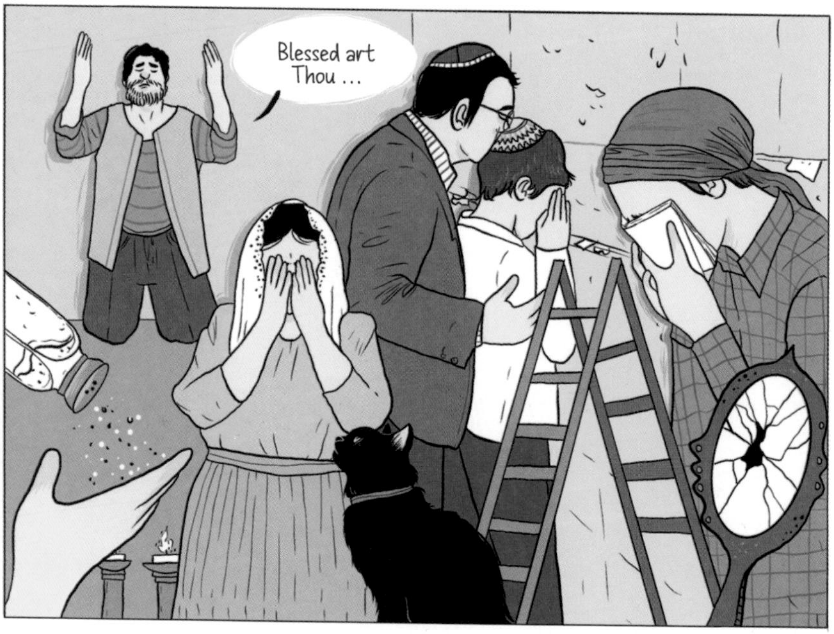
Blessed art Thou …

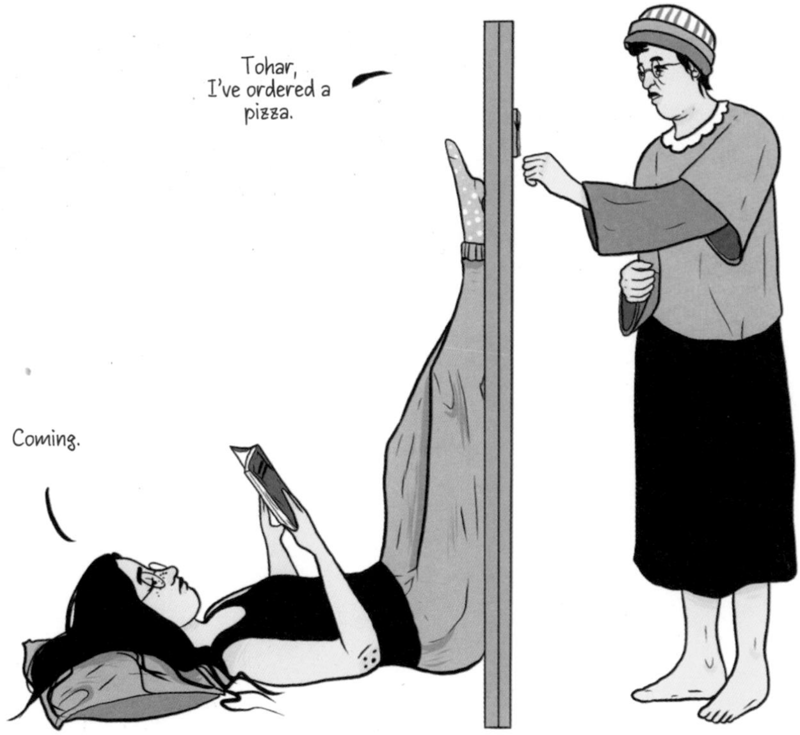
Tohar, I've ordered a pizza.
Coming.

As she went away, she kissed the mezuzah* as usual.

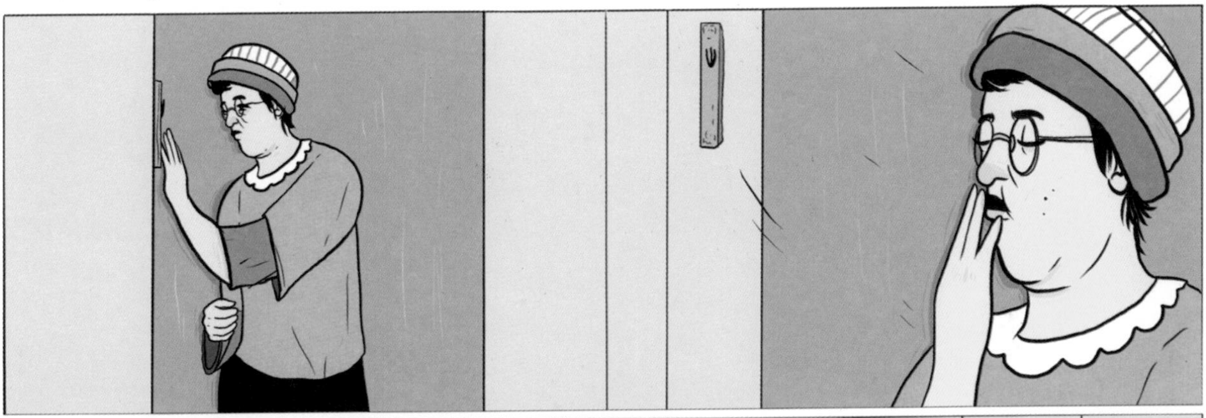

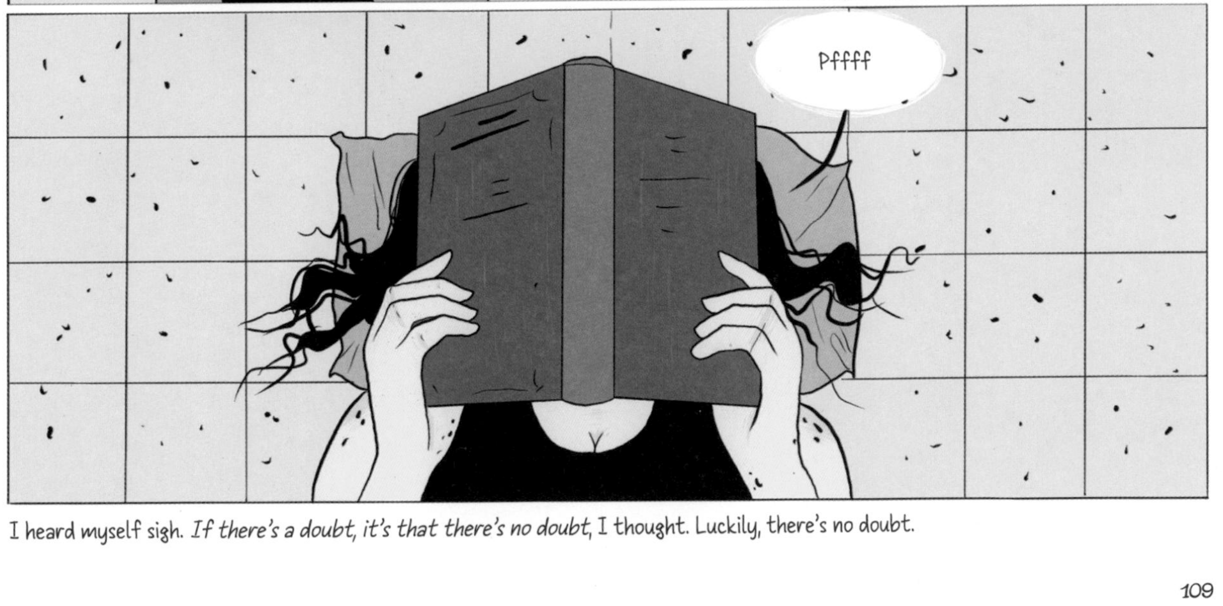
Pffff

I heard myself sigh. *If there's a doubt, it's that there's no doubt*, I thought. Luckily, there's no doubt.

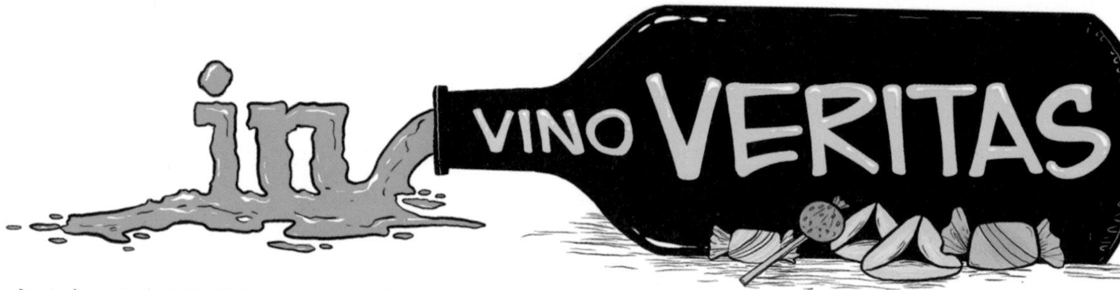
in VINO VERITAS

The Purim* carnival at the Oulpena is a time of release. All the corridors are decorated in bright colors, and the Hassidic breaktime bell becomes a rhythmic song.

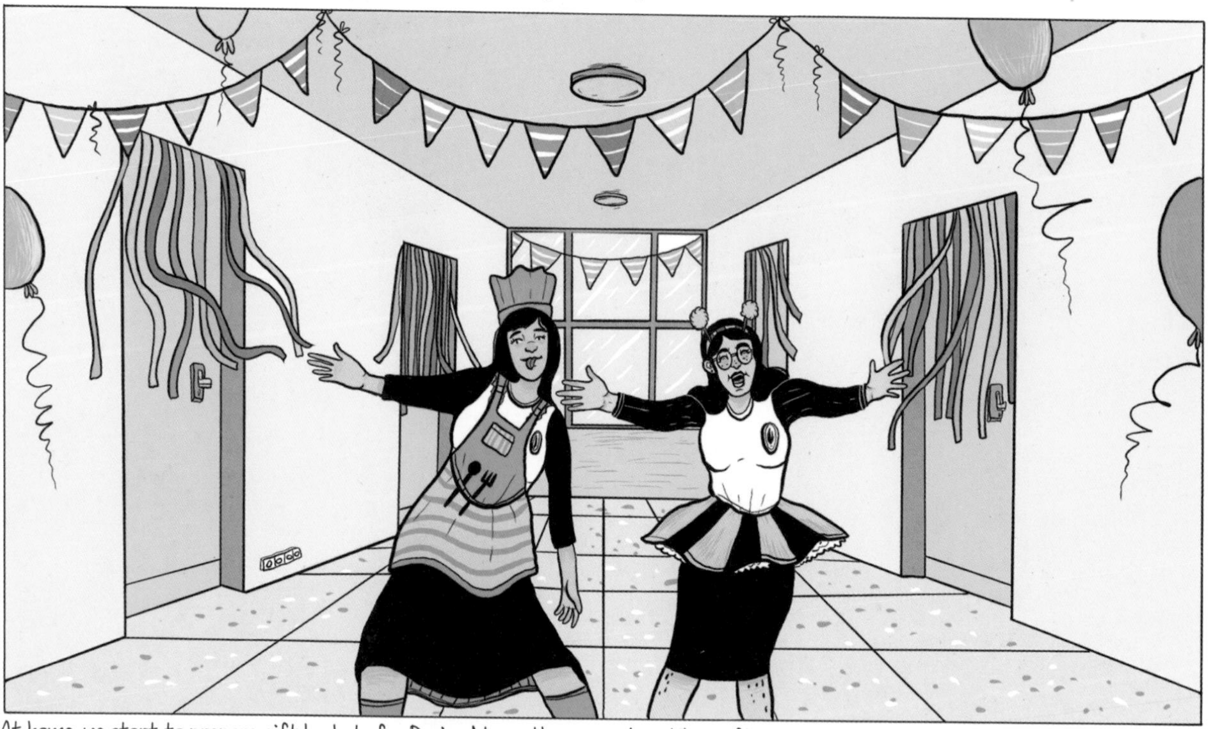

At home, we start to prepare gift baskets for Purim. My mother spreads out her gift wrap on the dining room table. Multicolored ribbons, lots of sweets and snacks. And me? I sit down and write personal letters to each of my friends. Because what's a gift basket without a personal touch?

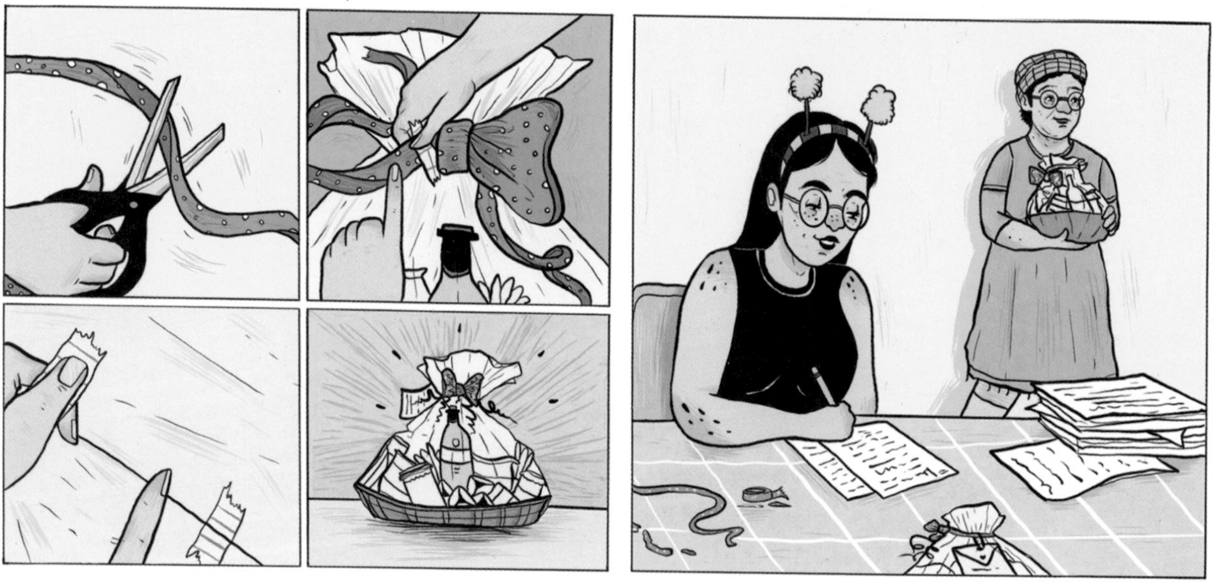

With all the preparations complete, I take all the wrapped parcels to hand out. One for Hadar who likes savory things, one for Eden who likes sweet things, a little something for Tchiya (because she's not wild about gifts), a really colorful one for Mariya, and one for Zimratt. At Zimi's house, I'd rather not go in, because her mother is a teacher at the Oulpena, and frankly, I'm not her favorite friend. My pants always make me stand out. And since I cut Zimratt's bangs, I'm finished …

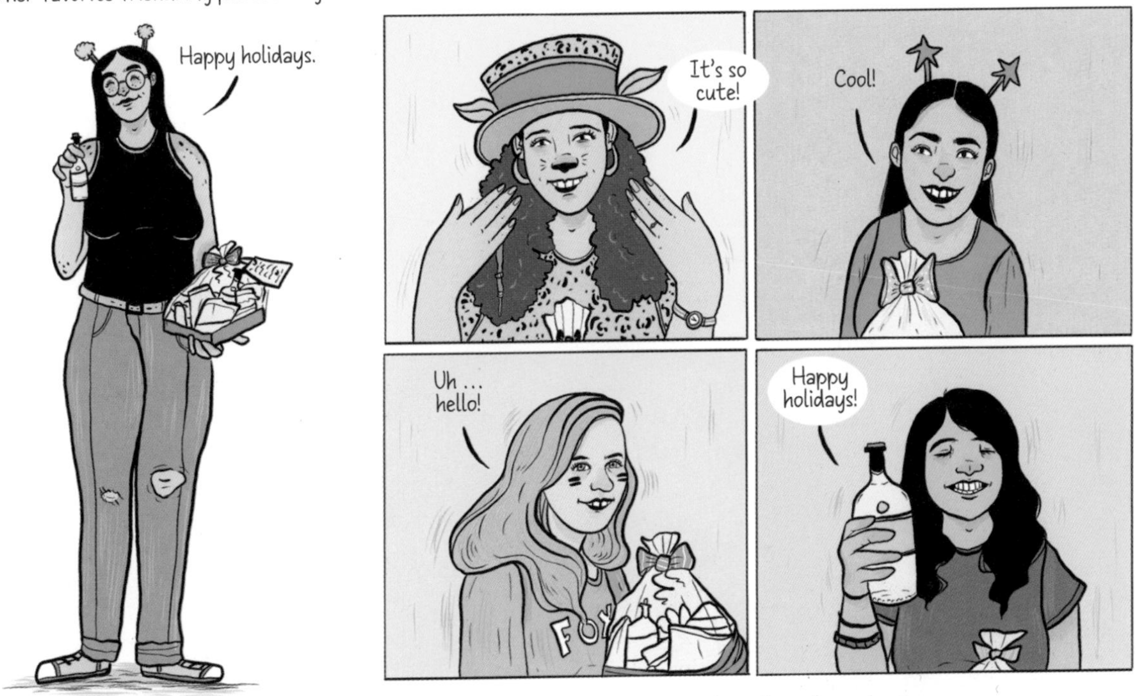
Happy holidays.
It's so cute!
Cool!
Uh … hello!
Happy holidays!

At the Kafashes' front door the smell of their Purim Tunisian Fricassee wafts out, one of my favorite moments in the distribution. Hadar and I sit down on the steps by her house, and we both enjoy the contents of her gift basket.

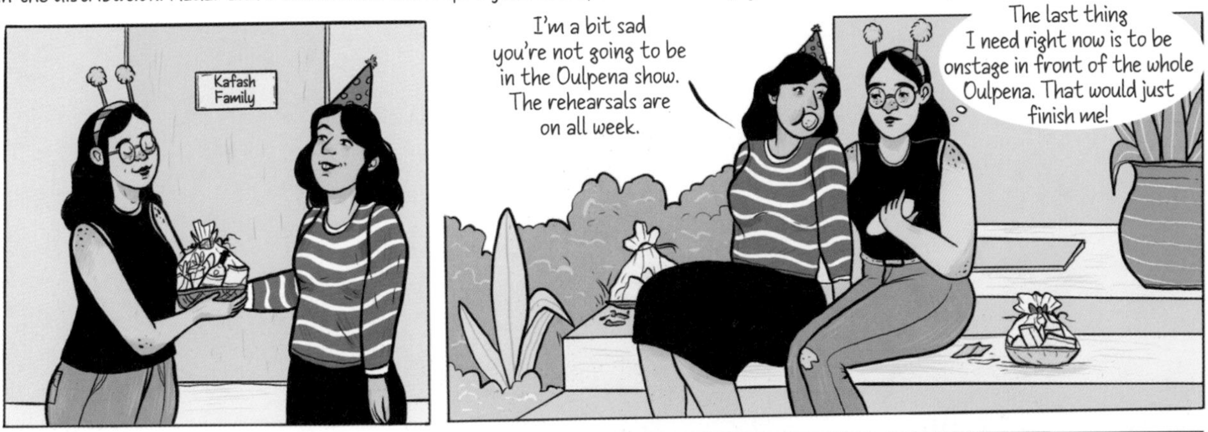
Kafash Family
I'm a bit sad you're not going to be in the Oulpena show. The rehearsals are on all week.
The last thing I need right now is to be onstage in front of the whole Oulpena. That would just finish me!

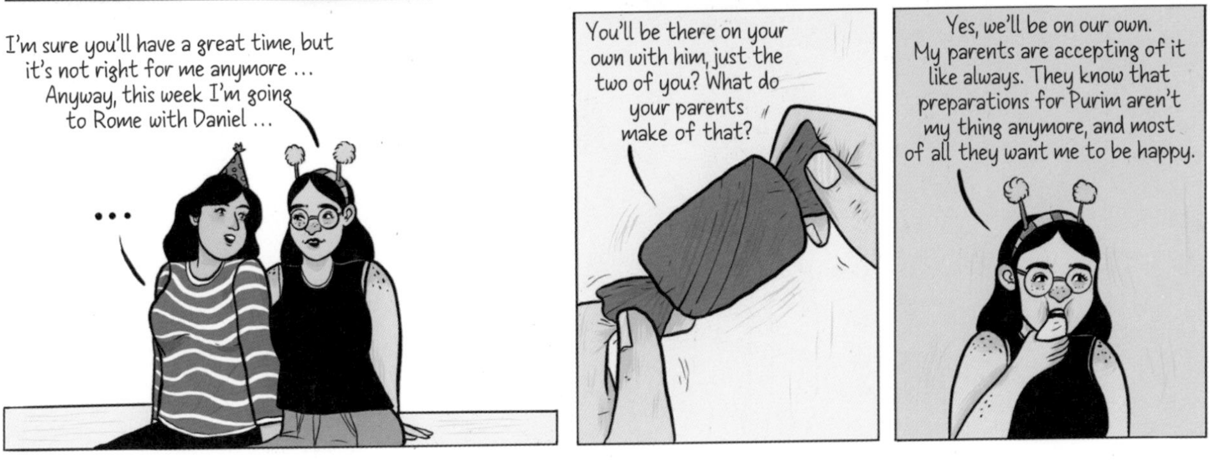
I'm sure you'll have a great time, but it's not right for me anymore … Anyway, this week I'm going to Rome with Daniel …
…
You'll be there on your own with him, just the two of you? What do your parents make of that?
Yes, we'll be on our own. My parents are accepting of it like always. They know that preparations for Purim aren't my thing anymore, and most of all they want me to be happy.

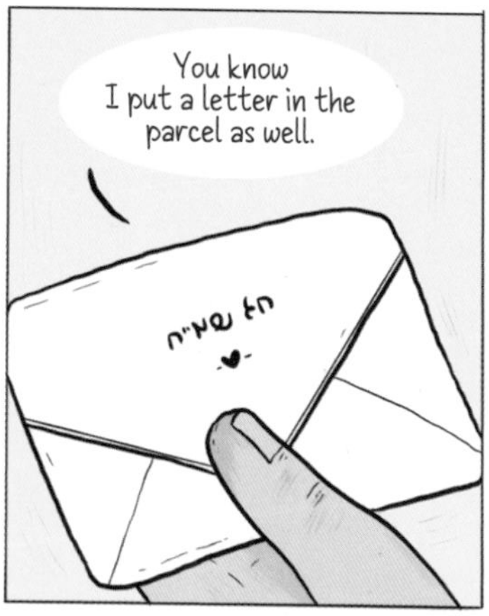
You know I put a letter in the parcel as well.
חג שמ"ח

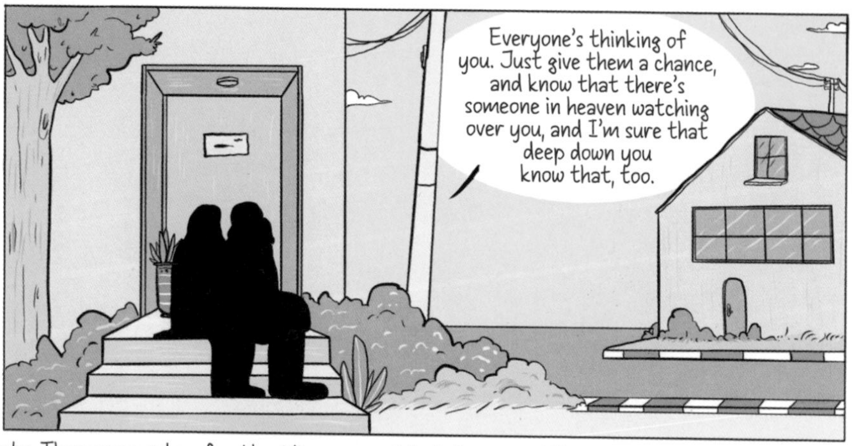
Everyone's thinking of you. Just give them a chance, and know that there's someone in heaven watching over you, and I'm sure that deep down you know that, too.

That evening we went to the Oulpena party. There were only a few Hassidic songs and Amir Benayoun's* music.
I brought some booze, because after all, it is one of the "days of joy and feasting."

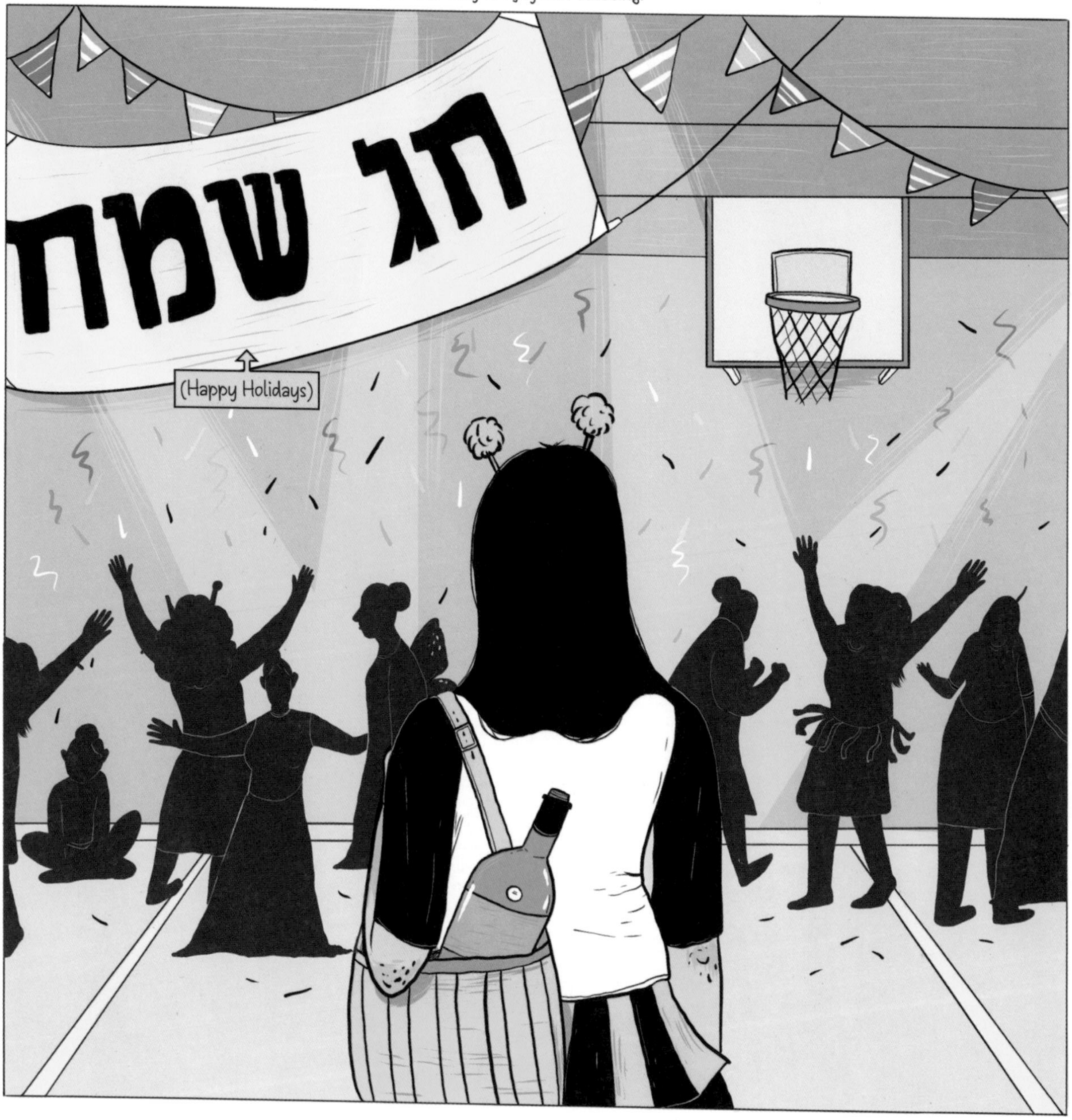
חג שמח
(Happy Holidays)

We danced on the lawn behind the main building, and we drank a bit … then a lot …
And when the wine goes in, the truth comes out … Our tongues had been loosened.

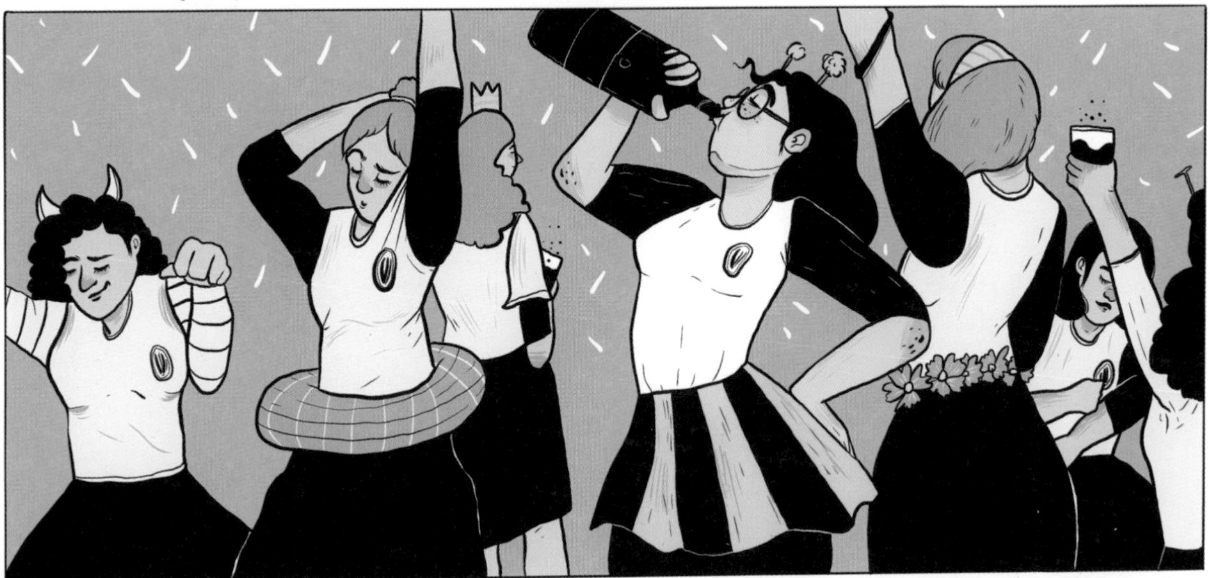

Mine a bit less than the others. But still, in that atmosphere I confided in them that my sister had recently tried to kill herself.
I don't know what they said anymore—I just remember that we cried together and then never spoke of it again.

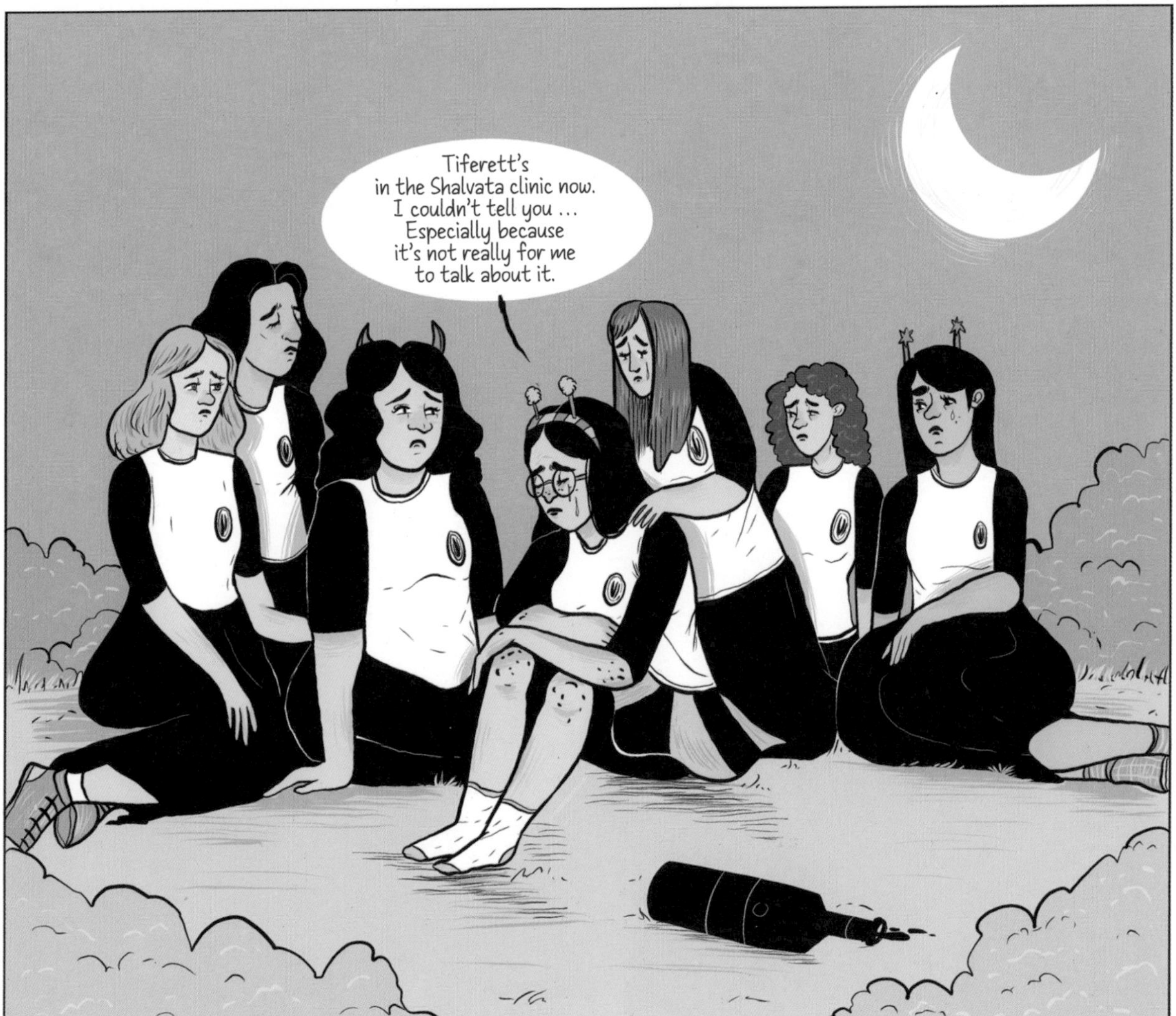
Tiferett's in the Shalvata clinic now. I couldn't tell you … Especially because it's not really for me to talk about it.

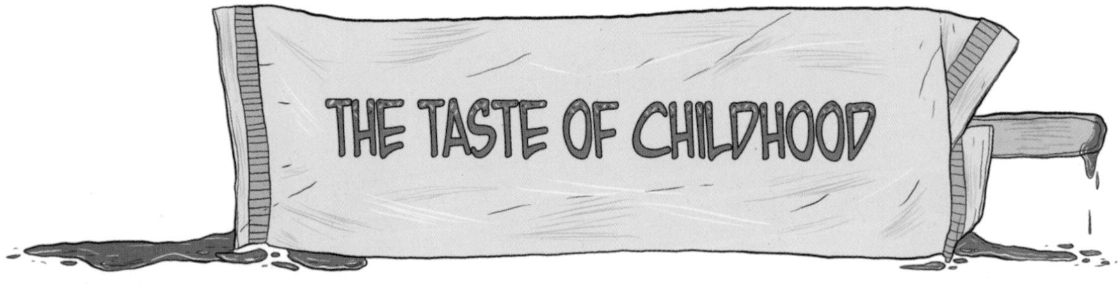
THE TASTE OF CHILDHOOD

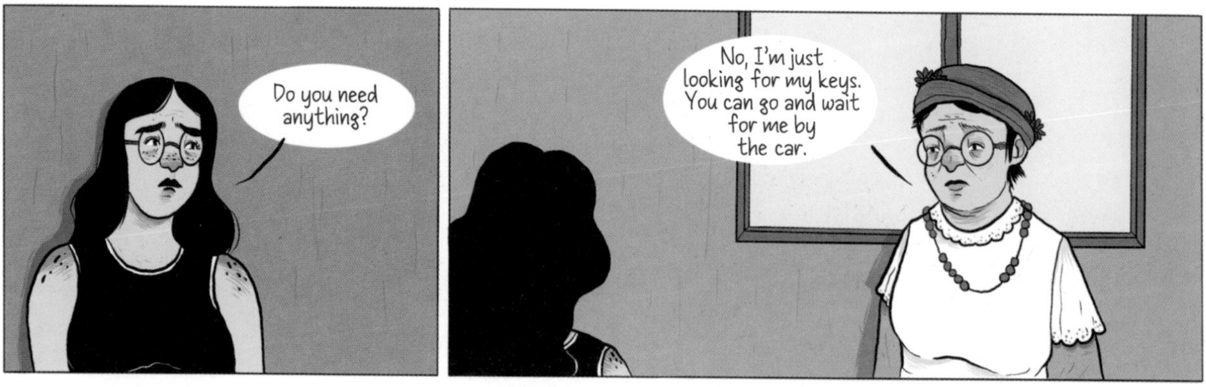
Do you need anything?
No, I'm just looking for my keys. You can go and wait for me by the car.

My mother grew up on a kibbutz where she had to share everything, and I think that's why I never wanted for anything. Anything I could ask for or want, I got, whether it was clothes, art supplies, or even tickets to rock concerts that my mother took me to. She made up for what was missing in her own childhood by giving us everything she didn't have.

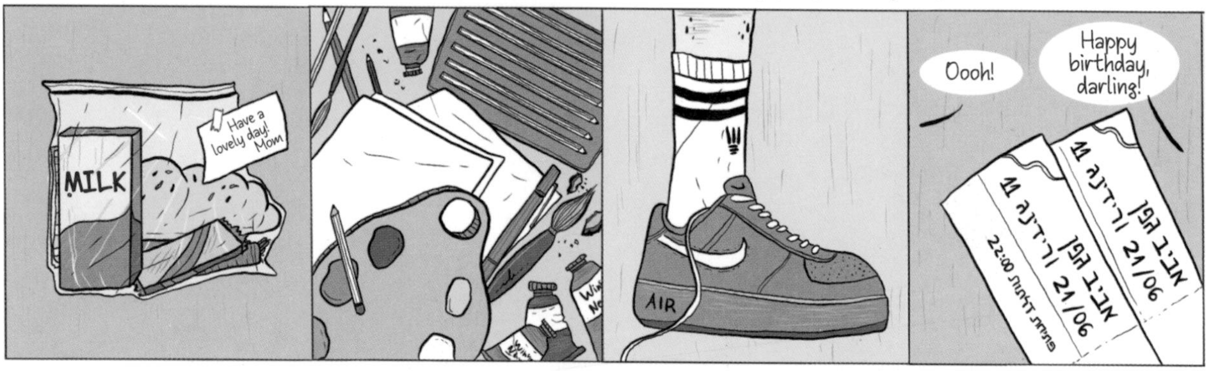
MILK
Have a lovely day! Mom
AIR
Happy birthday, darling!
Oooh!

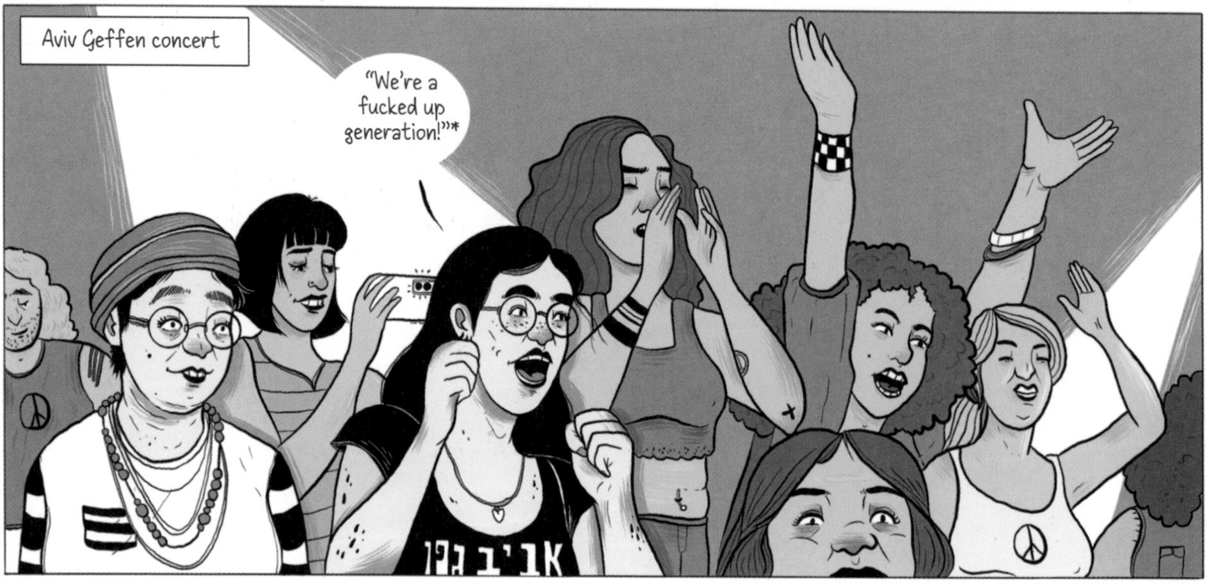
Aviv Geffen concert
"We're a fucked up generation!"*

My sister's suicide attempt really shook my family to the core. The sort of shock that is wrapped in an intense feeling of despair.

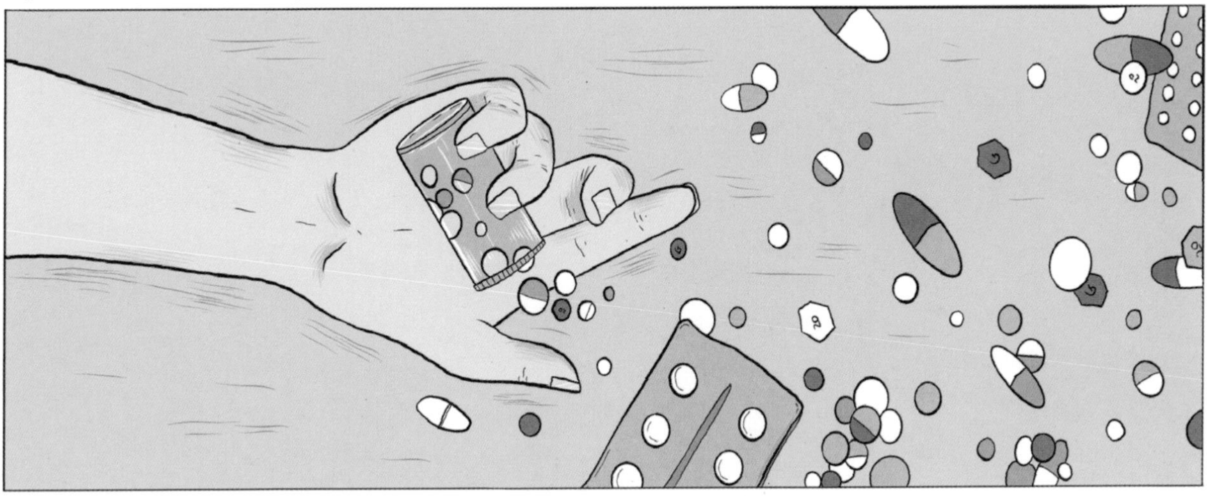

We went to see her at the clinic, we did her shopping and brought her little treats, we met all together for some private family comfort. My parents had sprung into action, managing the family crisis as a two-person team. I could see clearly that my mother wanted to fix things, but at this stage gifts were not going to do anything.

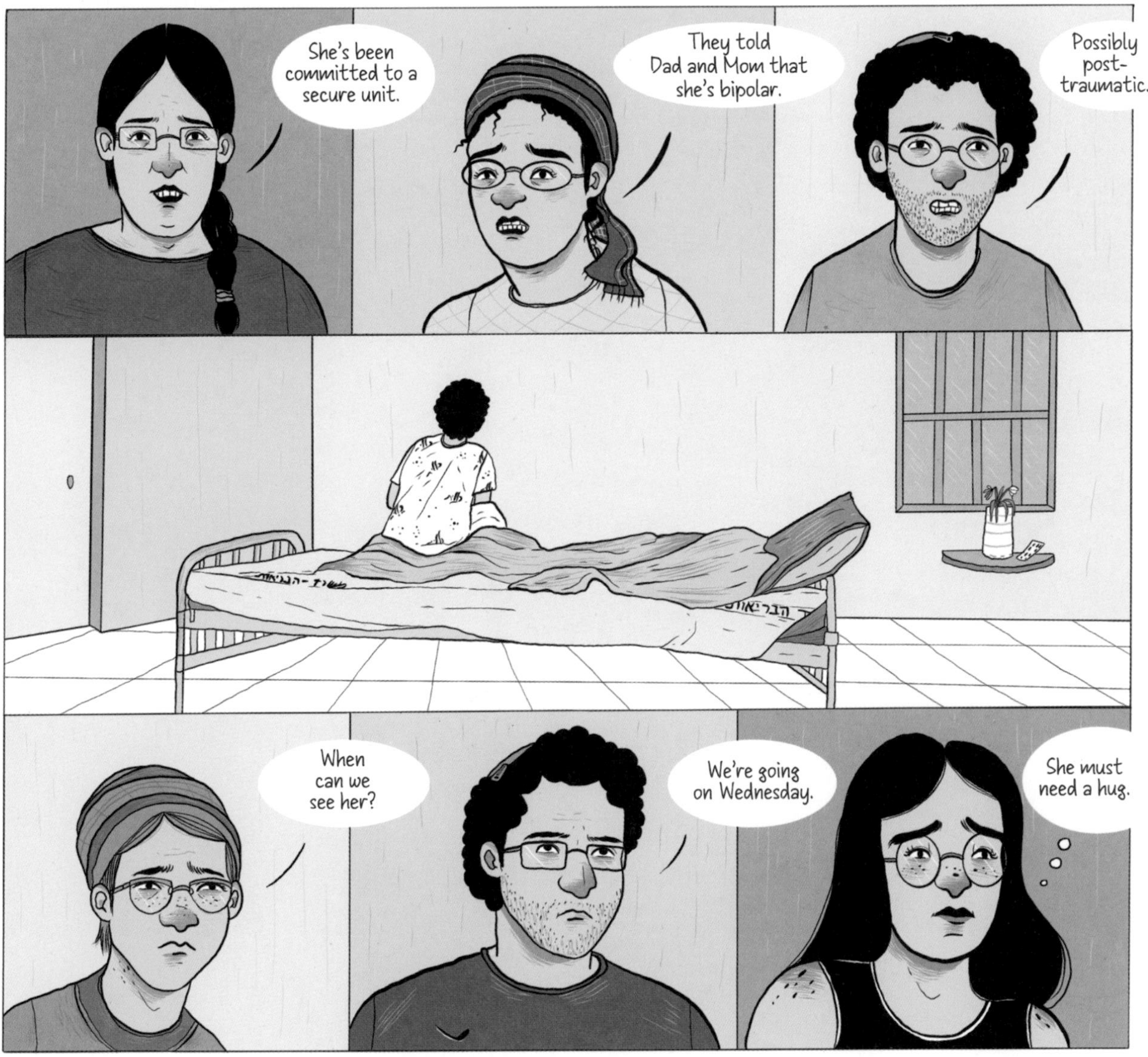

She's been committed to a secure unit.
They told Dad and Mom that she's bipolar.
Possibly post-traumatic.
When can we see her?
We're going on Wednesday.
She must need a hug.

I got in the car. My mother drove. She parked in front of the clinic, and we stayed right there, not saying anything for a while.

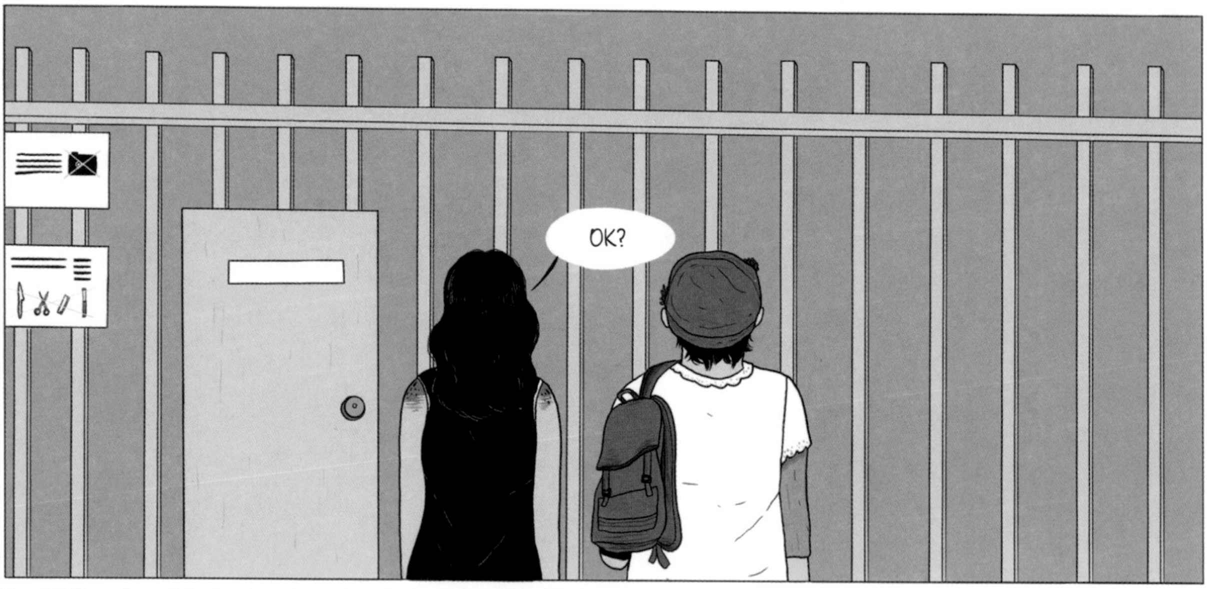
OK?

She didn't reply … What a stupid question, I thought to myself. Obviously she wasn't ok. All these years, she worked and supported us, and now it was all crumbling to pieces. Over the last eight months, new lines had appeared on her face. Worry lines above her eyebrows and under her mouth.
I took her hand, because there weren't any words to comfort her in the face of this new reality that had come crashing down on us.

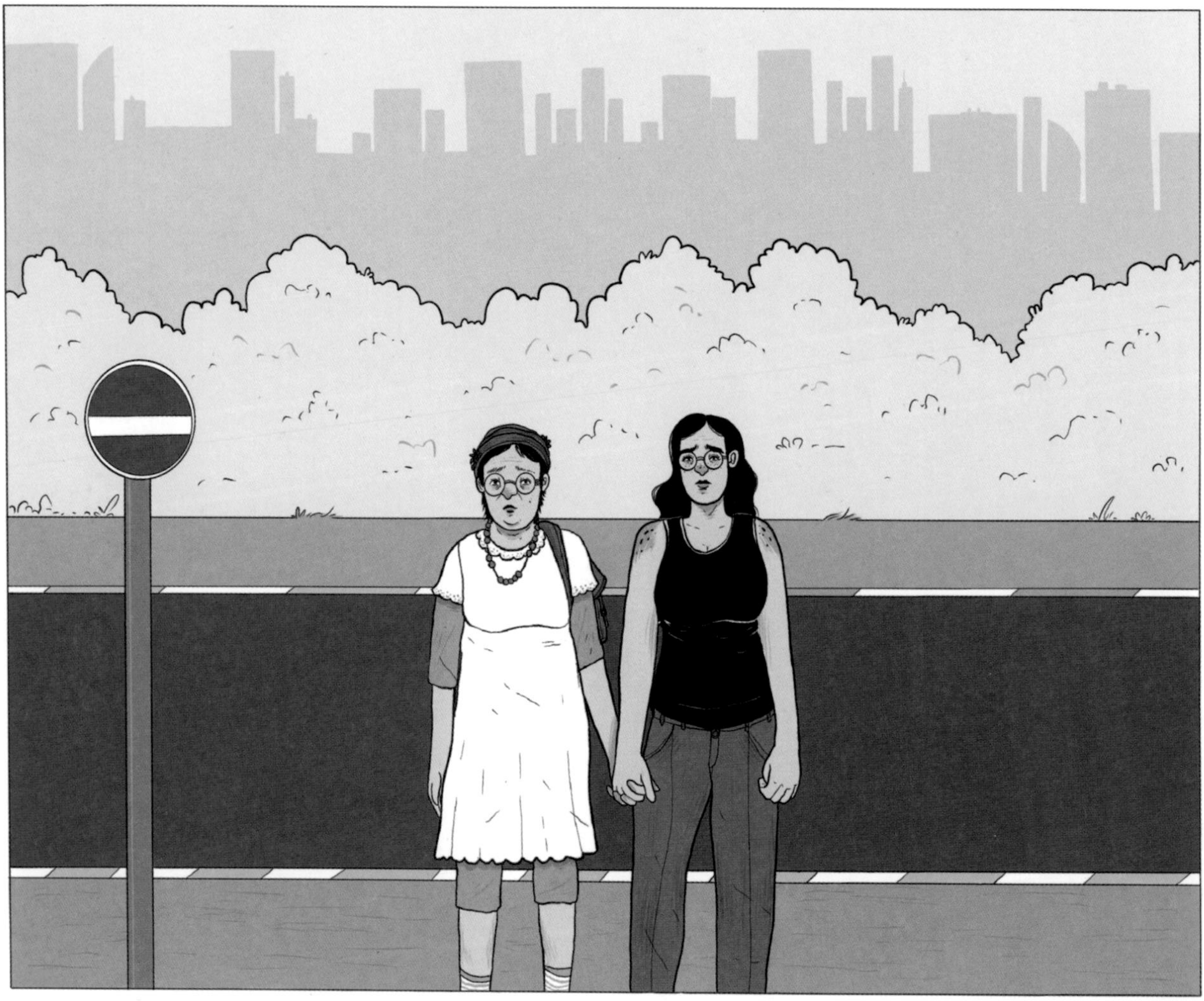

People walking by all wore yellow and blue gowns, like a uniform for lost souls.

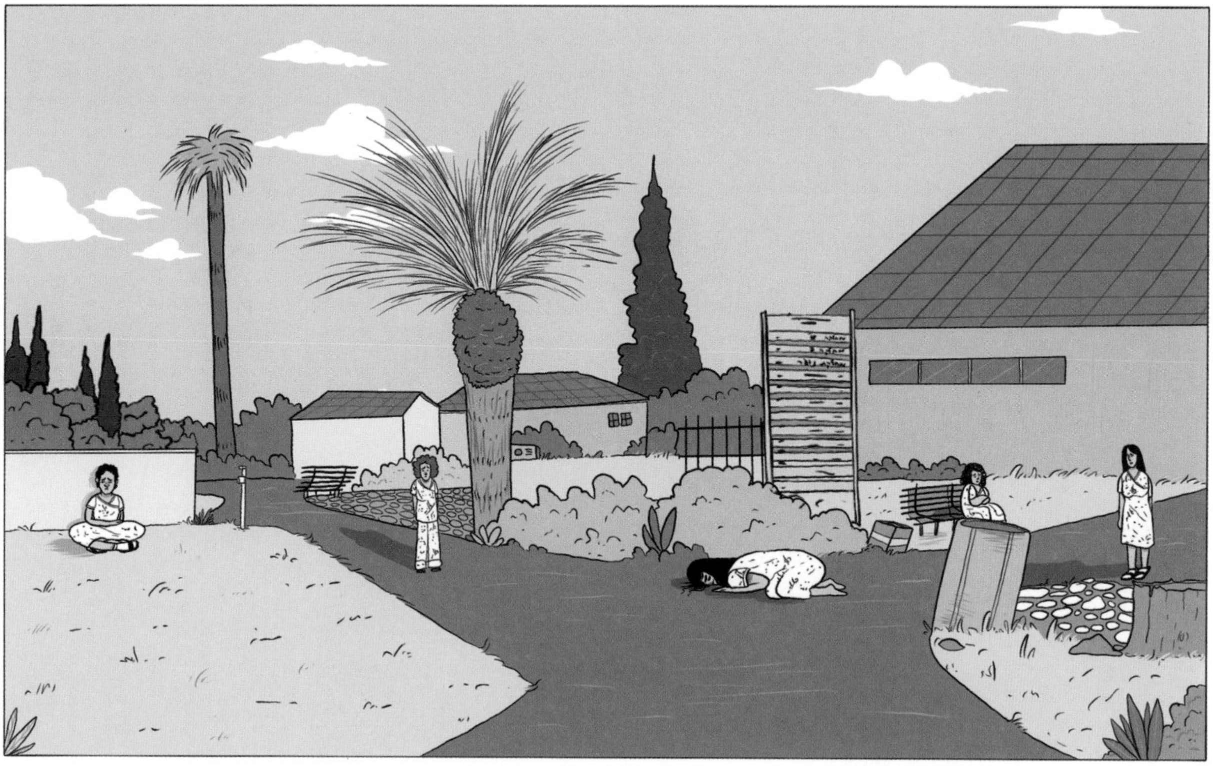

We had bought ice cream at the stall, dairy-free strawberry ice cream, and we took it in to Tiferett. She cried and said we were keeping her locked up, that we'd never understand, that we could never repair what her husband had broken.

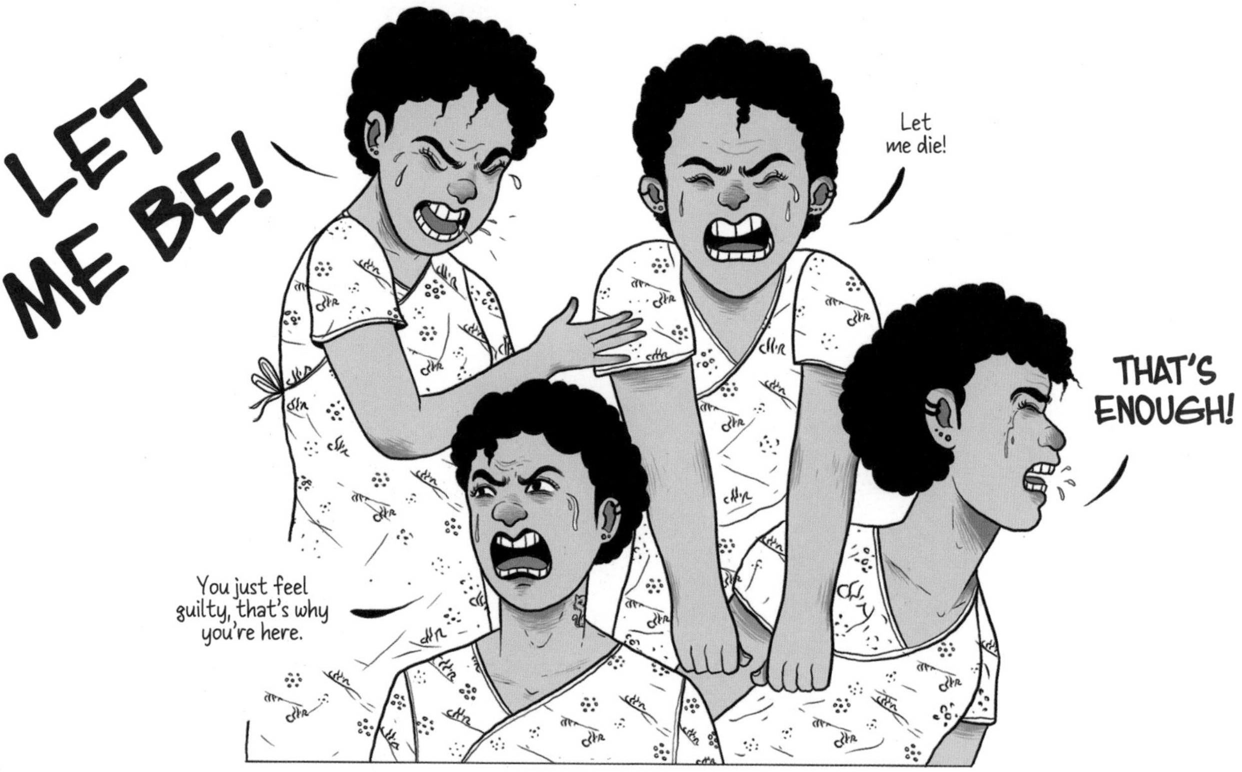
LET ME BE!
Let me die!
THAT'S ENOUGH!
You just feel guilty, that's why you're here.

On the way home, I felt that I needed to get myself under control, that I should give her my support, put my questions and troubles aside.

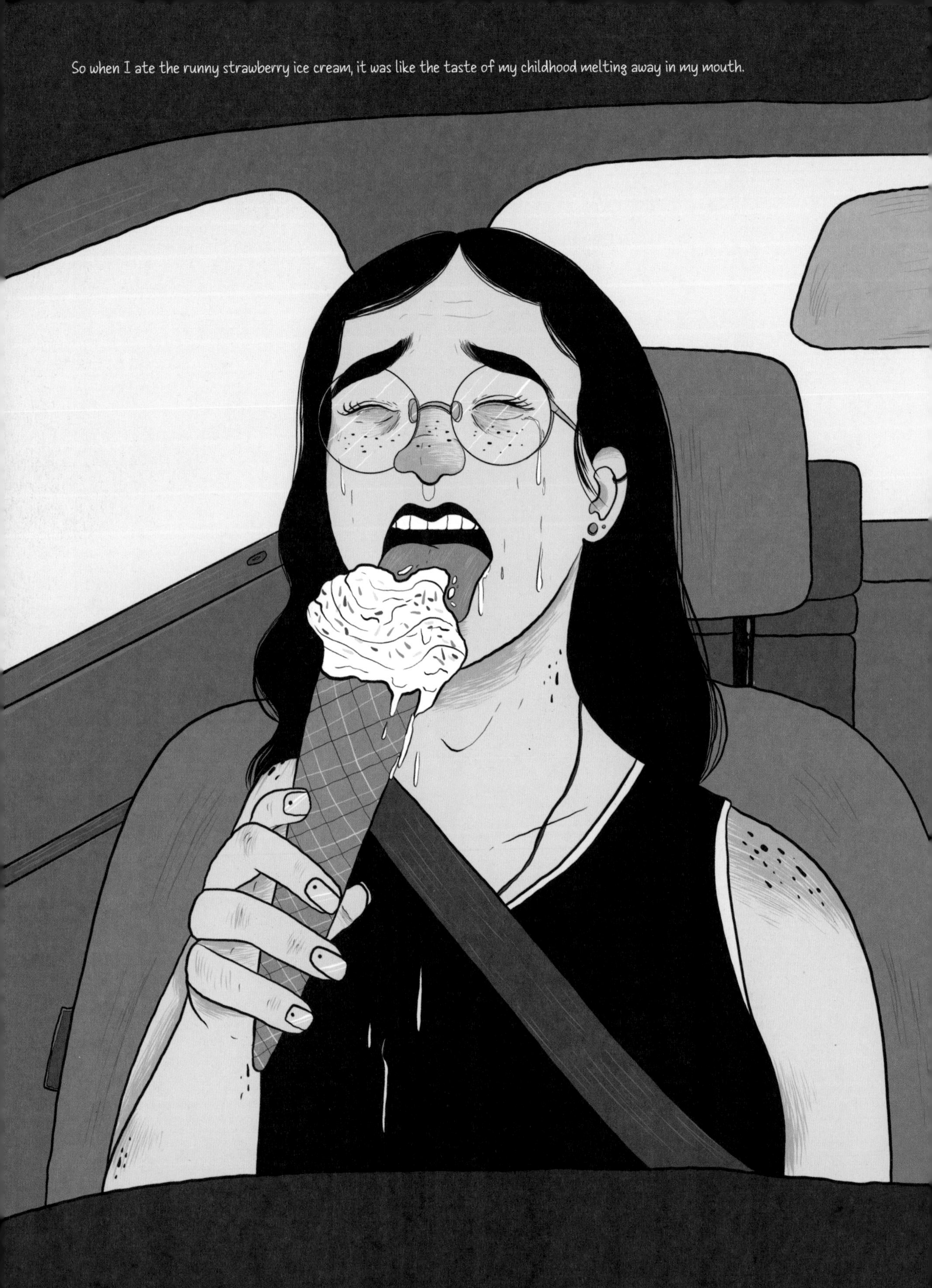
So when I ate the runny strawberry ice cream, it was like the taste of my childhood melting away in my mouth.

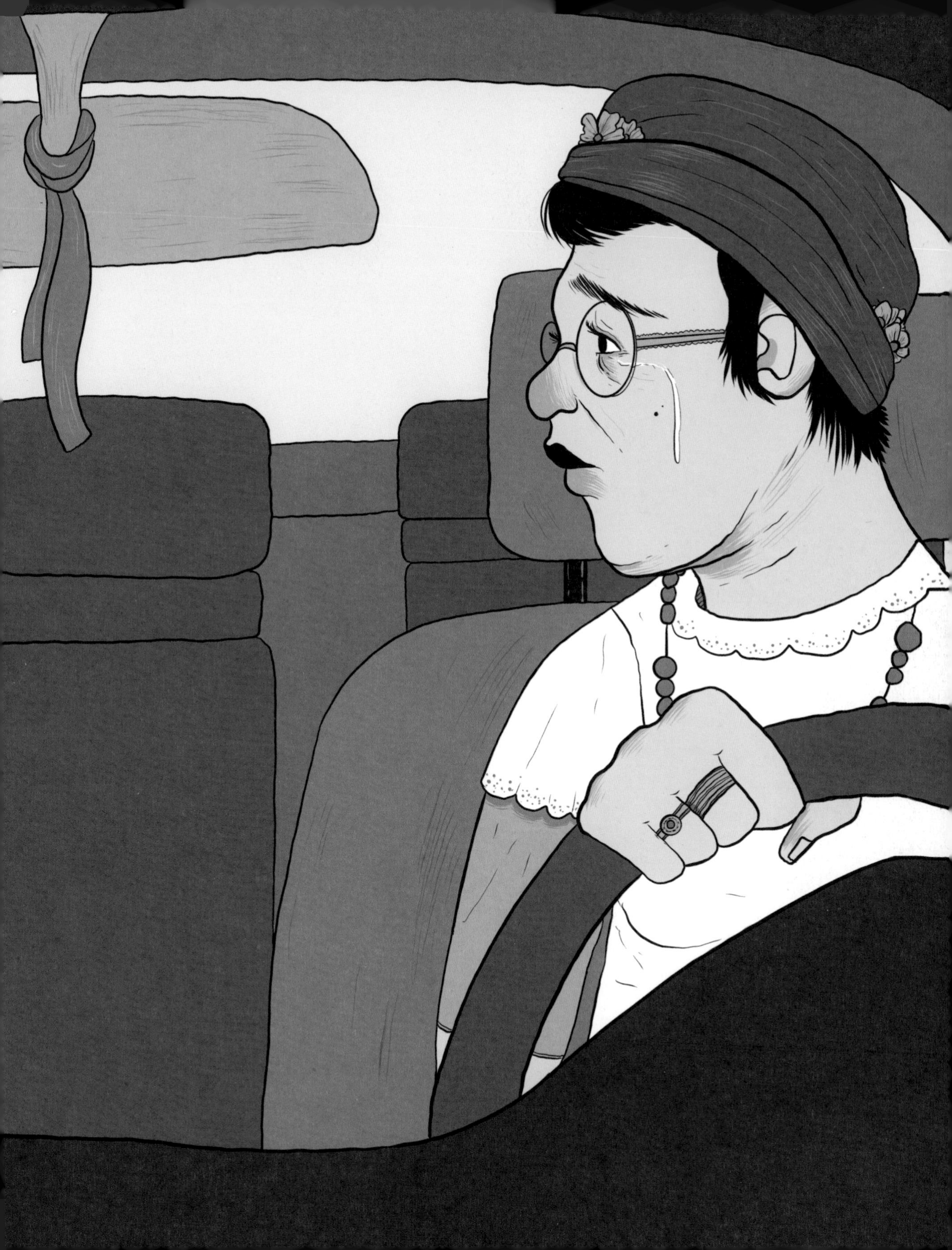

EPILOGUE

HERE IS A FAREWELL SONG

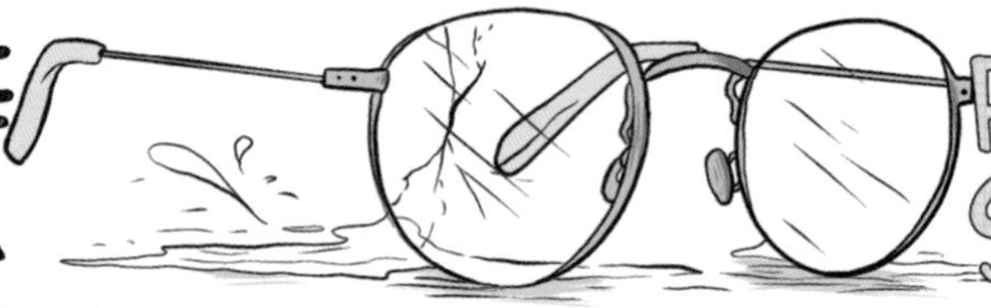

Sure, there's no real urgency. I could keep silent, maybe even forever.

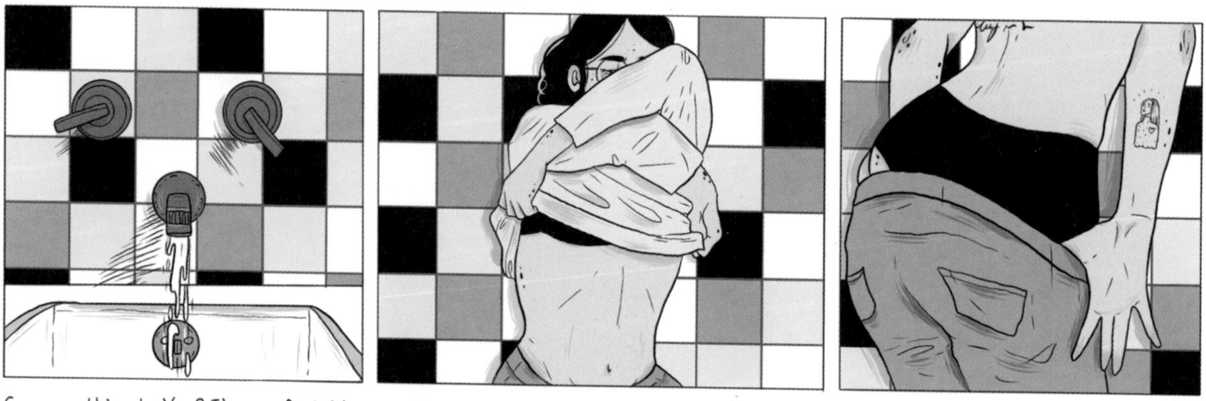

Say something to You? I'm comfortable with these silences—my lifeline when I have too much to say.

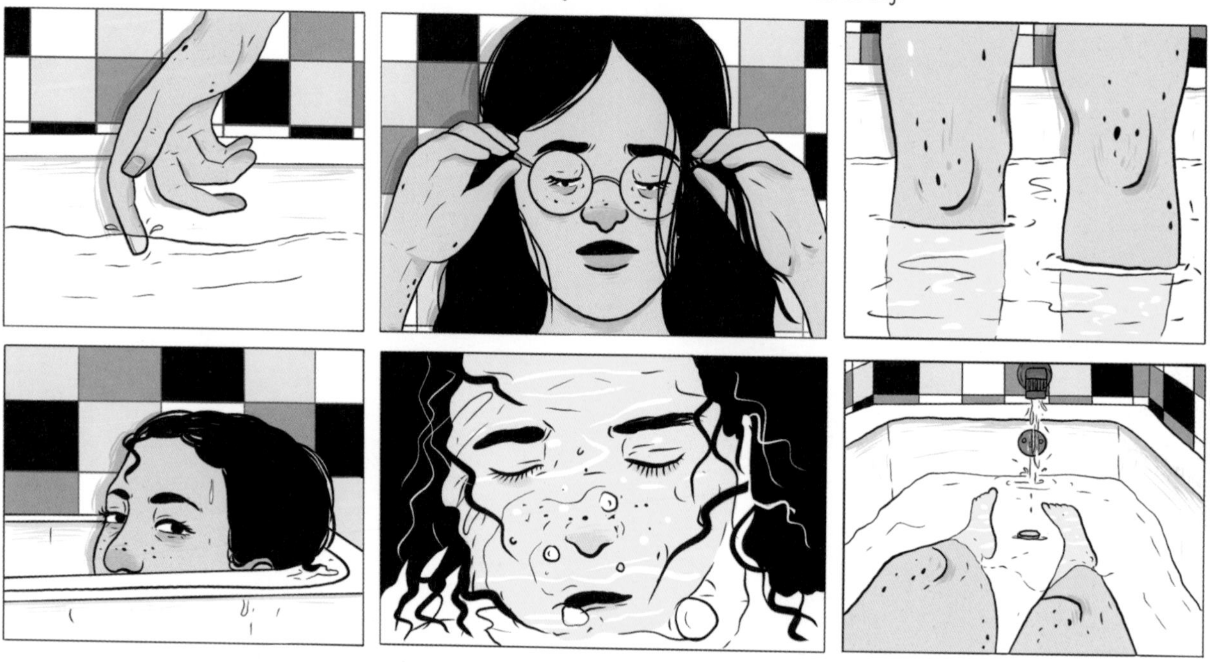

When I say nothing, I don't embarrass myself, I don't fall into the traps that scare me the most, but then here I am talking to You.

For weeks now I have prepared for this moment, I've thought about it under the shower, on the way to the Oulpena, at Friday night dinner, when we make Kiddush*. I've been waiting for this moment, waiting to confront You.

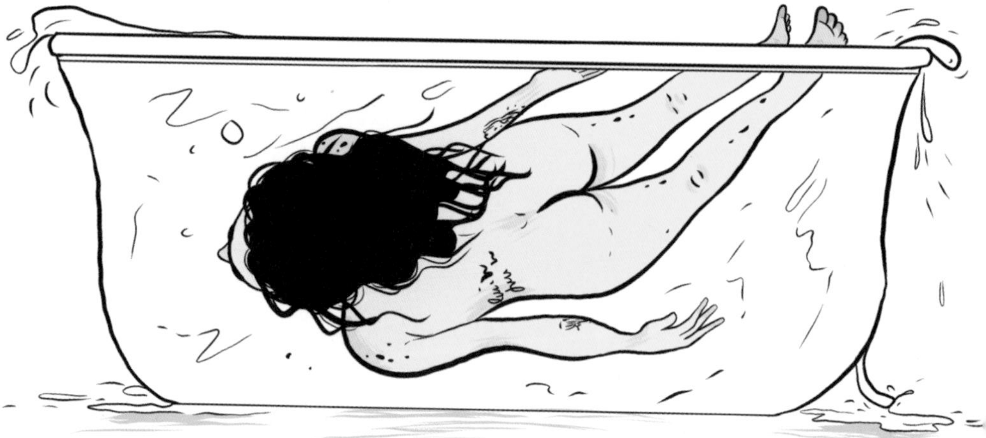

It's all the same to me if You get mad, if You get annoyed, if You scold me.

I'm almost waiting for You to say: "Where have you been, Tohar? These conversations are supposed to burst forth from you spontaneously, they are rooted in your body, inculcated in you from the moment you come into the world."

And when You ask me, I'd tell You that You have no special privileges down here.

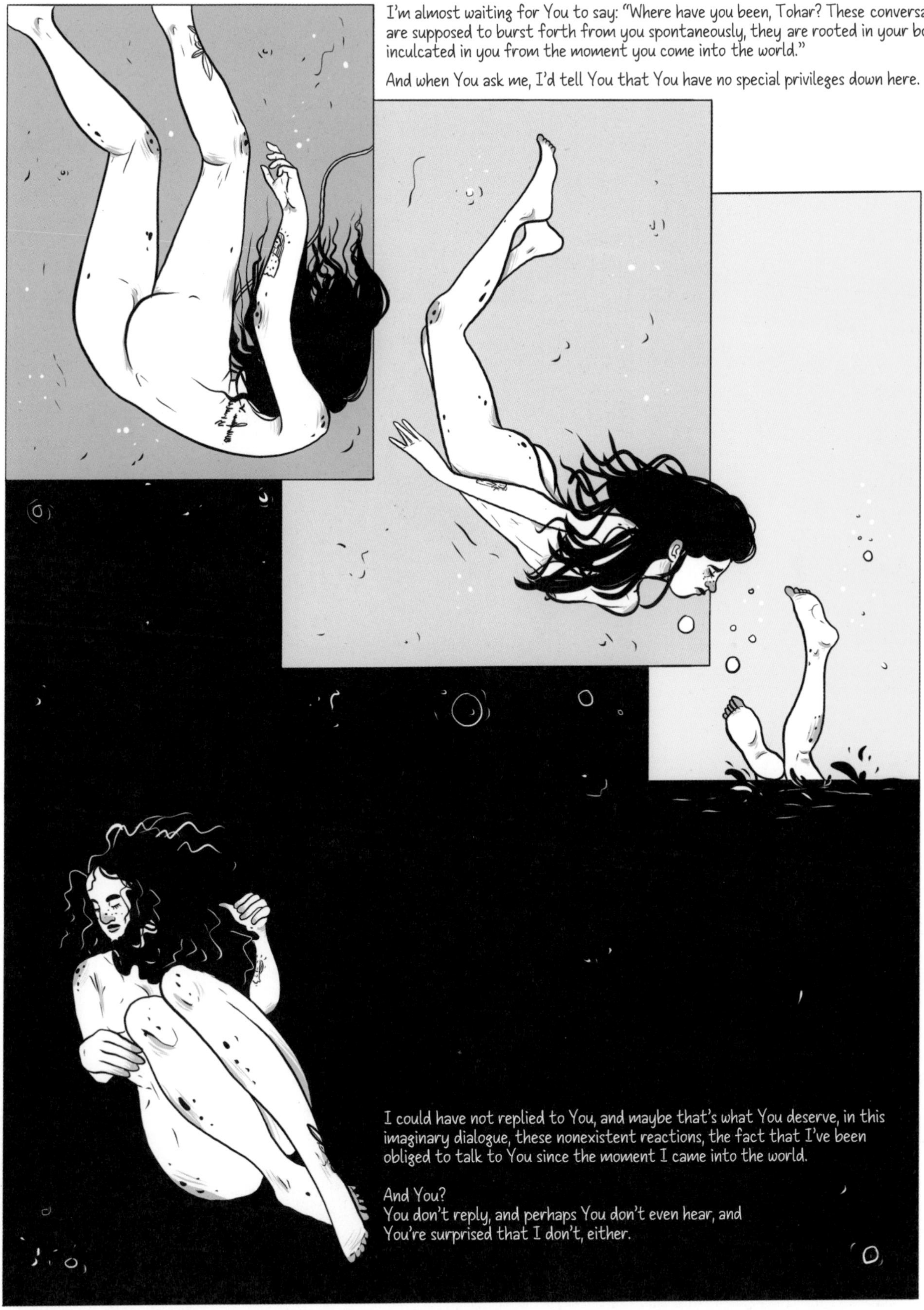
I could have not replied to You, and maybe that's what You deserve, in this imaginary dialogue, these nonexistent reactions, the fact that I've been obliged to talk to You since the moment I came into the world.
And You?
You don't reply, and perhaps You don't even hear, and You're surprised that I don't, either.

Do you know who I am? Do I know? No, and why's that?
Because I suddenly realized that You don't have an answer, that there isn't an answer at all.

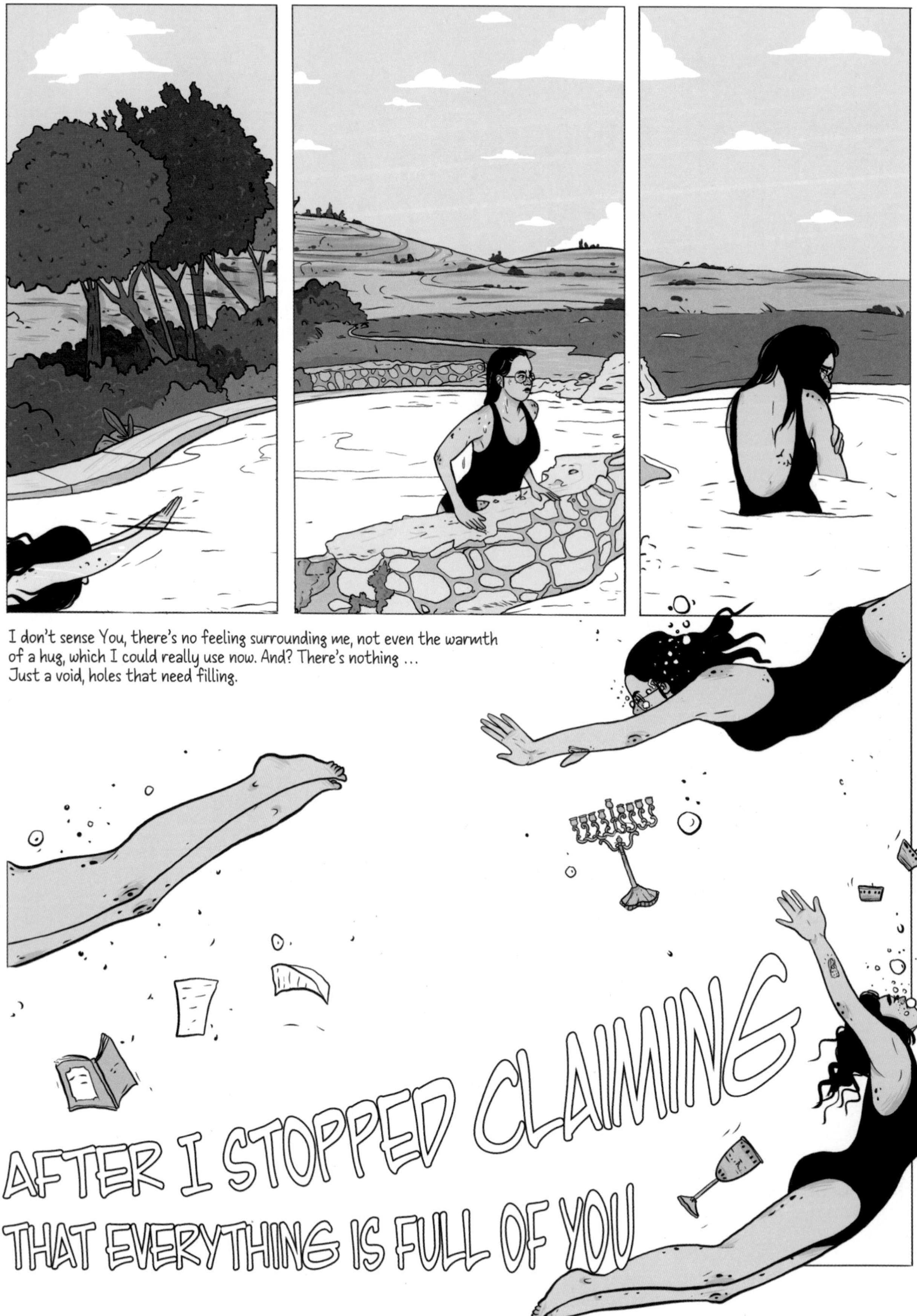
I don't sense You, there's no feeling surrounding me, not even the warmth of a hug, which I could really use now. And? There's nothing … Just a void, holes that need filling.
AFTER I STOPPED CLAIMING
THAT EVERYTHING IS FULL OF YOU

And we come to the crunch point—are You ready? God, Lord, Yahweh, Hashem? I'm saying farewell to You.

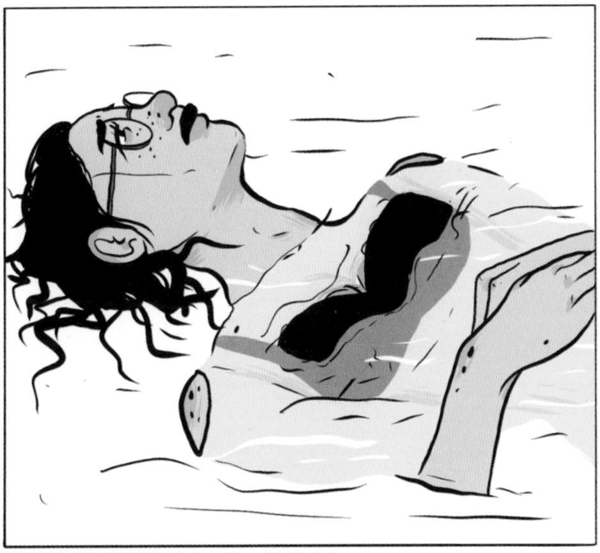

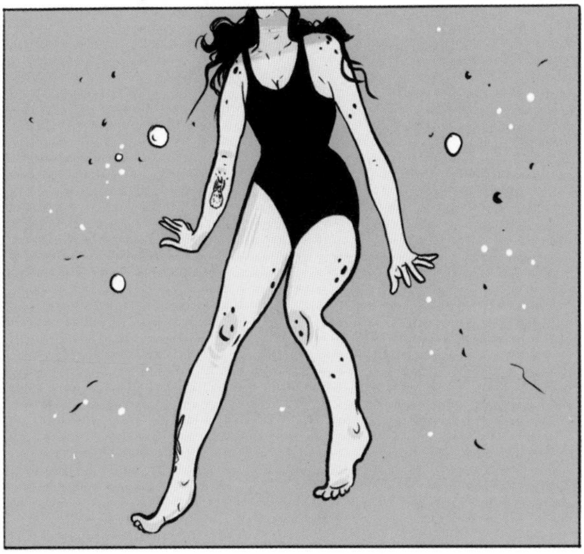

I tried beating around the bush, saying that we were just taking a break, that perhaps we'd come back to each other, that we could fix this relationship.
It's always difficult to admit that it's over. But now it's me taking that step.
I'm emptying the holes, I'm shaking off the feelings. I've stopped expecting a reply, I'm cleansing myself of You.

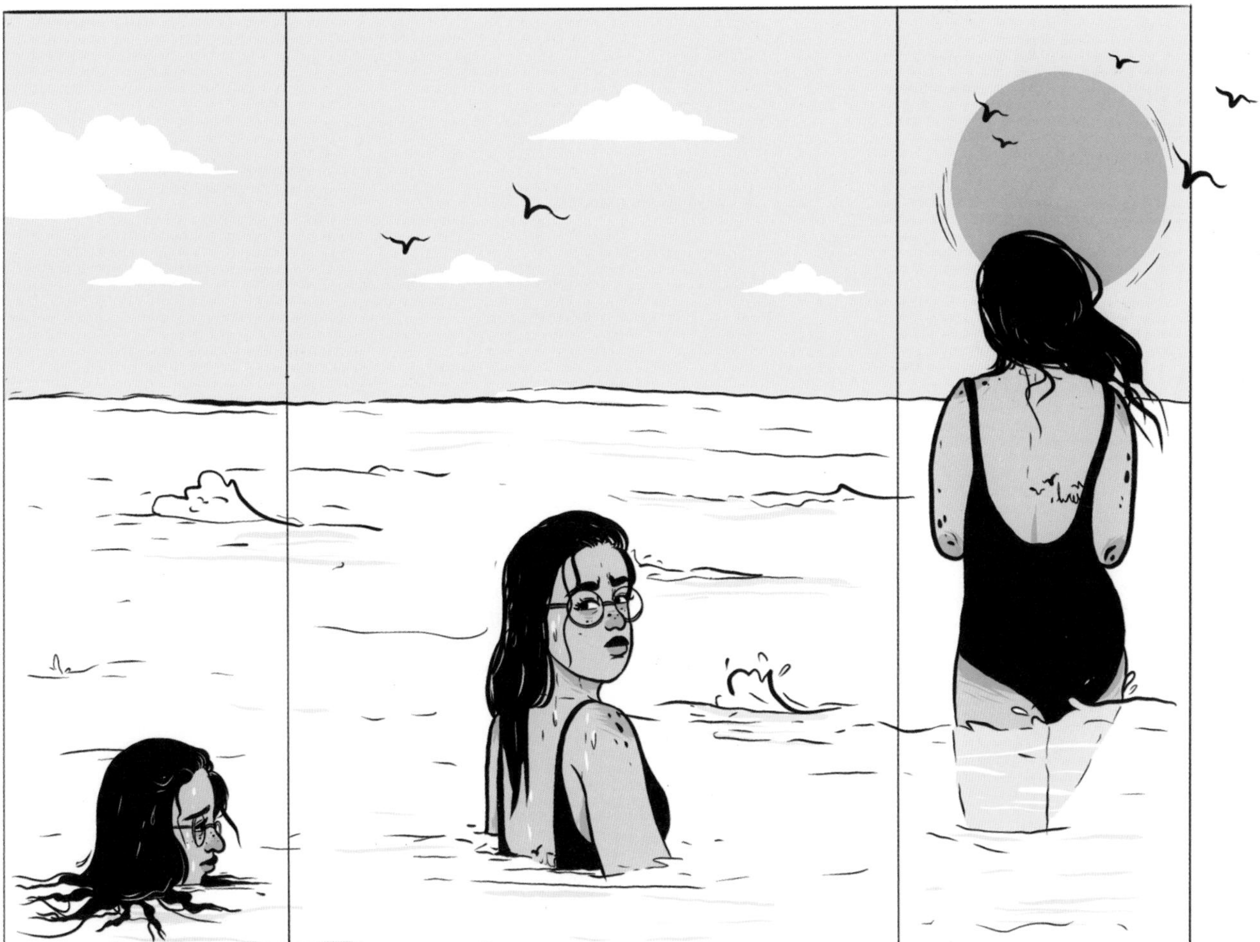

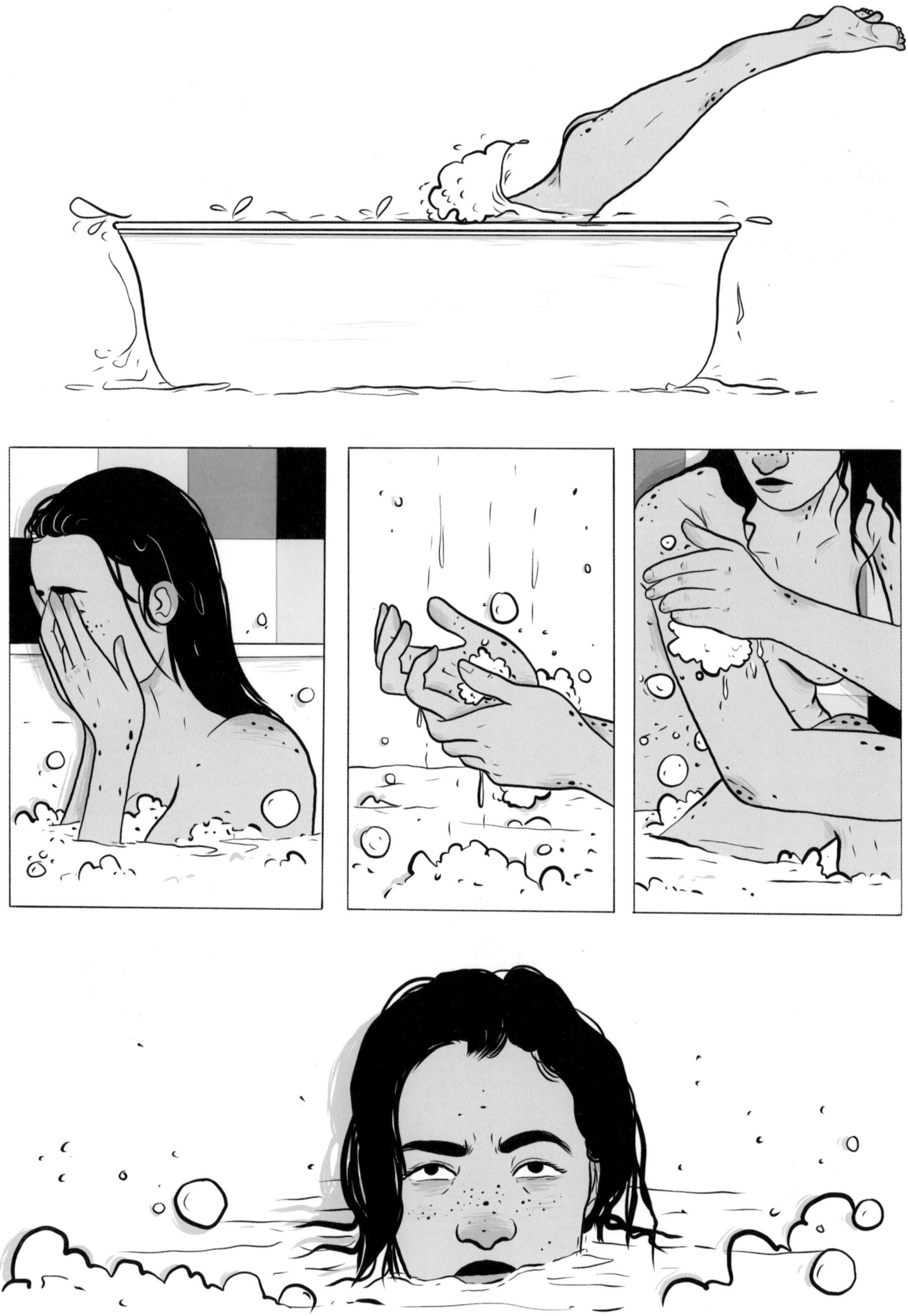

I thought I would feel dirty, but the truth is—don't You get annoyed now—I feel more pure than ever before.
I don't belong to You anymore, or to anyone else.
Tohar.

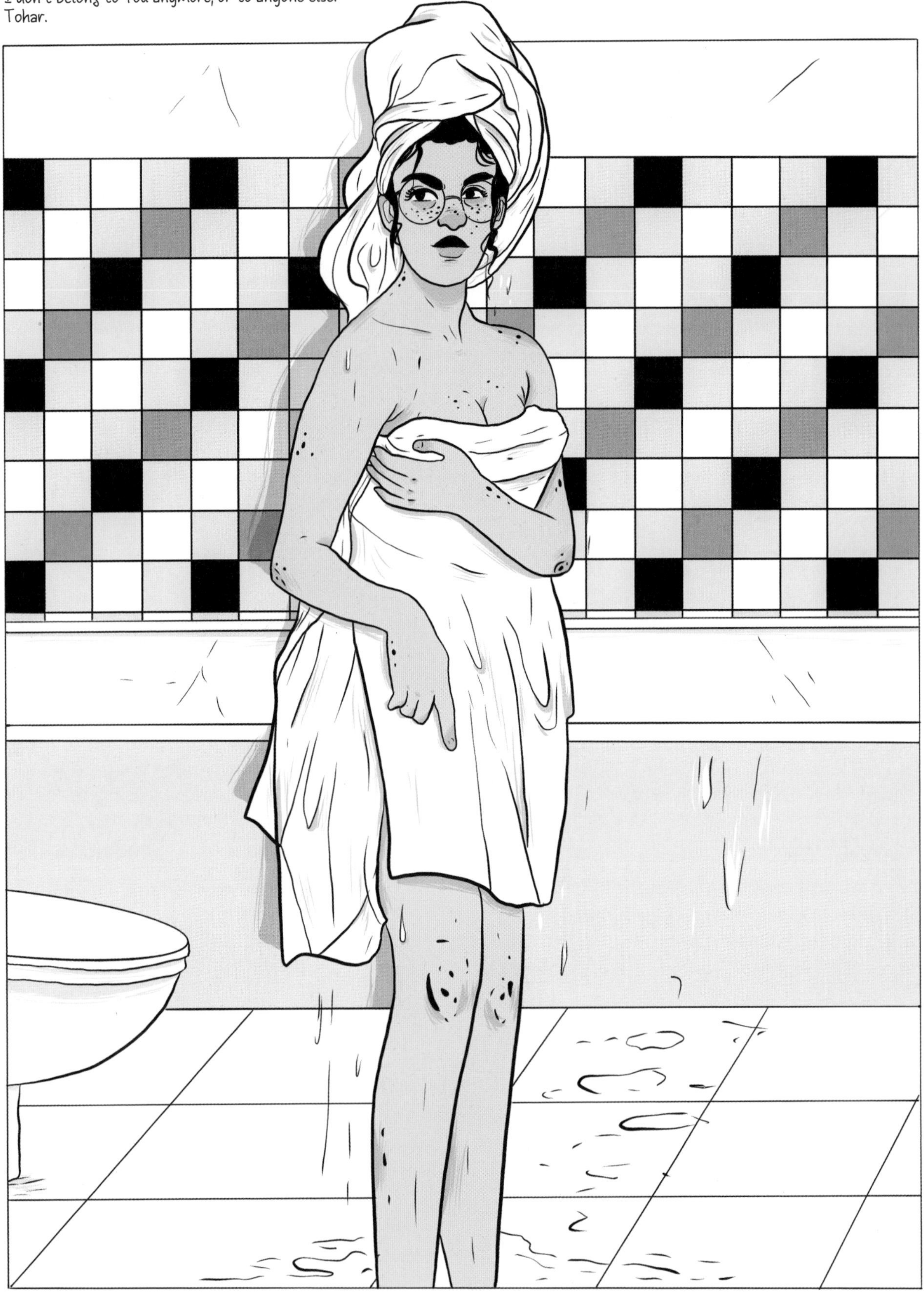

NOTES
(notes are indicated in the book with an asterisk)

Page 2 "The Shouts of Joy":
"The shouts of joy over your ripened fruit and over your harvests have been stilled" (Isaiah 16:9, NIV). The original Hebrew title of this image, "It is sad to die in the month of Tammuz," is based on the title of a song by Naomi Shemer, a well-known songwriter and composer in Israel. It so happened that she died that same month years later. She herself was inspired by Isaiah's verses in the Old Testament.

Page 3 "In the month of Tammuz":
Tammuz is a month in the Hebrew calendar, at the beginning of the summer, and very hot … It is a month of 29 days, spanning June and July of the Gregorian calendar. The other months of the Hebrew calendar are: Tishrei, Cheshvan, Kislev, Tevet, Shevat, Adar, Nissan, Iyar, Sivan, Av, and Elul.

Page 10 "The Color Orange":
The color orange rallied settlers opposed to the plan to evacuate settlements from the Gaza Strip, ordered by Ariel Sharon in 2005. This protest color was inspired by the flag of the Gaza Strip Regional Council, which united all the settlements in Gush Katif, all of which were evacuated in favor of the Palestinian Authority. The population was split between the left, which supported a peace movement and advocated more concessions—"two peoples, two states"—and the right, which represented those who see the territories as biblical lands that have belonged to the Jewish people for thousands of years.

Page 18 Maimonides (Rambam):
Rabbi Moshe ben Maimon (1138-1204) was one of the greatest sages of all time and one of the most important and revered scholars in Judaism. He was also recognized as a philosopher and physician in Arab and European cultures. Maimonides was the great architect of the interpretation of Jewish law for generations, and his many writings deal with various disciplines.

Page 18 Graffiti on the walls:
The graffiti on the walls reads "Love your neighbor as yourself" and "It is a great mitzvah to be joyful":
A mitzvah, according to Judaism, means a commandment or a good deed. There are estimated to be 613 different mitzvot, derived from the written and oral Torah. They usually refer to God's commandments to the Jewish people (i.e., the dos and don'ts).

Page 21 "The concept of Niddah":
According to Judaism, Niddah refers to a woman during her menstrual bleeding. During her period, intimacy and sexual relations are prohibited. These prohibitions end when she is purified by immersion in a Mikvah (ritual bath) after seven days without bleeding. This immersion is done at night, on the evening of the seventh day.

Page 21 Shabbat:
Shabbat (Saturday) is the seventh day of the week, a day of rest (official in Israel) for Jews. It symbolizes the seventh day of rest after the six days of the Creation of the world. Shabbat begins on Friday night, shortly before sunset, and ends the next day when the stars appear. According to Judaism, the Sabbath is considered the most sacred time, and the Torah considers its desecration a sin.

Page 21 "The 'shmirat negiah' law":
Negiah, literally "touching," is a concept in Jewish Law that prohibits or restricts sensual physical contact with a member of the opposite sex (except for a spouse, outside the period of Niddah, and certain relatives for whom one is presumed not to have sexual attraction). A person who complies with this law will be considered a Shomer Negiah. The laws of the Negiah are generally followed by strict Orthodox Jews, with varying degrees of observance. Some Orthodox Jews take steps to avoid accidental contact, such as avoiding sitting next to a member of the opposite sex on a bus, train, or plane, or in other similar situations. Others are more lenient, only avoiding intentional contact. The followers of Conservative and Reform Judaism do not observe these laws.

Page 24 Yom Kippur:
Also known as the Day of Atonement, Yom Kippur is a holy day in Judaism. Set on the tenth day of the first month of the Jewish calendar year, it is marked by fasting and completely refraining from all work. Yom Kippur is the day of repentance, considered the holiest and most solemn day of the Jewish year. Its central theme is forgiveness and reconciliation.

Page 26 Bamba:
Bamba is an Israeli brand of peanut- and corn-based snack.

Page 51 "One third of heaven":
A belief—which, however, has no source—that "if two people are brought together, if they become a couple, the person who created this union would deserve one third of heaven."

Page 107 "The Birkat Hagomel prayer":
A prayer to thank and bless God for being spared from danger, for getting out of various situations safely.

Page 109 "She kissed the mezuzah":
The mezuzah is a small case containing two passages from Deuteronomy that Jews place on the right side of the door of their home. Many observant Jews kiss the mezuzah when they pass through the doorway.

Page 110 Purim:
Purim is a Jewish holiday with biblical origins that celebrates the joy of deliverance from a large-scale massacre. The festival is celebrated every year in February or March of the Gregorian calendar. The holiday features many traditions and customs, including special foods, shaking rattles, giving gifts, and other joyful and carnivalesque activities.

Page 112 Amir Benayoun:
Amir Benayoun is a singer-songwriter and musician very famous and well loved in Israel, whose parents are from Morocco.

Page 114 "We're 'a fucked up generation' ":
Aviv Geffen, great-nephew of Moshe Dayan, who advocates tolerance between religious and secular people, started his career being very provocative and had thousands of fans. His song "Achshav Me'unan" (It's Cloudy Now) ends with the line "We're a fucked up generation" (which was almost censored). It clearly highlights the despair of a generation.

Page 122 "At Friday night dinner, when we make Kiddush":
It is a commandment to mention the sanctity of the Sabbath day when it starts (i.e., on Friday night). Before the Friday night meal, the host recites the Kiddush while holding a glass of kosher wine. Each participant will drink a few drops and then will be given a piece of Shabbat bread (challah) before the meal is placed on the table.

Library of Congress Cataloging-in-Publication Data

Names: Sherman-Friedman, Tohar, 1996- author. | Morrison, Margaret
  (Translator), translator.
Title: Good girls go to Hell / Tohar Sherman-Friedman ; translated by
  Margaret Morrison.
Other titles: Filles sages vont en enfer. English
Description: University Park, Pennsylvania : Graphic Mundi, [2023] |
  "Originally published in French as Les Filles sages vont en enfer by
  Tohar Sherman-Friedman ©Editions Delcourt, 2021."
Summary: "A coming-of-age graphic memoir set in the West Bank,
  depicting the reality of growing up in a region split by religious
  tensions-and sometimes violent conflict"—Provided by publisher.
Identifiers: LCCN 2023022263 | ISBN 9781637790601 (hardback)
Subjects: LCSH: Sherman-Friedman, Tohar, 1996—Comic books, strips,
  etc. | Israelis—West Bank—Biography—Comic books, strips, etc. |
  Teenage girls—West Bank—Social life and customs—Comic books,
  strips, etc. | Jewish families—West Bank—Comic books, strips, etc. |
  Coming of age—West Bank—Comic books, strips, etc. |
  LCGFT: Graphic novels. | Autobiographical comics. | Coming-of-age
  comics.
Classification: LCC DS110.W47 S543 2023 | DDC 956.94/2092 [B]—
  dc23/eng/20230515
LC record available at https://lccn.loc.gov/2023022263v

Published by The Pennsylvania State University Press,
University Park, PA 16802-1003

10 9 8 7 6 5 4 3 2 1

 graphic mundi
drawing our worlds together

Graphic Mundi is an imprint of The Pennsylvania State
University Press.

Song lyric on page 60 panel 3 from So Far Away (2011) by Joyce L. Baker
& William Joseph Lervold.

Originally published in French as Les Filles sages vont en enfer by Tohar
Sherman-Friedman © Editions Delcourt, 2021.

Supplemental lettering: Indigo Kelleigh

The Pennsylvania State University Press is a member of the Association
of University Presses.

It is the policy of The Pennsylvania State University Press to use
acid-free paper. Publications on uncoated stock satisfy the minimum
requirements of American National Standard for Information Sciences–
Permanence of Paper for Printed Library Material, ANSI Z39.48-1992.